WORSHIP

(FROM THE GROUND UP)

BIBLICAL AND HISTORICAL LESSONS

STUART LEE SHEEHAN

FOREWORD BY DAN ODLE

About World Hope Ministries International and the
World Hope Bible Institute

At this moment, somewhere around the world, there is a pastor on his knees pleading with God to send him a mentor, a teacher, a scholar – to train him in the deepest doctrines of the faith. He has struggled for years to meet the ministry demands of his flock, and he is handicapped because his theological training is virtually non-existent. He has scraped together everything he's ever read in a spiritual magazine or heard on a Christian radio broadcast, and it has not amounted to much. How can he lead his congregation, nourish them on the Word of God, apply the scriptures to their daily needs, and grow in his walk with the Lord without sound biblical training? World Hope Bible Institute was founded to meet this pastor where he lives.

World Hope Ministries International (WHMI) exists to enable the Body of Christ to experience the Great Commission (Matthew 28:19-20). Since 1977, WHMI has worked with people from a variety of denominations and churches to spread the Good News of Jesus Christ. Obeying the Great Commission means going, reaching, *making disciples, and teaching* those who respond (Matthew 28:20). Globally, there are two to three million pastors (over 80%) who lack basic theological training. In 2008, WHMI established the World Hope Bible Institute (WHBI) to provide systematic theological training for pastors and leaders in remote or underserved areas.

We are committed to mobilize people to become engaged in the Great Commission. 2 Timothy 2:2 is a reminder that every pastor has a responsibility to help train other pastors. Pastors in developed nations who have received training should carry a burden for millions of pastors around the world who have no access to theological education. The World Hope Bible Institute can provide opportunities for you to do that effectively. WHBI provides the curriculum for the teacher, class notes for the students, and logistical support to put you in front of pastors who are hungry to learn. Each year requests for training go unmet. You can help—you can multiply the training God has given you by taking a week to go and teach for World Hope Bible Institute.

The curriculum is ready, the students are waiting...

World Hope Ministries International:
P.O. Box PO Box 11808
Spring, TX 77391-1808
P | 281-978-4570 – W | whmi.org

WHMI is a Fellowship of Baptist World Ministries Partner and works in cooperation with the International Mission Board, SBC and other like-minded Great Commission Christians around the world. WHMI is a 501(c)(3), non-profit corporation, and accredited by the Evangelical Council for Financial Accountability.

Responses to *Worship (from the ground up)*

"Once in a great while, a man brings together formal educational background in his discipline, a spiritual grasp of the Word of God, and profound thought about the nature of Christian worship. Stuart Sheehan, with his DMA from the University of Texas, has written this superb book, *Worship (from the ground up): Biblical and Historical Lessons*. In many ways, this book is the most thorough that I have read on the nature of worship. Sheehan understands that worship is far more than music. He also brings to the subject of music a trajectory for our own time. Sheehan also has a grasp of the 2,000-year history of Christian worship and formulates from that a method of enabling people to become more significantly involved in the worship of the church. In the process of doing so, he analyzes various worship forms that have been used by the church across the years and points the way forward. If you can only read one book on worship, Stuart Sheehan of World Hope Ministries International has written the book that you want to read."

PAIGE PATTERSON, President
Southwestern Baptist Theological Seminary

"Most Christians worship reactively rather than reflectively. Sheehan has done the church a great favor: he has reflected on our behalf. He has mined centuries of tradition and practice and demonstrated how historical worship can—and should—inform the worship of all types of modern congregations. Forget categories; any church can discover that meaningful and effective worship parallels that of the first century church—dancing between intellect, emotion, tradition, and innovation, and ultimately discovering worship that is biblical."

STEVE BEZNER, Senior Pastor
Houston Northwest Church, Houston, Texas

"Evolving styles of worship have probably created more tension and conflict in contemporary churches than doctrine. Stuart Sheehan has done a favor for the body of Christ in compiling objective and extensive historical and biblical research on worship. The reader will be tempted to skip to the final section on practical applications but to do so would forfeit benefiting from the insight and blessing provided by this experienced worship leader who writes from a scholarly approach with deep spiritual insight."

JERRY RANKIN, President Emeritus
International Mission Board, Southern Baptist Convention

"Many give precious little time and attention to what worship is, why worship matters and how worship happens. Through a careful biblical examination, a thorough and insightful historical survey, and a practical pastoral overview of the subject of worship, Dr. Stuart Sheehan has provided a volume that promises to breathe new life into the worship of the church. He combines keen scholarly insight with more than 30 years of pastoral experience to demonstrate that worship is (and always has been) more than something that the church does, but rather worship flows from the heart of what the church is. Whether you are just beginning your journey, or you are a seasoned scholar, *Worship (from the ground up)* will challenge you to reconsider many of the common myths and stereotypes that often cloud both how we view worship and ultimately how we 'do' worship."

MARK HOWELL, Senior Pastor
First Baptist Church, Daytona Beach, Florida

"Many are the stories of churches who have split over the issue of worship — often, if not primarily, because the 'worshippers' did not understand biblical worship. In this book, Stuart Sheehan takes us on a journey through the scriptures and church history to help us understand worship. This work is both informative and practical, written by a veteran worship leader. I commend it, especially to churches seeking to worship well in a rapidly changing culture."

CHUCK LAWLESS, Dean of Graduate Studies
Southeastern Baptist Theological Seminary

"Playing music and playing music well are different. Any child can bang a tambourine but to learn the discipline, the scales, and the theory that allow you to play well and play multiple genres takes thoughtful devotion. Stuart Sheehan offers an opus on worship blending theology, scripture, and tradition in an artful balance that provides a path for the future through a window of the past. I would have loved to have had this approach and texture when I was in Seminary… so fluid without letting go of Scripture or tradition."

JEFF HARRIS, Senior Pastor
Grace Point Church, San Antonio, Texas

"Having met Stuart Sheehan for the first time on the international mission field training indigenous pastors and church planters, I can testify that he is a man who genuinely loves the Lord Jesus with all his heart, soul, mind, and strength and cares deeply for His church. It comes as no surprise then that one of his most profound concerns is to see our Lord's bride firmly grounded on biblical truth when it comes to her most essential practice: worship. In *Worship (from the ground up)*, Dr. Sheehan has done the church a tremendous service in outlining biblical worship and its significance from its earliest roots in the Old Testament all the way through its New Testament fulfillment and various expressions in church history. If you have been looking for a comprehensive, scholarly, Christ-centered, and church-focused resource on this subject, you should read this book and then thank Dr. Sheehan for writing it!"

NICK MOORE, Lead Pastor
Redemption Hill Baptist Church, Fisherville, KY

"If you are looking for a historical and biblical approach to the topic of worship, coupled with spiritual and practical insights for the church today, then search no further. Stuart Sheehan has been teaching this material at the Rocky Mountain Campus of Golden Gate Baptist Theological Seminary for the past 12 years. Responses from students convey that his class and the material contained in this book revolutionized their view and approach to worship."

STEVE VETETO, Director, Rocky Mountain Campus
Golden Gate Baptist Theological Seminary, Denver, Colorado

WORSHIP

(FROM THE GROUND UP)

BIBLICAL AND HISTORICAL LESSONS

STUART LEE SHEEHAN

FOREWORD BY DAN ODLE

Published by the author
P.O. Box 11808
Spring, TX 77391-1808
P | 281-978-4570
W | whmi.org (World Hope Ministries International)

ISBN 978-0-9892212-0-7 ——— ISBN 978-0-9892212-1-4 (electronic version)

Unless otherwise noted, Scripture quotations are from the *New American Standard Bible®, Copyright © 1960, 1962, 1963, 1968, 1971, 1972, 1973, 1975, 1977, 1995 by The Lockman Foundation.* Used by permission (www.Lockman.org).

Any words bolded in Scripture quotations have been added by the author. Block Scripture quotations are set in 10 point font rather than 9 point font.

Unless otherwise specified, all translations are by the author.

The author has maintained the original spellings, punctuation, and formatting of block quotations whenever possible.

Cover Design by Randy Stewart
Cover image by Janaka Dharmasena, © 2013
Used under license from Shutterstock.com

ISBN 978-0-9892212-0-7
ISBN 978-0-9892212-1-4 (electronic version)

For more information about World Hope Ministries International or to learn about opportunities to teach underserved pastors with World Hope Bible Institute, visit the WHMI website: whmi.org

Printed in the United States of America.

To Amy,
who has loved me, supported me,
patiently encouraged me, and, like Jesus,
has shown me extraordinary grace.

As an undergraduate, I took my first ministry position long before I had any good sense, even lacking enough good sense to know how ignorant I was. Through my years in college and graduate school, I continued to serve in various churches. Shortly before taking my comprehensive exams, I finally settled the issue of my call and surrendered to full time ministry. When I finished my dissertation, and graduated, I had a degree in Church Music and masters and doctoral degrees in music. I was well trained, but I really had no idea what I was doing as a pastor who had oversight over congregational worship. Without a few great examples to imitate, I would have been in a mess.

I loved theology, but in those days, it seemed uncommon for 'music guys' to think about theology—theology was for preachers and seminary professors. That did not quell my hunger. I believed that unless I understood the theology behind the activity, I would have no real platform from which I could lead others. Thankfully, my professors in graduate school taught me how to learn, to think critically, to read, and research. Beyond that, God placed around me some choice men who had given themselves to the deep things of God and were not selfish with what they had learned. To this day, I have been fed good books and a great deal of wisdom by a network of wonderful friends, mentors, teachers, and fellow pastors.

A few years into this journey, I was asked to teach a seminary course on Christian worship. I began to prepare for that first class, searching for books that would adequately serve as my textbook. I wanted something to span the gap between classically oriented Church Music (as I was taught it) and a flood of emerging worship styles in the 90s. Finally, I wanted something that spoke of what I was learning about the biblical nature of worship. My study was teaching me that the only thing that could span the wide gaps that existed among so many worship styles was the truth of the Bible. Theological truth opened up to me as a thing of beauty—its beauty extended beyond worship. To study the nature of God on any subject is to learn of Him in every other, for the totality of all His character is found wherever He is.

If that weren't enough, God opened my eyes to see something else. Years of studying music, its history and development, began to take on a new meaning. In Western Civilization, the history of music is, to a great extent, a history of the development of Christian worship. History and my growing understanding of biblical theology began to coalesce. I could see that biblical truths about worship had been practiced at times and discarded at times. And, as a result, I saw patterns that were repeating themselves, often to the detriment of the Church. In the subsequent years of teaching seminarians, my lectures included the biblical foundations I was learning and an increasing number of lessons from history. This book is a product of that journey. My students and friends have suffered its long birth over the last ten years. As you will note from the bibliography, many others have provided extensive scholarship to make this volume possible.

Additionally, I have both apologies and thanks for all the churches where I have served through the years, as well as the pastors with whom I have served. I wish I had faithfully practiced all that is in this book and I am deeply grateful for the grace shown to me by thousands of dear people as I learned.

In the end, the necessity of knowing and understanding biblical theology opened my eyes to the plight of millions of pastors around the world who have no access or opportunity to learn those things which so radically have impacted me. This ultimately stirred my heart to help provide theological training for them. It is now my joy to serve as the leader of an organization that places a high value on providing theological training to pastors in remote and underserved areas as a key component of accomplishing the Great Commission.

As you read this book, I encourage you to avoid skimming through to the 'practical stuff.' I started my ministry rushing to the 'back of the book'—to get on with the doing, causing me to make many mistakes. If you are a preaching pastor, I pray that you will read, understanding that you occupy a key role as a leader of God's people in worship. You should know and be facile with the truths in this book as much or more than anyone who serves on your staff. If you are a practitioner of worship in your church, I pray that you will work your way through this material, as well. Your understanding of biblical worship—what God wants and how He wants it done—is more important than any skill set you can have.

To every reader, I invite you to take the journey with me—to become a lifelong student of biblical Christian worship. May God use this book to help enrich your practice of one of the most beautiful gifts that God has given to us— the privilege of worshiping Him for our salvation through Jesus Christ.

Gloria tibi, Domine
S.L.S.

FOREWORD

The last thing the church needs is another book on worship... methods. *Try this. Sing that.* It seems that we in the worshipping community love to talk a lot about techniques and we're always looking for that new book telling us about what "will work."

This is not that book.

What we in the worshipping community do need, however, is to think biblically, theologically and historically about worship. We need a rich biblical theology that will serve as fuel on the fire of our worship. But this will not happen by accident. It will come only through careful study and interpretation of God's Word. "What works?" must be replaced with "What has God said?" It takes effort to mine lessons from the pages of church history and then to apply those lessons to our own ministries—but the effort is worth it.

In so many areas of life, we often want the product without the process. We want to be healthy, but we do not want to exercise. We want to go on vacation, but we are not disciplined enough to save. In the worshipping community, the temptation is the same. We want to be in on the latest fads of what's "working" without doing the diligent work of studying what God has revealed to us.

In this immensely helpful book, Stuart Sheehan challenges us to place our concern for methodology in its rightful place:

> *Worship is essentially connected to the recognition and display of God's glory – something that is already maintained and protected by the Godhead, which exists in a perpetual state of glorification. For nearly two thousand years, the Church has often been more passionate about how we worship than who we worship. Our continuing obsession with method and form indicates that we often make our practice of worship the focus rather than God* (p.10).

As a worship pastor, I've often heard it said that worship is for "an audience of One." Fundamentally, it may more properly be said that in worship, God invites us to have an audience with Him. God speaks; we respond. He initiates; we submit. So often, it seems we approach worship with our mouths open and our ears closed. We are eager to offer God our "sacrifice of praise," without regard to what He is saying to us. Sheehan rightly encourages us to open our ears – to listen to what God has said, and what He is saying.

When our ministries lack this kind of scriptural rootedness, there are many temptations that may easily overtake us. We can begin to think worship is all about us and our gifts. It's also possible to go through the motions of worship without the heart of a worshiper. Amos 5:23 warns of this kind of empty ritual: "Take away from me the noise of your songs; to the melody of your harps I will not listen." We may be doing the right things, but if disconnected from a genuine passion and love for the Savior, God says He will not even listen. We must be careful that we do not substitute sincerity for truth, but rather that our strong biblical foundation leads us to a deep and holy affection for God.

I love so many things about this book. It begins with a solid foundation of the biblical definition and understanding of worship. It points us toward a more God-centered, Christ-focused, and gospel-saturated approach to worship. But it is not merely a biblical theology. As the subtitle makes clear "Biblical *and* Historical Lessons," this book also seeks to draw from the deep well of church history. We are not the first generation of believers to seek to rightly worship God. There is much we can learn as we stand on the shoulders of those who've gone before, seeking to understand and "to contend for the faith that was once for all delivered to the saints" (Jude 3). Ultimately, with our understanding of worship anchored in the truth of scripture and tempered by the wisdom of church history, we can begin to move forward with a sense of humble confidence:

> *It is a sobering thought that the decisions we make will directly affect how those who come after us may worship and how effective their corporate worship experiences might be. Therefore, it is crucial for those who make decisions about worship to do so with godly wisdom* (p.275).

Sheehan writes with the precision of careful scholarship (he has done the hard work), but also with the heart of a pastor. His concern is not merely for truth, but for an application of that truth that informs and transforms:

> *Our charge remains: we are responsible to take the clear guidelines in Scripture and deal with them. We cannot afford to ignore them. If nothing else, we must be able to say that we have taken what the Bible says and have applied it fully to our ministries. I do not want to stand before God knowing that I made worship into what I wanted it to be, rather than what He wants it to be* (pp.304-305).

Through the spread of the gospel, God is redeeming for Himself men and women, boys and girls, from every tribe, tongue, people and nation. He is building for Himself an army of worshippers that will forever voice the praise of the redeemed from Revelation 5:12: "Worthy is the Lamb who was slain, to receive power and wealth and wisdom and might and honor and glory and blessing!"

This book will make you long for that day when our worship *by faith* becomes worship *by sight*. Read it. Learn from it. In the process, you will learn to love the gospel more – to love Jesus more.

And then let that be your call to worship.

Dan Odle
Birmingham, AL

CONTENTS

SECTION 1:

THE BIBLICAL FOUNDATION FOR DEFINING AND UNDERSTANDING WORSHIP

CHAPTER 1

WORSHIP: JUST WHAT
ARE WE TALKING ABOUT?

How do we start?

The subject of worship can be an unruly one to tackle. Varied as the styles in which it is expressed, there are a multitude of opinions about what worship is or should be. Because of this, many discussions on worship first occur in the realm of methods. This is unfortunate because the real beauty of worship is not in its form but in its purpose and splendor—the rightful response to the only true God. In the course of this book, we will explore form and travel the roads of our worship forefathers. Yet any hope of evaluating form or understanding history will be cut short without understanding the fundamental truths that guide this precious practice of the Church. For this reason, our discussion must begin with foundational truths and basic biblical vocabulary.

Just as a complex chemical formula can be broken down into basic elements, so worship is best understood if we look at its most fundamental elements. If we can identify those things in Christian worship that make it genuinely Christian and genuinely worship, we can make a meaningful assessment of our own practices. For many of us, the connection between our

3

personal experiences and our understanding is so profound that separating the two seems impossible; but it is not. We can see the simple and profound beauty that is Christian worship if we set aside our cultural practices and look once again to the scriptures. In the Bible, we can rediscover what worship truly is. Our methods may have temporal benefits but if anything in our own practices has real eternal value, it will be because in them are the true fundamentals of worship. After we have rediscovered those, we can evaluate historical forms and then return to our own practices with renewed zeal and, where necessary, set them aside for something better.

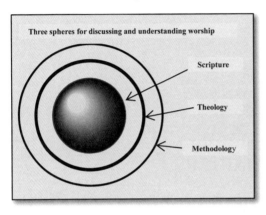

A healthy understanding of worship begins with what we *believe* rather than what we *do*. Therefore, the first key factor in developing our understanding of worship is to determine what authority will superintend our beliefs. Worship, if it is to be pleasing to the Lord, must be in agreement with His Word. Therefore, developing a solid worship theology must always begin with God's Word. Having established what God has said about worship, we can then begin to evaluate our own beliefs and develop our theology of worship. Only then are we able to evaluate our preferences, methods and forms. By looking at worship in this way, we can break it down into three components. The first is scriptural, what God has said about worship in the Bible. The second is theological, what we understand that to mean—how we organize and interpret what God has said. The last is methodological, how we express our understanding in our own practices.

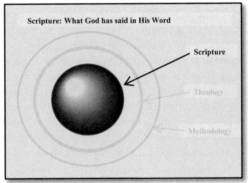

Scripture

Theoretically, a true and complete theology of worship would accurately represent God and everything He has said on the subject of worship. We need the disclaimer, *theoretically,* because, despite our best attempts, God and all that He has said is more profound than the human mind can grasp. Our only true hope for gaining understanding is found in the Scripture and the work of the Holy Spirit to help us understand its truth.[1] As we develop our worship theology, we are not doing so by discovering newly revealed truth. We are actually gaining understanding about what God has already revealed in His Word. God has spoken by His written Word and by His Living Word.[2] He continues to speak by illuminating what He has already disclosed through the pages of Scripture.[3] The benefit in starting the discussion with the Bible is that what God has spoken is consistent with His character—it never changes. Truth is static. For students of worship, this is encouraging. God has given us the source document—the truth of His Word. Developing our worship theology need not be dependent on our own traditions or the traditions of others. We can certainly learn about worship from our traditions, both present and past, and a significant portion of this book will illustrate that. However, we have the privilege of going to the original source, discovering in our time what the Bible has to say about worship. While its truth is more ancient than our faith, it can be as fresh for us as it was to those who first heard it.

Theology

What we think or believe—how we organize our thoughts—about what God has said represents our theology. We can look at how other believers have understood God's truth in the past and how others seek to understand it today. We are not seeking to develop our worship theology without a keen awareness that

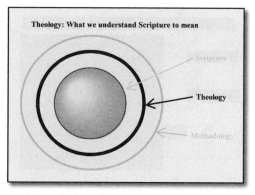

we are part of a river of the redeemed that flows from Calvary to the consummation of history. At the same time, we must take into account that human understanding of worship has been neither consistent nor complete. Theological changes that have occurred over the course of Christian history have been, at times, both good and bad. Any changes in theology demonstrate how human understanding has changed, rather than how truth has changed—again, truth is static. At times whole systems of thought have changed, not because humankind had discovered new truth, but because they gained a fuller or renewed understanding of God's truth. For example, the Reformation was a result of a renewed commitment to God's Word. Changes in the way people

---

[1] John 16:13.

[2] Hebrews 1:1-2: *God, after He spoke long ago to the fathers in the prophets in many portions and in many ways, in these last days has spoken to us in His Son, whom He appointed heir of all things, through whom also He made the world.*

[3] Our view of what God has said in His Word will determine what we think about it and ultimately how we will apply it. This makes a high view of Scripture essential. If our opinions displace God's Word as the central focus, God's Word becomes subject to human thought rather than subjecting human thought to God's Word.

thought about God's Word impacted how people understood the theology surrounding worship.

Our theology is the connection between what God has said and what we actually do in practice. For this reason, changes to theology generally have enormous impact and, as a result, are not always positive innovations. At times, changes to theology are a result of changes in societal or academic opinion, potentially making God's truth subordinate to human opinion rather than keeping human opinion subject to God's Word. Any change in theology is susceptible to human error and can have a massive impact. For this reason, theological changes should be approached with caution.

Methodology

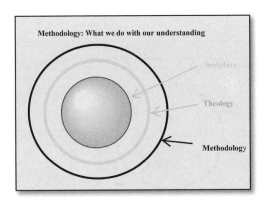

Methods are the outward expressions of what we believe. They are often based on traditions and closely related to our culture. As such, methodology may vary greatly from generation to generation or from one geographical region to the other. As we employ our methods we are answering the question, *What do our beliefs look like when expressed in our time, in our language or region?* As we unpack the subject of worship, we will find that the Scripture does not have a great deal to offer in the way of actual methods or liturgies for Christian worship. This makes the historical study of worship important because we can see how other believers in previous generations have interpreted the Scripture and applied it. This makes methodology the most subjective and, therefore, the area most problematic. The lessons we will learn from the history of worship will illustrate this very clearly. For nearly 2,000 years, Christians have fought, at times killing or dying, over a particular method.

The key to developing healthy worship is to ensure that theology and method never ignore Scripture. Unhealthy worship happens whenever theology or methodology infringes on or adds to the center circle of Scripture. Healthy worship never sets aside any portion of God's truth, nor does it ever view human understanding or method equal to it. This does not mean that theology and methodology cannot change.

The diagram to the right illustrates how there can be flexibility in method and understanding while including the whole core of Scripture. Some aspects of theology and especially methodology can change safely as long there is no distortion to what God has said. The key is to keep both theology and methodology subject to the totality of God's Word. This allows for wide

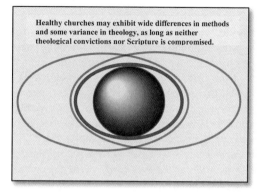

Healthy churches may exhibit wide differences in methods and some variance in theology, as long as neither theological convictions nor Scripture is compromised.

possibilities of practice that still encompass all of God's directives. We will see the significance of this over the course of worship history.

When discussing and debating issues of worship it is helpful to know which of these areas we are discussing. For instance, we should be able to discuss and agree on what God has said (Scripture) with believers who lived 200 or nearly 2,000 years ago. Even as it relates to a large body of Christian orthodoxy, we would agree as well. The person and work of Christ, the Trinity, salvation by grace through faith, the nature of the Atonement, etc., are part of our historical theology because those teachings are so clear in Scripture that the one who distorts them places himself outside of biblical Christianity. In such areas as these, our theology cannot change because it is clearly taught in Scripture. Yet, moving our discussion with the same believers beyond Christian orthodoxy into other areas, particularly into our methodology, could result in a great deal of misunderstanding, if not outright disagreement and division. Even within Christianity today, we could find cultural expressions of genuine orthodox theology that are widely varied. How this variety occurs among churches is important. Variety should never occur because we vary in our subjection to scriptural authority or in our orthodox beliefs. However, variety in methods can safely occur if both of these are carefully maintained.

The life-long task of each believer is to learn what the Scripture says about worship (represented by center circle), seek to understand its meaning (theology), and how best to apply that to our own time and practice (methodology). Doing so helps us to avoid discarding something that God's Word clearly specifies as essential to our worship theology or, just as dangerous, adding to it by placing our opinions or methods on par with or above God's Word.

THE ESSENTIAL ELEMENT

For several years, it has been my privilege to teach on the subject of worship to seminary students. The interaction with the students is always stimulating. To see their love for Christ and observe their discovery of biblical theology is a wonderful thing. Besides the face to face interaction with the students, one of my favorite learning activities is to give them a question that provides an opportunity for rigorous discussion. Hopefully, through the discussion process they learn something important in the end. One of those questions that has produced a great deal of interaction is: *What is required for the true God to be properly worshiped?* This question has garnered many noteworthy responses. Students often mention humility, spirit and truth, a scriptural view of God, and the like. To be sure, all of these are wonderful answers. However, these responses, as well as others we could list, actually answer a different question. Namely, *What is required for willing human beings to worship the true God?* Or, *What is required for willing humans to enhance their worship of the true God?* When it comes to determining what is necessary for God to be worshiped and adored, the truth is much more fundamental and profound.

Willing hearts are not essential

We often think in terms of God being adored, loved, glorified, and obeyed as something that we provide Him. We wrongly assume that somehow our devoted hearts, our love and adoration, our willful submission are all important components in ensuring that God is glorified. The truth is that God does not need our willingness to ensure that He receives our worship. While we may believe that willing or submissive hearts are essential for God to be worshiped, they are not an essential part of the worship equation. This is clearly demonstrates from the scriptures.

Paul gives us this glimpse into future worship:

> For this reason also, God highly exalted Him, and bestowed on Him the name which is above every name, so that at the name of Jesus EVERY KNEE WILL BOW, of those who are in heaven and on earth and under the earth, and that every tongue will confess that Jesus Christ is Lord, to the glory of God the Father.
>
> Philippians 2:9-11

Likewise, Paul references Isaiah 45 when he states:

> For it is written, "AS I LIVE, SAYS THE LORD, EVERY KNEE SHALL BOW TO ME, AND EVERY TONGUE SHALL GIVE PRAISE TO GOD."
>
> Romans 14:11

Both of these texts use the image of bowing to illustrate worship. The Bible teaches that all will bow in worship before Him, all creatures, human or otherwise. This act of worship, described in the scriptures above, will occur at the consummation of history. It will come from both the redeemed and the unsaved, not just from the angels but also from the demons. There is a day coming when this truth will be apparent: a lack of willingness to worship God will be no impediment to His being worshiped by every one of His created beings. This is not dependent on a heart of love and affection toward Him. Every knee will bow down to the triune God. That does not void the desire that God has for true, willing worshipers (John 4:23). Instead, it demonstrates that all beings, human or otherwise, will ultimately observe the proper order in the universe, one where God is honored for occupying the sole place of supremacy.

Human beings are not essential

Just as willing hearts are not a required component for worship to exist, human beings are not an essential component of the worship equation. The Bible clearly teaches that angels are worshiping Him. In Isaiah's translated moment of worship (Isaiah 6), the prophet witnesses the seraphs undertaking what presumably is their eternal task—to worship the LORD. Angelic worship is not an isolated encounter in Scripture. The Revelation of Jesus Christ given through John provides numerous tableaus of angels engaged in worship. In addition to the angels, creation itself declares the glory of God (Psalm 19:1-6). And even with all of that, Jesus says that if He is not praised then inanimate objects can be conscripted to cry out if need be (Luke 19:40). Since God is worshiped by angels and can command worship from inanimate objects, the worship of God is not dependent on human beings. What a mystery that from the redeemed and the angels, as well as the damned and the demonic, God will receive *glory*.[1] This all underscores the foundational truth that we are beings who live in a universe superintended by the God who deserves all glory and will receive the glory that is rightly His. This fundamental truth must precede any growing understanding of worship. The created order—not willing hearts—ensures that God's supremacy must ultimately be acknowledged in everything.

Only God is essential

God's glory is perpetually self-sufficient and self-sustaining—He exists in an eternal state of glorification, which cannot be diminished by the fickle hearts of human worshipers. This is clearly demonstrated within the Trinity itself, where the Godhead is eternally glorified and adored. The Father loves the Son (John 3:35), is pleased with Him (Matthew 3:17; Matthew 17:5), glorifies Him (John 8:54) and honors His eternal obedience (Philippians 2:9). The Son glorifies the Father by laying aside His Divine prerogatives and humbling Himself to the point of death (Philippians 2:5-8; John 17:1). Jesus' obedience to the Father, to humble Himself and die, is the purest picture of the biblical concept of worship in all of Scripture.[2] Likewise, the Spirit glorifies the Son,

---

[1] Phil 2:11, glory, δόξα [*doxa*].

[2] The Hebrew word for worship is *shachah* and connotes the humbling of self. See pages 11 and ff.

not by drawing attention to Himself, but by disclosing that which He receives from Jesus (John 16:13-14). The self-perpetuating glory of the Trinity is a fundamental truth that is crucial in understanding our place in the worship equation. Knowing that God has always received glory and always will be glorified apart from anything else confirms that God's desire for us to worship Him is not self-serving. It is an expression of His pure love.

There are really two types of worship—one demanded by God's glory in which all will participate and one that He desires from those who are willing. God desires worship but He does not need it—He is eternally glorified. How unlike us God is. Our desire for things we do not need drives us to reach for that which is excessive or impure. Yet, God desires what He does *not* need to prove His love. Once we realize that God needs nothing yet desires our worship, we can begin to gain some perspective on God's incredible love for us. He does not need us but He truly wants us!

Worship is essentially connected to the recognition and display of God's glory—something that is already maintained and protected by the Godhead, which exists in a perpetual state of glorification. For nearly two thousand years, the Church has often been more passionate about *how* we worship than *who* we worship. Our continuing obsession with method and form indicates that we often make our *practice of worship* the focus rather than God. In doing so, we ascribe greater weight to our own importance in the worship equation when, in fact, we are not even an essential component. God lacks nothing and, therefore, needs nothing. God has the power to command worship from believers and unbelievers, angels and demons. He has the ability to command worship from inanimate objects and, beyond all of that, the glory of the Triune God is self-perpetuating. So, in the end, the only essential element for worship to exist is God. Therefore, giving our worship to God is a privilege—it is not something God needs for us to do in order for Him to be adored, loved or glorified. Instead, worship is something God desires from us and something in which we are privileged to participate—a way for us to enjoy this one and only perfect and perfectly glorified God.

So WHAT IS WORSHIP?

Obviously, worship is giving God His due but, what do we mean when we talk about worship? Language is dynamic. While we may know what we mean when we say *worship*, the meaning of that word continues to change. Since the word *worship* is employed to communicate so many different things, we may not all be thinking of the same thing when we use it. Like the Greek word for *baptism*,[1] which historically meant to immerse and now means other things, so it is with the word *worship*. In the evangelical tradition, *worship* has come to mean an event in which people offer devotion to God, usually carried out in an

---

[1] Βαπτίζω, *baptízō.*

assembly. Or more recently, worship has come to mean the music within that assembly.

As a worship leader for many years, I often heard someone say something like this: *The worship was really great today*, meaning they liked the music. I certainly hope that the music glorified God but, it is equally important that all other aspects of the corporate gathering are genuine expressions of worship as well. Just as a song can be glorifying to God, so also is the delivery of the sermon an act of worship. Are not the testimonies worship? Are not the prayers worship? In each case, the one who leads those elements is the worship leader. Music is not worship, only a tool that may be useful to express it. Our confusion in the way we use the word *worship* demonstrates that its meaning has lost clarity. There is no better place to go than the Bible to discover exactly what the word *worship* means.

The word most commonly translated *worship* in the Old Testament is the Hebrew word שָׁחָה [*shachah* /shaw·khaw/], meaning to prostrate one's self—face to the ground. It is first used in Genesis 22:5 when Abraham says to his servants, *stay here with the donkey, and I and the lad will go over there; and we will worship and return to you.* Perhaps the idea is somewhat lost on us. If we applied many of our privately held definitions of worship, we might assume that Abraham and Isaac were going to say some prayers, sing songs, give an offering and come back. When instead, it could read, *I and the lad will go over there, put ourselves on the ground in humility, and return to you.*

Our English word *worship* means to ascribe worth to someone or something. While this is part of the concept, it lacks an important component. *Shachah* is reflexive. This verb is both the subject (the one doing the action) and the object (the one to whom the action is done). In other words, a reflexive verb indicates that the one who performs the action does so to himself. The greatest adjustment we need to make in our understanding is that worship is something we must first do to *ourselves* before we can point any acceptable action toward God. Worship certainly acknowledges the worth of God. But what is the appropriate response to His worth? What will a man do to himself because he recognizes the worth of God? The believer who truly worships responds to God by doing something to himself—he humbles himself; he submits. Just as the Hebrew word indicates, he lowers himself and submits himself to God. This is *worship from the ground up.*

For this reason, worship can never begin at eye level with God. That is not to say worship is groveling and nothing else. It is only when one humbles himself before God that he finds himself lifted by God's gracious hand to do the unthinkable, to interact face to face with the Almighty. This type of communion was the type Moses understood—a full portrait of complete intimacy and total reverential awe. While the LORD hid Moses in the cleft of the rock as He passed by, He spent time speaking to Moses face to face as a man does his own friend.[1]

---

[1] Exodus 33:11-23.

Biblical worship is always demonstrated by a higher view of God in the estimation of the worshiper, and, at the same time, has a humility that yields an indescribable intimacy with the Most High. It is to the humble that God grants both His grace and the intimacy of His presence.[1] When we worship, as this biblical word instructs us, we recognize God's greatness and, in response, we *shachah*, or lower ourselves in subjection to Him, obediently yielding to His will for us. Therefore, while the English word *worship* means to ascribe worth to another, the Old Testament word includes both recognizing God's worth and humbling ourselves as a response to Him.

In the Ten Commandments, the significance of submitting to another is illustrated in the command not to make any idols (Ex. 20:4-6). God declares that we are not to *shachah* (that is, bow down before or make ourselves subject to) any idol. This helps us understand God's jealousy. He is not jealous as an insecure lover would be. Rather, if we truly worship anything besides Him, we have made ourselves subject to it; when, instead, God is the only appropriate object of our submission. In other words, the fundamental concept of true worship is not acknowledging one greater or ascribing value to one greater but subjecting ourselves to One greater.

In the New Testament, the word most commonly translated *worship* is προσκυνέω [*proskuneo* /pros·koo·neh·o/]. It is a contraction of two words, *pros* (toward) and *kuneo*, which means to kiss or adore. The meaning of this word is best understood when placed in its cultural context.

> The ancient oriental (especially Persian) mode of salutation between persons of equal ranks was to kiss each other on the lips; when the difference of rank was slight, they kissed each other on the cheek; when one was much inferior, he fell upon his knees and touched his forehead to the ground or prostrated himself, throwing kisses at the same time toward the superior. It is this latter mode of salutation that Gr. [Greek] writers express by *proskunéō*.[2]

While a believer may adore God, he cannot do so in biblical terms unless, considering the extreme difference in rank between himself and God, he lowers himself. The difference in rank between God and human beings is infinite. Even the illustration of a dog licking the master's hand[3] does not adequately communicate our inferiority to Him. Recognizing God's superiority causes the worshiper to humble himself in order to adore Him. *Proskuneo* communicates subservience from the worshiper as well as the mutual affection that exists between him and God. Again, unlike the English word *worship*, which only ascribes worth to one greater, the New Testament word goes further. Like the

---

[1] James 4:6-8.

[2] Spiros Zodhiates, ed., *The Complete Word Study Dictionary: New Testament* (Chattanooga: AMG Publishers, 1992), 1233–34.

[3] James Strong, *Strong's Exhaustive Concordance of the Bible* (Peabody, MA: Hendrickson Publishers, 2007), 4352.

Old Testament word, it demonstrates one who recognizes a superior and, in response, performs a reflexive action—the humbling of self.

Shachah and *proskuneo* carry the same essential component of submission. Both go beyond a general acknowledgement of God's greatness to fully embrace His greatness *and* fully submit to His authority. The Apostle Peter highlights this difference when he describes the power of the devil (like a roaring lion) but commands us to resist him.[1] This illustrates that to acknowledge the worth or power of something is not necessarily to worship it. Even the demons clearly understand and acknowledge the power of God—but they neither lovingly nor willfully worship.[2] When Jesus was tempted in the wilderness, Satan invited Jesus to fall down and worship him (Matthew 4:9). Here the word translated *worship* is *proskuneo*. The temptation Satan offers is not for Jesus to recognize Satan's power; certainly Jesus knew the power of Satan and its limits. Rather, Satan is asking Jesus to submit to his authority.

In our culture, submission is seen as weakness. Because of that, we learn to resist submission by asserting ourselves. However, it was in Jesus' submission that we see His unparalleled strength and by that submission, He was rewarded with the complete approval of His Father.

> Have this attitude in yourselves which was also in Christ Jesus, who, although He existed in the form of God, did not regard equality with God a thing to be grasped, but emptied Himself, taking the form of a bond-servant, and being made in the likeness of men. Being found in appearance as a man, He humbled Himself by becoming obedient to the point of death, even death on a cross. For this reason also, God highly exalted Him, and bestowed on Him the name which is above every name, so that at the name of Jesus EVERY KNEE WILL BOW, of those who are in heaven and on earth and under the earth, and that every tongue will confess that Jesus Christ is Lord, to the glory of God the Father.
>
> Philippians 2:5-11

For us, submission to God should never be viewed as weakness. It is the way we express our true devotion to God. When we submit to God, we have lowered ourselves to the place where willing participation in worship really begins. Luke 7:36-50 gives one of the most beautiful pictures of what lowering one's self looks like and, in doing so, paints a beautiful picture of worship.

> [36] Now one of the Pharisees invited Jesus to have dinner with him, so he went to the Pharisee's house and reclined at the table. [37]When a woman who had lived a sinful life in that town learned that Jesus was

---

[1] 1 Peter 5:8-9.
[2] James 2:19.

eating at the Pharisee's house, she brought an alabaster jar of perfume, [38] and as she stood behind him at his feet weeping, she began to wet his feet with her tears. Then she wiped them with her hair, kissed them and poured perfume on them.

[39] When the Pharisee who had invited him saw this, he said to himself, "If this man were a prophet, he would know who is touching him and what kind of woman she is—that she is a sinner."

[40] Jesus answered him, "Simon, I have something to tell you."

"Tell me, teacher," he said.

[41] "Two men owed money to a certain moneylender. One owed him five hundred denarii, and the other fifty. [42] Neither of them had the money to pay him back, so he canceled the debts of both. Now which of them will love him more?"

[43] Simon replied, "I suppose the one who had the bigger debt canceled."

"You have judged correctly," Jesus said.

[44] Then he turned toward the woman and said to Simon, "Do you see this woman? I came into your house. You did not give me any water for my feet, but she wet my feet with her tears and wiped them with her hair. [45] You did not give me a kiss, but this woman, from the time I entered, has not stopped kissing my feet. [46] You did not put oil on my head, but she has poured perfume on my feet. [47] Therefore, I tell you, her many sins have been forgiven—for she loved much. But he who has been forgiven little loves little."

[48] Then Jesus said to her, "Your sins are forgiven."

[49] The other guests began to say among themselves, "Who is this who even forgives sins?"

[50] Jesus said to the woman, "Your faith has saved you; go in peace."

Jesus did not shun her love and adoration. He accepted her worship. There is an interesting progression in verse thirty-eight. First, notice that as the woman *stood behind him* [Jesus] *at his feet weeping, she began to wet his feet with her tears.* We do not know if her sobs were silent or audible; but from where she stood, her tears fell onto His feet. Next, she washed His feet with her hair. As was the custom, her hair was likely long. She would have accomplished this by kneeling, using her long hair to wipe the mixture of tears and dust from Jesus' feet. Then, she began to kiss His feet. To do this, she must have bent even lower. Finally, she gave her offering by applying perfume to Jesus' feet. Her posture changed—from standing, to kneeling, to bending low. In that moment, she was unconcerned with the critics. While pride worries about such things, her humility kept her attention on the object of her affection. In order to show her love for Jesus, she had to lower herself. Just as it is for all worshipers, true worshipers must lower themselves. That is the reflexive nature of worship. Jesus explains to

Simon the reason for her love and gratitude—forgiveness. Like the one who owed much and found himself released from debt, she had been forgiven much. Nowhere in this passage is the word *worship* used. Nevertheless, Jesus accepted what we should hope to bring in worship: devoted love and overwhelming gratitude.

This raises significant questions about our understanding of worship. What is lacking in our professed love for Christ that keeps us from lowering ourselves and loving Him with abandon? Jesus answers that question in His dialogue with Simon. He asks, *Now which of them will love him more?* Jesus affirms Simon's answer, *the one who had the bigger debt canceled.* Jesus' parable is an indictment to many of us who have become comfortable with our own forgiveness and as a result, sloppy with the grace of God. We no longer love deeply because we have forgotten the greatness of debt we once had. Like Simon, we easily see the sinfulness of others but have long since disconnected God's just wrath with the gravity of our own sin.

This raises a second question. If we could imagine ourselves without Christ, how far would we see ourselves separated from God? The distance we see between God and ourselves before we were saved reveals how much debt we think needed to be canceled. Despite what we may profess with our mouths, the conduct of our lives often reveals a slapdash reckoning of our sin and God's forgiveness. To paraphrase Jesus' words, we love little because we have come to think that we were forgiven little. Perhaps, even worse, we have never really understood the depth of our lostness apart from God's intervention. To correct this requires each worshiper to see God higher and holier than anything he had ever imagined, to see ourselves, apart from redemption, more thoroughly sinful and hopeless than we ever believed, to see the gulf that once separated us from Him wider than we could ever comprehend. Only then will we love greatly and worship rightly.

This makes the lowering of self even more important for the worshiper. If we are to see God bigger, we must see ourselves smaller. The Psalmist said, *O magnify the Lord with me, And let us exalt His name together.*[1] How can we magnify the Lord? Can we make Him bigger than He is? Of course, the answer is *no.* While it is not possible to make God any bigger than He is, we can adjust our perspective. The photographer who wants to make the building look its tallest sets the eye of the camera as low to the base as possible. While he is incapable of making the building any larger than it is, the resulting photograph provides the viewer the best opportunity to grasp the building's height. This is what worship does for the believer and why the reflexive element is essential. By lowering ourselves, we change our perspective. To go a step further, worship is the telescope by which we view God and ourselves. Looking at God from the small end, He is magnified and we see His greatness. Reversing the telescope, we look at ourselves from the large end and we look unbelievably small in comparison. When we magnify Him and minimize ourselves, we see how unlike

---

[1] Psalm 34:3.

Him we are and come to understand something of the gulf God crossed through Calvary. Submission exceeds mere duty and becomes privilege and joy. At that moment, our love and gratitude take breath again and exhale in adoration of our Redeemer.

The significance of both the Old Testament and New Testament words for *worship* is crucial for any believer desiring to *behold the beauty of the Lord.*[1] This can help correct inadequate definitions based on culture and ignorance. God is to be acknowledged as God and we are to submit ourselves to His power and authority. To be sure, there is a balance in this. We are not to exist in cowering fear of God—as if He were an arbitrary monster apt to injure us at any time. Both of these words for worship communicate nearness. However, it is clear that we often separate our knowledge of who God is from our submission and obedience. While many definitions of worship exist, the Scripture makes it clear that worship is far more than ascribing worth to Him.

For our discussion, we will define worship for the believer in the following way:

> *Worship is the proper state of submission before God:*
> *it acknowledges who He has been, is now, and will be; and*
> *it recognizes who I was, am now, and will be.*

Worship begins with *being*—existing in a state before God that is submissive to His authority and properly acknowledges Him. Such a state of being is impossible apart from redemption. The ability to exist in a submissive state before God and be in union with Him was how man was created. Yet Adam's sin, or self-will—the antithesis of submission—is the inheritance of every human being. Only by God's intervention can we become new creations, who in the power of Christ can rightly acknowledge and submit to God. From the moment of redemption, our acknowledgement and submission grows deeper and richer any time we gain a higher view of God.

Worship is also *doing*. First and foremost, worship brings God to the forefront of the mind and heart, recalling the work of God in our own history and His interaction with humankind. This draws our attention to His faithfulness and perpetual goodness. In a very real sense, this is the record of Scripture—the story of God's activity toward humankind. Our God is the God of all that has ever been. But, we do not only acknowledge God for what He has done. God is also the I AM, the Ever Present One. As a result, He is the One with whom we have to deal in the here and now.[2] We worship Him in the here and now because He is presently surrounding and sustaining us. Finally, worship also looks to the

---

[1] Psalm 27:4.
[2] Hebrews 4:13.

16

future, to God's activity in the culmination of human history, which finds its end in Him.

As we worship, we are not able to ignore our own condition: past, present and future. In looking at who we have been, we are enamored again with God's work in redemption—the chasm once separating us closed and His gracious hand sustaining our lives. When we lay our lives before God and gain an understanding of who we are today, we can say with the Psalmist, *Search me, O God, and know my heart.* Knowing that nothing is hidden from His eye, and, despite all we are at this present moment, He loves us as His children. Finally, worship looks to our future, who we will be when He has completed His work in us. We rejoice in Him because He will be faithful and continue to work in us until all of His purpose is accomplished.[1]

OTHER COMMON OLD TESTAMENT WORDS

Besides these two key words, the Bible contains many others associated with worship and its practice. A brief description of each of these is included below. From these words we gain a broader picture of what worship looks and sounds like. While many of these words suggest an audible sound or a visible action, they are acceptable only in as much as they reflect the heart of one who worships in *the proper state of submission before God.*

praise- from the Hebrew root הָלַל, *halal* ☐ This word suggests boastful rejoicing, perhaps even to the point of making a fool of one's self—to be so proud of who God is and what He has done for us that we rejoice in Him with abandonment. This abandoned joy is a result of acknowledging and submitting to God and is so consuming that there is no fear of looking foolish. Such joyful abandonment is demonstrated in Psalm 150:

> **Praise** the LORD!
> **Praise** God in His sanctuary;
> **Praise** Him in His mighty expanse.
> **Praise** Him for His mighty deeds;
> **Praise** Him according to His excellent greatness.
> **Praise** Him with trumpet sound;
> **Praise** Him with harp and lyre.
> **Praise** Him with timbrel and dancing;
> **Praise** Him with stringed instruments and pipe.
> **Praise** Him with loud cymbals;
> **Praise** Him with resounding cymbals.
> Let everything that has breath **praise** the LORD.
> **Praise** the LORD!

---

[1] Philippians 1:16.

bless- בָּרַךְ -- *barak* suggests extolling God's character or actions by speaking favorable words of Him or to Him. The idea is generally related to giving something of value as a sign of love or devotion. In this sense, we both bless God and are blessed by Him. Our favorable words toward Him, the recognition of His greatness, our submission to Him, are characteristic of the kind of worshipers the Father seeks. The act of speaking favorably to (or about) the Lord was particularly important for a Hebrew culture that used oral tradition as a means to pass on the valued story to subsequent generations. Reciting God's attributes to Him and to one another provided a way to keep God's truth in front of the people. Many of the Psalms are built around the simple construct of recalling the mighty acts of God, particularly toward Israel.

> **Bless** the LORD, O my soul,
> And all that is within me, **bless** His holy name.
> **Bless** the LORD, O my soul, And forget none of His benefits.
>
> Psalm 103:1-2

Archetypical of this genre, this Psalm then continues by recounting the benefits of God's character and His many benevolent acts toward His children. One of the functions of worship within the congregation is to remind one another regularly of the gracious acts of God toward His people.

sing- רָנַן -- *rā·năn* is used to describe singing in public that is both rhythmic and loud.

> Let the nations be glad and **sing** for joy;
> For You will judge the peoples with uprightness
>
> Psalm 67:4

זָמַר -- *zā·măr* a chanting melody either sung or played and related to the concept of striking an instrument.

> Shout joyfully to God, all the earth;
> **Sing** the glory of His name;
> Make His praise glorious.
>
> Psalm 66:1-2

שִׁיר -- *šîr* a term that indicates using the voice as an instrument.

> Then Moses and the sons of Israel sang this song to the LORD, and said, "I will **sing** to the LORD, for He is highly exalted."
>
> Exodus 15:1-2

Serve- עָבַד -- ʿā·ḇǎḏ may signify almost any activity performed with intensity but is often used in the context of one in servitude to another.

> Shout joyfully to the LORD, all the earth.
> **Serve** the LORD with gladness;
> Come before Him with joyful singing.
> We are His people and the sheep of His pasture.
>
> Psalm 100:1-2

OTHER COMMON NEW TESTAMENT WORDS

praise-

αἰνέω -- *aineo* to extol or commend.

> And a voice came from the throne, saying, "Give **praise** to our God, all you His bond-servants, you who fear Him, the small and the great."
>
> Revelation 19:5

ἔπαινος -- *epainos*, related to the above but more intense, it may be understood as giving full commendation to someone.

> He predestined us to adoption as sons through Jesus Christ to Himself, according to the kind intention of His will, to the **praise** of the glory of His grace, which He freely bestowed on us in the Beloved.
>
> Ephesians 1:5-6

glorify - δοξάζω -- *doxazo,* to celebrate, honor, or clothe with splendor. Since this word shares a common etymology with the root word for glory, it highlights the truth in which we may participate, drawing attention to the self-perpetuating glory of God.

> My Father is **glorified** by this, that you bear much fruit, and so prove to be My disciples.
>
> John 15:8

This word also may be translated *praise*:

> Now when the centurion saw what had happened, he began
> **praising** God, saying, "Certainly this man was innocent."
>
> Luke 23:47

bless (blessing)-εὐλογία -- *eulogia*, meaning to speak favorably of, to eulogize.
The connotation can be one of excessive flattery.

> Worthy is the Lamb that was slain to receive power and riches
> and wisdom and might and honor and glory and **blessing**.
>
> Revelation 5:12

serve (service)-
> λατρεία – *latreia* is translated variously as *service, worship* and *service of
> worship.*

> Therefore I urge you, brethren, by the mercies of God, to
> present your bodies a living and holy sacrifice, acceptable to
> God, which is your spiritual **service of worship**.
>
> Romans 12:1

λειτουργία -- *leitourgia* may be translated service or ministry and is used
in reference to acts of worship by believers as well as by the administration
of priestly functions (including those of Jesus). *Liturgy* (the order of
events in corporate worship) comes from this word.

> Therefore, since we receive a kingdom which cannot be shaken,
> let us show gratitude, by which we may offer to God an
> acceptable **service** with reverence and awe.
>
> Hebrews 12:28

Considering the meaning of the New Testament word *proskuneo*, the
significance of the New Testament words for *serve* should not be overlooked.
Both of them, *latreia* and *leitourgia,* stem from the same root. They are both
from the Greek word λατρίς – *latris,* which indicates the lowest menial servant,
and reflects the nature of submission and service. Even our service, the work we
do as a people on behalf of God, is given as humble and loving worship.

Each of these words helps clarify our concept of how worship is expressed.
Scriptural words associated with worship, translated *praise, bless, glorify, serve,*
etc., should all be understood in light of our understanding *shachah* and
proskuneo. Actually, these two words deal with our *being* (the proper state of

20

existence before God), while the other biblical words associated with worship help us understand *doing* (how we outwardly express that). It is impossible to *do* worship without *being* a worshiper. Otherwise, we find ourselves like the Children of Israel of whom God said, *they honor Me with their lips, but have removed their hearts far from Me.*[1] A common difficulty for all believers is that outwardly we can *do* actions that look like worship without *being* a worshiper.

The Worship God Desires

The fact that we as a fallen race can even participate in worship is a great privilege. We have already stated that God does not need our worship—but it is equally true that God desires our worship. Our unworthiness makes the words of Jesus in John 4 amazing.

> But an hour is coming, and now is, when the true worshipers will worship the Father in spirit and truth; for such people the Father seeks to be His worshipers. God is spirit and those who worship Him must worship in spirit and truth.
>
> John 4:22-24

Worship, as the state of proper submission (being) before God, is the foundation of all our proper dealings with Him. Worship cannot merely consist of outward acts. God is spirit and, therefore, the essence of our interaction with Him must be spiritual. Our interaction with God must first take place in our *being*—who we are, rather than in what we do. While we are commanded to glorify God with our physical being, such expressions are only acceptable if they represent the spirit of one who is truly inclined to the Lord. It is in our spirit, that part of us which will live forever, that we can have communion with God both in this life and the next. The truth is clear: there is no outward action we perform that makes our approach to God acceptable. Before our actions can be acceptable to Him, He first looks at the condition of our hearts. This makes the work of Christ an essential component. By the atoning work of Jesus, we are made acceptable to God and therefore have the means by which to approach Him.

As we discussed earlier, there is a type of conscripted worship in which all, redeemed or not, will engage. For the believer, however, worship is not conscripted. It is how we live day by day, how we acknowledge and respond to God in the core of our being. Worship is living life in such a way that we appropriately engage and experience His presence moment by moment. Worship is not a scheduled event on a church's calendar nor is it an activity that we undertake. It is a result of being recreated by the redeeming work of Jesus Christ. We have been given a new nature, a new spirit, in effect a whole new being. One may engage in activities that express worship, but those expressions cannot satisfy God's desire for willing worship unless they come from one who is first a

---

[1] Isaiah 29:13.

21

new creation. We are recreated to be living sacrifices.[1] In other words, what we do for God proceeds out of who we are. This makes worship, our proper state of existence before Him, the substance of our relationship with Him. The substance of our relationship must be constantly renewed so that we are living as God has recreated us to be. When our spirit is in the proper state of being, our actions can be genuine and acceptable expressions. This is worship in spirit.

Jesus not only says that we must worship in spirit but, we also must worship in truth. If we are to be genuine worshipers, it means all aspects of the relationship that we have with God must be on His terms. Our worship must line up with truth, His Word. God's Word guides us. God's Word sanctifies us[2] and makes our spiritual responses acceptable. It is essential that our worship be guided by Scripture. Unless worship is on God's terms, it is not acceptable at all. But truth in worship is not just about God's truth. It is also about truth inside the worshiper. That is only realized when our outward expressions are in agreement with our hearts. For the redeemed who have been recreated, outward actions must be in harmony with the new nature we have been given.

This is spirit and truth—being right before Him and responding sincerely, according to the truth of Scripture.

THE ESSENTIAL ELEMENTS FOR WILLING WORSHIP

We have answered the question of what is essential for worship to exist and seen that God alone is all that is needed. We understand that every knee will bow to Jesus, simply to acknowledge the created order. But, what is required for us to worship God out of desire rather than conscription? It will be helpful for us to break this down to the most fundamental elements. We have looked at spirit and truth, yet both of these presuppose several fundamental components of worship. Simply stated, the interaction between God and willing man begins with three essential components:

1) God must reveal Himself.

2) We must respond to Him.

3) We must have sufficient truth to guide this encounter.

First, God must reveal Himself to us. If God had not chosen to reveal Himself to us, we could have no hope of ever knowing Him, no hope of ever having fellowship between our spirit and His Spirit. Sometimes in our own overestimation of ourselves, we think that we are the ones who sought and found God. Nothing could be further from the truth. No person seeks after God apart from being drawn by Him.[3] Although the Apostle Paul says that God is not far from us,[4] had He chosen not to disclose Himself to us, it would be impossible to

---

[1] Romans 12:1.
[2] John 17:17.
[3] Romans 3:11; John 6:44.
[4] Acts 17:27.

ever find Him or know Him. Paul underscores the desperate nature of the situation in the first chapter of Romans. He reminds us that there is sufficient general revelation to demonstrate to all humankind that there is a God. Yet that knowledge alone is not enough to save us. It is only enough to confirm that, whatever God there is, He is not like us and we stand condemned apart from His gracious intervention.[1]

Second, we must respond to Him. Worship is not an initiative, it is a response. In other words, worship is never something we initiate and then get God's attention. A view like that would be more akin to the methods employed by the prophets of Baal on Mt. Carmel. Everything they tried was in hopes of getting their god(s) to respond, but *no one answered, and no one paid attention.*[2] Unfortunately, this misconception has been common throughout the history of the Church. No matter how we approach God in our worship, whether through personal piety, inspiring music or fervent prayers, we can never initiate an encounter with God. Even when Adam and Eve sinned, God's judgment of the Serpent revealed He already had begun the work of redemption.[3] Nothing humanity does can predate the work of God. Therefore, any worship we offer is a response to what God has already done.

Finally, truth must guide our response to God and His interaction with us. For God, that is not a problem; He is truth in every way. This is not the case for humankind—truth is not our nature. Because of the deceitfulness of the human heart, we are not even capable of knowing our own motives.[4] This makes Scripture an essential component. Without the objective truth of Scripture, we may find ourselves responding inappropriately to God; i.e., not responding on His terms. Unless we respond on God's terms, all our efforts are in vain because they are unacceptable to Him. Even more tragic, without truth to guide us, we may respond to something with our worship that is not even God at all. The truth of Scripture provides a constant by which the believer can evaluate those things to which he gives his devotion. This is crucial since worship is to *shachah* or submit one's self to something or someone. Truth is essential because it reveals both Whom we should worship and how to worship in an acceptable way.

Without God's self-revelation, there is nothing worthy of worship—He must begin the interaction. If we do not respond to Him, we cannot worship. Unless our response is in line with His truth, our responses will be unacceptable. These three essentials are interdependent. The absence of any one invalidates the human worship experience. The Old Testament often shows how God's people failed to respond to God or to do so appropriately. Likewise, the Church has shown her own confusion about these three essentials. As later discussions will demonstrate, Church history tells an often repeated story of attempts to get God's attention through intricate and complex worship forms or personal piety.

---

[1] Romans 1:18-20.
[2] 1 Kings 18:29.
[3] Genesis 3:15.
[4] Jeremiah 17:9.

These may represent well-meaning efforts to approach God but they prove insufficient since, above all, worship is simply our proper response to God. In many churches, believers invite or invoke the presence of God into a service of worship as if they are initiating contact with the Most High. Worship is not something to which we invite God. While the motive may be sincere, this represents a fundamental misconception and robs us of one of the most astounding truths that we can find in all of Scripture. The Mighty One, the Sovereign King of the universe, has lovingly summoned His subjects to come. He is the One who initiates and invites; ours is the privilege of response.

Isaiah's vision of God is archetypical of these three elements.[1] When God revealed Himself to Isaiah, it was extraordinary, allowing the prophet to see a fuller glimpse of his true Master. Struck by this clearer view of God, Isaiah responds in genuine humility, *Woe is me!* But this response is far more than acknowledging his weakness in the presence of the Almighty. He responds with genuine submission. Notice what happens to Isaiah:

> Then one of the seraphim flew to me with a burning coal in his hand, which he had taken from the altar with tongs. He touched my mouth with it and said, "Behold, this has touched your lips; and your iniquity is taken away and your sin is forgiven."
>
> Isaiah 6:6-7

No matter how many times we read this text, it still seems amazing that Isaiah stands without flinching, waiting for the burning coal to touch his lips. Is it not human nature to flinch or turn aside from God's work in our lives? When worship really works as God has designed it, He discloses Himself and then it is the worshiper's task to submit to the work of God in his or her life. Isaiah's submission to God is demonstrated in his willingness to stand still and allow God to work in his life. Isaiah's verbal response to God, *Here am I. Send Me* (v.8) is no surprise. He had already demonstrated a high view of God that resulted in a proper view of himself. His willingness to allow the burning coal to touch his lips was an expression of trust and submission. Isaiah goes far beyond words of commitment and surrenders all to the Lord's will. In such an atmosphere of surrender and trust, it is only natural that Isaiah volunteers for his commission and obediently fulfills its demands.

Perhaps no other passage in Scripture is more often referenced in a discussion on worship than the sixth chapter of Isaiah. This is for good reason since it gives a close camera angle of a one-on-one encounter between a human being and the LORD.[2] The way God discloses Himself and the way Isaiah responded demonstrates an important truth that can help us evaluate our own

---

[1] Isaiah 6:1-13.

[2] Isaiah's vision of the LORD was the second person of the Godhead, Jesus Christ. See John 12:41.

worship encounters: the intensity of a worship experience, whether personal or corporate, depends on how fully God discloses Himself and how deeply we respond. This is why Isaiah's encounter is so meaningful to us—God gloriously revealed Himself to Isaiah and Isaiah deeply responded to God. It is no accident that Isaiah is declared forgiven during this encounter. Whenever a believer responds to God in worship, there are always issues in the life of the worshiper that need correction. After all, the worshiper is standing before the Most High. Unlike Isaiah, who worshiped under the Old Covenant, the believer's forgiveness is already appropriated in the work of the cross. Nevertheless, there are still relationship issues between the believer and God that can only be right when the believer walks fully in agreement with God. This makes repentance an ongoing part of the New Covenant—the believer continues to turn from his own ways as he submits to the ways of God. As Isaiah discovered, worship provides an opportunity to check the heart and come into full conformity with God's will.

FOUNDATIONAL ISSUES FOR WORSHIP

Since worship is the state of proper submission before God, it is a fair question to ask how this is even possible since God is holy and we are not. Above all, this illustrates the necessity of Christ's work. When we look back at the cross, we see the death of Jesus as the means by which an unholy human being can be reconciled to a holy God. However, the crucifixion was not the beginning of God's interaction with humankind. It was a culmination of something planned before the world was created.[1] From the beginning, neither God's nature nor the way He interacts with human beings has changed. Even in Isaiah's encounter, there had to be some way to deal with his sin before his conversation with God could continue. Throughout God's interaction with humankind, man's sin has been an impediment to relationship. The means by which God addressed this demonstrates principles that are essential for building a proper theology of worship.

The opposing natures of God and fallen man

All truth flows from the person and character of God. He is the essence of all that is true and right. By contrast, human beings in their fallen state are the antithesis of truth.[2] And while God is pure and holy,[3] human righteousness is something else. Isaiah summed it up in these words:

> For all of us have become like one who is unclean, And all our righteous deeds are like a filthy garment; And all of us wither like a leaf, And our iniquities, like the wind, take us away.
>
> Isaiah 64:6

---

[1] Revelation 13:8.

[2] Jeremiah 17:9.

[3] Leviticus 11:44.

The fact that God by nature is transcendent and holy and man by nature is unholy and finite, places their natures in opposition to one another. That would not be of particular importance if God did not love human beings and desire to have ongoing interaction with them. We have already established the fact that God does not need us nor does He need our worship to be perfectly complete in Himself. He does seek our worship, however, and desires to reconcile us to Himself. In fact, the relationship God desires with humankind is not just one of servitude, though God's supremacy demands that. The relationship He desires with human beings is unique among all of His creation: Father to child.

The barrier between God and man

The dilemma is apparent in the fact that God will not co-mingle His holiness with the sinfulness of man. The kind of worship that is not conscripted—God desires willing worshipers—requires two fundamental elements. First, since God is sovereign, any relationship with Him requires His willingness. Because of God's holy nature, His desire to have a relationship with us who are sinners cannot violate His nature, neither His justice nor holiness. Second, humankind must be willing to approach God on His terms. This requires humble submission on man's part but leaves him in the untenable position of having nothing to offer to God that is acceptable—no way to close the barrier of separation between himself and God. This leaves a large gap between God and man. It is the distance between God's holiness and our unholiness.

God's solution

The solution is revealed in the way God allows for substitutionary atonement. For those of us who know Jesus, it is clear that His death on the cross was the mediation between God's holiness and our sinfulness, spanning the gap between God and man.[1] In Christ, God forever satisfied His own requirements for justice, a task that was beyond all human capability. That is the message of the New Covenant.[2] However, the death of Jesus was not only the beginning of the New Covenant; it was the final fulfillment of the First Covenant. The writer of Hebrews identifies Jesus as the completion of the First Covenant when he says:

> Every priest stands daily ministering and offering time after time the same sacrifices, which can never take away sins; but He, having offered one sacrifice for sins for all time, sat down at the right hand of God, waiting from that time onward until His enemies be made a footstool for His feet. For by one offering He has perfected for all time those who are sanctified.
>
> Hebrews 10:11-14

---

[1] 1 Timothy 2:5-6.
[2] Matthew 26:28.

The First Covenant is important to us because it demonstrates the way God chose to deal with the separation between Himself and humankind. It was rooted in a system of sacrifice that made interaction with God possible and yet did not compromise His holiness. God established a system whereby a sacrifice could be presented as a substitute for the guilty one. This system presumed the fact that human beings had nothing within themselves that could acceptably be offered to atone for guilt. In the **Sacrificial System**, God provided a way for man's guilt to be absolved by allowing that guilt to be transferred to an acceptable sacrifice. This sacrifice, unlike the guilty one bringing it, was clean and without blemish.[1] Guilt was transferred to the sacrifice and upon the death of the animal through the shedding of its own blood, God's justice was satisfied.

The first sacrifice offered in the Bible was not offered by humans; it was provided and offered by God on behalf of Adam and Eve. In the story of man's fall in Genesis 3, the Bible says that Adam and Eve realized they were naked and were ashamed. This shame was an outward sign of their newfound guilt. God showed great compassion by covering them with animal skins.[2] It is interesting that God could have provided clothing for them with some plant byproduct. The significance of God's choice is notable. Because of their sin, Adam and Eve would eventually experience physical death. But slaying an animal to provide a covering for them demonstrated two important lessons: that the wages of sin is death,[3] and that God's way of dealing with sin requires blood.[4]

Just as God provided and offered the first sacrifice, He provided and offered the last sacrifice as well—Jesus Christ. All the blood sacrifices given by the Children of Israel as part of the Sacrificial System reflect the basic parameters of the first sacrifice and point to the last. The death of Jesus on the cross conforms to God's own pattern established in the Sacrificial System. Like the first man and woman, humankind can never solve the sin problem on its own. We must go beyond ourselves to one who is clean and without blemish. By faith in God's provision our guilt was laid upon Jesus and, through the shedding of His own blood, God's justice was satisfied. Thus, God is both the *just and the justifier*.[5] The importance of this in a discussion on worship is paramount. God desires our relational worship but that is not possible without addressing the sin problem. Our ability to approach God is made possible by God's provision.

---

[1] See Chapter 2, *Old Testament Archetypes.*

[2] Like God's decision to remove them from the garden, lest Adam and Eve be immortal in their broken state, God's provision of a covering shows His compassion despite their sin.

[3] Romans 6:23.

[4] Hebrews 9:22.

[5] Romans 3:26.

Since God is eternal and is eternally worshiped, worship has neither beginning nor end. It has always been and always will be because God *is*. If we choose to acknowledge His greatness and submit to His authority, we can willfully and joyfully participate in this eternal activity. It requires we enter into it on His terms, in compliance with His Word. The worship God desires from those who love Him does not consist merely of what we *do*; it is grounded in who we *are*, whenever we are in the proper state of submission to Him. On our own, it is impossible to reach any state of being that is proper or acceptable to God. However, He has taken care of that for us by allowing our guilt to be placed on another, providing forgiveness and restoration to us. Before Calvary, God accomplished this through the sacrificial animal, each sacrifice looking forward to one final and sufficient sacrifice. Since the crucifixion, we find our provision for a relationship with God by looking back at the holy altar where God in Christ shed His own blood for the Church.[1] What more can He do to draw us to worship, since He who is our Prophet, Priest, and King is also our sacrificial Lamb? In light of that, every believer should make worship his life pursuit. Worship is not only the proper state of existence before God, it is the true fulfillment of our lives—the reason God created us.

---

[1] Acts 20:28.

28

CHAPTER 2

OLD TESTAMENT ARCHETYPES
AND CHRISTIAN WORSHIP

While it is possible for a New Testament believer to worship God without understanding the details of Old Testament worship, such a study has great value to us. God's actions are always consistent with His character. Because of that, studying the ways God interacted with people in the Old Testament helps deepen our understanding of who God is. We have two Testaments in our Bible but that should not obscure the fact that we have one God, who acts consistently toward humankind. The implications of God's relationship with His chosen people are more than we can cover in the scope of this discussion. For our purposes, we will focus on how three practices of the Jewish people provided the primary forms through which they understood and expressed worship both in their personal lives and when they assembled. Each of these has something to teach us about God and what He desires from us in worship. These three practices are observing the Sabbath, keeping the Feasts, and participating in the Sacrificial System.

From the vantage point of many evangelical Christians, it is difficult to separate the observance of the Sabbath from Sunday worship gatherings. Some see the practice of meeting on Sunday as a continuation of weekly Jewish worship and obedience to the fourth commandment.[1] However, the Christian observance of the Lord's Day (assembling for worship on Sunday) is a practice distinct from the Jewish Sabbath.[2] To illustrate this point, I have often asked my students to discuss and defend their scriptural rationale for weekly corporate gatherings. Invariably answers will include God's fourth commandment to *remember the Sabbath and keep it holy.* Growing up in a Baptist church, I, like many of my students, was taught that coming to church on Sunday was exactly what the fourth commandment required. However, the biblical command to remember the Sabbath did not mean a weekly gathering for the purpose of corporate worship, at least not to the Jews who originally received it. To understand the Jewish Sabbath, it is important to recognize that the Sabbath was not initially a gathering of any kind. To be sure, weekly worship (in fact daily, continual worship) is certainly a biblical concept and one with which the Children of Israel would have been well acquainted. God had rested on the seventh day from His labors and had set the day apart as holy (Genesis 2:2-3). Later, when chiding the Israelites for attempting to gather manna on the Sabbath day, God clearly commanded them to stay at home (not even to leave the house) on that day:

> Then the LORD said to Moses, "How long do you refuse to keep My commandments and My instructions? See, the LORD has given you the Sabbath; therefore He gives you bread for two days on the sixth day. Remain every man in his place; let no man go out of his place on the seventh day."
>
> Exodus 16:28

The perception that observing the Sabbath means gathering for corporate worship each week is not correct. Whatever God intended for the Sabbath, it was possible to accomplish that without gathering for corporate worship. What this does tell us is that the key ingredients of the Sabbath were rest from labor and spending time with family. By staying home on the Sabbath, the Children of Israel could focus on a day of rest and, presumably, give themselves to their families and to remembering the mighty acts of God. In fact, Jews were commanded to make their homes the hub of all spiritual instruction.[3]

---

[1] Exodus 20:8.

[2] The observance of the Lord's Day is discussed in Chapter 3, *The New Covenant and the Early Church.*

[3] Deuteronomy 6:1-9.

Though not mandated by Scripture, weekly gatherings for corporate worship had developed within Jewish culture by the time of Christ. These weekly gatherings did not occur at the Temple but rather at a local meeting place called the Synagogue. The practice of a local gathering place to observe the Sabbath began during the Babylonian exile, when Temple gatherings were not possible. At the Synagogue, Jews could meet to sing, fellowship with one another, pray, and hear Scripture read and explained. Because these practices did not require the use of the Temple, Synagogues could be located within the communities where Jews lived. During the inter-testamental period, the Synagogue became firmly established as the central hub of Jewish culture. Although there is no Scripture establishing the Synagogue in the Old Testament, there was evidently not anything wrong with this extra-biblical practice since Jesus participated in it.[1]

As for what we as Christian worshipers should take from the Jewish observance of the Sabbath, it is not that the Old Testament commands a weekly gathering for corporate worship, nor that we are bound to observe the Sabbath as the Jews did. The lessons from the Old Testament Sabbath are much more basic and profound. First, within a group of the faithful, regular observance of worship begins in the home, not in a church building. This is something that has disappeared from the consciousness of many Christians, seeming almost archaic in light of present notions of what worship should be. The results of this are unfortunate, placing the primary responsibility on the local church for cultivating worship in the hearts of people, or more specifically, on a weekly service, instead of in the home where it belongs. Using our weekly assemblies as a replacement for prayer, Bible reading, and teaching about God in the home violates God's intent that worship be rooted in our family life.

The second lesson runs even more contrary to our present culture. While we are no longer bound to a Sabbath day, God has designed us with a need to break from the everyday grind in order to remember what He has done for us. God created for six days and on the seventh day, He ceased from His labors. He was not tired; His strength is without limits. The Scripture explains that God was demonstrating an important cadence that we are to imitate:

> Six days you shall labor and do all your work, but the seventh day is a Sabbath of the LORD your God; in it you shall not do any work, you or your son or your daughter, your male or your female servant or your cattle or your sojourner who stays with you. "For in six days the LORD made the heavens and the earth, the sea and all that is in them, and rested on the seventh day; therefore the LORD blessed the Sabbath day and made it holy.
>
> Exodus 20:9-12

---

[1] See Matthew 4:23 and John 18:20.

Just as the rests in a musical score allow us to hear the rhythm and beauty of the notes that are played, breaks in the busy cadence of life help us find order and beauty in the life we live. Breaks from our busy cadence are as important as the railroad crossing sign that reminds us to *stop, look, and listen.* As the Scripture above says, the cadence that God has created is to remind us that He is the maker of heaven and earth. As if we could so easily forget, all we see—the beauty of the earth, the cycle of days and seasons, the order of the cosmos—declares the glory of God.[1] If we live with no regular cadence that includes resting from our labors, we have robbed ourselves of a God-ordered cycle by which we may be constantly reminded that we are the creatures who live in a creation made by our Creator.

Even as church leaders, we need to be careful about seeing our day of worship as one to fill up with activities. Congregations that evaluate their own success by the number of people involved in a full day of Sunday programs may be working against the basic principle of helping people see and embrace the importance of a cycle of labor and rest. In many of our churches, the gathering time for corporate worship is just another activity in a full day. It is not that activities on Sunday are wrong. After all, the Lord's Day is not the Sabbath and, furthermore, believers may benefit from such programs. However, we should carefully consider that a fundamental, biblical concept of spiritual health includes a systematic break from the normal level of activity. As leaders, we should understand that spiritual maturity in our people is not measured by how many hours they spend at church gatherings. Most of us, like those whom we lead, struggle with integrating the concept of spiritual rest into our lives.

Just as the sacrificial system pointed to a final sacrifice, the weekly observance of a Sabbath pointed to a coming rest found in Jesus Christ:

> So there remains a Sabbath rest for the people of God. For the one who has entered His rest has himself also rested from his works, as God did from His. Therefore let us be diligent to enter that rest, so that no one will fall, through following the same example of disobedience.
>
> Hebrews 4:9-11

The writer of Hebrews reminds us that the rest God has for us is far more than ceasing from physical labor or activity. As an archetype, the Old Testament Sabbath reminds us that we must constantly adjust our focus and allow the Lord to draw us back into close fellowship with Him. This happens when believers are diligent to enter into the rest provided in Jesus Christ. Thankfully, this rest is no longer limited to one day in a week; for one day is no holier than any other

---

[1] Psalm 19:1.

is.[1] Instead, this rest is the proper state of existence before God and lived day by day in obedience to His Word.

THE JEWISH FEASTS AND CORPORATE WORSHIP

While the Old Testament did not command a weekly gathering for corporate worship, God instructed the Jews to assemble in conjunction with feasts and celebrations that occurred throughout the year and, in each case, corporate worship played a significant role. This made the Jewish feasts and annual celebrations significant both spiritually and culturally. Just as the Sabbath was the spiritual hub for families, so the Feasts and Holy Days were the spiritual hub of the nation. Holy Days could be called for special reasons or as a part of the regular calendar like the *Passover, Day of Trumpets* or the *Day of Atonement.* Gatherings of the people could also last for more than one day. The Jewish calendar specified three week-long feasts: *The Feast of Unleavened Bread* which began with the *Passover, The Feast of Weeks*, and *The Feast of Booths.* A brief description of these is included below. As for the cultural significance, it is noteworthy that the Feasts provided a means by which the identity of the whole nation as favored and chosen could be celebrated. Since three of the feasts required a pilgrimage to the Temple, they were part of the common cultural experience of the nation and key components in shaping Israel's identity.

HOLY DAYS AND FEASTS

Passover and The Feast of Unleavened Bread was a commemoration of the deliverance of Israel from bondage in Egypt, followed by a weeklong feast. The Scripture describes how the Passover begins these eight days:

> In the first month, on the fourteenth day of the month at twilight is the LORD'S Passover. Then on the fifteenth day of the same month there is the Feast of Unleavened Bread to the LORD; for seven days you shall eat unleavened bread. On the first day you shall have a holy convocation; you shall not do any laborious work. But for seven days you shall present an offering by fire to the LORD. On the seventh day is a holy convocation; you shall not do any laborious work.
>
> Leviticus 23:5-8

---

[1] Romans 14:5-6: *One person regards one day above another, another regards every day alike. Each person must be fully convinced in his own mind. He who observes the day, observes it for the Lord, and he who eats, does so for the Lord, for he gives thanks to God; and he who eats not, for the Lord he does not eat, and gives thanks to God.*

The feast began with the Passover meal and was to last for seven days during which no heavy work was done and only unleavened bread was to be eaten. The Passover was a perpetual reminder of God's deliverance of the Israelites from Egypt. Since leaven is a common biblical symbol for sin, this feast speaks of cleansing and true relationship with God.[1] Each of the seven days a burnt offering was given; the fire representing purification. With respect to corporate worship, the significance of this festival was that the first and the last day called for a sacred assembly, also known as a *holy convocation*. The whole week was a common experience for everyone and these sacred assemblies provided special times of corporate worship.

First Fruits: During this celebration, the Children of Israel made an offering of the first sheaf of grain from the harvest. The offering not only included the first sheaf of the harvest but also called for a burnt offering, a grain offering, and a drink offering. As a perpetual statute, this day served as a reminder that God was the provider and that He was due the full devotion of His people:

> Then the LORD spoke to Moses, saying, "Speak to the sons of Israel and say to them, 'When you enter the land which I am going to give to you and reap its harvest, then you shall bring in the sheaf of the first fruits of your harvest to the priest. 'He shall wave the sheaf before the LORD for you to be accepted; on the day after the sabbath the priest shall wave it. 'Now on the day when you wave the sheaf, you shall offer a male lamb one year old without defect for a burnt offering to the LORD. 'Its grain offering shall then be two-tenths of an ephah of fine flour mixed with oil, an offering by fire to the LORD for a soothing aroma, with its drink offering, a fourth of a hin of wine. 'Until this same day, until you have brought in the offering of your God, you shall eat neither bread nor roasted grain nor new growth. It is to be a perpetual statute throughout your generations in all your dwelling places.
>
> Leviticus 23:9-13

The Feast of Weeks, also known as Pentecost:

> You shall also count for yourselves from the day after the Sabbath, from the day when you brought in the sheaf of the wave offering; there shall be seven complete Sabbaths. You shall count fifty days to the day after the seventh Sabbath; then you shall present a new grain offering to the LORD. You shall bring in from your dwelling places

---

[1] In Luke 12:1, Jesus specifically used leaven to describe the sin of hypocrisy among the Pharisees. The removal of leaven, then, may be understood as a figure of true relationship with God rather than merely outward religion.

two loaves of bread for a wave offering, made of two-tenths of an ephah; they shall be of a fine flour, baked with leaven as first fruits to the LORD. Along with the bread you shall present seven one year old male lambs without defect, and a bull of the herd and two rams; they are to be a burnt offering to the LORD, with their grain offering and their drink offerings, an offering by fire of a soothing aroma to the LORD. You shall also offer one male goat for a sin offering and two male lambs one year old for a sacrifice of peace offerings. The priest shall then wave them with the bread of the first fruits for a wave offering with two lambs before the LORD; they are to be holy to the LORD for the priest. On this same day you shall make a proclamation as well; you are to have a holy convocation. You shall do no laborious work. It is to be a perpetual statute in all your dwelling places throughout your generations.

Leviticus 23:15-19

This feast occurred fifty days after the first Sabbath of Passover. The timing of the feast (late spring/early summer) coincided with the year's first grain harvest and was a reminder that God was the source of their life. The use of burnt offerings and the waving of bread served to remind God's people that they were dependent on Him for both sustenance and forgiveness. This feast included a one day sacred assembly. It is not hard to imagine Jews gathering to glorify God for once again allowing a productive harvest.

The Feast of Booths (also called the Feast of Tabernacles), like the Feast of Unleavened Bread, lasted for seven days and included burnt offerings for the Lord:

Speak to the sons of Israel, saying, "On the fifteenth of this seventh month is the Feast of Booths for seven days to the LORD. On the first day is a holy convocation; you shall do no laborious work of any kind. For seven days you shall present an offering by fire to the LORD. On the eighth day you shall have a holy convocation and present an offering by fire to the LORD; it is an assembly. You shall do no laborious work."

Leviticus 23:34-36

This Feast began with a sacred assembly and ended with one as well on the eighth day. During this time, families made shelters of tree branches and camped in them for the week. The significance of this was to remind Israel that they had once sojourned in the wilderness, kept by God until the people reached the Promised Land.

The Day of Trumpets occurred just before the Day of Atonement. Blowing of the ram's horn (*shofar*) signaled a time of preparation for the upcoming national day of humility and repentance and included another sacred assembly:

> Again the LORD spoke to Moses, saying, "Speak to the sons of Israel, saying, 'In the seventh month on the first of the month you shall have a rest, a reminder by blowing of trumpets, a holy convocation. You shall not do any laborious work, but you shall present an offering by fire to the LORD.' "
>
> Leviticus 23:24

The **Day of Atonement** occurred just five days prior to the Feast of **Booths.** This was observed only one day each year:[1]

> The LORD spoke to Moses, saying, "On exactly the tenth day of this seventh month is the day of atonement; it shall be a holy convocation for you, and you shall humble your souls and present an offering by fire to the LORD. You shall not do any work on this same day, for it is a day of atonement, to make atonement on your behalf before the LORD your God. If there is any person who will not humble himself on this same day, he shall be cut off from his people. As for any person who does any work on this same day, that person I will destroy from among his people. You shall do no work at all. It is to be a perpetual statute throughout your generations in all your dwelling places. It is to be a Sabbath of complete rest to you, and you shall humble your souls; on the ninth of the month at evening, from evening until evening you shall keep your Sabbath."
>
> Leviticus 23:26-31

This day served as a national day of repentance and forgiveness during which each individual was to humble himself before the Lord. On this day and only this day, the High Priest would enter the Holy of Holies. First, he offered a bullock for his own sin. The blood of the bull was taken into the Holy of Holies and sprinkled on the Mercy Seat. For the congregation, he used two goats. The first goat was slaughtered and burned as a sin offering. Just as he had used the blood of the bullock as a propitiation for his own sin, the priest used blood from the goat for the sins of the people. He took it into the Holy of Holies and sprinkled it on the Mercy Seat. Then, combining blood from the bullock and the slaughtered goat, the priest smeared it over the horns of the altar. The other goat, also a sin offering, became the scapegoat. The High Priest laid his hands on the head of the animal and confessed the sins of the entire nation. The goat was then

---

[1] For a more detailed description, see Leviticus 16.

36

driven out from among the people. The reason two goats are used *is to be found purely in the physical impossibility of combining all the features that had to be set forth in the sin-offering, in one single animal.*[1] Both the satisfaction of God's justice and the removal of the people's sin guiltiness are vividly demonstrated in the use of two animals as one sin offering.

The Feast of Purim was established by Mordecai. This day of celebration marked the deliverance of Israel from Haran's threat of slaughter.

> Then Mordecai recorded these events, and he sent letters to all the Jews who were in all the provinces of King Ahasuerus, both near and far, obliging them to celebrate the fourteenth day of the month Adar, and the fifteenth day of the same month, annually, because on those days the Jews rid themselves of their enemies, and it was a month which was turned for them from sorrow into gladness and from mourning into a holiday; that they should make them days of feasting and rejoicing and sending portions of food to one another and gifts to the poor. Thus the Jews undertook what they had started to do, and what Mordecai had written to them. For Haman the son of Hammedatha, the Agagite, the adversary of all the Jews, had schemed against the Jews to destroy them and had cast Pur, that is the lot, to disturb them and destroy them. But when it came to the king's attention, he commanded by letter that his wicked scheme which he had devised against the Jews, should return on his own head and that he and his sons should be hanged on the gallows. Therefore they called these days Purim after the name of Pur.
>
> Esther 9: 20-26a

Although this is the only post-exilic feast, it was established by Mordecai as a permanent ordinance under the Law. This was a day of joy and feasting. The benevolence of this feast included taking food to friends and relatives and giving special gifts to the poor. In its goodwill, it might have resembled something akin to a non-commercialized Christmas.

While other extra-biblical feasts became part of Jewish ritual as well, our focus is only on the Feasts prescribed in Scripture, and particularly how they provided opportunities to gather for corporate worship. Besides the Festivals and Feasts, many other Old Testament passages do show various assemblies that could be described, at least in part, as corporate worship gatherings. However, these corporate worship times were most always in conjunction with special events, i.e., a dedication or cleansing of the Temple, special times of corporate repentance, or spontaneous times for corporate worship following a mighty display of God's power.

---

[1] Carl Friedrich Keil and Franz Delitzsch, *Commentary on the Old Testament* (Peabody, MA: Hendrickson, 1996), 405.

So what may we infer about corporate worship from the Jewish Feasts? Perhaps most significant and easiest to miss is the priority God placed on a need for corporate worship. Since the Sabbath was not designed to address the need for corporate gatherings, God made sure that the Children of Israel were called to assemble as a regular expression of their faith. Because the Pilgrimage Feasts required everyone to go to Jerusalem, the entire week was a protracted meeting that included food, sacrifices, and special times of assembly. These feasts were clearly times of fellowship and huge social events, often occurring around meals. Food, as a hub of communion between family and friends, is a common element in Scripture. The meals celebrated around these Feasts provided a true sense of closeness and intimacy between both God and His people and between the celebrants themselves.

As for other spiritual functions of corporate worship in the Old Testament, the Feasts and Holy Days provide some worthy objectives for our corporate worship today. All the Feasts shared some common objectives. Because of the way they were conducted, they all had a strong element of fellowship. More importantly, each of these Feasts and Holy Days recalled God's mighty acts toward humanity and pointed directly to His character. Finally, the Scripture had a significant role in these corporate gatherings for several reasons. First, considering the intricate ceremony that surrounded these Feasts, the Word of God was essential to ensure that they were properly observed. God harshly judged worship activities that were not in strict adherence to His Word.[1] Additionally, Old Testament worship included the public reading and expounding of Scripture as a featured component of corporate worship. And, finally, God instructed His people to recite the Law regularly in the home.

Besides the regular elements of the Scripture and fellowship, three other themes recur in the Feasts: repentance, testifying of dependence on God, and giving praise and thanks for God's deliverance. These five basic elements shaped corporate worship for the Jews. The table that follows shows how each of these was spread among the various Feasts.

For today's believers who are seeking a renewed vision of God, the Old Testament themes of *fellowship*, the reading and proclamation of *Scripture,* as well as *repentance, testimony* and *praise/thanksgiving* remain worthy objectives for corporate worship.

---

[1] For example see Leviticus 10 where Nadab and Abihu were struck dead for offering strange fire before the Lord, or see also, 2 Samuel 6 where Uzzah was struck dead while the Ark of the Covenant was moved on a cart rather than being carried on poles as God had directed.

The Primary Focus of the Major Biblical Feasts:

	Repentance	Testifying	Praise/ Thanks	Scripture	Fellowship
Passover		X	X	X	X
Unleavened Bread	X	X		X	X
First Fruits			X	X	X
Pentecost		X	X	X	X
Trumpets	X		X	X	X
Atonement	X			X	X
Booths		X		X	X
Purim			X	X	X

SACRIFICES AND OFFERINGS

Since the fall of man, the Sacrificial System has governed the whole of God's interaction with humankind. The concept of this system has already been discussed. In laying out the system to the Children of Israel, God specified five primary types of sacrifices, each one having a function within the relationship between God and His people. The sacrifices fell naturally into two categories, mandatory and voluntary. They were as follows:

Burnt Offering was the most common of all offerings. It was generally a sign of devotion or surrender and was a voluntary act of worship. In this offering, the animal was one without defect, usually a bull, ram, or male bird (for the poor). The custom was to slaughter and skin the animal. After being cut into pieces it was placed on the altar and, except for the hide, was fully consumed (see Leviticus 1:3-17, 6:8-13, 8:8-21).

Grain Offering acknowledged the goodness of God and showed gratitude for His provision. Like the Burnt Offering, it was a voluntary act of worship. It consisted of flour, or young heads of grain, baked loaves, or cakes cooked on a griddle. The flour could contain no honey or leaven but could include oil or incense and salt if baked as a symbol of the covenant between God and His people (see Leviticus 2, 6:14-23).

Peace Offering was also a voluntary offering and could include a variety of clean animals within the herd or, in some cases, bread. This offering was a symbol of devotion in which one gave a portion of the animal for a burnt offering and kept a portion to eat. This is significant because the whole animal was given to the Lord,[1] yet God shared a portion of the meat with the one who had made the offering. The symbolism was powerful. Once the worshiper was right with God, there was a communal meal between God and the worshiper, one in which God would provide the main course (see Leviticus 3, 7:11-34).

Sin Offering was a mandatory offering to make atonement for unintentional sin as well as for cleansing from defilement. It is notable that in the Sacrificial System there was no available sacrifice for malicious intentional sins. This sacrifice was to make atonement for breaking God's law without premeditation or intention. That being said, it is significant to note that there were different animals specified for different persons: for the high priest, a young bull; for a leader, a male goat; for the common person, a female goat or lamb; a dove for the poor; and a tenth of an ephah of flour for the very poor (Leviticus 4:1-5:13; 6:24-30; 8:14-17; 16:3-22).

Guilt Offering was much like the Sin Offering and, in some instances, it is difficult to differentiate between the two. Both are mandatory and primarily used for unintentional sin. The difference seems to be that the Guilt Offering was appropriate when the worshiper sought forgiveness for an infraction that required both sacrifice and restitution. In such a circumstance, it was necessary to sacrifice the animal (a ram or bull) and pay any fees associated with restitution (Leviticus 5:14—6:7; 7:16).

While there were other offerings (wave, libation, as well as various votive and freewill offerings), these five comprised the majority of offerings in the Old Testament. When more than one offering was given, the sin or guilt offering came first followed by the burnt offering, the grain offering and, finally, the peace offering. In other words, the mandatory offerings that dealt with sin had to come before any voluntary offerings. When the sin was forgiven, the door opened for fellowship and, therefore, the whole process could end with a peace offering and communal meal celebrated before the Lord.

For believers, the Sacrificial System provides a beautiful symbol for those who desire to offer acceptable worship to Jesus Christ. In Jesus, God has satisfied all the mandatory requirements of the Sacrificial System, by providing the perfect High Priest and a perfect sacrifice:

> For it was fitting for us to have such a high priest, holy, innocent, undefiled, separated from sinners and exalted above the heavens;

---

[1] See Leviticus 7:20.

who does not need daily, like those high priests, to offer up sacrifices, first for His own sins and then for the sins of the people, because this He did once for all when He offered up Himself. For the Law appoints men as high priests who are weak, but the word of the oath, which came after the Law, appoints a Son, made perfect forever.

Hebrews 7:26-28

When we come to worship, we are not coming to offer mandatory sacrifices to satisfy God's justice. The guilt and sin offerings have been completely satisfied in Jesus. He has done what we were incapable of doing: to completely fulfill the legal requirements of the Law and by grace, through faith, His righteousness has been imputed to us. The need to offer the mandatory sacrifices no longer remains. Therefore, as archetypes, only the three voluntary offerings are still applicable for today's worshipers. Because the mandatory requirements are satisfied for all those who have placed faith in Jesus, our privilege is to worship out of devotion rather than to meet a mandatory obligation. As such, our worship can flow from love and gratitude rather than from legalism.

Both the order (Burnt Offering, Grain Offering, Peace Offering) and nature (voluntary) of the applicable offerings in the Old Testament help clarify our role as Christian worshipers. Just as the first freewill offering to be given was the burnt offering, one that was consumed in the fire, our first order of business should be wholehearted devotion to God. The fact that the burnt offering was completely consumed demonstrates to us that our role is one of unreserved surrender. For believers, worship should be an outward expression that our hearts are fully devoted to God. Fire, as the tool of the gold and silversmith, is a biblical symbol of purification.[1] In a similar fashion, God can use our worship encounters with Him to surface and remove the dross in our lives so that the precious gold of Christ in us shines all the brighter. Since it is no longer we who live but Christ who lives in us,[2] we are to be living sacrifices.[3] As believers, our role is to be conformed to the image of Jesus Christ. This is only possible as we continually put to death the deeds of the flesh.[4] This places before every believer the ongoing need for repentance and cleansing; not as a human work to maintain salvation, but as a work of God in the continued process of sanctification. The burnt offering stands as a symbol of believers continually offering themselves to the Lord so that anything not glorifying to Him is totally consumed. This keeps us in the place of surrender to the will of God and makes it possible to deepen our relationship with Him. Without devoted hearts, all of our words of praise and thanksgiving are meaningless.

---

[1] Zechariah 13:9, Malachi 3:2.
[2] Galatians 2:20.
[3] Romans 12:1-2.
[4] Romans 8:13; Colossians 3:5.

It is understandable that the burnt offering was followed by the grain offering, a symbol of gratitude and covenant relationship. Because this offering consisted of grain, itself a biblical symbol of sustenance, it represented returning to God a portion of that which God had given to sustain the worshiper. Our offerings of money can be such an offering, if in giving them we are reminded that we are returning a portion of what God has provided for our sustenance. Through such a gift we are reminded that all that we have belongs to the Lord. And even more than provision for our physical needs, we are recipients of His grace through the New Covenant. Among the most important functions of corporate worship is to acknowledge our dependence on God and express gratitude to Him for the covenant He has established for us in Jesus' blood. We are covenant people and the security of that covenant rests in God's perfect ability to maintain it. God's sustaining grace and mercy are the source of our continued forgiveness. Considering the fact that we were all hopelessly separated from God by our sin, that is, we were all equally lost, no believer can ever say he has been forgiven of just a little. Therefore, it is a contradiction to be ungrateful worshipers. As people who have been forgiven much, our appropriate response is love that expresses itself in generous gratitude.[1]

The last voluntary offering in the Old Testament sequence was the peace offering. The peace offering concluded with a communal meal, symbolizing that fellowship between God and the worshipers had been restored. In the peace offering, the whole animal was given to the LORD. However, God gave back a piece of the animal to be eaten during a time of joy and celebration:

> But you shall seek the LORD at the place which the LORD your God will choose from all your tribes, to establish His name there for His dwelling, and there you shall come. There you shall bring your burnt offerings, your sacrifices, your tithes, the contribution of your hand, your votive offerings, your freewill offerings, and the firstborn of your herd and of your flock. There also you and your households shall eat before the LORD your God, and rejoice in all your undertakings in which the LORD your God has blessed you.
>
> Deuteronomy 12:5-7

The result was a fellowship meal for which God provided the main dish and was the honored guest. During this meal the people rejoiced in the nearness of God and all of His blessings upon their lives. Since surrender, devotion and gratitude enabled those in the Old Testament to experience peace with God and rejoice in His presence, the goal of Christian worship should be no less. If worship produces nothing else in the life of the believer, it should yield a profound change of affections. When this happens, our joy in Him increases and our love deepens. From such love flows our obedience.[2] The result of following

---

[1] Luke 7:47.
[2] John 14:15.

42

the order of the three voluntary offerings takes the New Testament worshiper from giving thanks that Jesus has fulfilled the mandatory requirements into the joy that comes from close communion with Him. The purpose of worship is not to appease God through the diligent completion of duties, but to know Him in His fullness and rejoice in His nearness.

THE TABERNACLE AND TEMPLE

The observance of the Feasts and giving of sacrifices occurred primarily at one place, the Tabernacle or, later, the Temple. While there are examples of offerings given at other places, the Law established a system that required the appointments and architecture found in the Tabernacle or Temple. The difference between these two is not important for our discussion on worship. Prior to the colonization of the Promised Land, the Children of Israel sojourned in the wilderness. During this time, and until the Temple was built, the Tabernacle provided the essential elements necessary for observing the Feasts and making sacrifices, albeit in a portable package. Later, when the Temple was completed, it included the same basic architectural shape (the Courts, the Holy Place, and the Holy of Holies) and many of the same appointments. Since the Temple was not built until after King David, many of the Psalms and much of the Old Testament language associated with worship leans more heavily toward the Tabernacle rather than the Temple. Other excellent resources address the details of both the Tabernacle and Temple.[1] For the purpose of this discussion, we will only focus on the basic elements of the Tabernacle as they relate to our discussion of worship.

The Architecture and Appointments

Both the Temple and the Tabernacle were divided into three basic parts. The most sacred of these was the Holy of Holies (or Most Holy Place). It was a square room, divided from the outside by walls on three sides (north, south, west) and a curtain or veil on the east side, which separated it from a larger room known as the Holy Place. The Holy of Holies was the most holy site in all of Jewish ritual. It contained the Ark of the Covenant, the most holy artifact in Jewish worship. Inside the Ark were the tablets on which Moses had received the Ten Commandments, as well as Aaron's staff, which had budded, and a bowl of manna. The Ark itself was a beautifully crafted case topped by a gilded engraving of two Cherubim. Above the Cherubim resided the glory of God, a symbol of God's presence among His people.[2] Each year, the High Priest would

---

[1] For example see the updated publication: Alfred Edersheim, *The Temple, Its Ministry and Services as They Were at the Time of Jesus Christ.* (Grand Rapids, MI: Kregal Publications, 1997).

[2] God displayed His glory in both the Tabernacle and the Temple as a symbol of His presence among His people. See Leviticus 16:2 and 1 Kings 8:10-13.

enter the Holy of Holies on the Day of Atonement to sprinkle blood over the top of the Ark, between the Cherubim (a place known as the Mercy Seat). As the priest entered to sprinkle this blood, he would first introduce incense so that the glory of God might be veiled, even to the priest's eyes.

To the east of the Holy of Holies and separated by a heavy cloth curtain was the Holy Place, containing the Table of Showbread, the Altar of Incense, and Lamp Stand(s). The Table of Showbread (also called the Bread of the Presence) was to be a permanent memorial before the Lord. Twelve loaves of bread, one for each of the twelve tribes of Israel, were replaced weekly by the priests, who attended to the Temple as part of their regular duties. Also in the Holy Place was the light of the lampstand(s). In the Tabernacle, this was one stand with seven lights, while in Solomon's Temple it was ten single lampstands (five on each side of the Holy Place). The symbolism of constant light most likely represented God's ongoing guidance. Since only the High Priest could enter the Holy of Holies, and that only once each year, the candlelight was also a reminder that behind the veil dwelt the light of God's glory. Additionally, the Altar of Incense was kept burning as a fragrant aroma to both the Lord and to all who went to the Tabernacle/Temple. Together, the Holy Place and the Holy of Holies made one rectangular structure, the Sanctuary.

Surrounding this structure were the Courts that to the east contained the Laver(s) and an Altar of Sacrifice where offerings were burned. This area was accessible to all Jewish males of age. The Laver (later, more than one in the Temple) was a place of ceremonial cleansing and stood between the Altar of Burnt Offering and the entrance to the Holy Place.

Perhaps we miss the obvious: the court of the Tabernacle and later the Temple was a place of pungent smell, eerie sounds, and gore. The smell of incense, fresh blood and burning flesh, the sounds of prayers and the cry of animals being slaughtered, and the skinning and butchering of those animals must have made a deep impact on all who worshiped there. Early Jewish Christians must have easily seen the relationship between the mandatory sin offerings and Paul's words in Romans that *the wages of sin is death.*

The Structure of the Tabernacle

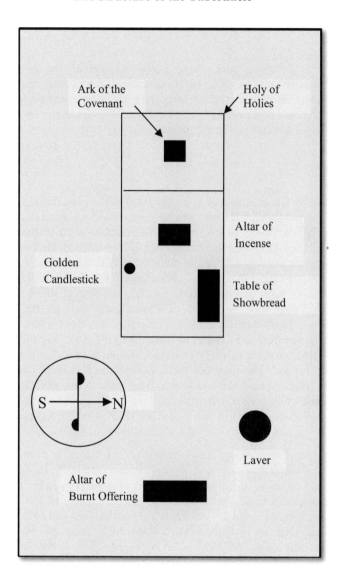

Ark of the Covenant

Holy of Holies

Altar of Incense

Golden Candlestick

Table of Showbread

S — N

Laver

Altar of Burnt Offering

As for applying all aspects of the Sacrificial System to Christian worship, there is a balance to strike. Dismissing all that God did to teach Isaac's descendants about worship is unfortunate. Each Feast, each appointment, each sacrifice was assigned from the truth of God's character and, therefore, its study has value for all believers. On the other hand, we must realize that the era of worship in an earthly Tabernacle/Temple has concluded, not because the Temple no longer exists, but because the purpose no longer exists. The writer of Hebrews contrasts the worship (λατρεία) of the priests in the old system with the work of Christ that superseded it.

> Now when these things have been so prepared, the priests are continually entering the outer tabernacle performing the divine worship, but into the second, only the high priest enters once a year, not without taking blood, which he offers for himself and for the sins of the people committed in ignorance.
>
> Hebrews 9:6-7

He continues:

> But when Christ appeared as a high priest of the good things to come, He entered through the greater and more perfect tabernacle, not made with hands, that is to say, not of this creation; and not through the blood of goats and calves, but through His own blood, He entered the holy place once for all, having obtained eternal redemption. For if the blood of goats and bulls and the ashes of a heifer sprinkling those who have been defiled sanctify for the cleansing of the flesh, how much more will the blood of Christ, who through the eternal Spirit offered Himself without blemish to God, cleanse your conscience from dead works to serve the living God? For this reason He is the mediator of a new covenant, so that, since a death has taken place for the redemption of the transgressions that were committed under the first covenant, those who have been called may receive the promise of the eternal inheritance.
>
> Hebrews 9:11-15

Because of this, it would be cumbersome to attempt to draw a connection between our faith practice and every minute detail of Tabernacle/Temple worship. Nevertheless, the imagery is rich, as evidenced by how often the writer of Hebrews used it to explain the work of Christ. There was specific work that only the High Priest could do, and Jesus has accomplished all of it. The fact that the veil was torn top to bottom when Jesus died[1] made the most holy of all places, one that could only rarely be occupied, open to anyone who comes through Christ. Perhaps even more profound, the tearing of the veil, representing the body of Jesus broken for us, announces *a new and living way* in which communion with God is no longer in a physical structure.[2] In the New Covenant,

---

[1] Matthew 27:51.

[2] *Therefore, brethren, since we have confidence to enter the holy place by the blood of Jesus, by a new and living way which He inaugurated for us through the veil, that is, His flesh, and since we have a great priest over the house of God, let us draw near with a*

God's people are the place where His presence resides, in the Person of the Holy Spirit.

There is rich symbolism in the Tabernacle/Temple that can enhance our understanding of how God interacts with His faithful ones. The death of Jesus as the perfect sacrifice meant that there would never be need for another sacrifice to make atonement for sin. Through our relationship with Him, we ourselves have entrance into the Holy Place. There no longer remains a need for a physical Holy of Holies in which to find the presence of God. By the work of Jesus, the presence of God dwells in His people in the person of the Holy Spirit. In fact, with the coming of the Holy Spirit one might say that the veil was torn not to represent that we have access to God as much as it represents that the presence of God among His people was to be in them, rather than *with* them in Holy of Holies. Similarly, the altar where the offerings burned no longer has a purpose. Like the burnt offering itself, worship is the place of sanctification where self is consumed with devotion to God. The Laver, no longer needed for ceremonial washing, still reminds us that the Spirit by the Word of God initially washes us in regeneration and continually washes in sanctification.[1] In the Holy Place, the appointments are reminders as well of truths that enhance our worship. The Lamp Stand is a beautiful figure representing the illumination given to us by the Holy Spirit and likewise the Bread of the Presence speaks of fellowship and covenant through the Bread of Life. The Altar of Incense rising as a sweet aroma to God is a beautiful picture of the prayers the saints.

It is interesting that each of these things just listed (the Word, the work of the Holy Spirit, Fellowship, and Prayer) is a key component of Christian worship to this day. This is no accident. The things that God held dear did not change with the coming of the New Covenant any more than God Himself changed. When understood this way, we can see Christian worship is a seamless continuum that began with the faithful of the Old Covenant, continues through us, and ends with the redeemed of every tribe and tongue who will sing, *Worthy*, in the age to come.

THE PRESENCE OF GOD

One final aspect of Old Testament worship that greatly affected the Children of Israel was an awareness of God's presence, or, at times, awareness that God had withheld His presence from them. By this, we are not saying that the faithful of the Old Covenant did not accept the omnipresence of God. As we will see, the scriptures of the Old Testament clearly teach this. However, more than once God removed Himself for a season from the lives of individuals or from the nation itself. Ezekiel's vision of the departing glory from the Temple (Ezekiel 8-11) and the prophetic return of His glory (Ezekiel 43-44)

---

sincere heart in full assurance of faith, having our hearts sprinkled clean from an evil conscience and our bodies washed with pure water [Hebrews 10:19-22].
[1] Titus 3:5; Ephesians 5:26.

demonstrates that God taught His people different aspects of His presence. Since the presence of God remains a topic of discussion in Christian worship, sometimes in unbiblical ways, it would be helpful to understand how God utilized His nearness (or lack of it) to direct and sometimes correct His children. The Scripture demonstrates three unique aspects of God's presence: His essential presence, His cultivative presence, and His manifest presence.

God's Essential Presence

God, as the Sovereign of the universe, is All-Knowing, Eternal, All-Powerful, and Ever-Present. The concept of God's omnipresence is a clear teaching of Scripture. The fact that He is from everlasting to everlasting and His knowledge extends from the heart of man to the furthest reaches of the universe indicates that He is fully present and knowledgeable in all places and at all times. [1] The lack of God's limitations was a constant assurance to the Children of Israel. The testimony of Scripture is very specific in describing God's omnipresence:

> Where can I go from Your Spirit? Or where can I flee from Your presence? If I ascend to heaven, You are there; If I make my bed in Sheol, behold, You are there. If I take the wings of the dawn, If I dwell in the remotest part of the sea, Even there Your hand will lead me, And Your right hand will lay hold of me. If I say, "Surely the darkness will overwhelm me, And the light around me will be night," Even the darkness is not dark to You, And the night is as bright as the day. Darkness and light are alike to You.
>
> Psalm 139:1-6

In other words, there is never a time or place where God is not. In this sense, God was equally present in the hills where the pagan Asherim stood and in the Holy of Holies above the Ark of the Covenant. He is equally present in our day as well. God *is*, so He is always present.[2]

God's Cultivative Presence

While it is true that God is always present, it is equally true that at times His presence is working deeply in one while to others He seems distant or not present at all. In the Old Testament, this contrast is demonstrated in the lives of David and Saul. In 1 Samuel 16:13-14, Samuel anointed David as king and immediately the text informs us that the presence of the Lord that had accompanied Saul departed. Instead, God had replaced His Spirit with a tormenting spirit. The anointing was both a symbol that David had been chosen to rule and also as a symbol of the presence of God at work in a special way in

---

[1] Psalm 90:2; Psalm 139:1-6; Psalm 147:4-5.
[2] Exodus 3:14.

David's life.[1] Shortly thereafter, Saul and David were together and the Scripture declares in 1 Samuel 18:12, *Now Saul was afraid of David, for the LORD was with him but had departed from Saul.*

In the New Testament, the Holy Spirit indwells all believers. While it is true that the Holy Spirit never leaves the believer, it is also true that at times some believers may have a much greater awareness of His work in their lives. This is partially due to the sovereign choice of God to work in believers in various ways and, in part, because at times individuals can quench the work of the Spirit.[2] In either case, it is clear that God may choose to reveal His presence to someone in a significant way, while others who are in the same place may be unaware of any special work of God in their own lives. While God digs deeply in the heart of one believer, the heart of another believer may lay fallow. Most of the patriarchs and prophets from Abraham to Ezekiel experienced special portions of God's presence at work in their lives. For this reason, I have chosen to use the term, *cultivative presence.*[3]

God's Manifest Presence

As sure as God sometimes chooses to reveal Himself to some, there are times when God draws the curtain back from heaven and reveals Himself in a way that affects everyone. This type of manifestation of His presence is nearly undeniable and many times overwhelming. God manifested Himself in this way after Aaron and his sons were consecrated for the priesthood and went to the Tabernacle to offer sacrifices:

> Moses and Aaron went into the tent of meeting. When they came out and blessed the people, the glory of the LORD appeared to all the people. Then fire came out from before the LORD and consumed the burnt offering and the portions of fat on the altar; and when all the people saw it, they shouted and fell on their faces.
>
> Leviticus 9:23-24

---

[1] David understood that the presence of the Lord, in this particular sense, could leave him just as it had left Saul. Following the debacle with Bathsheba, he prayed in Psalm 51:11, *Do not cast me away from Your presence And do not take Your Holy Spirit from me.*

[2] 1 Thessalonians 5:19.

[3] I first heard and discussed the terms, *essential, manifest,* and *cultivative* in a conversation with evangelist and author, Richard Owen Roberts, around 1995. Since that time, he has written an article that describes the terms *essential* and *manifest* with respect to God's presence. See Richard Owen Roberts, "When God Comes Near - Online Magazine Archives - NavPress," NavPress Home, http://www.navpress.com/magazines/archives/article.aspx?id=14745 (accessed December 01, 2010).

In a similar way, God manifested Himself at the dedication of Solomon's Temple:

> Now when Solomon had finished praying, fire came down from heaven and consumed the burnt offering and the sacrifices, and the glory of the LORD filled the house. The priests could not enter into the house of the LORD because the glory of the LORD filled the LORD'S house. All the sons of Israel, seeing the fire come down and the glory of the LORD upon the house, bowed down on the pavement with their faces to the ground, and they worshiped and gave praise to the LORD, saying, "Truly He is good, truly His lovingkindness is everlasting."
>
> 2 Chronicles 7:1-3

Moses understood the difference between God manifesting Himself to the whole nation and revealing Himself in a limited fashion. In Exodus 33, Moses pleaded with God to continue with the nation on its journey to the Promised Land, making His presence known to the whole nation. God was so angry with the Children of Israel that He told Moses if He went up with them to the Promised Land, in His wrath, He might destroy them. Instead, God offered to Moses what could only be described by today's standards as ministerial success. In Exodus 33:1-3, God offers him the Promised Land, angelic protection, and victory over his enemies:

> Then the LORD spoke to Moses, "Depart, go up from here, you and the people whom you have brought up from the land of Egypt, to the land of which I swore to Abraham, Isaac, and Jacob, saying, 'To your descendants I will give it.' "I will send an angel before you and I will drive out the Canaanite, the Amorite, the Hittite, the Perizzite, the Hivite and the Jebusite. "Go up to a land flowing with milk and honey; for I will not go up in your midst, because you are an obstinate people, and I might destroy you on the way."

For Moses, succeeding in human terms simply was not enough. Going into the Promised Land apart from the active presence of God was not acceptable to Moses. It is interesting to note that this offer was also unsatisfactory to the people. Despite their rebellion, they knew that the Promised Land was more than a place. Moses continues to intercede for his people and in response, God offers to grant a particular portion of His presence to Moses alone.

> And He said, "My presence shall go with you, and I will give you rest." Then he [Moses] said to Him, "If Your presence does not go with us, do not lead us up from here. For how then can it be known that I have found favor in Your sight, I and Your people? Is it not by

Your going with us, so that we, I and Your people, may be distinguished from all the other people who are upon the face of the earth?" The LORD said to Moses, "I will also do this thing of which you have spoken; for you have found favor in My sight and I have known you by name." Then Moses said, "I pray You, show me Your glory!"

Exodus 33:14-18

God makes a second offer. He promises a special portion of His presence to Moses—what we might understand as God's cultivative presence in his life—without manifesting Himself to the whole nation. That was not enough for Moses either. He insisted that if God did not go up with him and the people (*If Your presence does not go with us…*), making His presence known to them, there would be no use in going to the Promised Land at all. For Moses, there was no Promised Land unless God would manifest Himself to His people. At that point, God granted Moses' request.

With all the conveniences we have in ministry today, it is sobering to consider whether or not we carry the same sense of necessity when it comes to the active presence of God in our own lives and in the lives of our people. For Moses, ministerial success, even a special portion of God's cultivative presence for him alone, was not enough. As a leader, he desired for the entire nation to know of God's presence. There is simply no Promised Land without the presence of God.

For believers it is important to understand how God's presence affects worship, particularly for those who lead. By the indwelling of the Holy Spirit, we have something greater than a visible manifestation that God is with us: we have the presence of God living inside of us.[1] For this reason, we should have a good and growing understanding of the cultivative presence of God. I know many times I have preached or taught and heard someone indicate that they were deeply touched. But, it is equally true that others might just as quickly admit that they thought the message was flat. The truth is that every message preached, every song sung, and every act of corporate worship is flat apart from the cultivating work of the Holy Spirit in the heart of the *hearer*.

As for the omnipresence and manifest presence of God, let us first settle the issue that human beings have absolutely no control over either one. God by nature is omnipresent—it is one of His attributes. There is nothing anyone can do to change that. Similarly, no man can obligate God to manifest His presence at a given time or place. That is something totally dependent on the Divine prerogative. Both the essential presence of God and the manifest presence of God are totally beyond the realm of human control. In a time when we have so many external means by which to affect the emotions of people, responsible leaders must be careful not to manufacture a false sense of God's presence. If we

---

[1] Romans 8:11; 2 Timothy 1:14.

do so, we are manipulating instead of leading, giving honor to idols of our own making, and in the end, we are robbing people of the potential of seeking the real beauty that only comes when God manifests Himself.

This does not mean that leaders should not long for and pray for God to manifest Himself in our day, among our people. This was Moses' desire for the Children of Israel. Perhaps the best scenario for us today is to be mindful of God's essential presence and accountable because of it, knowing He sees and knows all. We must also be faithful in the practice of our ministry, trusting God's cultivative presence to move in the hearts of people as He chooses, always knowing that God honors His promise to be at work in the lives of His people— even when we cannot see it. And, finally, to live with a deep thirst that can only be quenched in the refreshing rain of God's manifest presence. May our hearts echo the prayer of Isaiah, *Oh, that You would rend the heavens and come down.*[1]

---

[1] Isaiah 64:1.

CHAPTER 3

OLD COVENANT EXPRESSIONS IN
THE NEW COVENANT CHURCH

For those of us who live on this side of the death and resurrection of Jesus, it is difficult to appreciate the struggle that practicing Jews had in determining how they were to accomplish corporate or group worship and how that worship was to be appropriately expressed. Steeped in ancient spiritual traditions, Jewish believers saw Christianity in a way that may be difficult for us to understand. Jewish believers did not see their faith in Jesus as a new religion that drew them away from Judaism, but as a fulfillment of their own historic faith. This was the message delivered to those living in Jerusalem by the Apostle Peter in Acts 2:14-40 and Acts 3:11-26. For this reason, there was a time of transition for Jewish believers between practicing the ways of the historic faith and discovering what aspects of those practices were no longer necessary or appropriate. In some instances, this meant setting aside their practices and, in some instances, it meant seeing the ancient customs in a new light rather than doing away with them altogether. For instance, the Sacrificial System and its blood sacrifices were no longer necessary; that was a clear teaching of the Early Church.[1]

---

[1] It is probable that some Jewish Christians continued the liturgy of sacrifice. Perhaps that is the reason the writer of Hebrews explains so clearly that the need for

Nevertheless, there were many other practices deeply ingrained into the Jewish worship culture which influenced the Early Church. As a result, Christians incorporated many Jewish expressions of worship into early Christian worship, passing them on to believers who had no Jewish background. Some of those have survived to this day. Our focus in this discussion will be two-fold. We will look at the expressions of worship found in the Old Testament and common in Jewish worship; and, we will discuss how the Early Church transitioned from festival corporate worship to gatherings that were more frequent.

BIBLICAL EXPRESSIONS OF WORSHIP

We began our discussion of worship in the first chapter by stressing that worship is first being, not doing. This does not mean that worship is passive, i.e., that it does not *do* anything. Being in the proper state of submission before God will outwardly express itself in a God-honoring life, whether in a corporate worship gathering or not. Within the framework of corporate worship this may be displayed in a variety of postures, gestures or vocal expressions, sung or spoken, many modeled in Scripture. Expressions used in public worship may be widely varied across different cultures. This variety may raise questions about what is appropriate or even acceptable. As for cultural appropriateness, it is not possible to make a definitive statement about what is or is not appropriate within a given culture. However, when it comes to what is acceptable to God, it is possible to be more specific. If a posture, gesture, or verbal expression is sanctioned in Scripture, we may assume that it is acceptable to God, given the stipulation that the heart is right. That does not mean God has mandated the use of every biblical expression for each Christian. It does mean that if God has sanctioned any expression as acceptable, we should be careful about declaring it inappropriate. For that reason, our discussion will focus specifically on what is described in the Scripture. This leads us to explore the various postures and gestures that were part of Jewish worship and were incorporated into the practice of the Early Church.

BIBLICAL POSTURES

Face to the Ground
To Jewish believers (and therefore to the Early Church) the posture of the body was an integral part of expressing a heart of worship. In Eastern culture, lowering one's self in the presence of another was, and is, a sign of respect. As we discussed in the first chapter, the word most often translated *worship* in the Old Testament describes one lowering himself before the Lord. *Shachah* literally means to put one's face down on the ground, signifying total submission. This

---

sacrifice no longer exists. We do not know whether this would have continued to be an issue because the Temple was destroyed in AD 70.

concept of lowering one's self continued in New Testament worship practice, not just in the meaning of the Greek word, *proskuneo*, but in actual responses to God as well. Note Paul's (Saul's) response on the road to Damascus:

> Now Saul, still breathing threats and murder against the disciples of the Lord, went to the high priest, and asked for letters from him to the synagogues at Damascus, so that if he found any belonging to the Way, both men and women, he might bring them bound to Jerusalem. As he was traveling, it happened that he was approaching Damascus, and suddenly a light from heaven flashed around him; and he fell to the ground and heard a voice saying to him, "Saul, Saul, why are you persecuting Me?" And he said, "Who are You, Lord?" And He said, "I am Jesus whom you are persecuting."
>
> Acts 9:1-5

Notice the similarity of John's response during his encounter on the Isle of Patmos:

> I was in the Spirit on the Lord's day, and I heard behind me a loud voice like the sound of a trumpet, saying, "Write in a book what you see, and send it to the seven churches: to Ephesus and to Smyrna and to Pergamum and to Thyatira and to Sardis and to Philadelphia and to Laodicea." Then I turned to see the voice that was speaking with me. And having turned I saw seven golden lampstands; and in the middle of the lampstands I saw one like a son of man, clothed in a robe reaching to the feet, and girded across His chest with a golden sash. His head and His hair were white like white wool, like snow; and His eyes were like a flame of fire. His feet were like burnished bronze, when it has been made to glow in a furnace, and His voice was like the sound of many waters. In His right hand He held seven stars, and out of His mouth came a sharp two-edged sword; and His face was like the sun shining in its strength. When I saw Him, I fell at His feet like a dead man. And He placed His right hand on me, saying, "Do not be afraid; I am the first and the last."
>
> Revelation 1:10-17

To be very clear, this is not an example of what some might call being slain in the Spirit. Instead, this is the response of someone who, fully cognizant, viscerally reacts to the presence of God by lowering himself as far as possible—a clear picture of what the biblical words for worship indicate. In today's westernized evangelicalism, it might seem a strange thing to fall on our face before the Lord. However, it is difficult to determine whether or not that is a cultural difference between these two Apostles and us or if, in reality, we are so filled with pride that we could not bring ourselves to do such a thing. While God never commands that all Christians must lie face down on the ground in worship, public or private, He has commanded us to have the same submission and humility before Him and, therefore, we should not find this practice out of place as a proper posture of worship.

Kneeling

For many Christians, kneeling is a posture that is more acceptable than being face down on the ground but, in non-liturgical churches, it is almost as rare. The biblical posture of kneeling was a worship practice of the Jewish faithful.[1] Various versions may translate the words *bow* or *kneel* interchangeably since the meaning is essentially to bend low (either body, knee or both). Because it physically illustrates humility and supplication, it is common to find kneeling used as a posture for prayer in both the Old and New Testaments. For example, King Solomon kneels to pray at the dedication of the Temple:

> Now Solomon had made a bronze platform, five cubits long, five cubits wide and three cubits high, and had set it in the midst of the court; and he stood on it, knelt on his knees in the presence of all the assembly of Israel and spread out his hands toward heaven. [2]
>
> 2 Chronicles 6:13

In the New Testament, the Apostle Paul described his own practice in praying for the Church at Ephesus:

> For this reason I bow my knees before the Father, from whom every family in heaven and on earth derives its name.[3]
>
> Ephesians 3:14

Finally, note the posture used by the leper to entreat the Lord Jesus in Mark 1:40-41:

> And a leper came to Jesus, beseeching Him and falling on his knees before Him, and saying, "If You are willing, You can make me clean." Moved with compassion, Jesus stretched out His hand and touched him, and said to him, "I am willing; be cleansed."

In our day, kneeling still carries the connotation of supplication and submission. In light of that, both liturgical and non-liturgical worshipers can

---

[1] Psalm 95:6.

[2] This occurred during the dedication of the Temple. It must have been an impacting sight to see the King kneel down before God in humility and supplication.

[3] Paul continues in an extended prayer for the Ephesians.

look for ways to utilize this expression more effectively. For liturgical churches that prescribe kneeling as part of corporate worship, it is important to remember that the knee can bend without the heart. Therefore, teaching on the meaning of kneeling is important to keep the practice from becoming perfunctory. For freeform worshipers, the practice of kneeling is one that should be looked at again with fresh possibilities, understanding that bending the knee can be a beautiful outward expression of a heart that submits itself to God.

Sitting

Sitting may symbolize one who sits down to judge[1] or one who rests from his labors, not because he is tired but because he has completed his task.[2] Sitting is also an appropriate posture for worship, both in sadness[3] and in high ceremonial worship as demonstrated in Revelation chapter four. In this scene in heaven, the twenty-four elders first sit then later fall on their faces before the Lord:

> Immediately I was in the Spirit; and behold, a throne was standing in heaven, and One sitting on the throne. And He who was sitting was like a jasper stone and a sardius in appearance; and there was a rainbow around the throne, like an emerald in appearance. Around the throne were twenty-four thrones; and upon the thrones I saw twenty-four elders sitting, clothed in white garments, and golden crowns on their heads.
>
> Revelation 4:2-4

The scene continues:

> And when the living creatures give glory and honor and thanks to Him who sits on the throne, to Him who lives forever and ever, the twenty-four elders will fall down before Him who sits on the throne, and will worship Him who lives forever and ever, and will cast their crowns before the throne, saying. "Worthy are You, our Lord and our God, to receive glory and honor and power; for You created all things, and because of Your will they existed, and were created."
>
> Revelation 4:9-11

Sitting during worship can become a way to disengage. However, it does not have to be so. The elders who sat around the throne of God must have been

---

[1] Matthew 19:28.

[2] Hebrews 10:12.

[3] See Psalm 137 where the Children of Israel recall how they sat down and wept before the Lord.

anything but bored. In other words, it is possible for a congregation to sit attentively and remain engaged in the congregational experience. This should relieve some leaders from worrying that people are not worshiping if they are not standing. That is not necessarily the case. Sitting is an acceptable posture for worship.

Standing

After the exiles returned from Babylon, they came to Jerusalem to celebrate The Day of Atonement. As they assembled for worship, Ezra opened the scroll to read:

> Ezra opened the book in the sight of all the people for he was standing above all the people; and when he opened it, all the people stood up. Then Ezra blessed the LORD the great God. And all the people answered, "Amen, Amen!" while lifting up their hands; then they bowed low and worshiped the LORD with their faces to the ground.
>
> Nehemiah 8:5-6

This picture represents both the posture of standing and of bowing low. In much the same way a gallery in the court rises when the judge enters, they stood to accord honor to God and His Word. There are numerous other examples of standing before the Lord in worship[1] and in each of them it is apparently to accord honor as is the case here:

> After these things I looked, and behold, a great multitude which no one could count, from every nation and all tribes and peoples and tongues, standing before the throne and before the Lamb, clothed in white robes, and palm branches were in their hands; and they cry out with a loud voice, saying, "Salvation to our God who sits on the throne, and to the Lamb."
>
> Revelation 7:9-10

While standing is a common posture for worship among both liturgical and freeform worshipers, the meaning has been somewhat lost. I remember as a child standing each Sunday at the conclusion of the offering to sing the *Doxology*. A small asterisk in the worship guide informed us when we were to stand. The thought that we were standing for any particular spiritual meaning was certainly lost on me. Since we were not taught the reason for standing, I was most likely not the only one who was ignorant as to why we might be standing at all.

---

[1] For example see Leviticus 9:5, 1 Kings 8:22, 2 Chronicles 29:26, Psalm 135:1-4.

In our culture, we still stand at specific times to demonstrate honor. When the judge enters the court room, the bailiff declares, *All rise.* Similarly, when the President or a member of a royal family enters the room, people stand to accord honor to that position or person. One of my students reminded our class what he was taught as a soldier—it is the responsibility of every soldier to call *attention* as soon as an officer enters the room. At once, all the soldiers are to rise in honor of the officer who has entered the room. And so it should be for those of us who recognize and know the presence of our King. It is our duty to call attention to His presence by our own demeanor and focus. In a day when standing is common at gatherings such as concerts and sporting events, leaders should remind their congregations from time to time that standing in worship is a biblical posture meant to express honor to God or His Word.

Dancing

Physical movement in worship is common to many cultures today and evidently was a part of the Jewish custom of worship. The fact is that many passages in Scripture indicate movement far beyond what might be acceptable in today's evangelical churches. The two words translated as *dance* in the Old Testament give insight into this ancient practice.

מָחוֹל (*mā·ḥôl*) generally means to whirl or turn in a circle. This dance was one of celebration and was *likely segregated by sex, possibly accompanied by rhythm instruments and/or musical instruments.*[1] Psalm 30:11-12 demonstrates that this dance is a joyful one since it is the antithesis of mourning.

> You have turned for me my mourning into dancing; You have loosed my sackcloth and girded me with gladness, That my soul may sing praise to You and not be silent. O LORD my God, I will give thanks to You forever.

The other word for dancing is רָקַד (*rā·qăd*), which means to skip or leap.[2] The most familiar occurrence of this word describes David dancing after he had brought the Ark up to Jerusalem.

> It happened when the ark of the covenant of the LORD came to the city of David that Michal the daughter of Saul looked out of the window and saw King David leaping and celebrating; and she despised him in her heart.
>
> 1 Chronicles 15:29

---

[1] Swanson, James: *Dictionary of Biblical Languages With Semantic Domains: Hebrew (Old Testament)*. Electronic ed. Oak Harbor: Logos Research Systems, Inc., 1997, S. DBLH 4688.

[2] This word can also be translated as *skip,* as in Psalm 29:6.

It is unclear from the text exactly why Michal reacted as she did. Even so, it is clear that she took no pleasure in seeing her husband skipping and leaping. Whether or not God approved of David's dancing is also unclear. What is clear is that David, taken with joy that the Ark was finally in Jerusalem, could not contain himself. And, he was not concerned with the opinions of others. In this, all worshipers could learn something of value: namely, that we do not worship for the approval of others but as a response to the goodness of God. Truth must always guide this reaction for worship to be acceptable. Even so, worship is much more than an intellectual exercise. It can be a visceral reaction to God. Even in the postures we have already discussed, expressions of worship are often reactionary and quite full of emotion.

In general, many evangelicals find themselves more in the company of Michal than in the company of David. This is unfortunate since the Bible does sanction some type of dancing. However, does that mean that everybody should dance? We should always be reticent to prohibit what the Scripture describes as acceptable. Admittedly, there are issues with dance in our culture that were not part of Jewish culture. The primary difficulty in incorporating spontaneous dance into worship today is the context of dance in much of Western civilization. While dance was a part of Jewish culture, it was uncommon for unmarried men and women to dance with one another, especially as a romantic expression. While there is nothing intrinsically wrong with *clean* dancing, the strong sexual connotations associated with some forms of dance today create a significant barrier for some in the West to accept dancing as a part of worship at all.

Apart from an approach that totally embraces all forms of dance, there are generally three approaches to addressing this issue among American churches. A very common response is to frown on dance and avoid it completely. Churches that take this position may feel that any unscripted movement is less than dignified, distracting to the whole, and therefore should not be incorporated into corporate worship. The second, practiced by many freeform churches and made more popular by charismatic influences, is to accept some movement by individuals within the context of corporate worship. In this approach, a local congregation generally strikes its own balance between freedom to move and some restraint for the common good. Churches that adopt this method, whether consciously or not, have generally accepted limits. Finally, liturgical churches and, more recently, a few freeform evangelical churches have resolved this issue, not by avoiding dance, but by using classical forms of movement and dance as a component of worship. While the use of dance is sanctioned as acceptable in Scripture, it ultimately falls to the local church to determine how or if to utilize it in corporate worship.

BIBLICAL GESTURES

Gestures were common as an expression of worship in the Old Testament. Like the postures previously discussed, gestures are typically a part of a cultural language, and used as non-verbal communication. While Christianity was not a faith based on Jewish culture, the Jewish cultural forms of communication significantly affected the Christian faith. This is evident in how gestures were incorporated into worship. Many Old Testament gestures became part of Christian worship and have been handed down to us. Clearly, using hands to worship God is not always required. When Scripture describes the use of hands in worship, there are two primary expressions: clapping and lifting or raising hands.

Clapping

The use of clapping is widespread among many cultures, at times as applause to show approval or affirmation and, even more widespread, as a rhythmic component of music. Scripture models both of these. When Solomon is crowned king, the people erupted with applause.

> Then he brought the king's son out and put the crown on him and gave him the testimony; and they made him king and anointed him, and they clapped their hands and said, "Long live the king!"
>
> 2 Kings 11:12

Whether or not this was only an affirmation of the king or an act of worship expressing gratitude to God is unclear in the text. However, the same word[1] is used in the context of worship in Isaiah 55:12:

> For you shall go out in joy and be led forth in peace; the mountains and the hills before you shall break forth into singing, and all the trees of the field shall clap their hands.
>
> Isaiah 55:12

The other word that is used in the Old Testament translated *clap* has a slightly different connotation. This word[2] is used to describe the sound of a trumpet blast as well as to strike the hands together. Since it is onomatopoetic, it further suggests the use of the hands in a rhythmic fashion. This would indicate that it is biblically acceptable for a congregation to participate in worship by clapping in rhythm to the music.

---

[1] נָכָה (nā·ḵā(h)).
[2] תָּקַע (tā·qǎʿ).

O clap your hands, all peoples;
Shout to God with the voice of joy.
For the LORD Most High is to be feared,
A great King over all the earth.

Psalm 47:1-2

While the use of clapping may vary culturally, the practice is widely accepted in many evangelical churches. The cultural meaning of clapping, particularly applause, becomes the most problematic issue in the context of worship. Applause has become a nearly universal response to a performance. In many houses of worship, applause follows a song, just as it would in a concert. Since God did not intend for worship to be a performance for people, use of this type of clapping runs contrary to His design. So, how should congregations handle the use of clapping? As with dance, some congregations who are concerned about the potential for mixed messages avoid all expressions of clapping and/or applause in worship. Other congregations more concerned about utilizing biblically acceptable modes of worship need to deal with the differences between worship and performance. This relates less to clapping as a form of musical participation and more to the use of applause. Leaders of congregations who use applause in corporate worship must exercise care. Applause, whether following a song, a testimony, or a rousing point in the sermon, should not be for the singer, the one testifying, or the one speaking. Since people should never be the focus of worship, the best use of applause in worship is as the congregational *amen*[1] or as a spontaneous expression of honor to the Lord.

Lifting Hands

Through Christianity, the Middle Eastern custom of lifting hands in worship has spread across many cultures. The Jewish custom, evidently incorporated into New Testament worship, has at least three meanings. The first is that of lifting hands as an oath or a promise as used in Genesis 14:21-22: *The king of Sodom said to Abram, "Give the people to me and take the goods for yourself." Abram said to the king of Sodom, "I have **sworn** to the LORD GOD Most High, possessor of heaven and earth."* Here the NASB translates the word as *sworn* but the literal phrase is *lifted my hand.* The use of the hand lifted toward God as an oath is serious business. As an expression of a devoted worshiper, it may signify one who lifts his hand to pledge allegiance to the LORD.

Two other meanings of *lifting hands* are much more common in the context of worship. The first is associated with joy, as in Psalm 63:3-5:

---

[1] The Hebrew word אָמֵן (*ā·mēn*), meaning *that is true*, or *we agree* was a common verbal expression signifying acceptance or affirmation.

Because Your lovingkindness is better than life,
My lips will praise You.
So I will bless You as long as I live;
I will lift up my hands in Your name.
My soul is satisfied as with marrow and fatness,
And my mouth offers praises with joyful lips.

Psalm 141:1-2 provides an example of the second. It expresses supplication:

O Lord, I call upon You; hasten to me!
Give ear to my voice when I call to You!
May my prayer be counted as incense before You;
The lifting up of my hands as the evening offering.

The Apostle Paul likewise references the lifting of hands for supplication when he declares; *Therefore I want the men in every place to pray, lifting up holy hands, without wrath and dissension.*[1]

In any case, it is clear that in all of the above instances, the intent of the gesture is to honor God. In both joy and in supplication the lifting of hands was an appropriate gesture for worship. It is not difficult to understand the beauty of hands lifted to the Lord from His perspective as our Father. As I have heard others muse over their own children, so have I with my three. When they were just two or three years old, I would come in the door from work to a beautiful sight: little hands lifted and little voices saying, *Hold me!* In this instance, there was no pretense from any of my children, just a joyous desire to be close to their father. That is how it should be when God sees His children lift their hands to Him: no show, just sincere love, longing to give and receive.

Waving

Waving before the Lord was a practice particularly associated with the Sacrificial System. As a gesture of worship, a portion of an animal that had been sacrificed, sheaves of grain, or loaves of bread were lifted and waved toward heaven. While the New Testament provides no reference to waving as a worship gesture, it does not mean it would be inappropriate to do so. Most likely, the wave offering fell out of use with the New Covenant since it was specifically associated with the Sacrificial System.

---

[1] 1 Timothy 2:8.

Singing

Singing is common to people all over the world. God created the voice to be a very expressive instrument and, through song, the human voice can express a wide variety of emotions. In the Bible, singing plays a key role in worship expression. The Bible demonstrates the wide variety of emotional expressions possible through singing. The Psalms (the songbook of the Bible) express everything from great joy, broken-heartedness and, at times, the raw emotions of people struggling with their own faith. As believers, we draw a great deal of comfort from them. We are afforded an honest look at the spiritual struggles of others, their joy, hurts, fears, and faith, and then given the opportunity to discover the hand of God in the process of their lives. One of the reasons songs are an integral part of worship is that they are able to convey the vulnerability of the worshiper. Like the Psalms, worship songs can exhibit the good, the bad, and the ugly of human beings while revealing the consistent faithfulness of God. We see our own struggles and join the singer in confessing our faith in God to rescue us. In such instances, the song becomes not only a way to express human emotions, but a vehicle for testimony. Many of the Psalms are personal or national testimonies of God's goodness.

Singing in worship is not just a way to express our emotions or tell our story. A worship song can be both prophetic and didactic, as it displays the truth about who God is. Prophetic songs can declare and explain the Word of God. Like the book of Habakkuk that was intended to be sung, a prophetic song can deliver a strong or confronting message. Like the Psalms, which consistently recall the attributes and character of God, a didactic song can teach us about God, reaffirm important tenets of the faith, or help us memorize a Scripture. When songs move our focus from the temporal to the eternal, they remind us where our priorities should be. In recalling the character of God and His attributes, we are telling His story more than our own—and while our story has value, His story is the only one that can lead to salvation. Worship songs that repeat God's story teach the next generation who He is and how He has been at work through human history.

A song may accomplish many of the above at the same time. A song can at once be the expression of a wide variety of human emotions, a testimony of trust in God, a prophetic declaration, and a tool for teaching about God. When worship accomplishes these things, it can be a powerful tool for evangelism. I am not suggesting that the intent of worship is evangelism; but, evangelism is a potential by-product of worship. Genuine worship is a meaningful declaration of God's truth for those who do not know Him. Worshipers of the Old Covenant understood this. Notice how Psalm 95:1-10 blends the function of worship (W), evangelism (E), and the prophetic/didactic (P):

W- Sing to the Lord a new song;
   Sing to the Lord, all the earth.

64

Sing to the Lord, bless His name;

E- Proclaim good tidings of His salvation from day to day.
Tell of His glory among the nations,
His wonderful deeds among all the peoples.

P- For great is the Lord and greatly to be praised;
He is to be feared above all gods.
For all the gods of the peoples are idols,
But the Lord made the heavens.
Splendor and majesty are before Him,
Strength and beauty are in His sanctuary.

W- Ascribe to the Lord, O families of the peoples,
Ascribe to the Lord glory and strength.
Ascribe to the Lord the glory of His name;
Bring an offering and come into His courts.
Worship the Lord in holy attire;

P- Tremble before Him, all the earth.

E- Say among the nations, "The Lord reigns;

P- Indeed, the world is firmly established, it will not be moved;

E- He will judge the peoples with equity."

God gave the Children of Israel different themes to use in songs of worship as a means for them to maintain the proper view of Him, ascribe to Him glory, and to communicate His message to the nations. With such a rich tradition of singing among the Jewish people, it is not surprising that Christianity became a faith expressed in songs as well. To both the church at Colossae and Ephesus Paul gives similar instructions. To the Church at Ephesus he writes:

And do not get drunk with wine, for that is dissipation, but be filled with the Spirit, speaking to one another in psalms and hymns and spiritual songs, singing and making melody with your heart to the Lord; always giving thanks for all things in the name of our Lord Jesus Christ to God, even the Father.

Ephesians 5:18-19

Many have conjectured about the meaning of *psalms, hymns, and spiritual songs*.[1] In doing so, many have attempted to affirm three distinct genres. This may be forcing the text since *psalms, hymns, and spiritual songs hardly refer to different kinds of texts*.[2] Nevertheless, there is value in looking at the individual words for clarification. The first word, *psalms,* is the Greek word ψαλμός [*psalmos*], which means to pluck or strike, as in the sounding of a stringed instrument, and may suggest the use of a song with instruments. There is nothing in the New Testament that would prevent the use of instruments in the context of worship. In the Jewish tradition instruments often accompanied the Psalms themselves. This word may also indicate the actual singing of Psalms from the Old Testament. While it is possible that Paul is suggesting singing the actual Psalms of the Scripture, it would seem more plausible if this letter had been written to believers in Jerusalem who would already have an established custom of singing the Psalms. While we know that there were Jews in Ephesus and Colossae, it is not likely that a majority of the believers there would have been devout practicing Jews. For those who were, the tradition of Psalm singing would have been familiar to them. Perhaps the best lesson to glean from this is that whether actually singing a Psalm from the Old Testament or not, singing Scripture is a wonderful practice. This could include a translation of a biblical text or a poetic versification of a biblical text.[3]

The second word, *hymn,* is from the Greek word ὕμνος [*humnos*]. It is likely that this word is a song of praise or honor. It comes from an archaic word meaning to celebrate,[4] so this may indicate that the Apostle was suggesting songs to celebrate God and His work. One does not need to look far in the Psalms to understand that joyous singing would have been a customary practice for Jews. Furthermore, Christians who had recently been witnesses to God's redeeming work through Jesus Christ must have had renewed joy. Just as Psalms were familiar to the Hebrew culture, hymns were common to Greek culture, appearing often as songs to pagan deities. While history has obscured the actual sound of the music, we know the tradition was a rich one. The pre-Christian

---

[1] The same terms are found in Colossians 3:16. The primary difference between the passage in *Ephesians* and the one in *Colossians* is that Paul highlights the didactic possibilities of singing in *Colossians*.

[2] Gerhard Kittel, Gerhard Friedrich and Geoffrey William Bromiley, *Theological Dictionary of the New Testament*, Translation of: Theologisches Worterbuch zum Neuen Testament., (Grand Rapids, Mich.: W.B. Eerdmans, 1985), 12226.

[3] Versification is a practice of taking the words of Scripture, usually the Psalms, and rewording them so they fall into a poetic meter. For more information on this topic see CHAPTER 8, LESSONS FROM HISTORY: REFORMATION WORSHIP, *The Role of the Congregation*.

[4] Strong, James: *The Exhaustive Concordance of the Bible: Showing Every Word of the Text of the Common English Version of the Canonical Books, and Every Occurrence of Each Word in Regular Order*. electronic ed. Ontario : Woodside Bible Fellowship., 1996, S. G5215

hymn texts were often metrical, following some poetic scheme and therefore served as natural predecessors to Christian hymnody.

The final word, *song*, ᾠδή [*ode*] is the Greek word for a common everyday song. This word would have been used to describe either a popular song or a praise song to a pagan deity, but in a Folk style. This may support the idea that this was music for the faith community to sing together—commonly shared songs. The qualifier, *spiritual*, πνευματικός [*pneumatikos*] could suggest that the song is from the spirit and, therefore, extemporaneous. Scripture does demonstrate that God can give an extemporaneous song.[1] However, since extemporaneous songs are just that, it is unlikely that Paul is commanding everyone to sing extemporaneously to one another. Therefore, it is more likely that the term *spiritual* speaks of a song that is from the spirit and has the ability to speak to and nourish the spirit of others. The use of the common word for *song* indicates that Christian songs could be in a popular or Folk style. This contradicts an assumption by some that music must be classical or sophisticated to honor God.

Whether God intended these three words to create separate genres or whether He meant for them to enhance our understanding of the single genre of worship songs makes for interesting speculation but misses the thrust of the text. He wants His people to sing! Having led music in churches for more than thirty years, it is apparent that the Church as a whole has much room to improve in this area. Countless times I have heard believers say, *I like to listen but, I am just not a singer.* This text is not a call for singers but for worshipers. While it is true that God has gifted some to sing very well, in all different styles, I believe He enjoys hearing the voices of His children praising Him, no matter how it sounds. When our children were small, we loved to teach them all sorts of songs. Many times, we heard our children confuse the words and alter the melody, nearly beyond recognition. Never once did we meet such a song with disdain or criticism. On the contrary, our hearts warmed to hear their little voices attempting to approximate the song, no matter how it sounded. That experience is common to almost every parent. If we know how to enjoy the efforts of our little ones to sing songs, how much more our heavenly Father knows how to enjoy the singing of His children. He does so, not because it meets some human standard of excellence but, because He loves to hear His children sing.

Speaking and Shouting

Congregational expressions are not limited to music but include spoken words as well. At times, the congregation should shout these words and at times, they should whisper them. There are so many references in the Psalms that indicate shouting or declaring loudly; one must assume it was a common practice. At times, such shouts were associated with battle.[2] Shouts were also

---

[1] For example, see the Song of Moses, Exodus 15:1-18, or Miriam's song in Exodus 15:21.

[2] See 1 Samuel 17:52.

associated with times of great joy as when David brought the Ark up to Jerusalem.[1] There are many examples of speaking as an act of worship as well. In Psalm 105:2, the Scripture commands us to *speak of His wonders* and Psalm 145 declares that men will speak of God's wondrous acts, of His glory and praise. God created the human voice to be a flexible instrument, able to speak, whisper, and shout—all to His glory. One other type of speaking in the context of group worship is the public reading of Scripture. Paul tells Timothy not to neglect this important task.[2] Surely, Timothy understood that this meant reading the Scripture in the assembly for all to hear. In addition, it can and should mean unison readings as well. Congregations should be encouraged to employ their voices in a wide variety of ways and not be limited to hymn/song singing only.

Silence

Obviously, we are not to use our voice at all times. Sometimes silence is good, so good, in fact, that the Scripture instructs us to use it. Habakkuk 2:20 says: *But the LORD is in His holy temple. Let all the earth be silent before Him.* Numerous references to meditation in the Psalms assume silence—lips quiet, mind and spirit fully engaged. Silence is not a soft dynamic level where instruments play in the background, but a complete absence of any programmed sound. Often, we do all in our power to avoid any moments of silence in our worship services. The constant sounds during most evangelical worship services demonstrate that we have either forgotten how to be quiet or we do not understand its power. In a culture saturated with aural stimuli, silence can be profound. At times, it is in moments of quiet that the thunderous voice of God speaks the loudest.[3] For the one leading worship, silence may seem awkward. Nevertheless, even a few seconds of silence following a Scripture reading or a song can be a powerful component of corporate worship.

God gave the voice a wide range of possibilities. It is no accident that Scripture models the full spectrum of vocal expression, including shouts and silence, songs and spoken words. Leaders who struggle with disengaged congregations would do well to consider the wide vocal palette offered in Scripture.

SUMMARY THOUGHTS ON EXPRESSIONS OF WORSHIP

Perhaps leaders today would do well to make worshipers more aware of the variety of expressions found in biblical worship. The goal is not to force an outward action. However, a large gap exists between the wide variety of postures, gestures, and vocal expressions found in the Old and New Testaments

---

[1] For example, see 2 Samuel 6:15. Also see Ezra 3:11 when the foundation for the Temple was set.

[2] 1 Timothy 4:13.

[3] 1 Kings 19:11-13.

and what is culturally acceptable in many churches. Corporate worship is a participatory event and God has sanctioned many different expressions for that purpose. While each congregation needs to find its personality, within that personality, it is helpful to draw upon expressions found in Scripture to keep congregational worship from becoming stale.

Worshipers should not be required or coerced to exhibit any or all of these expressions. The benefit in considering what options are scripturally approved gives those who plan and lead worship a wider variety from which to choose. If the goal of the leader is willing participation, educating congregations about what types of expression are in the Bible gives them more opportunities. In some churches, the freedom to experiment with a variety of biblically sanctioned expressions is severely limited. Such limitations may inhibit participation. This is not just an issue of more contemporary styles versus more traditional styles. I have witnessed excellent participation in both and a lack of it in both. The style employed in a local congregation is not the determining factor in participation. Churches of all styles will benefit from expanding the use of expression that God has provided. Cataloging the wide variety of worship expressions in the Bible is a way for those who lead to think creatively about what is possible.

WORSHIP GATHERINGS

The Method of Gathering

We know from our previous discussion that Jewish believers *did* assemble for worship. We know that these worship gatherings primarily occurred in conjunction with the Feasts, happening only a few times each year. We also know that beyond the demands of Scripture, the system of attending weekly services in the Synagogue was common practice when the Church was born. So how did the Early Church assimilate previous Jewish practices and adapt them for Christian use? The answer is not a simple one.

At the time of Pentecost, Jews gathered in the Synagogue each week. As a result, Paul often found such gatherings a natural place for engaging his fellow Jews with the gospel. Whether or not those converted continued the custom of Sabbath gatherings at the Synagogue is not addressed in the Scripture—likely, some did. For completed Jews living in Jerusalem, the Temple remained a central hub of their life. The book of Acts tells us that believers in Jerusalem gathered daily at the Temple and in homes,[1] and that the Apostles were there preaching daily as well.[2] The gathering at the Temple was most likely in conjunction with the tradition of morning and afternoon prayers. However, as a hub of religious and social culture, the Temple did not last. About 40 years after the birth of the Church, the Roman army razed Jerusalem and destroyed the Temple. Even before this, the Temple had already begun to lose its draw for

---

[1] Acts 2:46.
[2] Acts 5:42.

Jews who had received Jesus as Messiah. They no longer needed to go there to make sacrifices. Therefore, the Temple gave way to homes as the central hub of Christian culture. This may not have been an altogether unusual development since a great deal of spiritual activity in Jewish culture was based in the home. It was primarily in homes that early Christians met on the first day of the week,[1] though, most likely, home meetings were happening more frequently than that. The gatherings on the first day of the week were eventually referred to understandably as gatherings on the *Lord's Day*,[2] commemorating the resurrection of Jesus. Such gatherings included offerings, preaching and teaching of the Scripture, prayer, congregational participation and typically a weekly breaking of bread, commemorating the Last Supper.

On the surface, this sounds much like worship gatherings today. However, nowhere in Scripture do we have a record of large weekly gatherings. By and large, we are speaking of a gathering that would not exceed the capacity of a home. Historical data suggests that would have been less than 100 in a single gathering. It was these house gatherings that believers were exhorted not to forsake by the writer of Hebrews.[3] The Church in Jerusalem alone apparently reached tens of thousands within the life of James, who was the chief elder there. So, while quite large in number, the church in Jerusalem existed, worshiped, and grew in much smaller units than many of today's large churches. They did this without buildings, property, pulpits, sound systems, or even a place outside of the home to assemble regularly. This is not to say that today's practices are wrong, but rather to illustrate that the accoutrements of corporate worship in the Early Church were very different from ours. The Early Church grew without many of the comforts we consider essential. Even the ability to gather weekly in large numbers was a privilege not enjoyed by first century Christians. Just as the Jews had not practiced large weekly gatherings before synagogues developed, the Early Church did not practice large weekly gatherings. These did not happen regularly until after the conversion of Constantine in the fourth century.

Functions of Gathering

Because early Christians devoted themselves to similar activities, their gatherings served to solidify the practice of the faith. This began to occur immediately after Pentecost as described in Acts 2:42-46:

> They were continually devoting themselves to the Apostles' teaching and to fellowship, to the breaking of bread and to prayer. Everyone kept feeling a sense of awe; and many wonders and signs were taking place through the Apostles. And all those who had believed were together and had all things in common; and they began selling their property and possessions and were sharing them with all, as anyone

---

[1] See 1 Corinthians 16:2 and Acts 20:7.
[2] Revelation 1:10.
[3] Hebrews 10:25.

might have need. Day by day continuing with one mind in the temple, and breaking bread from house to house, they were taking their meals together with gladness and sincerity of heart, praising God and having favor with all the people. And the Lord was adding to their number day by day those who were being saved.

These shared elements became the glue of the Early Church, uniting them on a foundational level. For instance, it is not likely that all gatherings had access to the same teaching of the Apostles but, they all were devoted to their teaching. Similarly, it is not likely that all congregations sang the same songs but, it is likely that they all sang. In other words, the true unity of early Christians was built around a growing understanding and practice of New Covenant truth, not a specific method. While there was no one style of worship that was common to all early Christians, there were similarities in the basic elements of worship gatherings. These elements are worthy of our study and sincere imitation.

The **Ministry of the Word** was a central focus of Early Church worship. This was not limited to reading or quoting the Scripture, but to preaching and teaching it as well. This subject alone warrants its own volume. For the purposes of our discussion, it is important to understand that preaching is a component of corporate worship rather than something separate from it. Just as singing, prayers, testimonies, and the like are components of a corporate worship gathering, so is preaching and teaching the Word of God. Because hearing the preaching and teaching of the Word are essential to the spiritual health of all churches and are, in themselves, appropriate acts of worship, they should consume a significant portion of any corporate worship gathering.[1]

Preaching and teaching the Word was a customary practice at the Synagogue prior to the coming of Jesus and became part of the New Testament practice. With the coming of the Messiah, believing Jews must have been eager to hear the scriptures taught and to understand them in light of the death and resurrection of Jesus. The sermon of Peter at Pentecost (Acts 2:14-36) and Stephen's defense before the High Priest (Acts 7:1-53) provide examples of how the Early Church preached the Jewish scriptures in light of Christ's coming. Both of these sermons exhibit that the Apostles' teaching, to which the Early Church was devoted, included the exposition of Old Testament texts.

The Early Church circulated the writings of the Apostles as they became available. The combination of Old Testament texts with writings that the Church ultimately recognized as part of the New Testament provided the foundation for faith and practice. They were taught, preached, and read in the context of corporate worship as evidenced by Paul's instructions to Timothy: *Until I come, give attention to the public reading of Scripture, to exhortation and teaching* (1 Timothy 4:13). This commitment to the Ministry of the Word provided much

---

[1] See *Mono-Directional Communication [Preaching Teaching]*, p.93 and ff. for a discussion of peaching teaching as components of corporate worship.

needed theological stability. The importance that the Early Church placed on the Scripture, both its preaching, teaching, and public reading, should challenge today's churches to give the Word similar importance when they gather for worship.

It may seem a foregone conclusion that **prayer** was an important part of spiritual life for early Christians. Considering the rich tradition of prayer common among Jews, it is not surprising that prayer was a custom of the Early Church. Acts tells us about gatherings for the purpose of prayer[1] and Paul offers several churches instruction on prayer.[2] Paul's instructions concerning prayer indicate that it was a regular function of gathering. Apart from the enormous power of prayer, it is an important participatory component of worship. In many of our churches today, prayer has become little more than filler between things we consider more important. Prayer is part of the liturgy of the people in worship and, as such, deserves a place of prominence among Christian worshipers. It is important to note that prayer can take many forms in worship besides those most familiar to us, such as offertory or pastoral prayers. Prayer can also be the sweet incense that rises toward God in the silent thoughts of a congregation as well as the words of one who stands on behalf of the congregation to lift a shared burden to heaven. Prayer can be a song of devotion or praise that addresses God, whether sung by one or by all. Many times, I have observed a worship leader complete a hymn or song that addresses God in the first person and then say, *Let us pray.* I have wonder if the leader recognizes that the congregation has been praying. If they have been addressing the Lord in spirit and truth then, it is prayer whether spoken or sung.

The Early Church shared the bond of common **fellowship**. This closeness was, in part, explainable—they were experiencing similar hardships and joys. As we have previously discussed, Christianity was birthed into a rich Jewish culture. New Christians, particularly Jewish ones, were in somewhat of a no-man's-land. They no longer fit within the customary practice of Judaism and they were not yet sure of what it culturally meant to be a believer in Jesus Christ. The separation between Christian Jews and those not yet believing pushed Christians further from their native culture. From a practical standpoint, this meant that in a time when Christians belonged to no one else, they belonged to one another. But the bond of Christian fellowship was deeper than common beliefs or experiences. Their fellowship was spiritual at the core. Because of the indwelling of the Holy Spirit, they shared a truly profound and supernatural union. Therefore, gatherings for worship allowed believers to experience both a very practical form of human fellowship and a supernatural bond that went beyond a commonly held set of beliefs and experiences. Today, the size of many gatherings makes genuine fellowship a challenge. Leaders should make every

---

[1] For an example, see the gathering at the home of Mary, the mother of John in Acts 12.

[2] In the letters to the churches at Corinth, Ephesus, Colossae, and Thessalonica, Paul clearly presumes that the believers to whom he writes are praying. He gives them instructions that include when to pray, what to pray for, and how to pray.

effort to facilitate both the practical and spiritual benefits of fellowship in worship.

As we have studied, the faith practice of the Old Covenant was a tradition of Feasts, Festivals, and Sacrifices. The Jewish faithful who came to Christ exchanged the intricate ceremonies of Judaism for a much leaner and simpler faith practice. Jesus established only two ordinances and both became vital practices for the Early Church: **Believer's Baptism** and the celebration of the **Lord's Supper**. Apparently, Baptism was not initially part of the weekly worship gathering. Baptisms originally occurred more in conjunction with the time of conversion than a weekly gathering.[1] There were instances of gathering for baptism in the first century and these were likely a time of worship and celebration. By the second century, baptism was included as a regular part of weekly Christian gatherings.[2] The earliest preserved baptismal font dates from this era and is located in the remains of a house church in Dura Europos.[3] For the Early Church, baptism was the public profession of faith in Christ. As the vehicle for public profession, it was the point of demarcation between one who might be an inquirer after the faith and one who truly believed. By the end of the first century, it was a prerequisite for participation in the Lord's Supper. Evangelical churches that utilize an altar call must be careful not to supplant the importance of baptism as the biblically prescribed means of publicly professing faith in Christ.

As for the Lord's Supper, the testimony of history and Scripture indicate that it was widely observed by all Christians with some regularity, likely celebrated weekly, if not more frequently. When Jesus instituted this memorial, He did not specify how frequently it should be observed. He did specify that whenever we celebrate the Lord's Supper it must be to remember Him. This was not an elaborate ceremony. In keeping with Paul's instructions to the Church at Corinth,[4] the supper was a reenactment of the Last Supper instituted by Jesus on the night before He was crucified. The meaning of His broken body and shed blood, represented in the bread and wine, was to be the focus.

Since the Lord Jesus gave both Baptism and the Lord's Supper to us, they deserve a place of prominence in the Body of Christ. Baptism in the New Testament is the public profession of faith in Jesus Christ and an occasion for the Church to give praise to God. It is a beautiful drama in which one tells the story of Jesus' death and resurrection as well as his own story of conversion. While believing faith initiates one into the Body of Christ, water baptism provides the new believer a means of openly declaring his faith in Jesus and identifying with the New Testament Church. This profession does not save but,

---

[1] For examples see Acts 2:41, 8:36-38. At times, Believer's Baptism occurred as soon as was practicable, see Act 19:3-5.

[2] The *Didache* indicates that baptism had become a part of regular worship.

[3] Brian D. Spinks, *Early and Medieval Theologies of Baptism: From the New Testament to the Council of Trent*, Ashgate Press, 2006, 16.

[4] 1 Corinthians 11:23-34.

in obedience to Jesus, identifies the new believer with others who have also confessed Christ, presumably within a local assembly. While this may not mean that baptisms must occur within the context of the weekly assembly, they should receive the full attention of the Body.

Similar significance must be accorded to Communion. For many freeform worshipers the fear of entering into this celebration lightly has led them to limit its frequency. This concern is warranted. At the same time, Jesus clearly gave the Supper to the Church as a tool to remember His atoning death. The infrequent use of the Lord's Supper in some congregations may violate its purpose as much as frequent celebrations may violate its meaning by becoming perfunctory. This illustrates the tension that exists for both sides of Christendom. For those whose faith traditions call for a weekly Eucharist, there is the constant challenge of avoiding a rote celebration of this Holy Supper, disobeying the command to enter into it carefully. For those who celebrate it infrequently comes the challenge of sufficiently remembering what Christ has done without using the tool He gave us to keep us from forgetting. If a church only celebrates the Eucharist every few weeks or months, it would be preferable that it take the focus of the entire meeting so that it receives the appropriate prominence.

Giving **offerings** and alms was a common practice in the Synagogue and in the Temple. It is not difficult to imagine that this culture of giving, including the Old Testament tithes, would have found a corollary practice in Christianity. When planning for a mission offering to be taken in Corinth, Paul instructs the Church at Corinth in 1 Corinthians 16:2, *On the first day of every week each one of you is to put aside and save, as he may prosper, so that no collections be made when I come.* Just as giving was an act of worship for Jews, so it was for early Christians. The Scripture instructs the local assembly to give for the support of those ministering locally, to missionaries and missionary causes, and to special needs within the greater Body of Christ. What makes giving an act of worship is not the ceremony with which it is offered or received. Giving is a matter of the heart.[1] In other words, including giving as a component in a worship service by passing an offering plate or singing a *special* song does not make giving an act of worship. In some churches, it may be unpopular to discuss money. If giving is to be an act of worship, no matter how the offering is collected, congregations will need clear biblical teaching on how financial gifts that are given may truly be offerings to God. In the best case, they represent the free-will offerings of believers who see themselves as stewards of what God has entrusted to them.

Summary Thoughts on Worship Gatherings

In our earlier discussion of Scripture, theology, and methodology, we examined the importance of continually digging deeper into the Word. The Scripture gives ample information to keep our gatherings headed in the right direction. A continual assessment of our own local practices is an important part

---

[1] See Matthew 6:1-4 and 2 Corinthians 9:7.

of our faith. As we will see in the unfolding of Church history, we are apt to forget important things and to replace them with our own traditions. The study of the Scripture is the only place we can go to ensure that we are giving attention to what is right and to continually strip away meaningless tradition. There are many things modeled in Scripture that we do not utilize and many things we hold dear that the Scripture does not model. The Bible is silent on much of the method for *how* or *when* we worship corporately. However, it has much to say about our motive for gathering. Gatherings for corporate worship should be an expression of love rather than an attempt to satisfy a biblical command.

For believers today, this may raise the issue of why we gather each Sunday as we do. It is not because large weekly worship gatherings are prescribed or modeled in Scripture. Certainly, there were house meetings modeled in the New Testament. But why do many Christians gather in large crowds for the Lord's Day? As a boy, I was taught that Scripture commanded us to remember the Sabbath by coming to church. While this approach may give a pastor some leverage in getting people to attend Sunday services, it really is an unfortunate distortion of Scripture. Oftentimes we direct our people to do things for less than the best reason. Moreover, at times, we ourselves practice our faith out of cultural habit or a desire to meet a self-imposed legalism. Now, as a father with children of my own, I worship in an assembly weekly, much larger than a home gathering, and I invite others to do the same. I do this without a clear scriptural command to do so. Certainly, the Bible teaches me to be in regular fellowship with other believers. However, it does not require me to attend a gathering of dozens, hundreds, or thousands of believers to worship. I do it because I *can*! It is my joy to do so, simply because I "get to" out of love for the family of faith and the One who has redeemed us. The freedom granted by the lack of scriptural mandate to *attend church* creates the opportunity to gather corporately to exercise a privilege rather than to perform a duty.

The privilege we have as the redeemed is no clearer demonstrated than in Revelation 7:9-12. The scene is in heaven; the time is after the Tribulation. Notice the characters present in this heavenly drama:

> After these things I looked, and behold, a great multitude which no one could count, from every nation and all tribes and peoples and tongues, standing before the throne and before the Lamb, clothed in white robes, and palm branches were in their hands; and they cry out with a loud voice, saying, "Salvation to our God, who sits on the throne, and to the Lamb." And all the angels were standing around the throne and around the elders and the four living creatures; and they fell on their faces before the throne and worshiped God, saying, "Amen, blessing and glory and wisdom and thanksgiving and honor and power and might, be to our God forever and ever. Amen."

The multitude is those who have come out of the Great Tribulation. Like you and me, they were saved by the blood of Jesus Christ, redeemed by the

Father, and brought into His presence. As they stand before the Lamb of God, they erupt with a thunderous cry, *Salvation to our God who sits on the throne, and to the Lamb.* It is interesting that in such a moment of worship the angels are silent: *And all the angels were standing around the throne....* It almost seems disrespectful that they do not participate. However, the angels cannot sing the *Salvation Song;* they do not know the words. Angels worship God eternally but they cannot praise Him for their own redemption. The Apostle Peter indicates that salvation is something *into which angels long to look.*[1] To the angels, our salvation must have seemed a peculiar and wonderful thing. They knew how some of their own had rebelled against God. There was no second chance, no grace, no mercy. God irrevocably cast from His presence all of the angels who rebelled to await no other possibility than an eternal future in torment. The same angels who saw the rebellion of their own and God's subsequent judgment saw the rebellion of humankind as well. However, they did not see God cut off humanity from hope. Instead, they saw Jesus Christ, God in the flesh, shed His own blood so that He could restore human beings to fellowship, adopted as sons. Surely, the angels would join their voices if they had ever known the blessedness of redemption.

As human beings, we occupy a unique place in God's entire universe. While we are not the only beings to rebel, we are the only ones that God chose to redeem. I have often heard the quip, *unbelievers cannot worship.* Of course they can and they will, as will all the demons of hell! However, as the redeemed of the Lord, we have the privilege of doing something the unsaved can never do, nor can the demons, nor the entire angelic host. We have the privilege to sing the *Song of Salvation*, to thank Him for doing what He did for no others, pouring out His own blood to redeem us.

---

[1] 1 Peter 1:12.

SECTION II:

LESSONS FROM WORSHIP HISTORY

AN INTRODUCTION TO SECTION II

That which has been is that which will be,
And that which has been done is that which will be done.
So there is nothing new under the sun.

Ecclesiastes 1:9

We live in a world that is constantly changing and seems full of 'new' things. However, the Bible teaches that there is really nothing new. The struggles we face in life and in ministry are the same ones that have been there since the beginning. The same obstacles we face with worship today are the same ones shared by Christians who came before us. In some cases they dealt with those well and in some cases they did not. In studying how previous generations faced a variety of problems, we can see what approaches they took to solve some of them. In the laboratory of history, we can examine the effects of their decisions. This can help us look at the challenges we face today with the added wisdom of others. Additionally, we can look at what we are now doing and gain some sense of what effect those practices might have on subsequent generations. If we fail to look at history as a teacher, we forgo the opportunity to learn its significant lessons. The treasure of what we can learn from history is second in value only to what we can learn from the Scripture. While many fret about the complex issues facing today's worshipers, solutions are lying quietly embedded in our own history.

This section will not attempt to recount the development of Christian worship; others have done that very well. Instead, we will paint the history of Christian worship with broad strokes, attempting to glean some valuable lessons. Therefore, the amount of history included is limited, providing the reader only enough to contextualize the lessons. This may raise some objection since I have chosen to recount only those portions of history which support my conclusions. Granted, worship history—as I have summarized it in my interpretation—is subjective. But, no recounting of history can be objective—none reports everything. Each writer must edit somehow and thereby tell the parts that he or she believes to be most important. Therefore, the hope is that my own subjective telling will benefit other believers. If nothing else, perhaps the reader will study the history for himself and find more or different lessons than I have found. For this reason, a companion reference of Church history, as well as a reference on the development of Christian worship, will enrich the experience.[1]

Through this next section, we will examine thirteen lessons from the last twenty centuries of Christian worship. Throughout this section we will illustrate the lesson from history and give some application of that lesson to today's practice of worship. We can learn from our worship forefathers and benefit from the wise choices they have made while avoiding some of their errors.

---

[1] For example, Justo González's excellent history of Christianity: *The Story of Christianity. Volume 1, The Early Church to the Reformation;* and *Volume 2, The Reformation to the Present Day* (New York, NY: HarperOne/HarperCollins, 2010); and for the history and development of Christian worship, see: Geoffrey Wainwright and Karen B. Westerfield Tucker. *The Oxford History of Christian Worship* (Oxford: Oxford University Press), 2006.

CHAPTER 4

THE AGE OF THE APOSTLES
AND EARLY CHURCH FATHERS (AD 30-312)

The years after Pentecost were formative for the practice of Christian worship. The birth of the Church and its subsequent geographic expansion and numeric growth brought multiple issues of faith and practice to the forefront. Followers of Jesus had to figure out what Christian worship looked like without the benefit of historical practice to inform them. Some questions were settled by the Apostles or by the scriptures of the New Testament, and some issues were worked out regionally without the benefit of Scripture. Although there was access to the scriptures of the Old Testament, the scriptures of the New Testament were not completed until just before the death of the Apostle John, around AD 100. For the first generations of believers, the task of deciding what was appropriate or even expected in Christian worship was not a small one. The way in which the first generations of believers worked out the practice of Christian worship, and the results produced by those decisions, have much to teach us today. Where Old Testament and available New Testament scriptures were prescriptive concerning worship, we can see how believers understood and applied their teaching. In circumstances where Scripture was less specific or unavailable, we can see how practices developed through trial and error. In both instances, there were successes and failures. In this chapter we will examine five lessons from the years during which there were still Apostles living and Scripture was being written, and one final lesson from the century immediately following the death of the Apostles.

The first generation of Christian worshipers shared neither a common culture nor ethnicity. The rapid expansion of the Church meant that different cultures and ethnicities were, at once, faced with many of the same questions. What does Christian worship look like? What makes Christian worship distinctly Christian? What aspects of our own culture are contrary to the teaching of the Apostles or to the Scripture? Is there a single cultural approach to worship that we all must adopt? Answers to some of these questions came almost as soon as the Church was established and they provide our first lessons from the history of Christian worship.

LESSON 1: CHRISTIAN WORSHIP IS ATTACHED TO NO PARTICULAR CULTURE

BACKGROUND

If the first Christians chose a specific cultural expression for worship, it could indicate God's preference and, therefore, be of great importance to us. There was certainly no shortage of cultural expressions from which to choose. At the time of Christ, the Greco-Roman world was a tapestry of religion and culture. The Romans considered themselves heirs to Hellenistic thought. They developed their own versions of the Greek gods and venerated them with various monuments and temples in nearly every city of any size. Roman polytheism provided an almost endless supply of deities, none having the supreme spot, but each being worshiped as it might seem most beneficial to the worshiper.[1] This extended a religious culture of polytheism to the far reaches of the Empire. Additionally, Rome was a pluralistic society. Despite the fact that many prided themselves in being Roman citizens, there was no single Roman society, no shared Roman culture, only factions and subcultures held in the fragile balance of the *Pax Romana.*

Just the little strip of land called Palestine could serve as a microcosm of Roman cultural diversity at the time of Christ. There were a variety of factions within Palestine and several within Judaism itself: Jews by lineage and practice, devout proselytes from many cultures, as well as a variety of inhabitants from other lands that did not practice Judaism at all. Within Judaism there were both political and religious factions: Romanists, Separatists, Zealots, Zionists, Sadducees, Pharisees and more.[2] While we may refer to *the Jews* as if they were a homogenous group, they were far from it. Even so, if Christianity were going

---

[1] For a summary of Roman religious beliefs, see John Scheid, *An Introduction to Roman Religion,* trans. Janet Lloyd (Bloomington, IN: Indiana University Press, 2003).

[2] For a more complete discussion see, Merrill Chapin Tenney, *New Testament Survey, Revised* (Grand Rapids, MI: Wm. B. Eerdmans, 1985), 105 & ff.

to base its worship practice in any culture, something from within Judaism would be the logical choice. Jesus was the God of the Jews in the flesh, the fulfillment of God's promise to Israel. The Apostles taught from the Jewish scriptures and were, of course, Jews themselves.

Following Pentecost, the birth moment of the Church, development of Christian worship could have taken one of three courses. It could have: 1) become a subset of Jewish culture, 2) become identified with a pagan culture, or 3) developed a new and distinct Christian culture that would spread with the faith. None of these occurred. In retrospect, we know that Christianity did not bond to a single culture but was received and practiced in a variety of cultures. From the beginning, Christianity was multi-lingual and multi-cultural: one Truth shared and experienced by a broad array of cultures and ethnicities. The diversity was so great on the day of Pentecost that without the miracle of tongues, many could neither have understood nor participated.

> They were amazed and astonished, saying, "Why, are not all these who are speaking Galileans? And how is it that we each hear them in our own language to which we were born? Parthians and Medes and Elamites, and residents of Mesopotamia, Judea and Cappadocia, Pontus and Asia, Phrygia and Pamphylia, Egypt and the districts of Libya around Cyrene, and visitors from Rome, both Jews and proselytes, Cretans and Arabs—we hear them in our own tongues speaking of the mighty deeds of God."
>
> Acts 2:7-11

Culture and *Cultus*

Our English word *culture* comes from the Latin word *cultus*, which was used to describe the various religious practices of people. The common ground between our present understanding of the word *culture* and the use of the Latin word *cultus* is important for our study. There is an inescapable connection between the *cultus* of Christian worship and the culture in which the worshiper lives. The outward expression of all worship practices, to varying degrees, is tied to the customs and communication methods of the people who express it. This connection includes language and goes to the core of how each culture uniquely expresses itself. This might seem strange considering we spent three chapters emphasizing biblical foundations of worship that transcend all cultures. Nevertheless, our languages, our social interactions, our songs, our means of verbal and nonverbal communication are all connected to the ways in which we live and worship. For first century Christians, this connection is of particular interest. As Christianity spread around the Mediterranean rim and west to Rome, people had to choose how they would express worship. The only precedent they had for understanding how worship looked or sounded was their experience as Jews or as worshipers of pagan gods.

For those who had Judaism as a backdrop, it must have been difficult to determine how a new faith in Christ would modify religious practices that had been woven into the cultural fabric for centuries. To us, we can see the seamless work of the One true God. Our understanding of the Temple and Sacrificial System is bathed in the light on this side of Calvary. For the first Jewish believers, it was a different story. Some of them continued to practice Jewish ceremony until the Temple was destroyed in AD 70. Understandably, they saw Jesus as Messiah, the Son of David, Yahweh's anointed One. As a result, they were not quick to set aside their system and sought to require other Christians from non-Jewish backgrounds to adopt it—much like the requirements for proselytes. The confusion in Jerusalem was such that it took a gathering of Apostles and elders to clarify that the practice of Christianity was not synonymous with Jewish culture and ceremony.[1] This confusion continued and would prompt the Apostle Paul to write the church at Colossae to avoid, among other things, the yoke of legalism concerning Festivals, New Moons, and Sabbaths.[2] Nevertheless, the consistent message of the Apostles and Early Church leaders was that Christianity was based neither on Jewish culture nor *cultus*.

Outside of Judaism, Christians struggled to determine which pagan practices could continue and which should be set aside. For those who came to Christ from something other than Judaism, their cultural backgrounds were widely varied and the spiritual background was often Roman polytheism. Even after coming to Christ, some of them likely continued some of those practices, just as Jews continued their cultural practices. This created a scenario where elements of the Christian faith were combined with unacceptable pagan practices. On more than one occasion, the Apostle Paul dealt with the issue, advising Christians in Corinth and Rome to set aside some of those customs.[3] Just as the Apostles limited the association of Christianity with Jewish culture, they also limited its connection to pagan rituals. In effect, they were teaching the first generation of Christians that their newfound faith was tied neither to a specific culture nor an existing *cultus*. It quickly became apparent that the *cultus* of both Judaism and paganism contained cultural aspects that were incompatible with Christian practice. Therefore, as new styles developed, they were shaped to be neither distinctly pagan nor Jewish.

If Christian worship would not be built on Jewish culture or a specific pagan culture, then how would it develop? Could it become a combination of a specific culture and *cultus*? To answer the question simply: *No*. As the gospel spread across cultural lines, new converts maintained their own cultural practices and developed unique worship practices within those cultures. A diversity of worship styles developed with the spread of Christianity.[4] The Early Church

---

[1] See Acts 15.

[2] Colossians 2: 11-23.

[3] For example, see Romans 14 and 1 Corinthians 8.

[4] For a discussion of various geographical areas where liturgical styles developed see below, *Lesson 2: Flexibility in Worship Starts with Theology.*

came to understand that the gospel was not about creating a distinctly Christian culture or *cultus*. It was not about becoming Jewish or adopting pagan cultures. The gospel was about transforming individuals. Where lives were changed cultural practices that were in conflict with the Scripture changed. Otherwise, cultural uniqueness remained. Christianity flourished without a separate Christian culture and without a fixed or universal *cultus*.

Christians, who were changed by the power of the gospel, were not distinguishable by adopting an existing culture or forming new ones, but by displaying the truth of Jesus Christ in the communities where they lived. This is a distinguishing mark of our faith and was clearly illustrated in its first thriving decades. The letter, *Epistola ad Diognetum*, most likely written in the first half of the second century, illustrates this truth:

> For the Christians are distinguished from other men neither by country, nor language, nor the customs which they observe. For they neither inhabit cities of their own, nor employ a peculiar form of speech, nor lead a life which is marked out by any singularity. The course of conduct which they follow has not been devised by any speculation or deliberation of inquisitive men; nor do they, like some, proclaim themselves the advocates of any merely human doctrines. But, inhabiting Greek as well as barbarian cities, according as the lot of each of them has determined, and following the customs of the natives in respect to clothing, food, and the rest of their Ordinary conduct, they display to us their wonderful and confessedly striking method of life.[1]

The believers described above did not make a lasting impact on their world by instituting a new culture or society. Nor did they make an impact by becoming part of one new monolithic Christian culture. Instead, as to cultural practice (clothing, food, and cultural conduct), Christians were generally indistinguishable from unbelievers. What made them noticeable was not a separate Christian culture, but a *wonderful and confessedly striking method of life*. The writer of this letter to Diognetus goes on to describe lives that are lived with moral uprightness, integrity, and a community characterized by uncommon love—a distinct righteousness characterized these believers. We understand this righteousness to be the fruit of a life surrendered to God, one that is markedly different from the ordinary because it shines with the radiance of the Treasure it contains. Thus, the sincerity of early Christ worshipers was validated by their Christ-like character.

---

[1] Alexander Roberts, James Donaldson and A. Cleveland Coxe, *The Ante-Nicene Fathers Vol.I : Translations of the Writings of the Fathers Down to A.D. 325, The Apostolic Fathers with Justin Martyr and Irenaeus* (New York: Cosimo, 2007), 26.

Instead of a distinct culture, Christianity proved itself as the embodiment of truth that transcended culture. The impact this has on worship is enormous. There is no *one culture* of Christian worship. It can find expression in any culture. Because man is sinful, there are aspects of every culture that dishonor the Lord and would be completely inappropriate as expressions of worship. But, it is also true that many aspects of culture are neither good nor evil. Since the expression of worship always has some relationship to the culture of the worshiper, healthy worship will be as varied in the way it looks and sounds as those who are expressing it. Scripture does not mandate that Christians look the same culturally or practice the same *cultus*. Instead, our uniqueness comes from lives that reflect the glory of God. Our distinctive is far beyond cultural. It is living a holy life in an unholy world. It is not in the peculiarity of our culture or customs, but in the peculiarity of who we are as a people—a priesthood that expresses worship in the way we live-*shachah* before God.

> But you are a chosen race, a royal priesthood, a holy nation, a people for God's own possession, so that you may proclaim the excellencies of Him who has called you out of darkness into His marvelous light.
>
> 1 Peter 2:9

It is tempting to assume that the perplexing problems of religious pluralism we face today are unprecedented, but nothing could be further from the truth. The world of the New Testament was characterized by social, intellectual and religious ferment.[1] The power of the gospel was able to speak to, be received by, and transform aspects of every first century culture where it took root. It is equally able to address the ferment of today's culture. This should encourage today's church leaders, who tire of trying to figure out corporate worship by chasing culture or running from it. As our own world becomes more diverse, we have the opportunity to demonstrate that genuine worship transcends culture and ethnicities. Its power, demonstrated in the lives of changed people, will set aside cultural practices that are contrary to the Scripture. It is able to do this with sufficient precision to remove what God finds offensive without obliterating the uniqueness of a people. True Christianity is monolithic in its doctrine, but varied in its expression. Sadly, the Church more often practices just the opposite. When Christian worship is practiced rightly, it is possible for there to be as many cultural expressions of worship as there are congregations; and, yet, if a congregation has been diligent with the Scripture, each unique expression will share the same elements that make worship pleasing to God.

---

[1] Harold A. Netland, *Encountering Religious Pluralism: the Challenge to Christian Faith and Mission* (Denvers Grove, IL: Intervarsity Press, 2001), 26.

BACKGROUND

God has given us a gift that defies explanation: He has given us the ability to express worship to Him who is eternal with something very temporal: our own culture, our own language. How does Christianity have the ability to be expressed with such enormous variety? Since God and His truth are attached to no particular culture or ethnicity, His truth is equally applicable to all people groups. As a result, worship, no matter how varied, can be acceptable to Him, so long as it is done according to the truth of His Word. It is this principle that we want to explore in this lesson.

As we discovered in the first chapter, Scripture is the foundation on which our understanding of worship must be built. When we are attentive to proper doctrine/theology, methods can develop protected by both the limits and liberties granted in the Scripture. We can see this in the way the Early Church applied doctrinal truth. The account of the Jerusalem Council, recorded in Acts 15, is the first prominent example of how the Early Church dealt with issues of conflict between liberty and restraint. Recent Gentile converts from Antioch, Syria, and Cilicia were being criticized for not keeping customary Jewish practices. This conflict was brought to the attention of the Apostles and elders in Jerusalem, with the hope that they would clarify exactly the extent to which Gentile converts to Christ needed to become Jewish. After their decision, they wrote a letter summarizing their findings. Their decision was as follows:

> For it seemed good to the Holy Spirit and to us to lay upon you no greater burden than these essentials: that you abstain from things sacrificed to idols and from blood and from things strangled and from fornication; if you keep yourselves free from such things, you will do well. Farewell.
>
> Acts 15:28-29

In summary, the Council curtailed pagan practices and addressed moral purity. But much more significantly, they liberated non-Jewish Christians from becoming functional Jews as they became Christians. Considering the enormous amount of Jewish tradition and ceremony that was under consideration, this was a very short list.[1] When the Apostles defined what was necessary, they were also saying what was not necessary. At that moment, the believers who received the instruction of the Council were released from hundreds of laws and regulations regarding the practice of Judaism. Imagine what the spread of Christianity would

---

[1] Numerous laws and regulations beyond those in the Scripture had been added to the practice of Judaism by the time of Christ. For an in-depth look at these see *The Cambridge History of Judaism: The Late Roman-Rabbinic Period, Volume IV,* edited by Steve Katz (New York: Cambridge University Press, 2006).

have looked like if each new convert needed to learn how to live and worship properly as a Jew before he or she could live and worship properly as a Christian. The rapid expansion of the Church would not have been possible if each new convert had been required to enter the long process of learning the ancient customs before they were ready to share the gospel with another. Instead of devoting their discipleship to teaching the scriptures in light of Jesus' work, the Church would have been bogged down in minutia, only giving lip service to what was important.

Paul drew on this same truth in his letters. Despite the Jerusalem Council's findings, over ten years later there were evidently Jews, either unaware of the decision of the Council or unwilling to abide by it, who were pressing new converts in Colossae to *do* life and worship the Jewish way. The Jerusalem Council occurred around AD 50 and Paul wrote the letter to the Colossians around AD 61. Evidently, old habits die hard.

> Therefore no one is to act as your judge in regard to food or drink or in respect to a festival or a new moon or a Sabbath day—things which are a mere shadow of what is to come; but the substance belongs to Christ.
>
> Colossians 2:16-17

Looking at this statement, it is easy to imagine what Paul's arguments might have been when he spoke to the Jerusalem Council ten years earlier.[1] The foundation of his argument was likely very similar to the words he wrote to the Colossians. In this case, theology expanded liberty that would otherwise be limited by cultural restraints.[2]

Truth not only has the power to expand freedom, it also has the power to limit freedom. In Paul's letters to the churches at Corinth and Rome, the same Apostle who argued for freedom curtailed cultural practices in order to maintain health within the church. He instructed both congregations that there are certain conditions when one should refrain from eating meat that had been sacrificed to idols.[3] He taught that it is not wrong to do so but, this practice might cause some to stumble. In other words, theological truth takes precedence over culture in determining what is appropriate. In this case, the cultural practice, eating meat sacrificed to idols, could violate a theological truth: God expects believers to be so concerned with the spiritual welfare of others that they are willing to refrain from cultural practices which are otherwise allowable.

---

[1] Acts 15:2-4.

[2] Paul made a similar argument in Galatians 2:14, also likely a reflection of his arguments before the Council: *But when I saw that they were not straightforward about the truth of the gospel, I said to Cephas in the presence of all, "If you, being a Jew, live like the Gentiles and not like the Jews, how is it that you compel the Gentiles to live like Jews?"*

[3] See Romans 14:14-23 and 1 Corinthians 10:23-33.

APPLICATION

So how does this lesson help direct our worship practices? Most importantly, the way in which the Council and, later, the Apostle Paul applied truth, gives us a pattern that we can readily apply to worship practice. By placing scriptural truth above cultural practice, both the Council and Paul assert that worship is not about religious culture, it is about Jesus Christ—the substance of our faith. Theology, not culture, is the standard by which a practice is accepted or rejected. This is important, not only in the evaluation of our own practice, but in how we view and appraise the practices of others. Our own worship practices are joined to our culture. As a result, we can execute the method flawlessly, without seeing that its real value is in the theological truth that undergirds it.

This can lead us to conclude that worship is defined by how *we* express it. When this happens, we often discount the practices of others and determine they are inappropriate based on our cultural perspective, just as the Jewish believers did to Gentile converts from Antioch, Syria, and Cilicia. At that point, we are dismissing the validity of other worship practices based on our own cultural definition rather than specific theological truth. This makes it difficult for us to accept a wide variety of worship practices and undermines the ability of the Church to be highly flexible. We are all likely to assume that the way we do things must be the best or only way and, therefore, others should do it that way as well. This limits our definition of worship to the way it looks or sounds to us.

The basis for understanding worship should be the Word of God rather than our culture. When we know and apply the Bible, we are refining our theology and discovering proper boundaries. The more clearly we define our theology, we can see aspects of our cultural practices that are unacceptable to God and, therefore, inappropriate for worship. A clearly defined theology also helps us see the broad liberty to express worship in a thousand ways in a thousand cultures. Within those scriptural boundaries worship can be both vibrant and highly flexible. As we understand our theology, we gain an important tool that can assist us in evaluating worship practices other than our own. We may find an alternate style of worship unpleasant or distasteful but, if it is grounded in Scripture, we do not have the authority to pronounce it unacceptable to God. Our goal should be to see worship, whether our own or another's, through the lens of God's Word, separating the wheat of biblical theology from the chaff of our methods. This grants us the ability to say with the Apostles, we desire *to lay upon you no greater burden than these essentials... the substance belongs to Christ.*[1]

When we worship in truth, we participate in something far greater than a cultural expression. In that moment, one action unites us with all believers of all races, classes, and customs—a human expression of communion with God. Whether we are in a cathedral, a storefront, or deep in a remote rainforest, worship may look and sound different but, it is worship nonetheless if it is accomplished in accordance with God's Word. When we think of worship in this

---

[1] Acts 15:28 and Colossians 2:17.

way, it has one single look: a perfect harmony with the Scripture that produces the proper submission to God. This is what made the gospel able to move from one culture to the next without encumbering subsequent Christian communities with the burden of reproducing another culture.

For church planters and missiologists, this is particularly important. It has been an oft repeated pattern for missionaries and church planters to share the gospel as well as their own culture and *cultus* simultaneously. In the absence of some clear demarcation between culture and theology, those who share the message and those who receive it are likely to confuse the two. When this occurs, host cultures receiving the gospel are quick to assume that the worship style of those who brought the gospel is the way Christians ought to worship. Aspects of the host culture which are not in conflict with Scripture are set aside to reflect the culture of those who brought the gospel. A clearly defined theology by those sharing the gospel will provide the safety and flexibility to encourage new forms of worship expressions to develop in the new culture. The Early Church needed to learn this lesson quickly to ensure the healthy development of faith and practice. Otherwise, they would have been pressing Jewish culture on new Christians or absorbing pagan practices as Christianity spread to new cultures.

LESSON 3: HEALTHY WORSHIP WILL REFLECT CULTURAL DIVERSITY

BACKGROUND

The first major test of Christianity's ability to survive in the middle of enormous cultural diversity came when Jerusalem was destroyed. As a reaction to uprisings in Palestine, Titus, the military commander, who would become emperor, sacked Jerusalem and destroyed the Temple in AD 70. The destruction of Jerusalem resulted in the *Diaspora*, the eviction and scattering of many from their homeland. For Jews, whose faith was attached to the Promised Land and whose worship was attached to a specific structure, the destruction of the Temple began a protracted sorrow that continues to this day. The taking of Jerusalem was no small task and required *nearly a fifth of the entire forces of the Roman Empire—altogether one of the most formidable forces so far assembled by the Romans.*[1]

Other prominent events also affected the lives of those living within the Roman Empire. In the twenty years surrounding the destruction of Jerusalem, there was a massive fire in Rome (AD 64), burning as much as two-thirds of the city. In the same year, Nero began persecutions against Christians, lasting four years. It would be the first of several state sanctioned persecutions. The atrocities leveled against Christians in that era would rival any in history. Nero died and in

---

[1] Warwick Ball, *Rome in the East: The Transformation of an Empire* (New York: Routledge, 2000), 57.

AD 69 Vespasian became emperor. Mount Vesuvius erupted in AD 79 destroying the entire city of Pompeii and Vespasian died leaving Titus as emperor. He would only last twenty-six months. All of this and more as Christianity lost its birthplace and many of its early leaders to martyrdom. In short, the first generation of Christians lived in a time of enormous turmoil. Add to all of this the barriers of cultural and religious division and, in human terms, engineering a worship methodology to account for so many variables would be impossible.

In the providence of God, the teaching and writing of the Apostles had relieved the burden for Christians to maintain Jewish *cultus* in such an environment. Imagine the plight of early Christians if they had not already settled this matter and, instead, the practice of Christian worship still required the Temple. What would have happened to the practice of the Faith if it had been dependent on a specific ethnicity, religious system, or geographical location? Thankfully, this was not the case. Separating the Christian faith from Jewish culture made it light for travel and had given it an inherent flexibility. When the Diaspora occurred, the size of the Christian community in Jerusalem was evidently large. By most estimates, it was in the tens of thousands well before Jerusalem was destroyed. As these believers went beyond the bounds of Palestine, the gospel spread around the Mediterranean rim. The direct contribution of the Diaspora to the growth of Christianity is unknown but, the speed with which Christianity spread is a matter of history. In 270 years Christianity grew from the eleven surviving disciples to an estimated 5-7.5 million.[1]

The rapid spread of the gospel meant simultaneously working out what Christian worship looked and sounded like in hundreds of communities. This had to take place locally, since there was not one approved method, nor any way to dispense it if there were. As a result, many of these communities developed unique aspects of Christian worship. The great variety of worship styles was regionally represented in five centers where various liturgies developed and thrived. They were Carthage and Rome to the west, and Jerusalem, Antioch, and Alexandria to the east. These cities developed influential forms of worship for the first several generations of Christians. The exception was Jerusalem, which, for a season, lost its place as a center for worship development after AD 70. Initially each of these areas was a hotbed of missions and evangelism and as a result, strong churches grew up in them. The large cities associated with these areas became regional centers for the spread of the Faith. It is not surprising that these cities produced leaders who participated in most of the major Church councils through the fifth century and provided much of the important writings of the post-apostolic era.

---

[1] Extreme estimates range from 1.5 million to over 15 million. The number we have used assumes a growth rate of roughly 40% for each decade between AD 40 and AD 300. See Rodney Stark, *The Rise of Christianity, A Sociologist Reconsiders History* (Princeton, NJ: Princeton University Press, 1996), 6.

APPLICATION

The adaptation of Christian worship into multiple cultures, producing multiple styles, was possible only because the Church was busy applying the truths contained in our first two lessons: Christian worship was attached to no particular culture, and, clearly defined theology had given it a safe flexibility. For us who are trying to gain helpful information from history, the presence of multiple centers of liturgical development was significant. We sometimes think of early Christian worship as a one-color painting. That is not the case. These five liturgical centers are only representative of a wide variety of worship styles that existed through this period. Christian worship was more like a tapestry of colors, distinguishable by local customs. The more Christianity spread, the more diverse worship became. While there were theological aberrations (we will discuss these later), generally speaking, worship within Christian communities was healthy and thriving. In other words, as Christianity was pressed into multiple cultures and spreading at a tumultuous time, it was healthy and becoming more and more diverse.

We often think that church growth is the replication of a method or style. Had this been the case in the Early Church there would not have been a variety of liturgical styles. The fact that there was enormous growth in the midst of this variety should demonstrate to us that in the face of cultural diversity, seeking stylistic conformity is not an effective approach. Merely transplanting a worship style may do more to slow church growth and hamper vibrancy than to help. This relates not just to our often repeated attempts to suppress local uniqueness in favor of broader stylistic homogeneity, but also calls into question the imitation of innovations. If people have greatly diverse cultures, it may be unhealthy to require or even encourage them to adopt a worship style from another culture. This truth is especially important for church planters who are struggling with how new churches should establish worship practices. If our desire is to see Christian communities be thriving and healthy, we would do well to encourage local communities to find worship expressions that fit their culture. Of course, this must be done with a clearly defined theology—one that is rooted in Scripture. It is the clarification of theology that makes such diversity safe and healthy.

LESSON 4: THE BASICS OF COMMUNICATION IN CORPORATE WORSHIP HAVE NOT CHANGED

Despite the rapid spread of Christianity and the development of diverse styles, healthy worship, however it looked and sounded, maintained a strong attachment to the components practiced from the birth of the Church. Acts 2:42 says the first believers devoted themselves to *the Apostles' teaching, fellowship, the breaking of bread and prayer.* These represent three types of communication, all integral to corporate worship, and became a pattern for subsequent generations to follow. They are *kerugma* (preaching and teaching), *leitourgia* (prayer), and *koinonia* (fellowship).[1] The maintenance of something so basic was clearly a focus of the Early Church, and the generations that followed built on the foundation laid by the Apostles. Each of these types of communication can be described in terms of direction, i.e., who is speaking and who is listening. In preaching and teaching, communication is mono-directional—one person speaks and all others listen. In prayer, communication is bi-directional, the people speak and listen to God speak, and God listens and 'speaks' to the people. Finally, omni-directional communication occurs in the context of fellowship, where communication is shared between God and His people and among the people themselves.

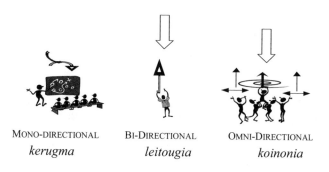

MONO-DIRECTIONAL	BI-DIRECTIONAL	OMNI-DIRECTIONAL
kerugma	*leitougia*	*koinonia*

These building blocks were foundational to the health of Christian worship from the beginning. Although we have discussed the wide variety of styles that developed with the spread of Christianity, there were commonalities. Among those was the imitation of the early Church's practice described in Acts 2. Because these three types of communication are still essential for healthy worship, we will look at them briefly.

Mono-Directional Communication [Preaching Teaching]
BACKGROUND AND APPLICATION

The most basic form of communication in corporate worship is mono-directional, one speaking and everyone else listening. The word used in Acts 2:42 for teaching is *didache* [διδαχή] and indicates that the Early Church was devoted to doctrine. The historical record and Scripture tell us how they expressed this devotion. Just as Paul instructed Timothy, one or more elders in a local assembly gave themselves to the study of sound doctrine and taught it to the congregation. Given the command of Jesus in Matthew 28 to *teach* those who responded to the gospel, this was essential. Transferring doctrine to new converts was an important component of the Church's early expansion. Paul stressed to Timothy the importance of both teaching the truth of the scriptures

---

[1] For more on this, see Barry Wayne Liesch, *The New Worship: Straight Talk on Music and the Church* (Grand Rapids, MI: Baker Books, 2001), 161 & ff.

and preaching the message of the gospel. In fact, one of the qualifications for elders (pastors) in the church is that they must be able to teach. In the historical context, this would have included both instruction and mentoring.

While the word *teach* in itself may not indicate mono-directional communication (a sermon), the word *preach* adds an important component to the concept of teaching. The most common New Testament words translated as *preach* indicate an intentional and clear proclamation of biblical truth. *Euaggelizo* [εὐαγγελίζω], as in 1 Corinthians 15:1, *means to speak of or proclaim good news*. This implies, at least to some extent, mono-directional communication, because one has something to say that others need to hear. Likewise, and even more to the point, *kerugma* [κήρυγμα] and the related word *kerusso* [κηρύσσω], mean to announce or cry out a specific message as a herald.[1] The herald had a specific announcement that had been entrusted to him. He was to cry out that message for all to hear. Such an announcement is certainly mono-directional. In this sense, preaching is distinct from teaching. While teaching may utilize a wide variety of techniques, including lecture and discussion, the focus of preaching is proclamation. Even in the Synagogue, the custom was to *preach* (expound in a monologue) the Scripture. Clearly, God intends for preaching to be a significant part of the believers' gathering and a portion of it is, by design, one person speaking and everyone else listening. Preaching/teaching are God-ordained acts of worship and Scripture is to be their primary focus.

Very few congregations grasp that teaching and preaching are acts of worship. I have heard many pastors through the years speak of *the worship* and *the preaching*. In this, they mean that worship is the music and prayers, normally done by the people, and the preaching is something distinct from 'worship' and done separately. To be sure, those actions of the congregation should be expressions of worship. But, the preaching/teaching times in the assembly should also be an expression of worship. The one who stands to speak must see himself first as a worshiper, ministering his gift in the *proper state of submission before God*. For the humanly gifted, this can be a challenge. It is one thing to preach in the power of the Spirit and another to use human talents to excite a crowd. It is not that preaching cannot or should not excite and motivate. However, that must never be the ultimate goal. The primary concern is to please God by being a faithful herald of the message, rather than to excite the listener. Neither the power nor authority of the sermon is in the messenger (the preacher), but in the message (the Word of God). Since it is impossible to worship God and promote self at the same time, preaching/teaching as an expression of genuine worship is the surest protection against human pride and the best way to ensure that the focus is on the truth of God's Word rather than the gifts of the preacher.

Listening to preaching/teaching is an act of worship for the congregation as well. God did not design preaching for passive observation. When we read that

---

[1] For *kerugma* see 1 Corinthians 1:21 and for *kerusso* see 1 Corinthians 1:23.

the Early Church *devoted*[1] themselves to the Apostles' teaching, we know that they were active listeners, passionate about the teaching they received. Throughout the history of the Church, there have been great orators who obviously had the talent to speak publicly and move crowds. Yet, the test of whether the ministry of preaching and teaching is truly an act of worship is not determined by stirred emotions, within either the one speaking or the one hearing. For the listeners, preaching and teaching is worship when they receive and apply the Word of God. God's Word is truth and it sanctifies.[2] For preaching to be the rich act of worship that God intended it to be depends on both the one speaking and the ones listening.

Mono-directional communication is not restricted to speaking in the context of the sermon. Others who lead should understand the importance of the role they have as well. When someone sings a solo, reads the Scripture or testifies, it must be a personal act of worship, as well. Leading in any way before the congregation carries the risk of becoming self-important. A sermon well preached or a song well sung can become an opportunity for pride. If you lead, never forget that any compliments you receive are not for you to keep. If God has used you, it is He who deserves the glory. Being aware of this can help insulate those who lead in public worship from misusing their position. When the one teaching or leading is first worshiping, the whole issue of pride becomes moot. When God is the One receiving all the glory, we have none left to misuse or keep for ourselves.

Bi-Directional Communication [Prayer]
BACKGROUND AND APPLICATION

Bi-directional communication can be best understood when we think of prayer, specifically what we may say to God and what He may say to us. We have previously mentioned the important role that prayer played in the Early Church. Often, we think of prayer only as what we say to God. However, any intense study of the subject reveals that prayer itself has the potential to speak to God and hear from Him as well. It is relational and as such, prayer is two-way communication and crucial to corporate worship. In some measure, each worship gathering should be a dialogue between God and His people.

To be clear, this conversation is not God speaking new revelation to us. Instead, on the most basic level, this worship dialogue includes what we say to God and what He says to us through the Word as it is illumined by the Holy Spirit. It also includes the way in which the Spirit may convict us, correct us, or provide us with wisdom, insight or direction. What we say to God in worship is not limited to scheduled prayers in the order of worship. Songs sung in corporate worship often address God directly, and, as such, they are corporate prayers. In addition, during the course of a worship gathering an engaged congregation is

---

[1] The word is προσκαρτερέω [*proskartereo*], describing the careful attention and focus the listeners accorded to the teaching of the Apostles.

[2] John 17:17.

also involved in an inner dialogue with God. While worship leaders and/or pastors may not know the private conversations happening between God and the congregants, they should take notice of what elements in a worship service address God directly. It is no more appropriate to approach a pastoral prayer with a lack of focus than it is to address the Almighty thoughtlessly in song. All words addressed to God are prayers. As such, we should both speak to God and listen for Him to speak to us, whether through His Word or by His Spirit. Therefore, whether sung or spoken, prayers are a dialogue with the Most High and deserve the focused attention of all who participate.

Each opportunity the congregation has to speak to God is important. At times, songs or responsive readings are the only opportunities the congregation has to join with others to address God. Congregations often miss the fact that they are addressing God through the words of a hymn or song. They may sing the words to an entire hymn like *How Great Thou Art* and never even give a thought to the fact that each chorus is directly addressing God Almighty. When worshipers begin to focus their attention on the One to whom they are speaking or singing, the total spiritual dynamic in corporate worship improves.

Two-way communication in corporate worship comprises the liturgy (*leitougia*[1]) of the people, the ministering work of the congregation before God. This makes bi-directional communication vital to worship. Without it, the congregation as a whole has little opportunity to engage and express themselves to God corporately. While unbelievers may benefit from observing worship, worship is never a spectator's activity for believers. When the congregation is engaged in two-way communication, it becomes their liturgy, i.e., their priestly service of worship before the Lord. If the dialogue between God and the people has become mundane through overuse or marginalized by those who plan, worship will suffer. Healthy corporate worship requires bi-directional communication.

Omni-Directional Communication [Fellowship]
BACKGROUND AND APPLICATION

The power of *fellowship* is one of the most visible signs of the New Testament Church. In human terms, fellowship is the interrelation among people. Human relationships are horizontal—person-to-person. In worship there is an added consideration of God's presence. This makes fellowship both vertical, person(s) to God, God to person(s), and horizontal, people to/from other people. When God and His people are in fellowship with Him and with one another, a unique bond occurs. In the Early Church, this bond with God and a deep love for one another was one of the telling marks of a changed people. Jesus told His disciples that such love between believers would be their hallmark.[2] In His priestly prayer (John 17), Jesus asked the Father for that union

---

[1] λειτουργία , see Chapter 1, 20.
[2] John 13:35.

to be shared between believers and the Triune God. In corporate worship, genuine *koinonia* ties Christians to one another and to their God. Through this spiritual union, believers share a common bond through joy and hardships. The gathering of early believers was a place of provision, celebration, solace, and mutual comfort. The first believers held all things in common.[1] This was far beyond money or goods. They lived out the Christian life with one another. They rejoiced with one another and when they hurt, they went to each other for comfort.[2]

The type of fellowship they practiced is illustrated by Paul in 2 Corinthians. Using comfort, received and shared, Paul illustrates the omni-directional nature of fellowship.

> Blessed be the God and Father of our Lord Jesus Christ, the Father of mercies and God of all comfort, who comforts us in all our affliction so that we will be able to comfort those who are in any affliction with the comfort with which we ourselves are comforted by God. For just as the sufferings of Christ are ours in abundance, so also our comfort is abundant through Christ. But if we are afflicted, it is for your comfort and salvation; or if we are comforted, it is for your comfort, which is effective in the patient enduring of the same sufferings which we also suffer; and our hope for you is firmly grounded, knowing that as you are sharers of our sufferings, so also you are sharers of our comfort.[3]
>
> 2 Corinthians 1:3-7

Both vertical communication (between God and people) and horizontal communication (person-to-person) are present in this passage. Blessings rise from people to God; comfort comes from God to His people. Then, believers can reciprocally pass comfort to one another and blessings rise to God. This interconnectivity gives Christian fellowship its unique power.

In a worship gathering, believers can express fellowship in a variety of ways. Certainly greeting one another, which was a custom in the Early Church,[4] is still appropriate. However, songs and readings that occur during corporate worship also provide opportunities for biblical fellowship. In many instances, songs themselves are not addressed to God, but to fellow worshipers. A hymn like *Amazing Grace* demonstrates this well. No one would say that *Amazing Grace* is inappropriate for corporate worship. But, since it does not address God, how does it function in corporate worship? The answer lies in how the song is

---

[1] Acts 2:42.

[2] Acts 4:23.

[3] The different forms of the word *comfort*, which occur ten times in this passage, are related to the word παράκλησις [*paraklesis*] and have the meaning of solace, encouragement, nearness, etc.

[4] Romans 16:16; 2 Corinthians 13:12; 1 Peter 5:14.

voiced, i.e., to whom it is addressed.[1] When we sing *Amazing Grace,* we are speaking to one another, and, by doing so, we are entering into fellowship with brothers and sisters in Christ. As we testify of God's blessings toward us, the words of our testimony bless one another and by that, we bless God. He returns to us even greater blessings and God's people then bless one another. Like the cycle of comfort within the Body, we share in the mutual blessings inherent in the bond of fellowship between God and His people when we worship together. This bond distinguishes private worship from corporate worship.

Final Thoughts on Worship Communication

Each of the three types of worship communication—teaching, prayer, and fellowship—has its place in worship today just as it did for the Early Church. They are to be constant components of biblical worship. God intends for us to hear His truth through the ministry of teaching and preaching. God desires hearts joined together to declare His greatness through the liturgy—the ministry of the people before God. Finally, God intends for the fellowship of His people to build up one another, demonstrating His grace to the lost. In short, we can summarize the purpose of corporate worship in the following way: *Corporate worship exists to hear from God and to express devotion to Him, to allow believers to remind each other of His grace, and to do so in such a way that they demonstrate the love of Jesus to the spiritually disconnected and lost.*

Healthy worship offers a healthy diet of communication. This does not mean dividing a worship service into thirds, one for each type of communication. It does mean that those leading should take care not to minimize the ministry of teaching, the ministry of the people, nor the ministry of Christian fellowship in the regular worship gatherings. Churches who do not give careful attention to each of these types of communication will create an unhealthy atmosphere for worship. For instance, the church that minimizes fellowship and teaching may have a very rich liturgy for believers to follow but, overall, corporate worship will lack the warmth of genuine fellowship and, in the absence of biblical preaching, be susceptible to theological error. Likewise, a church that maximizes the teaching/preaching event and does not cultivate biblical fellowship nor a robust liturgy for the people may develop a large, well-educated crowd without experiencing real vibrancy and participation.

The challenge to balance the various aspects of worship will not go away. Each new generation produces new threats to a healthy balance of worship communication. As leaders, it is our responsibility to address them. Two of these became more common in the twentieth century and for that reason, we will address them briefly. The first is the sheer size of some congregations. The number of larger congregations increased significantly in the 20th century. The rise of the megachurch presents a different twist on challenges to corporate worship simply because of the volume of people that gather weekly to worship.

---

[1] See Chapter 11, 291.

The Early Church may have numbered in the tens of thousands in particular cities but, they were not all meeting together each week. While a large church may be able to deliver excellent teaching to a large crowd, the bond of Christian fellowship can become impossible to maintain if there is no connection among the people outside of the worship gathering. This does not mean that larger gatherings are wrong. All methods of corporate worship have inherent strengths and weaknesses. The larger the gathering, the more challenging fellowship becomes. This makes it essential for leaders to help people find places to connect with other believers in genuine *koinonia*. Equally important, leaders of larger congregations should make sure that the services do not become large venue spectator events. This should be an area of constant vigilance for any who lead worship. In many larger churches, the level of excellence on the stage can become an invitation for the congregation to watch others worship on their behalf. The worship leaders then become priests who offer worship on behalf of the congregation. Based on personal experience, this is one of the greatest challenges in leading larger congregations in worship.

Another factor that threatens the health of worship communication is the advent of distribution technologies utilizing broadcast, web cast, and personal electronic devices. Through these media, it is possible to deliver excellent teaching and preaching to an individual without ever seeing them or knowing who they are. Furthermore, the church can record and produce live worship events in both audio and video formats and distribute them to other believers who may utilize them to have a *personal* worship experience. Such technologies may be helpful. However, they cannot replace the purpose of corporate worship. To utilize such technologies in this way ignores the congregation's ministry to the Lord and shortchanges biblical fellowship among God's people. By nature, believers can experience biblical fellowship and speak with a unified voice of praise only if they are together. There must be some level of person-to-person contact.

No matter how virtual our technology or how efficiently we can make the delivery of preaching and worship experiences, we cannot ignore the need to gather with other believers. This is a fundamental concept of New Testament theology and is in keeping with the importance God placed on corporate gathering in the Old Testament. God has created us to be relational creatures and has designed us to express that, at least in part, through fellowship in the Body of Christ—specifically in its local expression. New technologies may help churches be more efficient in some areas. Yet, without careful attention, our technological innovations will result in marginalizing other areas. As technologies proliferate, corporate worship will face new, unforeseen challenges. The consistent and balanced use of these three types of communication can ensure that corporate worship accomplishes the purposes for which God designed it, no matter what new challenges the Church encounters.

LESSON 5: APPLYING THE FUNDAMENTALS IS AN ONGOING PROCESS

BACKGROUND

By AD 100, the scriptures of the New Testament were complete. This made the years from AD 100-200 critical in determining what writings were truly Divine in origin. By AD 200, most of this had been settled for churches in the West (those more related to the liturgical centers of Carthage and Rome). The churches in the East (primarily related to the liturgical centers of Antioch and Alexandria),[1] as well as prominent churches in Asia Minor, were in substantial agreement less than a hundred years later. For the Church, struggling to understand who she was and looking for practical directions on faith practices, the writings of the Apostles were essential. Yet, they gave only limited direction on liturgy itself and left very few instructions concerning what was acceptable in Christian worship. Furthermore, few, if any, churches had access to the complete body of New Testament books before the end of the second century. To address this, the Early Church fathers used the scriptures they had, and, consulting with others when possible, began to produce writings that clarified appropriate practices. These works are valuable to us, not because they have the authority of Scripture but, because they show us how the protégés of the Apostles applied what they had been taught, and, applied that teaching to develop appropriate worship practices. A few representative works from this period demonstrate the type of instructions they offered for worship.[2]

Didache, circa AD 100

The earliest of post-Apostolic writings that survives is the *Didache*, probably written around AD 100. While historians are certain of the approximate date of the *Didache*, they do not know who compiled the material. The first section of the work appears to be a catechism and the second includes practical instructions for Christian living and offers some directions related to worship gatherings. These include instructions for a prayer offered before the elements of the Supper. This prayer would become known as the *anaphora.* Although it has taken on various theological functions, the prayer prior to taking the elements remains in almost all celebrations of the Eucharist to this day. A curious feature of the *Didache* is the order of the elements. The Cup is taken before the Bread, instead of afterward as Jesus had done and Paul had recounted to the Corinthians. This may suggest that the Church was still working out its practices in the years immediately following the death of the Apostles. After taking the Cup and Bread, a final longer prayer closes the celebration of the Eucharist.

---

[1] After its destruction, Jerusalem's influence as a center of liturgical development was greatly reduced.

[2] See Cheslyn Jones, Geoffrey Wainwright, Edward Yarnold SJ, and Paul Bradshaw. *The Study of Liturgy,* Revised ed. (London: SPCK, 1992), 80-97.

There is not a great deal of detail in the work, only rudimentary instructions. Nevertheless, it does provide a basic template for the Early Church to celebrate communion. The *Didache* stated that only baptized believers should take the Supper and stipulated that new converts should be able to affirm the *Didache* prior to baptism. This amounts to the earliest preserved pre-baptismal catechism—a set of truths one must affirm prior to being welcomed at the table. One other point of interest is that the *Didache* presumes a Sunday meeting for the purpose of worship, particularly for the celebration of the Lord's Supper. Since there is little instruction beyond that, we may assume that Church leaders viewed the Lord's Supper as a central feature of weekly worship gatherings at the close of the first century.

First Apology, circa AD 150

Justin Martyr's work is much more extensive than that of the *Didache,* both in its explanations of theology and practice. It includes more detail in its instruction for the Eucharist, laying out a simple form based on Scripture. In discussing the Lord's Supper, it is clear that there are gatherings just for this purpose but, Justin also describes a weekly Sunday gathering that would have included readings from the Old Testament scriptures and the writings of the Apostles (New Testament scriptures where available). Much like the Saturday services held in Jewish synagogues, the leader of the congregation would give a discourse based on the Scripture with exhortations and encouragements to the congregation. After this, the congregation stood, offered prayers, and then observed the Supper. After the congregation collected an offering for the poor, the meeting ended. Unlike the *Didache*, the *First Apology* indicates that all baptized believers would have first taken the Bread and then the Cup. It is also clear that all would have participated in corporate acts of worship such as prayer and giving. Though this work appears only about fifty years after the *Didache*, it is clear that attempts were being made to clarify what was appropriate and to develop a liturgy for worship. Considering the difference between the order of the Elements prescribed in the *Didache* and *First Apology*, it is likely that other significant differences existed between regions and even between churches within those regions. Various writings confirm differences in both practice and thought between churches in cities such as Antioch, Rome, Alexandria, Ephesus, and Corinth.

Apostolic Tradition c. AD 200

The appropriateness of the episcopate that developed in the second and third centuries is beyond the scope of this discussion. It is a historical fact that what began as an informal bishopric in the first and second centuries, eventually gave birth to patriarchal or perhaps even monarchical rule in the Eastern and Western Church. The Western expression of this became the papacy, which, in the Dark Ages, grew to its height of power by evil means. Initially, however, there were obvious reasons why the bishops sought to exert their influence over the churches. When examining writings like the *Apostolic Tradition*, written by

Hyppolytus of Rome, we can see a developing urgency from the Church fathers of this period. The push is clearly for more uniformity. The blight of various heresies in theology and practice, as well as intensifying rounds of persecution, most likely account for this urgency.

In the absence of a totally identified Canon of Scripture, churches were susceptible to aberrant teachings and methods. *Apostolic Tradition* demonstrates a concern for the Church to stay true to her calling. Hyppolytus goes much further than Justin in specifying aspects of both the persons and the process of corporate worship. In addition to covering most of what Justin had addressed, he included instructions for deacons and elders to pray specific prayers. Hyppolytus wrote out many of these prayers, suggesting his concern that those leading might lack sufficient doctrinal grounding. These prayers are interspersed with responses scripted for the congregation, perhaps recognizing that many newly converted worshipers needed help in knowing how to participate in corporate worship. This created a scripted dialogue between leader and congregation. This is the basis of chant and response that would become a staple method in the liturgical form of the Roman Catholic and Greek Orthodox Churches over the next several centuries.

APPLICATION

What do these and other writings teach us? Common among many writings of this era was a growing focus on appropriate worship expressions, specifying who could pray, what should be prayed, as well as who should distribute the Elements and how it was to be accomplished. For instance, Cyprian and Tertullian[1] gave high priority to directing aspects of the Eucharist. In *de Oratione* and *de Baptismo*, Tertullian describes corporate worship expressions that include kneeling, lifting of hands, standing, etc. It is difficult to say if the writings of the period represent a general concern that churches were not handling corporate worship correctly or if there were some sparring going on between various schools of thought, one hoping to set the definitive form. During this time, the influence of churches (like Rome in the West and Antioch in the East) was increasing throughout Christendom. Some of the instructions circulated in this period set guidelines beyond the bounds of Scripture. Perhaps, in a time of great pressure and change, some restrictions were inevitable. The instinct of the Early Church fathers was to place the foundations of the faith in front of the people—to apply truth as best they could. They did this in what they taught (the Scripture) and in what they practiced (the Lord's Supper). This may seem simplistic to us but, this served the Church well during a time of great difficulty.

Like the Christians who lived in the pre-Nicene era, we live in a time of enormous transition. And, as a result, some church leaders suffer from cultural

---

[1] Perhaps frustrated with the growing constriction of the Church in Rome, Tertullian eventually separated himself from orthodox Christianity and became associated with the heretical movement of Montanism.

panic. While there is little doubt that times of rapid transition and societal turmoil present significant challenges, it should be our first instinct to highlight the most foundational aspects of our faith, to constantly evaluate our practices in light of Scripture. The Early Church did not focus on the increasing turmoil of the day. Instead, they gave increased attention to the most fundamental elements that made worship meaningful—seeking to understand how to apply them. In retrospect, they did not get it all correct. Unlike the leaders of this period, however, we have a complete collection of Scripture to guide us. There should be no guesswork for us in identifying and constantly reapplying those things that are essential for worship.

Because the Church Fathers were intent on the fundamentals of the faith, the Church flourished, giving us a shining testimony that vibrant Christianity is indomitable. The difficulties the Church faced between its birth and the conversion of Constantine in AD 312 were enormous. We have mentioned several already: the destruction of its birthplace, Jerusalem, and the subsequent Diaspora that occurred, the lack of access to a complete New Testament, the influence of various heresies, the rapid spread of a single gospel across a geographically large and culturally diverse empire, and periods of intense persecution. For most of this period, it was either illegal or socially unacceptable to gather publically for Christian worship and, in many areas, there was active persecution.

Among numerous persecutions, those under Decius and Diocletian were enforced throughout the Empire making them especially brutal.[1] The persecutions reached their worst in the latter and made life miserable for many Christians for a decade. During periods of persecution, Christians gathered at their own peril, at times fleeing metropolitan areas or secretly meeting in the catacombs. Even when the Church was not under a statewide assault, Christians endured regular harassments, even brutal persecutions at the whim of local magistrates. Christians continued to assemble regularly to worship God and the numbers of believers continued to increase, all of this with the simple focus of Communion and studying the scriptures. If one knew nothing else about corporate worship during this period, we could at least surmise that the Church was getting enough of the real thing to endure great hardship and simultaneously be a part of the greatest expansion the Church has ever known.

As years separated believers from the time of the Apostles, many Church Fathers attempted to impose a greater degree of control on Christian worship, a regular progression toward more prescription and restriction. This was not all bad. The attempt of some episcopates to enforce control initially aided the Church in maintaining its focus. Judging from the vibrancy of the thousands of Christians who were willing to die for the name of Jesus, the negative effects of increased restraints were, at first, minimal. What they gained by applying the fundamentals outweighed any negative effects of a trend toward some liturgical

---

[1] Philip Schaff, *Ante-nicene Christianity: A.D. 100-325* (Grand Rapids: Wm. B. Eerdmans, 1950), 26.

conformity. The majority of negative impact came after the conversion of Constantine when the imposition of tradition became more significant.

While the written record of worship practices during this era may be limited, the effect of lives changed by genuine encounters with God is not. Many stood publicly to profess their faith in Christ and subsequently gave their lives in martyrdom. What pastor or leader would not hope to have men and women who were so committed to Christ that nothing could dissuade them from living out their faith, no matter the cost? Jesus had called His followers to surrender to Him with abandon, to take up their cross and follow Him. That is exactly what these men and women did. Again, the Church fathers and history are speaking and, hopefully, we are listening. For these who preceded us, a deep and profound commitment to apply the fundamental truths of corporate worship was sufficient to nourish their souls for the task of martyrdom.

This challenges the *laissez-faire* attitude of many believers today. Fresh and vibrant encounters with God, grounded in the Word, gave them what they needed to thrive. It was not in a complex or refined liturgy. In the few writings that have survived, it is clear that the Early Church was very concerned with clarifying basic doctrines and practices rather than debating intricacies of method and form. The result, committed lives of believers, should likewise be our goal. A deep commitment to the fundamentals of our faith can provide the necessary spiritual fuel for today's believers to flourish in time of cultural turmoil.

FINAL THOUGHTS ON THIS ERA

The years that followed the birth of the Church demonstrated how people received the gospel, interpreted it into an everyday life of worship and then passed it on to others. Never has there been a more vibrant time in Christendom. Rather than hinder the development of worship styles, the diverse culture of the Roman Empire demonstrated that the spread of the gospel was not a cultural phenomenon but a dissemination of transcendent truth. The same truth makes it possible for all people groups to express Christian worship without adopting one fixed Christian *cultus*. When the Early Church applied God's truth, they found the freedom to express worship in a variety of ways. In the same truth, they found protective limits that would keep unique cultural expressions from distorting or obscuring its message. This allowed the Church to flourish despite difficulty and intense opposition. Just as the truth of the gospel never changes, so it is with the basics of how we communicate in worship.

Today, when culture and change are no less prevalent, we must resist the urge to rally around a single form or a silver bullet method. There is none mandated or modeled in Scripture. Additionally, we must be willing to examine which aspects of our faith practice are cultural and which are genuinely biblical. Like the Jewish believers of the Early Church, we may continue to practice cultural aspects of our faith that do not conflict with the New Covenant but, we do not have the latitude to prescribe those practices for all believers. Our power and effectiveness in worship, like that of our forefathers, comes from biblical truth. The rapid rate of cultural change and growing diversity we see in our day may cause fear in many church leaders. They are truly concerned about whether or not Christianity will survive in a post-modern society. To this, let us say the obvious. While we may live in what sociologists call a post-modern culture, there can never be a post-gospel culture. If there is any lesson we must learn from the first three centuries of Christianity, it is that the worship of Jesus Christ transcends culture. The truth of the Bible is universal and eternal because it flows out of the character of God. We should never feel that it is time to circle the wagons and hope that we can just hang on to the end. The rapid changes in culture should excite all serious students of the Bible, knowing that no matter how diverse our culture becomes, the efficacy of the gospel will remain. As it touches the hearts of new believers, worship will find new expressions. Those expressions may look different from any we have known but, if they are grounded in the Word of God, they can be meaningful encounters with God.

CHAPTER 5

CHRISTIAN WORSHIP (AD 313-1500)

By comparison, the development of Christian worship between the fourth and fifteenth centuries was much slower than the first three hundred years. Originally, worship styles were developing quickly as Christianity spread around the Mediterranean rim and there was a strong focus on making the teaching of Scripture the foundation of worship development. This type of commitment to the centrality of doctrine did not continue. Christian worship in the era we are now discussing developed more along the lines of liturgical standardization rather than innovation driven by solid theology. This was accompanied by a clear and steady decline in the health of Christian worship. There were exceptions to this and we will note some of them. However, we can understand the lessons of this period best by recognizing a pervasive move toward establishing a fixed liturgy and a loosening of a deep commitment to Scripture as the authority for faith and practice. Other events, such as the fall of the Roman Empire, the rise of ecclesiastical authority, the birth of Islam, and the lack of literacy in the Dark Ages had enormous impact on worship practices, but none as great as liturgical standardization.

LESSON 6: STANDARDIZED WORSHIP PRACTICE IS BENEFICIAL ONLY IF THERE IS A STANDARDIZED CULTURE

BACKGROUND

Once the gospel had spread to the limits of the Empire the development of new styles began to slow. However, the greatest slowdown in the rate of change occurred after Christianity was no longer persecuted and, especially, after it was incorporated into the fabric of the Roman Empire.

No single event affected the course of public worship more than the conversion of Constantine in AD 312. Whether his conversion was immediately genuine is unclear. He was finally baptized just weeks before he died in AD 337. However, his sympathies for the Christian faith greatly increased after his purported vision of a cross prior to the Battle for the Milvian Bridge. Constantine won that battle and subsequently became the sole ruler of the Western Empire. His newfound confidence in Christianity and his imperial power combined to make him the primary benefactor of the Church, a role that continued to increase for the rest of his life. Constantine's impact became evident on several levels. Our interest is discovering the specific impact his change of affections had on Christian worship.

In the years prior to Constantine's conversion, Christians were experiencing intense persecution. Beginning in AD 303, Diocletian exacted the worst official persecution the Church had experienced. This persecution continued in earnest until AD 313, when an edict of toleration was issued for the Western Empire. This effectively ended the persecution and sought to decriminalize Christianity.[1] Several other edicts followed and Christianity became the official religion of the Empire in AD 380. Thus, within a few decades, believers went from suffering under severe persecution to tentative toleration, to favor and promotion by Constantine, to being the official religion of the government. For our brothers and sisters in the faith who suffered persecution, this change and the subsequent support of the newly converted Emperor could seem nothing less than Providence. Beyond the obvious benefits of a marked reduction in persecution throughout the Empire, the Church began to enjoy the resources Constantine and his successors provided, including property, buildings, and funds. Rome provided basilicas throughout the Western Empire, sometimes erecting new structures and sometimes refurbishing structures previously used for pagan worship. Perhaps the most significant change for the Church was an immediate social legitimacy. Almost overnight, a fugitive, underground faith became a religion of resource and considerable

---

[1] Not all persecution stopped immediately. Even after the agreement reached between Constantine and Licinius, the ruler of the Eastern Empire, to tolerate Christianity (AD 313), persecution continued intermittently until Licinius' death around AD 325. The persecutions by Licinius included edicts forbidding corporate worship within the city of Byzantium.

status. Corporate worship once practiced in the homes and the catacombs began to occur in grand structures paid for by the Roman government.

It may be difficult to understand how much this new status proved to be a heavy weight of social pressure on the Church. Perhaps it is needless to say but, the Emperor had great influence, whether intentionally or not, on a rapid expansion of pomp and ritual within church gatherings. The level to which pageantry was becoming part of Christian culture was evident at the Council of Nicaea in AD 325. In the opening ceremony, Constantine entered with great formality, clad in purple, and presided over the discussions.[1] It speaks volumes that Constantine was not a baptized believer at this time. Nevertheless, because of his position, he called for and oversaw the first ecumenical council of the Church. Such ceremony was also becoming part of worship gatherings, taking on an imperial flavor. The gathering of believers was becoming an event held in a grand location and with a great deal of pageantry.

Since Christianity had developed as a very simple faith practice, devoid of ceremony, this pageantry had to come from some place other than the New Testament or the practice of an underground Church. Rome certainly had plenty of religious ritual. However, most of it was of pagan origin and, therefore, not the first choice of Church leaders. Instead, to create this ceremony, they looked to the rituals of the Old Testament. In the Sacrificial System, they found ample ritual from which to create ceremony for corporate worship. From the vestments worn by the priests to temple architecture and the concept of sacrifice, the Church utilized increasing amounts of Old Testament ritual to create a new Christian ritual more suited to the imperial tastes.

By the fifth century, even Communion, which had once been a simple and intimate memorial, became an elaborate ceremony styled after the Sacrificial System of the Old Covenant. Like the atonement sacrifices made under the Old Covenant, the focus became the work of the priest rather than the liturgy of the congregation. In assuming the ceremony of the Sacrificial System, the Roman Church also assumed Old Covenant theology. Communion became more than a means to remember Jesus and, instead, became a means to offer the Body and Blood of Jesus each time Communion was celebrated. The pastor assumed the role of the Old Testament priest and the Body and Blood of Jesus, represented in the bread and wine, served as the sacrifice offered on behalf of the people to satisfy God's justice. In order for the bread and the cup to serve the function of a real sacrifice, their substance would need to be transformed. This was the genesis of the concept of transubstantiation—the bread and cup becoming the Body and Blood of Jesus.[2]

To some extent, the use of ceremony led the Roman Church into a new theological understanding of the meaning and function of Communion. Once the theology had adapted to the ceremony, the new theology pushed the ceremony to

---

[1] Timothy David Barnes, *Constantine and Eusebius* (Cambridge, Massachusetts: Harvard University Press, 1987), 215.

[2] See Chapter 6, *ROMAN CATHOLOC WORSHIP*.

become more complex. Believing the bread and wine were transformed into the actual Body and Blood of Jesus, the Church thought that they were too precious for the congregation to pass among themselves. By the beginning of the seventh century, it became increasingly uncommon for the congregation to participate in taking the Elements, especially the Cup. By the eleventh century, the congregational use of the Cup was banned in many places. The revitalization of the Old Testament ritual had functionally made a High Priest of the pastor, offering a sacrifice on behalf of the people. This transformed the role of the congregation from worshipers remembering Jesus' death to worshipers waiting on the absolution wrought by the offering. Just as the priests of the Old Covenant had been intermediaries for Israel, the priests of the Eastern and Western Churches became intermediaries for Christians. In the West this would reach its apex in function of the Bishop of Rome.[1] The Eucharist moved far from the simple supper instituted by Jesus. Instead of being guided by a shepherd, the congregation's communion with Jesus at the Table became separated by a human intermediary.

The increase in ceremonialism and lack of participation by the congregation was not limited to the Lord's Table. In addition to the ritual of sacrifice, other aspects of Jewish worship were also imported. In the synagogue, a common form of singing included a lead singer called a cantor. He served as the primary soloist in the synagogue service. At times, he sang or chanted a statement to which the congregation responded. This style was used when singing or chanting the psalms. The cantor made one statement and the congregation would offer a refrain as a response.[2] The Roman Church imitated this type of antiphonal singing as early as the latter part of the fourth century. The priest would sing or chant a phrase and the congregation would respond. This might have ensured congregational participation if the chant and response had not become increasingly complex. However, to match the ornate ceremony of Communion, singing itself became more complicated. This further reduced the ability of the congregation to participate. Other means of participation that had most likely been part of the first generation of Christians decreased as well. By the fourth century, freeform testimonies and prayers were totally scripted out of the liturgy. In the span of 200-300 years, congregational participation went from significant, at times excessive,[3] to very limited. Additional developments in singing and ceremony went so far that by the end of the eighth century, congregational participation was reduced to reciting the creed and an occasional response during the chant.

---

[1] The title *Pontiff*, used for the Pope (Latin, *pontifex*) is the word used in the *Vulgate* for the *High Priest* and for Jesus as our *High Priest* and intermediary (Hebrews 2:17): *unde debuit per omnia fratribus similare ut misericors fieret et fidelis pontifex ad Deum ut repropitiaret delicta populi.*

[2] For example, Psalm 136 would lend itself to such a responsive setting.

[3] Paul's letters to the Corinthians sought to curtail unhealthy excesses in congregational participation.

The dwindling role of the congregation was also attributable to the growing lack of literacy that followed the collapse of the Roman Empire. Latin was the language of the Church before the fall of the Western Empire. After the Roman Empire collapsed, Latin remained the language of the Church in the West, even though it fell from common use outside of the Church. Since the congregation had a diminishing role in corporate worship, the script for the Roman service (known as *Mass*[1]) was free to become more complex, with very little consideration for what effect that would have on individual worshipers. We will look at how the development of musical complexity affected corporate worship. It is enough in this lesson to understand that the dissolution of the Western Empire made a culturally diverse populous even more divided. The common language of Latin fell out of use and eventually developed into the various Romance languages. Thus, in a time when the liturgy should have been undergoing innovations to reflect a greater degree of diversity, the trend was just the opposite.

While our focus as Protestants is the Western Church, congregational participation also suffered during this period in the Eastern Church. They too had absorbed the ceremony and theology of the Old Covenant into their worship. While the prominence of the bishopric in Rome accounted for a growing conformity of style in the West, the East reached conformity through different means. They had rejected the concept that one bishop had any supremacy over the other and, thus, were open to accept approved styles from other regions.[2] Nevertheless, both Rome and their counterparts in the East addressed the massive cultural transitions of the Dark Ages with more rigidity than fluidity. This meant that both East and West generally sacrificed congregational participation for a fixed liturgy.

APPLICATION

So what can this teach us about the practice of Christian worship? It is clear that for over one thousand years a great deal of focus, both in the East and the West, was on developing and refining the liturgy. Beginning with the conversion of Constantine, the course of worship development changed forever. While there were differences between the East and West, the basics were the same. Liturgical complexity increased and congregational participation decreased. History does not indicate that Constantine had an agenda to make churches conform to a particular ceremonialism or opulence. Nonetheless, that was the result with the vast majority. Money flowed to almost every major city

---

[1] For a more in-depth understanding of the Mass, see Chapter 6, *ROMAN CATHOLIC WORSHIP.*

[2] It is remarkable that without papal oversight the East preserved their liturgy so well. The long lasting power of the liturgy in the East came, in part, from the longevity of the civil government rather than papal power. While the Western Empire had fallen by the middle of the fifth century, the Eastern Empire and its capital of Constantinople lasted another thousand years until it fell to the Turks in 1453.

to erect beautiful houses of worship. Gratitude to the Emperor, as well as the desire to honor him for ending the persecution and promoting Christianity, led many churches in the West to emulate the style used in Rome. After the Western Empire fell, the absence of a Roman civil government made way for the influence and power of the papacy to increase, thus setting a long-term course for a unified methodology.

There is nothing wrong with sharing methods between churches. However, the Church had thrived by being unified in theology and diverse in her methods. Conformity in methods can work if there is uniformity in culture. This was not the case in the Eastern or Western Empire. The reason that so many variants of liturgy had developed in the early years of Christianity was a testimony to the vibrancy of worship and the cultural diversity of the Roman Empire. This cultural diversity only increased in the years that followed the fall of the Roman Empire in the West.[1] The geographical area once under Roman rule disintegrated into a patchwork of city-states. The geographic size of these city-states was determined primarily by the military power of their individual rulers, who extended their influence as far as their limited power could reach. This not only resulted in a great deal of civil diversity but, also, laid the groundwork for a proliferation of cultural and linguistic diversity. This cultural and political instability was a primary characteristic of Western Europe for hundreds of years.

In hindsight, it is clear that the Roman Church made the wrong choice when facing the geopolitical struggles of the Dark and Middle Ages. Their approach was to help preserve the faith by pushing for greater standardization in form during a time of growing cultural diversity. Just the fact that the Church was comfortable with developing a highly complex liturgy in a language not spoken by the people is a clear indication that the Church had become dangerously concerned with standardizing worship practices while ignoring the needs of the people. As a result, the spiritual development of the Church and, therefore, the development of corporate worship came to a near standstill. That is not to say there were not bright spots in this thousand years of darkness; there were.[2] The fact remains: the people themselves had little voice, little participation, and very little understanding of what was happening in corporate worship. No matter how highly developed the music or liturgy became, as long as the people themselves could not engage, it was not a healthy situation.

---

[1] Some historians, such as Gibbons, date the fall of the Roman Empire in AD 476 when Augustus Romulus was deposed. It also may be acceptable to assign the date of AD 455 when Rome was sacked or in AD 480 when Nepos, the last legitimate claimant to the Western throne, died.

[2] Many would be familiar with men such as Thomas Aquinas (1225–1274) or Saint Francis of Assisi (1181/1182-1226). There were many others who thought and wrote on theological subjects. For examples, see Giulio D'Onofrio and Matthew J. O'Connell, *History of Theology: The Middle Ages* (Collegeville, MN: Liturgical Press, 2008), and William Carl Placher, *Readings in the History of Christian Theology* (Louisville, KY: Westminster John Knox Press, 1988).

In our present day, we must likewise be careful about seeking to standardize our methods when our culture is more and more diverse. Theological truth rather than methodological conformity is the power source of congregational worship. This is no less true for us than it was in the days of the Early Church. Constantine's influence on the Church yielded short-term benefits and put an end to the darkness of Roman persecution. Simultaneously, it marked the beginning of another type of darkness. It began a process of liturgical standardization that could not yield long-term benefits for a people so broadly diverse and standing on the precipice of a political and cultural meltdown. In the final analysis, it is no more possible for us to benefit from a single evangelical *style* amid our cultural diversity than it was for the Church of Rome.

LESSON 7: WORSHIP SUFFERS WHEN THE PRIMARY FOCUS BECOMES FORM AND STRUCTURE

BACKGROUND

The years between the Council of Nicaea (AD 325) and the Council of Chalcedon (AD 451) produced some of the greatest theological writings the Church has ever known. Theologians such as Ambrose, Athanasius, Augustine, John Chrysostom, and the Cappadocian Fathers (like Basil and Gregory of Nazianzus) struck down heresies that, had they been allowed, would have forever undermined orthodoxy. These men articulated important doctrines such as the complete deity and humanity of Jesus, the full doctrine of the Trinity, and salvation by grace. In short, there was a genuine focus on theology in the thinking and writings of many great theologians of this era. These men represented how both the Eastern and Western streams of the Church strengthened one another. In effect, they were applying the center circle of Scripture to define the concentric circle of theology.

Through these men the eye of the Church focused on orthodoxy. Unfortunately, that focus was lost as methodologies for worship developed. In fact, in the centuries that followed Constantine, the line between biblical theology and worship methodology became so blurred that nearly all distinction between them was lost. This was not a sudden process, perhaps even imperceptible to a single generation. Nonetheless, the broad retrospective of history reveals that the Church followed a course where a dogmatic commitment to biblical theology eventually became dogmatism over structure and liturgical practice. This resulted in a structure and form that displaced theology as the central focus of the Church.

Theological atrophy was so gradual and pervasive that it is difficult to summarize. However, the impact of this decline on corporate worship is clearly visible in three areas. They were:

1) the conflict over supreme authority,
2) the increasing complexity of the liturgy, and

3) the demarcation that developed between clergy and laity.

In each of these, it was obvious that structure, form, and method became more important than doctrine. In the end, developments in these three areas contributed to a sharp decline in the health of Christian worship and contributed to the theological aberrations that spawned the Reformation.

The Conflict over Supreme Authority
BACKGROUND AND APPLICATION

The New Testament does not give a definitive structure for a local church. What we can see in the New Testament are principles that govern structure but not a definitive road map. The Church, under the direction of the Apostles, was encouraged to deal with issues within the local congregation. In the post-Apostolic era, there was no single authority that controlled form or liturgy. Some of this may be attributable to the fact that the Church was intensely persecuted and therefore did not have a bishopric that spread across large geographical areas. However, it is more likely that such a structure was unnecessary as pastors looked to the Apostles' teachings as their final authority.

As early as the second century most of the New Testament books were already widely accepted.[1] The writings of the Apostles were largely silent with respect to governance in the Church, as well as style or form in corporate worship. The assumption seemed to be that where the Apostles gave direction, all were obliged to follow. Where they were silent, there was some degree of liberty. After the death of the Apostles, leading pastors within certain regions often settled issues between themselves, much as the Apostles had done at the Jerusalem Council. These leading pastors became known as bishops, because they assumed a roll of overseeing other pastors.[2] Should a particular bishop try to exert influence over churches in contradiction to the teaching of the Apostles, he would be called to accountability by other bishops. In fact, such scenarios precipitated several Church councils. When issues arose that were not addressed in Scripture, various regions determined their own practices without a great deal of interference from others. This created a balance of power that helped to hold the Church in theological check. Over time, the position of bishop became one of honor in these regions. Because Rome was the capital of the Empire, the

---

[1] The Canon of Scripture was finalized at the Council of Hippo in AD 393. One of the key tests for canonicity was the apostolic origin of the writing. Though they were no longer living, the authority of Apostles, rather than the authority of the bishops was final. The great theological writings of this era were authoritative not because of those who authored them, but because they sought to clarify Church doctrine based primarily on the writings of the Apostles.

[2] This was, itself, a mild departure from the New Testament use of the words *pastor, bishop,* and *elder.* The terms *elder* (πρεσβύτερος, *presbúteros*), *pastor* (ποιμαίνω, *poimaínō*), and *bishop* (ἐπίσκοπος, *episkopos*) are used interchangeably in the New Testament. See 1 Peter 5:1-3, Titus 1:5-9 and Acts 20:17, 28.

bishop in Rome was accorded added honor, even though he initially held no authority over any other bishop.

Within a hundred years after the conversion of Constantine, this parity and theological accountability among various bishops had begun to erode. It was only after the Emperor became the chief benefactor of the Church that this changed. In effect, the bishop in Rome was the Emperor's pastor. As a result, he became the most influential Christian leader in the Empire. During the years that Constantine ruled over both East and West, his influence stretched as far as a unified Roman Empire. This lasted for over fifteen years until Constantine relocated the capital to the eastern city of Byzantium (later called Constantinople) in AD 330. Relocating the seat of government further complicated the question of which bishop would have the most influence. When the imperial capital moved to Constantinople, the bishop there had direct access and input from/to the Emperor, giving him a similar claim of supremacy as the bishop in Rome.

As this structure emerged, churches were looking for and receiving guidance on worship practices from those outside of their local communities. In the West, churches looked to Rome alone, as the final authority, while in the East, they looked to Constantinople, Antioch and Alexandria, which all maintained strong influence.[1] This laid the foundation for a growing conflict between the worship styles of Rome and the Eastern churches. To bolster their positions, each became increasingly dogmatic. In the East, the Church maintained Greek, the language of the New Testament, establishing a liturgy based on the writings of Basil and John Chrysostom. In the West, the Church adopted the language of the Roman Empire and widely conducted worship in Latin by the end of the fourth century. From this point, a long, irreconcilable division began to develop between the Church in Rome and the Church in the East. Although Rome claimed preeminence above all other bishops, the Eastern Empire never accepted the supremacy of Rome, opting for a concept of parity among leading bishops. Thus, even though the Eastern Church developed a hierarchical bishopric, they still found the leniency to bless multiple Greek liturgies. Rome took a different path. When the Western Empire fell, the resulting vacuum of political authority was filled by the Bishop of Rome. By the end of the fifth century, an inseparable mixture of ecclesiastical authority and political power sealed the supremacy of the Bishop of Rome in the West and permanently established the power of the papacy. The differing views of East and West finally gave way to the Great Schism in 1054.[2]

---

[1] Both Carthage and Rome had originally been strong centers of liturgical development. By the end of the fifth century, the influence held by Carthage was already weakening.

[2] The *filioque* was the final breaking point between the East and West occurring in 1054. It is interesting to note that the *filioque* had appeared in confessions more than 500 years before the Great Schism. This leaves one to speculate as to the pretext for division when it finally happened. In fact, a deep division of liturgical preference as well as

A more centralized authority moved the consideration of theology and form further from the local church. We can applaud the theologians in the post-Nicene era, including several in Rome, for using their influence to settle many important doctrinal issues. Since the first century, Church leaders had gathered to confront and correct each other but, that type of local accountability began to erode. Following Constantine's conversion, the calling of Ecumenical Councils initially was the responsibility of the Emperor. As the Roman Empire faded, this power passed directly to the Bishop of Rome. While having an authority structure had been beneficial in dealing with heresies, this structure became a means to suppress variation in worship styles. This transition to conformity began prior to the collapse of the Roman Empire as many Christian practices became part of Roman civil law. Even the observance of the Lord's Day was mandated by the Roman government during Constantine's reign.

We should note that in the early years of the papacy, the claim of supreme authority over liturgical form was not necessarily demanded by those who held the position. Leaders like Pope Gregory the Great (AD 590-604) did not seek liturgical conformity but, his influence increased greatly after his death.[1] As the aura of previous popes increased, the expectation of sitting popes to be accorded similar honor also increased. The increasing honor and authority granted to the office was used to exert liturgical conformity. This could not have happened in the political landscape of a post-Roman-Empire Europe without some power of enforcement. Perhaps as a means to exert its power and stabilize the political landscape, the Roman Church entered into a political partnership in AD 800 that would become known as the Holy Roman Empire.[2] The Holy Roman Empire represented a fragile balance between political power and ecclesiastical rule. Both the Pope (the religious leader of the Western Church) and the Emperor (the political leader of the government) were mutually dependent on one another. The Emperor could not assume the throne without the blessing of the Pope. And without the political and military power afforded by this partnership, the Pope could not exercise his authority over Western Christianity.

By the tenth century, innovation could not occur in the Holy Roman Empire without the general consent of the papacy. A similar course of hierarchical control occurred in the East, so that innovation in the Byzantine Empire required the consent of the Eastern patriarchs. Thus, in both the East and West, authoritarian rule was pressing conformity in worship styles. From a local church perspective, decisions about worship—the *what* and the *why*—were no longer coming from a fundamental connection to Scripture but from human authorities. This dangerous situation ultimately led local churches further from

---

arguments over supremacy and authority had functionally separated the East from the West much earlier.

[1] Henry Chadwick, *The Church in Ancient Society: from Galilee to Gregory the Great* (New York: Oxford University Press, 2003), 674.

[2] The Holy Roman Empire began with the coronation of Charlemagne in AD 800 and ended with the death of Francis II in 1806.

the theology of the Apostles. The supreme authority was no longer Scripture and corporate worship was subject to extra-biblical mandates for worship practice.

The Developing Musical Complexity of the Liturgy
BACKGROUND AND APPLICATION

The development of the liturgy in the thousand years between the fall of Rome and the Reformation was a long but steady process. For the most part, the developing complexity of the Catholic Mass was the story of how music in the West developed. Originally, it is likely that Christian music emulated Psalm singing in the Jewish tradition. The Roman concepts of learning and understanding music came from Greek thought.[1] Little is known of ancient music since only a few fragments have survived. As late as the end of the third century, it is likely that congregational music was fairly simple and in a folk or common style. Even Gregorian chant, which to our ears sounds ancient, was a significant innovation from the music of pre-Constantine Rome.[2]

As the Church relocated worship from homes to public houses of worship, its basic shape changed. Prescribed elements of the liturgy increased and music became a focus of learning. This began in earnest with the innovations of Ambrose, Bishop of Milan (AD 374-397). His work represented a growing depth in musical style and theological content. Very little remains of Ambrose's musical work to study. However, he is clearly seen as the true father of formal Church Music and is credited with making antiphonal singing widely popular in the Western Church.[3] While this format originated in the Jewish synagogue, it clearly represented a new attention to the quality of the music in corporate worship. Ambrose is also significant for using music to teach theology to the congregation. Controversies over key issues, like the deity of Christ and the nature of the Trinity, prompted many Church leaders to set doctrines to music. Ambrose, a proponent of the deity of Christ and an outspoken opponent of Arian, wrote several hymn texts specifically designed to advance the orthodox view of Christ's complete deity. An outstanding example of such a hymn text is his well-known *Veni, Redemptor Genitum*.

The move to elevate the quality of singing and to make it more uniform resulted in the creation of the *schola cantorum,* founded in Rome by the end of the fifth century. This was a school specifically created to raise the level of musicianship in the Church. As the level of musicianship increased, what had been a dialogue between priest and congregation, imitating the Jewish tradition,

---

[1] Thomas Street Christensen, *The Cambridge History of Western Music Theory* (New York: Cambridge University Press, 2002), 136.

[2] While Eastern and Western Churches started with similar, simple musical styles, the Eastern Church did not develop on a parallel track with Western music. As a result, early chants of the Eastern Orthodox Church may provide a better example of Christian worship in the pre-Nicene era.

[3] In antiphonal singing, the leader would employ chant in a dialogue with the people.

became a dialogue between priest and choir. Pope Gregory, who led the Church in Rome from AD 590 to 604, greatly enhanced the importance of the *schola cantorum*. He worked to revise the liturgy and unify its practice in the West. From his work and writings, the whole body of Gregorian Chant developed. Gregorian Chant follows three basic forms: Psalm singing, where the leader would recite a phrase and the choir would respond with another; the strophic form, where several stanzas were sung or chanted to the same melodic formula (this is the ancient predecessor to hymns); and freeform, which would be used to chant longer, non-poetic texts.[1]

By the eighth century, the increased complexity in singing accelerated the move toward decreased congregational participation. With singing transferred to trained singers, the only obstacle to more complexity was the pace of musical innovation. By the twelfth century, vocal parts of what had once been the songs of the congregation became so complex that, if one still understood Latin, the words would have been obscured within intricate polyphony.[2] Sadly, this meant that for hundreds of years many of the faithful who gathered for worship were afforded very few opportunities to participate and could understand very little of what was being said. By the Renaissance, artistic achievements in music, painting, sculpture, and architecture were reaching their zenith. What could have greatly enhanced worship was lost on people functionally disengaged from a very intricate form of worship. Some of the greatest artistic achievements civilization has ever known were, in the end, a poor substitute for biblical theology and congregational participation. Complexity in musical form is not intrinsically evil. However, the lack of a place for the congregation to engage in worship is a distortion of the nature of corporate worship.

The Division between Clergy and Laity

BACKGROUND AND APPLICATION

The Bible tells us that when believers gathered for worship, it was a participatory event. The Apostle Paul's instructions on corporate worship, like those in 1 Corinthians 11-14, were not written to suppress the role of those attending, but rather to encourage them to participate, to engage in an orderly manner. In other words, the Scripture teaches that God did not intend corporate worship for spectators. Nevertheless, worship became highly ceremonial and complex, eventually making participation virtually impossible. This intricacy could not have developed without the division between those who led in worship, undertaking a priestly function, and those in the congregation, who became observers rather than participants.

Scripture established the office of deacon and elder, and history records that they both played roles in the leadership of corporate worship. The role of the

---

[1] See Donald Jay Grout, J. Peter Burkholder, and Claude V. Palisca, *A History of Western Music* (New York: W.W. Norton, 2006), 46.

[2] As a contrast to monody, which is one voice singing one melodic line, polyphony refers to multiple melodic lines intertwining simultaneously.

elder in corporate worship was to direct the gathering in an orderly fashion, teach the Apostles' doctrine, and oversee the distribution of the Lord's Supper. The deacons were to assist the elder(s) as was necessary. The assignment of different functions was intended to lead the congregation in a meaningful experience of *kerygma*, *leitougia*, and *koinonia*. With simple forms of worship, the pastor(s) could focus on presenting the Scripture and maintaining congregational participation. This changed as liturgies became more complex. By the second century, Church Fathers were becoming concerned whether or not those who led worship fully understood what they were doing. As we saw in the writings of the second and third centuries, the number of detailed instructions for leading worship increased significantly. In the post-Nicene period the liturgy became highly scripted. A more detailed liturgy required the leader to divide his attention between form and function. If there were some significance in accurately following the liturgy, then leaders needed to spend time studying and learning it, giving increased attention to accurately performing its intricacies. The leader's vigilance over the liturgy meant that his connection to the people through preaching suffered. Perhaps inadvertently, congregations were increasingly there to watch the liturgy be performed rather than being an organic part of it.

The division between the leaders and the congregation deepened as an ecclesiastical class developed in the Roman system. After the Apostles had passed on, the elders/pastors in the major liturgical centers, as well as those from churches that could trace their beginnings to the mission work of an Apostle, retained the most influence. This was the unspoken arrangement until the conversion of Constantine. To oversee the orderly Christianization of the Empire, Constantine set up an ecclesiastical hierarchy. He modeled the structure after Rome's regional, metropolitan, and rural government. This created an ecclesiastical-political class in the Church. As the influence of Christianity expanded in the Roman Empire, so did the power of the hierarchy. Eventually, leaders exercised authority in both civil and church matters. For this, they received compensation, not from the congregation(s) they served, but from the government. As the power at the top of this hierarchy strengthened, the decision making process moved further from the people, separating those who determined the liturgy far from the culture that gathered for worship. Whether those at the top of the power pyramid were ignorant of or disinterested in the fact that worshipers were being left behind by a universal standardization of worship practices is unclear. In the end, the outcome was the same.

Sacerdotalism

As bishops exercised more authority in deciding the form of worship, they also assumed more of worship's spiritual functions. Where once there had been both a desire and an understanding of the theological necessity for the congregation to participate, the congregation's role was absorbed into the priestly function. Eventually, the priest became known as the *celebrant* in Communion, illustrating that he was the one actually celebrating Communion,

119

thus performing a sacerdotal function on behalf of the people. With the rise of both a hierarchal and sacerdotal system, the kingdom of priests, as taught in the New Testament,[1] became a single priest who acted as an intermediary on behalf of the people. By the sixth century, it was common for the pastor-turned-priest to wear vestments in the performance of their duties. These garments were initially modeled after the garments of the Jewish priests and further illustrated the division that was occurring between clergy and laity.

Monasticism

As sacerdotalism divided the Church between those who participated (the priests) and those who primarily observed (the congregants), Monasticism divided the church between the common believer and the super-*devotee* of Christ. Monasticism was the practice of withdrawing from the culture in order to experience God on a superior plane through self-deprivation. It became so popular that many who sought to go into the priesthood withdrew from everyday life, at least for a season, to focus on the Divine. Various monastic orders developed beginning in the fifth century with Augustine, advanced by Gregory I, and were fully developed by the time of Benedict of Aniane (*circa* AD 750–821). On the positive side, those who chose seclusion provided significant scholarship to the Church as well as a great deal of hand copying before the invention of the printing press. Unfortunately, much of the scholarship was lost on the common believer, since the essence of the experience itself revolved around seclusion. Furthermore, had the scholarship been shared it would have been of little benefit to the many who were illiterate during the Dark Ages. Many monks and anchorets viewed the experience that came with seclusion to be a greater achievement than studying and understanding of the scriptures. Even Augustine, *blinded by the ascetic spirit of his age, says even, that anchorets, on their level of perfection, may dispense with the Bible. Certain it is, that this type of perfection stands not in the Bible, but outside of it.*[2] In some measure, just as the priest had become the celebrant of Communion on behalf of the people, those who chose the monastic life experienced God in a unique way, far beyond the experience of common people.

SUMMARY THOUGHTS ON THIS LESSON

The development of a clerical class and a complex liturgy revealed the Church's preoccupation with form and structure. The monastic movement confirmed that, in a deeper pursuit of God, the congregation had been left behind. This lesson does not teach that refinements in form and structure are evil in themselves. However, the purpose of all innovations in form and a deepening

---

[1] 1 Peter 2:9.

[2] Philip Schaff, *Nicene and Post-Nicene Christianity from Constantine the Great to Gregory The Great, A.D. 311-600* (Grand Rapids, MI: W.B. Erdman, 1974), 181.

understanding of God should advance Christ's Kingdom and build up His people, thereby bringing glory to Him. Our methods should never be an end in themselves. And, while every congregation hopes their leaders are having life-changing encounters with God, this is an excellent reminder to spiritual leaders, especially those who lead worship. It is possible to have a profound encounter with God during corporate worship and completely forget that we are there to lead the congregation. We are never to have an encounter with God on *behalf* of the people. Rather, it should be our goal to encounter God and the truth of His Word *with* our people.

With the sharp division that developed in the spiritual life between common Christians and their leaders, deeper issues of doctrine became the turf of the priesthood rather than the people. This only became worse as, by the eighth century, preaching was declining in both the East and West. While the Church was refining its grasp on form and structure, she was losing her grip on the theological constants that should have been driving worship. When the people most needed to hear the truth preached and participate in meaningful worship, they were cut off. This propelled the Church into a long period of mysticism, during which form and fable often stood on higher ground than the truth of Scripture.

Healthy attention to both form and doctrine has not proven to be the Church's legacy. The Church has exhibited the recurring tendency to vacillate between two positions. At best, she is firmly fixed to the scriptural constants that make worship vibrant, while being elastic with methods (as in Acts 15). More commonly, the Church increasingly becomes fascinated with form and structure and only nominally attentive to that which makes worship biblical. It is important to remember that people and the culture in which they live are neither perpetually relevant nor contemporary. Only God is worthy of that distinction. He and His Word alone are eternally contemporary. A preoccupation with form or concern over our own personal spiritual experiences, while turning a blind eye to our people, will have a disastrous effect.

As leaders we must ask, *What is our focus?* We can find some indication in how we allocate our time and energy. For many, finding a healthy way to balance being a worshiper and a 'lead worshiper' is difficult. Whether rehearsing a song or building a sermon, we naturally focus on the work at hand and may, without intent, move our focus away from the true calling upon our lives. It is our nature to become caught up in the mechanics. We lose sight of the reason we lead our congregation in song. As preachers, we forget that it is not the mechanics of the delivery, but the power of God's Word that makes a sermon have eternal value. We lose sight of the God we serve, the sheep we shepherd, and the reason for congregational worship. This lesson provides a vivid illustration of what continues to this day in many churches. Like those who continued to refine the liturgy, our worship may look great, even polished but, its weakness will inevitably become apparent in the lives of many who are taught lifeless motions. Everything we do as leaders in corporate worship should

lead the people into meaningful encounters with God and His Word. All forms
and traditions that do not accomplish this must be reexamined.

LESSON 8: WEAK WORSHIP PRODUCES WEAK BELIEVERS

BACKGROUND

Biblical worship, above all things, is enamored with the majesty and
wonder of God. The ceremony and hierarchy that followed Constantine's
conversion had an unforeseen effect, as the leaders apparently became enamored
with external things rather than with God. This was an unhealthy digression and
resulted in spiritual decline. The weakness of the Church was evident in
numerous ways, perhaps none greater than the spiritual malaise that
characterized the Dark Ages. Considering the Early Church's prosperity amid
great difficulties, we cannot blame the decline in the general health of the
Church on the social and political turmoil of the years following the collapse of
the Western Empire. What the Early Church had, which became lost, was a clear
delineation between form and theology. While the presence of structure does not
take away from spiritual life, any absence of theology does. The Church had
found freedom and vibrancy in clearly setting forth doctrine but, the post-Nicene
era blurred the lines between theology and form. Once that was done, the
congregation could be and was disengaged from corporate worship, leaving
believers in a spiritually weakened state. In the East, even with a more stable
political situation, the same disconnect occurred. A similar ceremonialism
displaced the awe of God in corporate worship.

The spiritual weakness came and was evident in many ways. Whereas
believers had once devoted themselves to the scriptures, post-Nicene believers
eventually accepted teachings from their leaders that were in direct conflict with
what the Bible taught. To see this, one must look no further than the fascination
that developed with various extra-biblical beliefs. The Church taught and the
congregation accepted mystical beliefs that had little or no foundation in
Scripture. As ceremonialism became a substitute for the awe of God, the
mystery of God was overshadowed by mysticism. The fascination with the
mystical resulted in several aberrations. Among these were praying to the dead,
the worship of Mary, and according importance to tradition that should only be
reserved for Scripture. We will only address these very briefly to illustrate how
they began and became part of the worship experience.

Praying to the Dead

The Church's fascination with the departed dead began soon after the
persecutions ended. The Church sought an appropriate way to honor the martyrs
who had stood firm in the face of fatal torment. The pagan systems of Rome
held various beliefs about the dead, including their ability to influence and affect
change in the lives of the living. In the absence of clear doctrinal teaching, some

of this concept was absorbed into the belief system of the Church. Surely, they believed, the saints who were martyred would be accorded some special recognition in the afterlife, some special ability to assist those who still remained here on earth.

> In the visionary revelation granted to him in exile on Patmos, St. John saw the martyrs beneath the altar crying 'How long, O Lord?' (Revelation 6:9-10.) By the fourth century, relics of the martyrs would be placed beneath the altar in the Christian basilica. Surely they were interceding for the faithful here on earth. Their acceptance by God was symbolized by the fact that while the ancient churches prayed for God's continuing grace for the faithful departed, they did not pray for the martyrs. The martyrs prayed for them.[1]

Combining Christian teaching with paganism, the Church concluded that the deceased could assist the living by interceding on their behalf and that the dead could also hear and respond to prayers. Veneration exceeded anything that Scripture could approve. As time passed, others besides the martyrs were accorded similar honor. To the names of the martyrs were added the names of any who, according to the Church, had lived with some special notoriety. What had begun as honor eventually became worship. This type of mysticism went virtually unchecked until the Reformation.

The Worship of Mary

Within the context of corporate worship, a similar development occurred with respect to the place of Mary, the mother of Jesus. Over a period of several hundred years, the Catholic Church went from venerating Mary because she was the mother of Jesus to deifying her. While the Scripture accords her a place of honor among all women,[2] it never suggests she is to be an object of worship. The most likely origin of this practice was an inadvertent result of the Nestorian controversy.[3] In an attempt to confirm that Jesus was fully God from conception, orthodox theologians referred to Mary as the *God Bearer*.[4] This term was originally used, not to bolster the place of Mary, but instead to confirm the deity of Jesus from conception. Some Trinitarian writers used the title *Mother of God* in reference to the hypostatic union, to illustrate that both the full essence of the Divine and the full essence of humanity joined in one substance conceived in the womb of the virgin, Mary.[5] Again, in the absence of clear theology, the

---

[1] John McManners, *The Oxford Illustrated History of Christianity* (Oxford: Oxford University Press, 1990), 45-46.

[2] Luke 1:41-42.

[3] Nestorius (AD 386-451) was Bishop of Constantinople and was expelled from the Church for heretical beliefs concerning the deity and humanity of Christ.

[4] θεοτόκος (theotokos), as used in the Chalcedonian Creed (451), referenced Mary in this way: θεοτόκου κατὰ τὴν ἀνθρωπότητα.

[5] Compare μητέρα τοῦ Θεοῦ with Elizabeth's address to Mary, μήτηρ τοῦ κυρίου, in Luke 1:43.

intent and meaning of these titles were lost and Mary became the object of prayers and worship. Although other extra-biblical concepts about Mary were centuries later in developing,[1] it is clear that the application of her role as the *God Bearer* or the *Mother of God* had gone far beyond the teaching of Scripture and the intent of those who used the terms originally.

Tradition

Passion for the Word of God was no longer the driving force of the Church. Instead, it was tradition. *The catholic principle of tradition became more and more confirmed, as the authority of the fathers and councils increased and the learned study of the Holy scriptures declined; and tradition gradually set itself in practice on a level with Scripture, and even above it.*[2] The effects of this were devastating. Without her organic connection to biblical truth, the Church suffered greatly, both in her vibrancy and in her geographical expanse. In Europe, the theologically weak Church became subject to all sort of aberrations, both in her liturgy and in her highest office. By the eleventh century, the papacy was at its deepest point of decline; at times, it was bought and sold as a commodity. Across the Mediterranean, to the south, the Church was not faring much better. When the seventh century pagan prophet Mohammad (AD 570-632) declared he had a vision and a new mandate for monotheism, he took sword in hand and set out to convert the nations. In a matter of a few decades, the Church in North Africa knelt to the Islamic demand to adopt the new belief or face the sword. Considering that Christianity in North Africa could trace its roots to the apostolic era and had withstood multiple persecutions, one is amazed to see how quickly the Church there almost completely vanished. This pattern was repeated to the north in Spain and around the eastern rim of the Mediterranean. Between the seventh and ninth centuries as much as half of the geographical area once covered by Christianity gave way to Islam and remains under that cloud today.

How could the cultural upheaval in Europe overwhelm the Church? How could the threat of death cause Christians in North Africa to bow to Islam? The worst Roman persecutions could not dampen the Church on fire. Obviously that type of passion to live for and die for the cause of Christ had significantly cooled. By the seventh century, form had replaced theology as the unifying hallmark of the Church and throughout the Middle East and Northern Africa, complete Christian cultures crumbled as Islam expanded.

---

[1] Many beliefs about Mary that are most disagreeable to evangelical Christians were not made dogma until many years after the Reformation. For instance, the idea that Mary was born without original sin, her Immaculate Conception, did not become dogma of the Roman Church until the middle of the nineteenth century.

[2] Philip Schaff, *Nicene and Post-Nicene Christianity from Constantine the Great to Gregory The Great, A.D. 311-600* (Grand Rapids, MI: W.B. Erdman, 1974), 366.

APPLICATION

In times of cultural, linguistic, or political changes, theology should shine the brightest. Instead, the Church minimized or marginalized biblical doctrine and provided the shiny, but lifeless, trinkets of form and mysticism. Worship without a steady diet of doctrine went hand-in-hand with weak worshipers, unable to stand in the face of adversity. What had once been a Church with little form and even less structure, but fueled by the power of God, became only a shell of its former self. She was rich in tradition, but became weak in the scriptures and devoid of the Spirit's power. It is difficult to determine whether the lack of theological focus contributed to weakness in corporate worship or whether weakness in corporate worship encouraged a lack of theological focus. Weakness in one will inevitably lead to weakness in the other. Corporate worship no longer contributes to the health of the worshiper when its focus is on anything besides God. Instead, it actually becomes a liability to spiritual health.

The way the Church lost its virility should serve as a warning to us. One of the ways Christians have dealt with cultural or political upheaval is to grab on to a form that is familiar. Tradition can be a beautiful thing when its meaning is vibrant in the hearts of the people who practice it. However, the power of worship is never in its form. We can spend a great deal of time honing and refining our structure but, this will not provide what our people need to deal with life's challenges. When our people face upheaval in their lives, they are in desperate need of much more than we can give in a structure or method. They need the same biblical truth that fueled the first generations of Christians. It is not enough to hold the truth of Scripture in our own hearts. It must be taught to our people. And, if culture changes, we must be aware of those changes. In the period we have studied, whole cultures and languages changed while the Church became more rigid in its means of communication. The surest safeguard against such a harmful disconnect is for leaders to stay connected to the people they lead, to know their hopes and fears, their successes and their failures. Had the Church in this era done that, they might have taken note of the spiritual condition of the people. Perhaps the course of worship development might have taken a different direction.

FINAL THOUGHTS ON THIS ERA

In each period of Church history there are remarkable parallels to our own time. This period is no exception. The thousand years between the fall of Rome and the Reformation is a case study illustrating what happens to corporate worship when biblical truth is distorted or obscured. It clearly undermined the vitality of worship. Schaff, writing of the Monophysite controversy of the fourth and fifth centuries, states the following: *The intense concern for practical religion, which animated Athanasius and the Nicene fathers, abated or went astray; theological speculation sank towards barren metaphysical refinements; and party watchwords and empty formulas were valued more than real truth.*[1]

In many ways this statement could be a summary of the entire period we have just examined. Sadly, it also serves as a stinging indictment of much in evangelicalism today. The lessons of this era should challenge every evangelical church, many of which are giving more attention to tradition or innovation in form and liturgy than to *truth*. The short-term benefits of maintaining our traditions or discovering new methods does not provide what the Church needs most. In the end, if God's people are encouraged to depend upon anything other than Him and His truth, they will be sorely disappointed. Neither tradition nor innovation can bring lasting vitality to God's people: as a result, they cannot bring lasting vitality to corporate worship. A church committed to Scripture can be traditional or innovative, liturgical or freeform and still be healthy. Truly biblical churches hold all *essential* things in common. Though they may look different, at the core they are observing the same set of biblical constants that never change. As long as a church employs the essentials and does not go beyond the bounds of liberty set by Scripture, their corporate worship can be healthy and honoring to God, no matter what style they employ.

Churches that define and understand these essentials and boundaries can find common ground with others who may choose different methods for worship, yet share the same theological essentials. This has the potential to make fellowship and partnership possible among different churches, while providing protecting from becoming involved with those who clearly do not embrace orthodox doctrine. Such partnerships were part of the early Church and should be welcomed again today. In many areas, Christian congregations remain isolated from one another and Great Commission partnerships are limited, often because their worship expressions look or sound different. Isolating ourselves from other Christians simply for stylistic reasons is unnecessary and harmful. Dogmatism over the essentials is right and reasonable—dogmatism over areas where Scripture grants us liberty is another thing, altogether.

As the diagram on the next page illustrates, there is a core of truth which all orthodox believers must hold in common. Beyond that, there is room for some variance and still remain within the boundaries of healthy worship.

---

[1] Ibid, p.453.

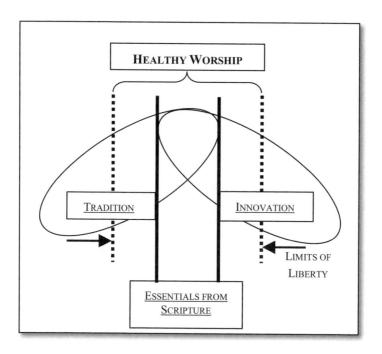

When a church moves beyond the limits of liberty in either direction, worship becomes unhealthy. Defining those limits is by no means an exact science. However, we have seen ample proof that there is a point when following a form or tradition becomes unhealthy. This occurs whenever the maintenance of the form takes precedence over Scripture. Similarly, those committed to be innovators are safe only as long as their attempt to innovate remains subject to Scripture. In every instance, boundaries are violated when the truth of what God says about worship becomes subject to anything else.

The absence of healthy worship diminishes the strength of the Church and makes her more vulnerable to conflicts within and adversaries outside of the Faith. Internal conflicts, both within local congregations and between believers, are rarely over the essentials from Scripture. The tension that exists between Modernism and Postmodernism, to some measure, may be tension between tradition and innovation. The outcome of this conflict will not be determined by what forms each side chooses, but by the doctrinal truth both groups affirm and practice. As the above illustration shows, real partnership—the place where divergent approaches overlap—can occur around the essentials from Scripture. The Postmodern view may yet prove to benefit the Church, but only if those within it find a close companion in biblical orthodoxy. Without embracing the propositional truth of Scripture, any innovation will rob itself of real possibilities and, following the pattern of all others, sink into a stylistic or cultural expedition that will pass as quickly as it comes. Even worse, innovations can become their own extra-biblical dogma.

Postmoderns need to see that embracing propositional truth from Scripture is not the same thing as embracing a declining Modernism. History teaches quite the opposite. In times of cultural shift, the unchanging truth of Scripture alone can give God's people the flexibility they need to be innovative. Without it, all innovations to worship run the risk of supplanting the purpose for which it exists. For many clinging to Modernism and trapped in traditions that have long since lost the connection to theological meaning, it is no better. Tradition in itself does not ensure that we are doctrinally right any more than innovation does. The real issue and the first issue is biblical truth. Otherwise, tradition becomes, in the words of Schaff, *party watchwords and empty formulas* and innovation becomes no more than *metaphysical refinement.*

The lessons of this era are some of the quickest forgotten, and, if ignored, can have the direst consequences. It is truly sad that the Eastern Orthodox and Roman Catholic Churches grew in resource and influence, art and beauty, while becoming progressively weaker as an agent of true spiritual transformation. The Church needs the strength that comes from Christ-centered worship which places the focus on the teaching and preaching of Scripture. Whatever style is used, those who lead must consistently fill that form with meaning and root it in biblical truth. Otherwise, it will lead to spiritual atrophy in the lives of believers.

While the liturgy in the early years of the post-Nicene era was sometimes extra-biblical, very little of it was unbiblical. In fact, major portions of both the Greek and Roman liturgies are biblical to this day. The problem was not in the use of a fixed form. The fact that form and tradition took on greater importance than God's Word is what made the situation dangerous. Had theology been properly maintained, it is probable that form and liturgy could have been embraced and spiritual vitality been preserved. Leaders must be aware of the dangers inherent in both the oldest and dearest and the latest and greatest. If we lead people to maintain tradition then we must not practice it without meaning. Even then, tradition is only effective when it can be improved or modified. We must be willing to modify or even discard a tradition that the Scripture does not model or mandate. Otherwise, we are in danger of repeating many of the mistakes of those who came before us. In this balance the Church finds its cultural relevance in the timeless truth of Scripture and is free to practice either tradition or innovation effectively.

CHAPTER 6

ROMAN CATHOLIC WORSHIP

Background

It is important at this point to take a pause from discussing historical backgrounds and how they can teach us lessons for today and deal directly with liturgical forms. The most prominent of these is that of the Roman Catholic Church. If one can get a handle on the Roman liturgy, then others like that of the Greek Orthodox Church as well as post-Reformation liturgies like that of the Anglican Church become much easier to understand. For many, studying the liturgy of the Mass seems a chore not worthy of the time and energy. To be sure, we have spent considerable time learning that a rigid commitment to form can prove unhealthy. That does not relieve ministers, Protestant evangelicals in particular, from the responsibility of studying and understanding the Mass of the Roman Catholic Church. This is important for several reasons. First, without some understanding of the Mass it is impossible for those who are Protestants to understand what they are protesting. In the West, our practice of any liturgy

129

other than that of the Roman Church is the continuation of a five hundred year protest. A careful study of the liturgy of the Mass should help us understand why our forefathers set aside a form that had been in use for several hundred years. The Reformation, at least in part, was about accessibility to Scripture and about Ecclesiology. However, among its most profound implications was how it affected Christian worship. Therefore, any well-balanced study of evangelical worship requires us to gain a deeper understanding of pre-Reformation liturgy.

Second, and equally important, is that despite what we will find theologically objectionable in the Mass, it is not without value to evangelicals. Several features of the Catholic Rite can benefit those who plan less liturgical forms of worship. Much of the text of the Mass is Scripture. If nothing else, studying the liturgy of the Mass will challenge us to utilize much more Scripture in worship. Considering the lack of biblical literacy among Christians, that would be a good thing. Furthermore, structure is not evil. The form of worship in the Catholic Church was not the primary issue with many of the reformers. Men such as Martin Luther and Thomas Cranmer, while vehemently opposing aspects of Roman theology and ecclesiology, were intent on retaining much of the Mass's form. Understanding the structure of the liturgy allows those who are free from the governance of Catholicism to use historical forms that are not in themselves evil, and to do this without embracing the theological aberrations they eventually contained.

To be fair, many Protestants have developed their own liturgies which are approached with all the inflexibility of the one blessed by Rome. The fact is, whether we are Protestant or Catholic, we find some security in a certain level of predictability and, therefore, almost all of us have a preferred liturgy for worship. Whether or not that is healthy is another discussion. Since it is clear that nearly all churches have some fixed liturgy, those whose worship liturgy is less Catholic may find it fruitful to experiment with liturgies other than those with which they have become comfortable. For this reason, we can all benefit from a closer look at forms that follow a fixed structure.

Additionally, there is something beautifully historic about the practice of Christian worship. Although we stand outside of the Roman Church, we share a common heritage. In its earliest forms, primarily in the ante-Nicene and early post-Nicene periods, the liturgies of the East and West are the true ancestors of our worship as well. We stand in a long stream of those who have come before us. It is true that many who practiced this form misused, altered, or even did great harm to the practice of the faith. Nevertheless, to understand the Mass is to understand something of our own history as Christians, albeit at times, the good, the bad, and the ugly.

Finally, we should study the Mass out of necessity. From a practical standpoint, it is foolish to plan worship or even practice ministry in North America without an understanding of Catholicism. If part of our job as pastors/worship leaders is to conduct our services in a manner that demonstrates an awareness of the culture around us, understanding the Mass is imperative. Studies indicate that as many as 67 million Hispanics, including those from

Mexico, Central America, and South America, will join the U.S. population by 2050, boosting those numbers from *35.6 million to 102.6 million, an increase of 188 percent. Their share of the nation's population* [will] *nearly double, from 12.6 percent to 24.4 percent.*[1] Of those entering the United States with Hispanic or Latin origin, most are Catholic. Surveys indicate that as many as 70% are practicing Catholics or have Catholic roots.[2] If you are not reaching those from a Catholic background, you are not reaching a rapidly growing portion of our population. Even if we cannot appreciate the history or structure of liturgical worship, our desire to unravel the misconceptions of those whom we reach should be motivation enough.

Various liturgies from both Eastern and Western traditions could serve as a pattern for study. Since evangelical worship grew out of the Reformation, it is most beneficial for us to examine the Roman Rite of the sixteenth Century. This will give us a foundation for studying the Protestant developments in the years following the Reformation.

The development of the Mass[3] was slow and steady, evolving for about 1,000 years prior to the Reformation. For most of that time, the liturgy used in Rome was generally accepted by all the churches in the West. Changes that occurred in Rome found their way to the local churches. Occasionally, developments that occurred in other dioceses sometimes found their way to Rome. The allegiance toward Rome created the bond that kept the liturgy intact. For this reason, during these thousand years there was not a single approved liturgy, just a strong adherence to its tradition by priests and bishops in the West. The Reformation changed this. The reformers called into question both the theology and form that had been widely accepted. This prompted the Church of Rome to respond by publishing a complete liturgy that had their approval. This response was the work of the Council of Trent (1545-1563). The liturgy that came out of this council, also known as the *Tridentine Mass*, was not a new invention, but was a statement of what had been the general custom and practice of the Roman Church for several hundred years.

As the focal point of Catholic worship for centuries, the Mass served as a primary influence in the development of classical art, literature, architecture, and music in Western Civilization through the sixteenth century. Although the

---

[1] By 2030, "Increasing Diversity Predicted in U.S. Population," America - Engaging the World - America.gov, March 18, 2004, http://www.america.gov/st/washfile-english/2004/March/20040318124311CMretroP0.4814264.html (accessed December 01, 2010).

[2] Paul Perl, Jennifer Z. Greely, and Mark M. Gray, "How Many Hispanics Are Catholic? A Review of Survey Data and Methodology," 2005, http://cara.georgetown.edu/Hispanic%20Catholics.pdf (accessed December 01, 2010).

[3] *Mass* is the term used to describe the celebration of the Eucharist and developed into three basic forms: the *Missa Solemnis* (High Mass), the *Missa Pivata* (Low Mass), and the *Requiem Mass.* The term *Mass* comes from a closing phrase of the liturgy, *Ite missa est* (*Go, you are sent*).

influence of the Mass decreased, particularly in countries where the Reformation was felt the strongest, it continued to impact a significant portion of Fine Art in Western Civilization through the twentieth century. The *Tridentine Mass* remained virtually unchanged until the major revisions of the *Second Vatican Council* (1962-1965).[1] In order to use a modern version of the Mass that predates the *Vatican II*, we will examine the 1962 edition of the *Tridentine Mass*. For our study, the differences between the 1962 version and the version originally released by the Council of Trent are not important. The key features are the same.

THE FIXED AND VARIABLE PARTS OF THE MASS

The Mass is the offering of the Bread and Cup as a sacrifice before God and is the centerpiece of Catholic worship. In every Catholic church, Mass is said at least weekly, as well as at other special times throughout the year. It is structured to provide consistency week in and week out and, at the same time, allow for variation according to different seasons. Both consistency and variety in the Mass occur within the context of a single celebration and within the context of an entire year. To achieve consistency, portions of the Mass remain constant no matter what the season; i.e., they are part of the Mass virtually every time it is celebrated. These parts of the Mass are called the *Ordinarium Missae,* or *Ordinary of the Mass*. There are five primary components of the *Ordinary*. They are the *Kyrie, Gloria, Credo, Agnus Dei,* and *Sanctus.* These five sections act as structural pillars around the elements of the Bread and Cup and, therefore, generally appear each time the priest conducts a Mass. The *Ordinary of the Mass* may be altered, but only for specific reasons. The two most common times the *Ordinary* is altered are during the Funeral Mass and seasonally, during the preparation for Easter (Lent) and Christmas (Advent). In the *Requiem Mass*, which constitutes the Catholic funeral and is recited for the dead, the *Gloria* and *Credo* are omitted.[2] During the seasons of Advent and Lent, the *Gloria* is generally omitted. This is designed to enhance the celebrative effect of the *Gloria* when Mass is said on Christmas and Easter.

The *Propium Missae*, the *Proper of the Mass,* contains the variable aspects of the Mass. The *Proper of the Mass* includes prayers and Scripture readings which change from week to week, as well as sermon topics and the recognition

---

[1] The liturgy of the Roman Catholic Church continues to undergo change, most recently in *the Second Ecumenical Council of the Vatican* (1962-65), also known as *Vatican II*. Despite the reforms, a comparison of the *Tridentine Mass* with today's Mass reveals that many of the elements that the Reformers found most objectionable still remain.

[2] The *Requiem Mass* is so named for the Latin phrase that is recited in the service; *Requiem aeternam dona eis Domine* (*Give them eternal rest, Lord*).

of various saints.[1] The Liturgical Calendar specifies these variations. The arrangement of the Liturgical Calendar is not haphazard. The calendar allots certain times within each year to focus on different aspects of the Faith. This creates a repeating cycle, which ensures that over the course of each year the congregation spends a set amount of time recounting the gospel Story, including among other things: the birth, life, death, and resurrection of Jesus. As a result, the major events in the gospel Story comprise the primary seasonal celebrations of the Catholic liturgy. The liturgical year begins with Advent, the preparation for Christmas. The primary celebrations of the liturgy are completed in late spring when the Church celebrates Pentecost, fifty days after Easter. The remainder of the liturgical year occurs without any major seasonal celebrations, but still varies in prayers, Scripture readings, and the celebration of saints.

The origins of the Mass date from the post-Nicene age, when the Church sought and found ceremony in the Old Testament Feasts and in the system of Tabernacle/Temple Sacrifice. A study of the Catholic liturgy reveals the extent to which the Church borrowed from the ceremonial aspects of the Jewish tradition. The concept of a sacrifice offered by priests, established in the Jewish tradition, is the foundation of the Roman Rite. While the substance of the sacrifice changed in the Catholic liturgy, there, Jesus is the Pascal lamb, the concept that one must continue to offer sacrifices to God for sins is the same. We will discuss this in depth with respect to the concept of sacrifice and priesthood later in this chapter. The influence of Hebrew tradition on the Catholic Church extended beyond the view of sacrifice. In addition to Communion, the rudiments of weekly Christian worship were based on post-exilic Judaism. It is likely that the format of gathering for reading and studying the scriptures, as well as singing/chanting Psalms and offering prayers, came directly from the weekly Sabbath meetings in the Synagogue.

The use of the Jewish calendar is also apparent in the liturgical calendar put in place by Rome. Just as all the Feasts in the Jewish tradition occurred between fall and late spring, so it was with the Liturgical Calendar used by the Roman Catholic Church. The following table shows the principle seasons of the Catholic liturgy and the principle Jewish Feasts as a point of comparison. The dates for some of the Catholic Feasts are fixed according to the Roman calendar and some are, like the Jewish Feasts, established by the lunar calendar. In both cases, there is an active period of special observances from the fall (equivalent to October in the Jewish system and November in the Catholic system) to late spring (May in both the Jewish and Catholic systems). In both systems, special observances were used to recount key aspects of the Redemption Story.

---

[1] Unlike its use in Scripture, the term *Saint* when used in the Catholic Church refers to those receiving special recognition and elevation after death.

133

THE PRINCIPLE SEASONS AND HOLIDAYS OF
THE CATHOLIC AND JEWISH YEAR

Month	Catholic Seasons	Fixed Calendared Celebrations	Old Testament Feasts[1]
October		All Hallows Eve (October 31)	Trumpets Atonement Booths
November	Advent (four Sundays before Christmas)	All Hallows Day or All Saints Day (Nov. 1)	
December	Christmastide (twelve days, starting on Dec 25th)	Christmas Day (Dec. 25th)	Lights[2]
January	Christmas Octave (eight days leading up to the celebration of Jesus' Dedication)	Epiphany (Jan. 6)	
February	Ash Wednesday (the first day of Lent-variable date)		Purim
March	Lent (40 days prior to Easter) Holy Week/Maundy Thursday/Good Friday		Unleavened Bread Passover
April	Easter (date set by Lunar Calendar)		First Fruits
May	Feast of the Ascension Pentecost (50 Days after Easter) Feast of Trinity/Sacred Heart		The Feast of Weeks
June			
July	No Extended Seasonal Celebrations		No Extended Feasts Days
August		Assumption of Mary (Aug. 15)	
September			

---

[1] For a description of the Feasts, see Chapter 2: *Old Testament Archetypes and Christian Worship*.

[2] The Festival of Lights (Hanukkah), mentioned in Maccabees, was not established until the inter-Testament period. This Feast, also known as the Feast of Dedication, was celebrated during Jesus' lifetime (see John 10:22). It qualifies as a biblical Feast for Catholics because 1 and 2 Maccabees were accepted into the Canon of Scripture at the Synod of Hippo in AD 393, as well as at the Council of Carthage in AD 397 and AD 419, although they had not been generally accepted as part of the most sacred Jewish writings.

DESCRIPTION OF THE PRIMARY SUNDAYS AND SEASONS IN THE CATHOLIC LITURGY

While the liturgical calendar establishes the times for various Feasts, the *Ordo Lectionum Missae,* or *Lectionary for Mass,* prescribes appropriate readings for each day from the Scripture. Before *Vatican II,* the prescribed readings were listed in the *Missale Romanum,* the Roman Missal. Below is a brief description of the Primary Sundays and Holy Days of the Church Year showing the scriptures prescribed in the *Missal* for the *Proper of the Mass.* For each Mass there are at least two readings specified. The first reading is often from one of the Epistles and the second is from one of the Gospels. The double forward slash (//) marks the division between the first and second readings.

Advent is observed on the four Sundays prior to Christmas. This time is set aside to anticipate the celebration of Jesus' birth. The symbolism of Advent recalls those who waited for the first coming of Jesus and recognizes the expectation of believers waiting for the Second Coming.

First Sunday: Romans 13:11-14a // Luke 21:25-33

Second Sunday: Romans 15:4-13 // Matthew 11:2-10

Third Sunday: Philippians 4:4-7 // John 1:19b-28

Fourth Sunday: 1 Corinthians 4:1-5 // Luke 3:1-6

Christmas Eve and **Christmas Day** are fixed on the Roman calendar as December 24th and 25th. Included are four Masses, one on Christmas Eve and three on Christmas Day.

Christmas Vigil (Christmas Eve): Romans 1:1-16 // Matthew 1:18b-21

Christmas Day (December 25th)

Midnight Mass: Titus 2:11-15 // Luke 2:1-14

Dawn Mass: Titus 3:4-7 // Luke 2:15-20

Daytime Mass: Hebrews 1:1-12 // John 1:1-14 and Matthew 2:1-12

Sunday of the Christmas Octave[1] The eight days following Christmas are called the Christmas Octave and always includes one Sunday. The significance of the eight days relates to the days of Mary's purification, leading up to the circumcision and dedication of Jesus.

Galatians 4:1-7 // Luke 2:33-40

The Holy Name of Jesus is observed when an additional Sunday occurs between Christmas and Epiphany.

Acts 4:8-12 // Luke 2:21

---

[1] In the liturgical calendar, all holy days are usually surrounded by eight days, referred to as the *Octave.* This ensures that each holy day is observed over at least one Sunday. The weeklong Jewish feasts also included eight days so as to encompass two Sabbaths.

Epiphany is observed on January 6 and marks the visit of the Magi to Jesus. Since the Magi came from the East and were not Jews, Epiphany highlights the fact that Jesus came not only for the Jews but for the Gentiles as well. The revelation of Jesus to the Magi is symbolic of His light shining on the Gentiles.

Isaiah 60:1-6 // Matthew 2:1-12

Sunday in the Octave of Epiphany continues the focus on the unveiling of Jesus and His mission. The next five Sundays are not Feast Sundays.

Isaiah 60:1-6 // John 1:29-34

Eight Non-Feast Sundays between the Octave of Epiphany and Lent

Ash Wednesday occurs 40 days prior to Palm Sunday and begins the season of Lent, the preparation for commemorating Jesus' death. During Mass on Ash Wednesday, the priest applies ashes in the shape of a cross on the forehead of the faithful. The ashes are symbolic of repentance.

Joel 2:12-19 // Matthew 6:16-21

Lent is the season of preparation leading up to the recounting of Jesus' passion. Observance of this season may include fasting from certain foods or activities. The intent is to enter the Passion Week in the spirit of contrition. There are four weeks in Lent and the scriptures for each Sunday are listed below.

First Sunday of Lent

2 Corinthians 6:1-10 // Matthew 4:1

Second Sunday of Lent

1 Thessalonians 4:1-7 // Matthew 17:1-9

Third Sunday of Lent

Ephesians 5:1-9 // Luke 11:14-28

Fourth Sunday of Lent

Galatians 4:22-31 // John 6:1-15

The First Sunday of Passion is preparatory for Palm Sunday.

Hebrews 9:11-15 // John 8:46-49

Palm Sunday (Second Sunday of Passion) commemorates the Triumphal Entry and marks the beginning of Holy Week.

Exodus 15:27; 16:1-7; Philippians 2:5-11 //

Matthew 21:1-9 & Matthew 26:1-75; 27:1-66

Holy Thursday (Maundy Thursday)[1] recounts the institution of the Lord's Supper, the washing of the disciples' feet, the watch of prayer in Gethsemane, and the betrayal of Judas.

1 Corinthians 11:20-32 // John 13:1-15

---

[1] In Anglican and other liturgical Protestant Churches, the day is called Maundy Thursday. It takes its title from the Vulgate text of John 13:34, *Mandatum novum do vobis ut diligatis invicem sicut dilexi vos.*

Good Friday is a day of prayer and remembrance. The Catholic Church forbids the taking of Communion on this day.[1]

Hosea 6:1-6 & Exodus 12:1-11 // John 18:1-40; 19:1-42

Holy Saturday (Easter Vigil) is observed after sundown on Easter Eve. It is the first Mass of Easter since, as in the Jewish tradition, the day being celebrated lasts from sundown to sundown.

OT: Genesis 1:1-31; 2:1-2; 5:32—8:21 (*passim*); 22:1-19; Exodus 14:24-31;15:1a; Isaiah 54:17; 55:1-11; Baruch 3:9-38; Ezekiel 37:1-14; Isaiah 4:1-6; Exodus 12:1-11; Jonah 3:1-10; Deuteronomy 31:22-30; Daniel 3:1-24 NT: Colossians 3:1-4 // Matthew 28:1-7

Easter Sunday

1 Corinthians 5:7-8 // Mark 16:1-7

White Sunday (First Sunday after Easter)

1 John 5:4-10 // John 20:19-31

Five Non-Feast Sundays between the Octave of Easter and Ascension Sunday

Ascension of the Lord (Thursday) occurs forty days after Easter and, unless the church has daily services, is usually observed on the following Sunday, one week before Pentecost.

Acts 1:1-11 // Mark 16:14-20

Sunday in the Octave of Ascension is the celebration of Ascension in churches without daily Masses.

1 Peter 4:7b-11 // John 15:26-27; 16:1-4

Saturday Vigil of Pentecost begins the celebration of Pentecost.

Genesis 22:1-19; Exodus 14:24-31; 15:1;

Deuteronomy 31:22-30; Isaiah 4:1-6; Baruch 3:9-38; Ezekiel 37:1-14; NT: Acts 19:1-8 // John 14:15-21

Pentecost Sunday occurs on the fiftieth day after Easter. In the Jewish tradition, Pentecost was the celebration of First Fruits. In the Christian tradition, Pentecost marks the birth of the Church and therefore the Church views it as a celebration of the gospel's First Fruits.

Acts 2:1-11 // John 14:23-31

Feast of the Most Holy Trinity (First Sunday following Pentecost) was added to the liturgical calendar after the Trinitarian controversy. This allowed at least one Sunday where the doctrine of the Trinity would take center stage.

Romans 11:33-36 // Matthew 28:18-20

---

[1] In the years following the Reformation, many in the Protestant traditions did utilize this day for the celebration of communion.

Corpus Christi (Thursday after Trinity Sunday) is also a feast to promote the theology of the Church, namely, that the bread of the Eucharist *is* the Body of Christ.

1 Corinthians 11:23-29 // John 6:56-59

Sunday in the Octave of Corpus Christi (Second Sunday after Pentecost)

1 Peter 5:6-11 // Luke 15:1-10

The liturgical calendar is less active through the rest of the year until October. While there is a celebration in August of Mary, the mother of Jesus, the rest of the liturgical year has no major Feasts or Holy Days until All Saints Day. Advent follows shortly thereafter and the whole cycle starts again. Even in times where there are no Feasts or Holy Days, the liturgy still calls for variations to the *Proper of the Mass*.

THE CONTENT OF THE MASS

Because the focus of the weekly service in the Catholic Church is the Eucharist, the five major components of the *Ordinary* highlight the preparation of the worshiper, the meaning of the sacrifice, and consumption of the Elements. A notated order of the Mass is included here with the full texts of the five sections of the *Ordinary of the Mass*: the *Kyrie, Gloria, Credo, Agnus Dei*, and *Sanctus*. These are provided in Latin with a parallel translation. Elements that are not part of the *Ordinary* are included but are summarized within the order. Both the complete text of the 1962 *Tridentine Mass* and the post Vatican II revision are widely available through online sources.[1]

THE ORDER OF THE TRIDENTINE MASS[2]
THE RITE OF PREPARATION

Asperge-cleansing prior to starting the Mass

Antiphons-various prayers ending with the *Gloria Patri*

In the Catholic tradition, ceremonial washing precedes the Mass. The parallels with the Jewish ceremony of sacrifice begin immediately. The Jewish tradition provided the Bronze Laver in the Tabernacle and the Molten Sea in the Temple to provide water for ceremonial washing.

---

[1] For example, see http://www.fordham.edu/halsall/basis/latinmass2.html and http://www.sanctamissa.org/en/resources/books-1962/missale-romanum-1962-pdf.html for the Tridentine Mass, and http://www.preces-latinae.org/Libelli/Missa.pdf for the Mass as released after Vatican II.

[2] All translations of the Mass are by the author, maintaining the word order of the original whenever possible. The condensed order of the Mass and the translations are based on the *Missale Romanum: Ex Decreto SS. Concili Tridentini Restutum Summorum Pontificum Cur Recognitum.* (Church Music Association of America, *Musica Sacra*: 1962).

THE MASS

PART I: MASS OF THE CATECHUMENS

The Mass is divided into two parts. The first is the Mass of the Catechumens and the second is the Mass of the Faithful. Both the faithful and the novice attend the Mass of the Catechumens. About midway through the service those who have not yet been confirmed in the Church are dismissed.

The Sign of the Cross

Psalm 42

The Confession of the Priest

The Confession of the People

The Mass is expiatory. It is intending to provide the sinful cleansing and forgiveness.. The Mass always begins with confession and supplication.

Introit Antiphon

KYRIE ELEISON[1]

Kyrie eleison.	Lord, have mercy.
Kyrie eleison.	Lord, have mercy.
Kyrie eleison.	Lord, have mercy.
Christe eleison.	Christ, have mercy.
Christe eleison.	Christ, have mercy.
Christe eleison.	Christ, have mercy.
Kyrie eleison.	Lord, have mercy.
Kyrie eleison.	Lord, have mercy.
Kyrie eleison.	Lord, have mercy.

Kyrie is a Latin derivative of the Greek *kurios* [κύριος]. Greek was the language widely used throughout the Roman Empire, at least until the third century. While the phrase in Greek is common to several other non-Latin liturgies, this form, using the repetitions of *Christe eleison,* is unique to the Roman Rite. It first appeared in Western liturgies in the sixth century and was well established by the time of Gregory.[2] This may have been used to underscore the deity of Christ.

---

[1] Often the *Kyrie* is done as a response where the Priest and the Servant, i.e., the one representing the congregation, speak back and forth to one another.
[2] See Fortescue, A. (1910). "Kyrie Eleison." in *The Catholic Encyclopedia*. New York: Robert Appleton Company. http://www.newadvent.org/cathen/08714a.htm, accessed December 17, 2010.

GLORIA

Gloria in excelsis Deo.	Glory to God in the highest.
Et in terra pax hominibus bonae	And on earth, peace to people of good
voluntatis. Laudamus te.	will. We praise You. We bless
Benedicimus te. Adoramus te.	You. We adore You. We glorify You.
Glorificamus te. Gratias agimus tibi	We give thanks to You
propter magnam gloriam	because of (the) great glory
tuam. Domine Deus, Rex coelestis,	of Yours, Lord God, King of Heaven,
Deus Pater omnipotens. Domine Fili	Father God omnipotent. Son of God
unigenite, Jesu Christe. Domine	only begotten, Jesus Christ. Lord
Deus, Agnus Dei, Filius Patris,	God, Lamb of God, Son of the Father,
Qui tollis peccata mundi,	who takes away the sin of the world,
miserere nobis. Qui tollis peccata	have mercy on us. [You,] Who takes
mundi, suscipe deprecationem	away the sin of the world, listen
nostram. Qui sedes	to our prayer. [You,] Who sits
ad dexteram Patris,	at the right hand of the Father,
miserere nobis. Quoniam tu solus	have mercy on us. Because You alone
Sanctus. Tu solus Dominus. Tu solus	[are] holy. You alone [are] Lord. You
Altissimus, Jesu Christe.	alone the Most High, Jesus Christ,
Cum Sancto Spiritu in gloria	with the Holy Spirit, in the glory
Dei Patris. Amen.	of God the Father. Amen.

Collect(s) for the day

These are prayers specified by the liturgy for the day.

The Reading of the Epistle

This reading, generally from one of the Pauline Epistles, would include several verses.

Gradual with Alleluia or Tract

This is a musical response. Whether it is the Gradual with Alleluia or a tract depends on the festivity of the season. During Lent, the Alleluia is omitted.

Munda Cor Meum (*Cleanse my heart*)

A prayer for cleansing is offered by the one who is about to read, asking that he might proclaim the gospel. In the less formal *Low Mass* the deacon reads. In the more ornate *Solemn Mass* (also called *High Mass*) the priest reads.

The Reading of the Gospel

Again, the Proper of the Mass directs the passage to be read (or sung if it is *High Mass*). This could be a few verses or a longer narrative. It is the most solemn reading in the service and the congregants stand.

Homily or Sermon

With each passing century, the Church added to the tradition of the Mass. By the Middle Ages, the teaching of Scripture in the context of corporate worship became obscured by the preparation and observance of the Table. Orders of the Tridentine Mass do not always include an entry for the sermon.

CREDO

Credo in unum Deum, Patrem omnipotentem, factorem coeli et terrae, visibilium omnium et invisibilium. Et in unum Dominum Jesum Christum, Filium Dei unigenitum. Et ex Patre natum ante omnia saecula. Deum de Deo, lumen de lumine, Deum verum de Deo vero. Genitum, non factum, consubstantialem Patri: per quem omnia facta sunt. Qui propter nos homines, et propter nostram salutem descendit de coelis. Et incarnatus est de Spiritu Sancto ex Maria Virgine: et homo factus est. Crucifixus etiam pro nobis; sub Pontio Pilato passus, et sepultus est. Et resurrexit tertia die, secundum Scripturas. Et ascendit in coelum: sedet ad dexteram Patris. Et iterum venturus est cum gloria judicare vivos et mortuos. Cujus regni non erit finis. Et in Spiritum Sanctum, Dominum et vivificantem: qui ex Patre Filioque procedit. Qui cum Patre, et Filio simul adoratur et conglorificatur: qui locutus est per Prophetas. Et unam, sanctam, catholicam et apostolicam Ecclesiam. Confiteor unum baptisma in remissionem peccatorum. Et exspecto resurrectionem mortuorum. Et vitam venturi saeculi. Amen.

I believe in one God, Father Almighty, maker of heaven and earth, and of all things visible and invisible. And in one Lord, Jesus Christ, Son of God the only begotten. And of the Father begotten before all ages. God of God, Light of light, true God of true God. Begotten, not made, of one substance with the Father. By whom all things were made. Who for us human beings and for our salvation descended from heaven. And became incarnate by the Holy Spirit of the Virgin Mary: and was made man. He was also crucified for us, under Pontius Pilate suffered, and was buried. And He rose on the third day according to the scriptures. And He ascended into heaven and sits at the right hand of the Father. He will come again with glory to judge the living and the dead. His reign will not end. And in the Holy Spirit, Lord and life-giver, who from the Father and the Son proceeds. Who with the Father and the Son, together, is adored and glorified, who spoke through the prophets. And one holy, catholic and apostolic Church. I confess one baptism for the forgiveness of sins and I await the resurrection of the dead and life in the world to come. Amen.

Previously we examined how the early writings of the Church Fathers increasingly called for pre-baptismal confessions (see Chapter 4). Similarly, the

Credo serves as a confession of faith prior to taking Holy Communion. The bulk of this text dates from the Council of Nicaea, AD 325, and the Council of Constantinople, AD 381. The implication is that if you cannot confess Christ, you cannot approach the Table. For this reason, the catechumens, those headed toward full membership in the Church but not confirmed through confession of belief and Baptism, along with any others not in the faith, were dismissed.

PART II: MASS OF THE FAITHFUL

Offering to the Secret

This includes several prayers of supplication directed to God. Specifically, the priest entreats God to accept the Blood and Body of Christ as a sacrifice for the sins of the people. It also includes the offering of the bread and wine in preparation for the consecration as well as ceremonial washing. A secret prayer uttered inaudibly by the Celebrant (priest) follows the congregational prayer.

Preface

This includes the *sursum corda* (lift up your hearts). The Preface dates back to the *anaphora* or Eucharist prayer and marks the beginning of the Communion Rite.

SANCTUS (with Benedictus)

Sanctus, Sanctus, Sanctus,	Holy, Holy, Holy
Dominus Deus Sabaoth. Pleni	Lord God of Hosts. Full
sunt coeli et terra	are the heavens and earth
gloria tua.	of Your glory.
Hosanna in excelsis.	Hosanna in the highest.
Benedictus qui venit in	Blessed is He who comes in the
nomine Domini.	name of the Lord.
Hosanna in excelsis.	Hosanna in the highest.

The text for the Sanctus comes from Isaiah 6:3 and was commonly recited in the Synagogue as part of corporate worship. The text of the *Benedictus* is taken from Matthew 21:9 and also has its origins in the Old Testament (see Psalm 118:26).

THE CANON OF THE MASS

The Roman Canon marks the portion of the Mass in which the bread and wine through transubstantiation become the Body and Blood of Jesus. It is so named because the Canon or rule of the Mass ensures that each entry from the *Sanctus* to the *Pater Noster* does not change. The priest offers both Elements to God as a propitiatory sacrifice. The priest then partakes of the Body and Blood, followed by the faithful (those who have been confirmed), both as a means to receive forgiveness.

Prayers Prior to the Consecration

The Canon begins by continuing the theme of earlier prayers, asking God to find the offering pleasing and acceptable, and it invokes the memory of Mary the Mother of Jesus, Joseph, the Apostles, and martyrs.

Consecration of the Body and Blood of Jesus

The priest then recites prayers and consecrates the Elements as he repeats the words of Jesus at the Last Supper, *HOC EST ENIM CORPUS MEUM* (*This is My body*). After the priest says these words, he kneels and lifts the Bread to be worshipped, invoking both the recollection of the Last Supper and demonstrating the belief that the bread has become the Body of Jesus. In the same way, the priest continues with the Cup quoting Jesus again, *HIC EST ENIM CALIX SANGUINIS MEI* (*This is the cup of My blood*). He kneels and lifts the Cup to be worshiped.

The Oblation Prayer

The priest prays that all who take communion may find grace.

Prayers after the consecration

Prayers are offered commemorating the dead and asking to share in the future fellowship with the Saints.

Final Doxology of the Canon and the Minor Elevation of the Host

The Bread and Cup are now referred to as the Host since they are now the flesh and blood of Jesus. Following a brief prayer of praise, the Host is lifted again by the Celebrant to be adored. This ends the Roman Canon.

The Lord's Prayer

The congregation prays the Model Prayer, ending with *sed libera nos a malo. Amen* (*but deliver us from evil, Amen*).

The Libera Nos and the breaking of the Host

The priest carefully takes the bread and breaks it over the cup. During this action he prays: *Libera nos, quaesumus, Domine, ab omnibus malis, praeteritis, praesentibus, et futuris, et intercedente beata et gloriosa semper Virgine Dei Genitrice Maria* (*Free us, we implore, Lord, from all evil: past, present, and future, and by the intercession of the blessed and glorious, ever Virgin Mother of God, Mary....*).

The Commixtio

The priest speaks *The Peace*,[1] as a small piece of the bread is broken and placed in the cup. The 'mixing' of the Body and Blood effectively means that the faithful need only to take only the Bread.

AGNUS DEI

Agnus Dei, qui tollis	Lamb of God, who takes away
peccata mundi,	the sin of the world,

---

[1] The priest says, *Pax Domini sit semper vobiscum* (*May the peace of the Lord be always with you.*) The congregation responds, *Et cum spiritu tuo* (*And with your spirit*).

Miserere nobis.	have mercy on us.
Agnus Dei, qui tollis	Lamb of God, who takes away
peccata mundi,	the sin of the world,
miserere nobis.	have mercy on us.
Agnus Dei, qui tollis	Lamb of God, who takes away
peccata mundi,	the sin of the world,
dona nobis pacem.	grant us peace.

Prayers

Three prayers follow, one each for peace, sanctification, and grace.

The Communion of the Priest

As the High Priest in the Jewish Rite of sacrifice first made atonement for himself, the priest who is leading the Mass receives the Body and Blood first, taking the Bread and then the Cup.

The Communion of the Faithful

The priest places the bread on the tongue of each of the faithful as he says, *Corpus Domini nostri Jesu Christi custodiat animam tuam in vitam aeternam* (*The Body of our Lord Jesus Christ keep your soul unto life eternal*).

Ablutions

Here the Celebrant cleanses the chalice from which he took the blood of Jesus then ceremonially washes his hands.

Communion and Post Communion Prayers

Two freeform prayers follow the taking of the Elements. Generally, these are prayers giving thanks for the forgiveness and grace communicated through the taking of the Supper.

Dismissal

Just prior to a final reading from the Gospel of John, the priest gives closing remarks including the phrase *Ite, Missa Est* (*Go, you are sent*) and a prayer of blessing.

The Last Gospel (John 1:1-14)

The service concludes with an extended passage from the Gospel of John, reiterating the deity of Christ and His power to save.

EVALUATING THE MASS

THE MINISTRY OF THE WORD

Those who examine the text of the Mass and the lectionary for the first time may be surprised at how much Scripture was actually included in the Mass. Considering that the *Proper of the Mass* specifies readings from the Old and New Testament for each Sunday, the typical pre-Reformation Catholic worshiper who attended weekly Mass would have heard roughly 250 verses from the Old Testament in a year. This is not counting the multitude of verses quoted from the Psalms. Additionally, in the same period, that worshiper would have heard over 1,300 verses read from the New Testament. When considering the addition of the Psalms and the many Scriptural phrases quoted or paraphrased in the *Ordinary of Mass*, it is likely that worshipers attending weekly Mass and the major festivals of the Catholic Church could have heard nearly 2,000 verses from the Scripture read during corporate worship in a year. This does not include any the priest might have used as part of his sermon or homily. Scripture reading remains a significant component of the Mass to this day. The variety of scriptures to which the congregation was exposed increased significantly following *Vatican II*. In the present lectionary, excluding the readings from the Psalms and references in the *Ordinary*, the number of scriptures read exceeds 3,300 different verses spread over a three-year cycle.[1]

What the Mass gained in the public reading of Scripture, it often gave away in the teaching and preaching of them. By the Middle Ages the message had become, in many instances, little more than a brief devotional. The scriptures were not taught in the context of the public worship gathering. The trend was to leave the serious study of Scripture to those who had given their life to the priesthood. For this reason, to say that there was not serious study of the scriptures by the Roman Church would not be true. We have already mentioned that bright spots of biblical study did exist. There were clerics and priests who studied the Scripture in a significant way. Furthermore, since the way in which the homily or sermon was conducted was dependent on the local priest, it is likely that in some churches the Word of God was preached. However, history demonstrates that such teaching was not pervasive.

In a form like the Mass in which there is such a large amount of prescribed content, there is simply not sufficient time for the exposition of Scripture. This is among those things that the initial reformers found troubling and remains one of the key sticking points between Catholics and many evangelicals. Unfortunately, without regular and significant teaching of the Word to the congregation, worshipers are left to draw their own conclusions about the spiritual meanings hidden inside the imagery of the Mass. While Rome made significant changes to the Mass during *Vatican II* to include a wider variety of Scripture reading, the malady that developed in centuries past remained. The Eucharist celebration continued as the primary focus of corporate worship, relegating the ministry of preaching and teaching to a place of inferiority.

Many evangelicals pride themselves in having a strong focus on Scripture. To be fair, whether or not preaching and teaching from the Bible occupy the proper place in many of our services is debatable. In addition, very few freeform worshipers hear as much Scripture read week in and week out as do those who follow the Roman Rite. In most Protestant churches, Scripture reading has dwindled to include only those scriptures examined in the context of the

---

[1] See "Lectionary Statistics," Catholic Resources - Felix Just, S.J., 2009, http://catholic-resources.org/Lectionary/Statistics.htm (accessed December 01, 2010).

message. One can only hope that the lack of Scripture reading is not intentional. Perhaps it is a lack of disciplined commitment to the public reading of Scripture.

This can and should be repaired. Pastors and other worship leaders can accomplish this by reading appropriate scriptures to introduce songs, playing pre-recorded passages of scriptures for meditation, or using scriptures that are printed or projected for corporate reading. Since freeform worshipers are not bound to a lectionary that requires them to read Scripture regularly, their leaders will have to make a concerted effort to ensure that they do not neglect the public reading of Scripture. In addition, this must be coupled with a commitment to teach and preach the scriptures themselves. Unless those of us who lead make this an ongoing commitment, freeform worshipers will never be exposed to a healthy amount of public Scripture reading and biblical preaching. In the end, corporate worship will suffer greatly.

AN ATMOSPHERE OF REVERENCE AND MYSTERY

In asking students over the years to observe different forms of worship, it is interesting to see that their observations have had some common themes. The most common is that liturgical forms, like those of the Catholic or Anglican tradition, inherently have a greater sense of reverence than the looser fitting forms of some Protestant churches. There may be several reasons for their observations. It is clear that among those things that the Mass does very well is to draw focus toward the holiness of God and the sinfulness of man. In part, the Mass accomplishes this by addressing God almost exclusively in terms of His holiness and transcendence. At the same time, both the Celebrant and the people often address God in suppliant terms that hope for His graciousness. The Mass constantly casts the worshiper before God with cries for help. Phrases such as *miserere nobis,*[1] *suscipe deprecationem nostrum,*[2] and *kyrie eleison*[3] are used throughout the service. This creates an effective juxtaposition between transcendent God and sinful worshipers, who plead frequently for mercy. Like the Penitential Psalms[4] that cry out to God for mercy, the structure of the Mass shows the disparity between sinful human beings and transcendent God. The Mass demonstrates this gap between Creator and created, and then closes it through Communion. The means by which the Mass accomplishes this are, in part, what evangelicals find theologically troubling about the Mass. The impression is that mercy and grace are not appropriated until the people receive the Elements through Communion. Therefore, the humility expressed in the Mass is so that God will grant mercy rather than because He has done so.

---

[1] *Have mercy on us.*
[2] *Hear our prayer.*
[3] *Lord have mercy.*
[4] Psalm 6, 32, 38, 51, 102, 130, and 143 are often referred to as the Penitential Psalms because of their cry to God for forgiveness and mercy. The Mass draws from several passages within these Psalms.

Two other reasons that the Mass evokes such reverence are its history and its mystery. For Christians who understand they are participating in a form celebrated for many centuries, there is an inescapable identification with those who have preceded us. Even though there are certainly issues with the theology of the Mass, reciting a text, prayer or creed that may have its origins in the early centuries of Christianity can have a profound effect. It is easy to forget that our faith is ancient. The strength of the Mass at this point demonstrates one of the weaknesses of newer forms; namely, they fail to communicate that Christian worship is steeped in centuries of practice. Portions of the text of the *Ordinary*, like the *Credo*, date from at least the fourth or fifth century and the concept of the anaphora (the prayer preceding the Elements) has its origin early in the second century. To be sure, some of the reverence and mystery felt by those who experience a Mass for the first time come from being unfamiliar with the liturgical form. However, the connection of the Mass to ancient Church history can evoke a deep sense of awe on its own.

Additionally, the intricate imagery and symbolism of the Mass are not immediately apparent without explanation. Since many who worship in this form are unaware of the centuries of embedded imagery, the worshiper may experience wonderment directed toward the complexities of the form itself rather than toward God. From the Middle Ages forward, the symbolism of the Mass continued to develop, resulting in extensive bodies of music, paintings, sculptures and grand architecture. Even today, these great master works of art and architecture still evoke a sense of awe, albeit, at times not necessarily toward God. While architecture, ceremony and the use of ancient texts may have helped create a climate in which the worshiper could stand in awe before God, all of them are poor substitutes for genuinely experiencing the wonder of standing before the Most High.

Similarly, the use of Latin, intended to keep the Church tied to its ancient origins, may have added mystery, but at the expense of comprehension and participation. After the general population no longer spoke Latin, worshipers were deprived of worshiping in their heart language. They observed the priests perform intricate rituals with little contextualization and spoke words and performed actions (kneeling, crossing themselves, etc.) without necessarily understanding the significance of what they were doing.

The mystery that surrounds God is an essential component of worship and one we must never discard. However, the reverence and mystery within a worship experience must concern the person and character of God. The Mass with its ancient form and intense symbolism may do this well for the worshiper who understands what is happening but, for the worshiper who does not have that understanding, the outcome could be quite different. No matter what form is used, a profound sense of awe and mystery in worship keeps the question of the Psalmist in our minds, *What is man that You take thought of him, And the son of man that You care for him?*[1]

---

[1] Psalm 8:4.

STRUCTURE AND FORM

From a structural standpoint, the Mass is well suited to accomplish a very specific purpose. In any planned worship gathering there should be a hoped and prayed for spiritual outcome. The components that are used should be placed intentionally with that outcome in mind. In other words, the components of a worship service should not be in competition or conflict with the purpose of the event. The way the Mass is structured makes it clear that the purpose of gathering is to restore the relationship between God and man through the shed blood and broken body of Christ. From the opening words of the priest in the Mass, *Introibo ad altare Dei,*[1] to the last words, *Deo gratias,*[2] the structure seeks to lead worshipers on a journey back to fellowship with God. The structure of the Mass is linear, moving the worshiper toward the act of receiving the Supper. As the time approaches for taking the Elements, the believer is drawn into a very personal focus. The Mass begins with all present hearing God extolled, the scriptures read, and the message or homily preached. Once the Mass of the Faithful begins, presuming the dismissal of those not yet confirmed in the Faith, the focus of the Mass tightens, leading those who have confessed Christ towards the celebration of His Body and Blood. Finally, both the most personally introspective moment of the celebration and the most climactic is the consumption of the Elements.

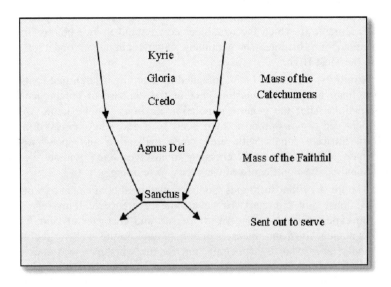

---

[1] *I will approach the altar of God.*

[2] *Thanks be to God.*

There are also clear rises in the emotional intensity of the Mass. Much of this comes through two significant episodes of congregational participation, both resulting in climactic moments. The first occurs during the Mass of the Catechumens when the congregation recites the *Credo*. We already know that pre-Communion confessions became an important part of corporate worship by the second century. This was necessary to ensure that those taking the Supper were all confessing the same Jesus. Thus, reciting the *Credo* provides a strong outward expression of union within the congregation around the most essential doctrines. In the second part of the Mass, the Mass of the

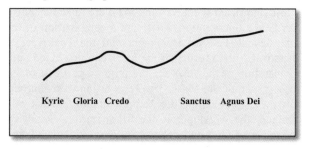

Dramatic peaks in the Mass come through participation. The *Credo* is the first climax of the service and the second, greater climax is the participation of the faithful, as they take the Bread and Cup and are commissioned to go out and spread the gospel.

Kyrie Gloria Credo   Sanctus Agnus Dei

Faithful, the climax is clearly the taking of the Elements themselves. Just as the *Credo* achieves its emotional and spiritual intensity by expressing union among believers, taking the Bread and Cup demonstrates the believer's individual union (or reunion) with God through Jesus Christ. The rises in emotional and spiritual intensity result in a dramatic form where ebb and flow find their highest moment after the worshiper is reunited with God and sent out to spread the gospel.

Because the form of the Mass is fixed, it shares similar difficulties with any worship form repeated over a long period. Whether Catholic or Protestant, we all share the same weakness. We all tend to forget why we do what we are doing when we worship. Repetition may make us better at performing the act of worship but, it does not ensure that the heart will follow. The use of any form that teaches, even by implication, that worship is accomplished through repetitive actions is counterproductive. Worship is the essence of the relationship between God and His people: *being in the proper state before God*. When it is real, worship is never mechanical at the core. True worship is the interaction between the individual and God, making it vibrant and dynamic. This does not mean that repetition is wrong; rather, we displease God when our repetition is vain or empty.[1]

Most of us have been in a service of worship and found ourselves addressing the Lord in prayer or a song, going through the motions, while our minds are elsewhere. Our familiarity makes it possible to perform the action while our hearts are far away. Many evangelical worshipers have developed their own forms that they repeat with as much rigidity as those who follow a liturgy.

---

[1] Matthew 6:7.

This is true for both traditional and non-traditional churches. Because of this, freeform worshipers share a similar risk to those who use a liturgy—both can make worship equally mundane. For congregations that are not bound to a liturgy, varying the form may be helpful to combat the staleness that accompanies repetition. For those who are committed to a liturgy, it is essential to teach and explain the form frequently.

THE THEOLOGY OF THE MASS

The Mass owes much of its theology to the practice of Jewish ritual. The most significant themes of the Mass are repentance/restoration and thanksgiving for God's intervention. These are a combination of the theological functions of two Jewish Feasts: Atonement and the Passover.[1] The primary function of Passover was to testify to the intervention of God and to give Him thanks. The preparation of the Jews for the pilgrimage Feast of Passover is reflected in the observance of the Mass. The Jews began their journey to Jerusalem from some distance, approaching the Temple singing Psalms of preparation.[2] In a similar fashion, the worshiper in the Mass starts at some spiritual distance from the presence of God and begins the approach toward the altar through confession and repentance. Portions quoted from the Last Supper blend themes from both Feasts. The relationship to the Passover is evident both in the fact that the Supper itself was instituted during the Passover and that participation of each individual worshiper is a testimony of God's intervention in their life. In many celebrations of the Mass, worshipers approach the front of the room to receive the Elements. Coming forward represents a personal confession of need and testimony of trust in the "flesh and blood" of Jesus as a means of deliverance. Like the Children of Israel who spent portions of each Passover recounting the deliverance of Israel from bondage in Egypt, the Mass is intended as testimony of the believer's hope in Christ's sacrifice for forgiveness of sin.

The function of the Jewish Feast of Atonement was personal and corporate repentance *for* the forgiveness of sin. The High Priest accomplished this when he confessed sins on behalf of the people, and then entered the Holy of Holies to bring the satisfactory offering of blood before God. Through this confession and sacrifice, the relationship between God and His people was restored. The parallel to this concept is clear in the Mass. As the priest speaks the words of institution, the bread and wine become the flesh and blood of Jesus and the priest offers them to God. This is the same concept of sacrifice used by the priest on the Day of Atonement. The parallel continues. Just as the High Priest on the Day of Atonement offered a sacrifice for his own sin first, the priest in the Mass takes communion for his own cleansing before he offers the sacrifice on behalf of the people. For the Roman Church this is the priest's journey into the most Holy

---

[1] See Chapter 2, *Old Testament Archetypes and Christian Worship.*

[2] The Psalms sung by the Israelites as they approached the Temple are commonly referred to as the *Psalms of Ascent* (Psalm 120-134).

Place, the altar, to offer a sacrifice to God. This is true both ceremonially and theologically since each celebration of the Mass constitutes a new atoning sacrifice of Jesus' Body and Blood.

For evangelicals, this represents some of the most troubling aspects of the Mass, specifically, and Catholicism in general. In the Old Testament system, a priest stood before God in the Holy of Holies to make an offering on behalf of the people. However, the Sacrificial System was not an end in itself. God had established the entire system to communicate His provision for forgiveness as it would ultimately be found in the coming work of Jesus.[1] Like the earthly Holy Place that represented a heavenly place not made with human hands, the earthly priest was only a shadow of God's choice of Jesus Christ as the final High Priest. Christ alone could stand before the Father on behalf of humankind and satisfy all of God's requirements. In the same way, the blood of the sacrificial animal pointed to the ultimate sacrifice of Jesus' blood. He was the complete fulfillment of the priestly system by becoming both our Sacrifice and High Priest. When He did so, He opened the way so that all who believe in Him might, by His righteousness and sacrifice, become a kingdom of priests who receive entrance into the Holy Place of fellowship with God.

Rather than celebrating this as a work already finished in Christ, the Mass renders a fresh sacrifice to God for the propitiation of sins. It is not a mere recounting of what has occurred. In the Jewish Rite, the priest stood at the altar before God on behalf of the people. Likewise, in the Mass the priest brings a sacrifice to God on behalf of the people. It is not the flesh and blood of bulls and rams. Instead, the priest offers the flesh and blood of Jesus. The portion of the Mass in which he does this is the Canon. During the Canon, he speaks the words of institution during which, according to Catholic theology, the bread and wine become the actual Body and Blood of Jesus. The words of Jesus from the Last Supper serve as the words of institution: *HOC EST ENIM CORPUS MEUM* (*This is My Body*) and *HIC EST ENIM CALIX SANGUINIS MEI* (*This is the cup of My Blood*).

This doctrine, commonly known as Transubstantiation, is essential to Catholicism because the system is rooted in the belief that forgiveness comes through the continued sacrificial offering of Jesus' Body and Blood. Without the Elements becoming the Body and Blood, there would be nothing acceptable to offer to God for the forgiveness of sin.

This leaves the theology of the Mass more in line with the practice and theology of the Old Covenant than the New Covenant. The true difference between the two lies in whether or not Jesus' work is already complete and therefore effective for all *believers* or if there is additional sacrifice needed to make it (and keep it) complete and keep it effective. This is significant because it

---

[1] The ninth chapter of Hebrews describes this in detail. The theme of the entire book deals with how Jesus fulfilled and superseded all aspects of the Old Covenant. For this reason, Hebrews remains one of the most important books of the Bible when discussing worship.

points to the most basic views of redemption and atonement found in Jesus' death on the cross. The sacerdotal work of an earthly priest (going to God as an intermediary), re-offering by his own hands the blood of Christ, strikes at the heart of a complete salvation by grace alone through faith alone in Christ alone. Instead, forgiveness is conditional—dependent upon an earthly priest's mediation. The clear implication of the Catholic Rite is that the sinner stands unforgiven before God. Then, through the fresh offering of Jesus' flesh and blood in the Eucharist, the believer hopes to leave forgiven and restored. While many theologians may vigorously debate the nuances of repentance and forgiveness or the meaning and substance of the Bread and Cup, in the end the evangelical view and Catholic view are substantially different. The Roman Rite celebrates the Eucharist in order to receive forgiveness, mercy, and grace, while evangelical believers celebrate the Eucharist because they have received it. This does not mean that sin should go unaddressed in the context of evangelical worship. Repentance and confession[1] (that is, the change of mind and heart to come into full agreement with God) are integral parts of the believer's life. However, the belief that the sin of the redeemed remains a debt against their account is troublesome. For Catholics, this created a theological dilemma and eventually led to the conceptual development of Purgatory, a place between this life and the next where those sins not forgiven could be purged from the believer's life before entering the presence of God.

Beyond these most fundamental problems, there are many others. The full text of the Proper of the Mass, while including much scripture and very forthright statements of the Trinity, includes prayers to the dead, the angels, and a consistent elevation of Mary, the mother of Jesus. Clearly, there is a large gap between the Mass and the evangelical view of the Eucharist.

CONCLUDING THOUGHTS ON THE MASS

Considering the irreconcilable problems with the Mass's theology, it is all the more important for Protestants, evangelicals in particular, to understand what it teaches. Many in our congregations may have come to Christ from a Catholic background and quietly hold views about Communion derived from Catholic theology. For many of those congregants, taking Communion is a means of grace, a way in which they can be sure to receive God's grace and mercy. I have often had those who grew up in Catholicism concerned that many evangelical churches do not offer Communion each week. Someone who has that concern may be operating from a belief that, without the sacrificial offering of the Body and Blood of Christ given anew in the Eucharist, they are building a cache of

---

[1] *Repentance*, μετανοέω (*metanoéō*), means a true change of mind and heart. *Confession*, ὁμολογέω (*homologéō*), means to say the same thing about our sin as God says about it—to fully agree with Him.

unforgiven sins. In their minds, they can only receive that forgiveness at the altar of God in the context of Communion. Understanding the Mass provides us the tools to help those who are living under the weight of a works salvation instead of a grace salvation.

For evangelicals, the most significant problems with the Mass are not as numerous as one might think. Of course, some freeform worshipers will struggle with any fixed liturgy. This should not keep us from learning from these forms. Our objections to the Mass should be few but, because they are primarily theological, they are significant nonetheless. The greatest objection is what the Mass teaches about the nature of the Atonement, i.e., the fundamental issues of salvation. For this reason, the differences remain a true barrier to genuine fellowship at the Table between Roman Catholics and Evangelicals. In light of this, pastors and worship leaders should be forthright in presenting the clear claims of the gospel when conducting Communion. While we have used the *Tridentine Mass* (1962) as our template for study, similar theological difficulties exist with the revisions since *Vatican II*. These theological issues and distaste for the wide-scale mysticism that pervaded the Roman Church fueled a growing unrest among many in the thirteenth and fourteenth century. The gross excesses of some leaders in Rome finally pushed the unrest to the boiling point and led to the Reformation.

In addition to those things which we discussed at the beginning of this chapter, there is something else positive that Evangelicals can glean by understanding the form of the Mass: to see how a fixed form can be very strong in accomplishing a specific purpose. While many Evangelicals eschew such rigidity from week to week, the shape of the Mass is an excellent template for celebrating Communion. The five primary components of the *Ordinary* provide a strong framework for the congregation to remember the sacrificial death of Jesus. The texts of those five segments are even appropriate for evangelical services with only slight modifications.

In my own ministry, I have structured Communion services according to the pattern of the *Ordinary of the Mass*: *Mercy, Glory, I Believe, Holy,* and *Lamb of God*. I did not do it to move our church toward Catholicism, but because these are excellent themes for such a service. The form begins in humility and then moves to extol the glory of God. There is a clear place to express one's own personal belief in Jesus Christ and then a time of reflection on the holiness of God. The last of the five culminates by drawing attention to Jesus; the *Lamb of God who takes away the sin of the world.* My hope is that by understanding the Mass, you will consider taking some of those ancient concepts, filter them through solid biblical theology, and use them to enhance corporate worship among your people.

CHAPTER 7

REFORMATION WORSHIP
(AD 1500-1650)

The Reformation, often dated from 1517 when Martin Luther published his *Disputatio pro Declaratione Virtutis Indulgentiarumon,*[1] was neither a sudden nor a systematic development. The Church in Rome, marked by abuses and corruption for centuries, had resisted attempts by earlier reformers like John Wycliffe (d. 1384) and Jan Hus (1369-1415). The devotion of these men is unquestionable. While they saw little change in their lifetime, the sixteenth century was much more situated for change than the centuries prior. The general rise of education, punctuated by the refinement of the university system during the fourteenth and fifteenth centuries, had sparked an interest in learning that had been dormant for centuries. This coincided with the invention of the movable type printing press in the first half of the fifteenth century.

The quest for discovery was not limited to knowledge. Europe's powers embarked on a race to discover and subdue new territory. The discovery of new worlds and their resources fueled a growing nationalism that shaped Western Civilization's map for centuries to follow. Various European monarchs, who saw the expansion of resource and geography as an extension of their own dynasties, advanced much of this nationalism. Additionally, the Renaissance was a period of unprecedented development in art, music and literature. This

---

[1] Commonly referred to as Luther's *Ninety-five Theses.*

155

represents a great deal of flux, considering that so much had been dormant during the Dark Ages. The force of change was lying just beneath the surface throughout the geographical expanse under the spiritual and political control of the Roman Church.

That is not to say that the Reformation was merely a natural progression of societal or cultural change. Western Civilization was bound to change significantly. What the Reformation did was shape how culture changed, specifically, how things changed in the Church. Because the Church still maintained its place as the most prominent influence in Europe, changes that occurred in the Reformation greatly affected European thought and culture. The impact of the Reformation was widespread, shaking both the Church and culture on multiple levels.

Our interest in these changes brought by the Reformation is specifically in the area of worship. As Protestant worshipers, we are the heirs of those changes. Many changes came for those who followed the lead of the reformers, including a new ecclesiology, new architecture, new music, new forms of worship, and a new emphasis on doctrine. We will examine how these developments changed the way many believers worshipped. All of the visible changes came from a shared desire to reform faith practice on the most fundamental level. For this reason, it is impossible to discuss or understand the outward developments in worship without seeing them as the results of fundamental adjustments to thought and theology. This raises an important point and leads to our next lesson from the history of Christian worship.

LESSON 10: WORSHIP RENEWAL ACCOMPANIES A RENEWED FOCUS ON DOCTRINE

BACKGROUND

Protestant worship in the years following the Reformation took one of three paths. The most conservative of these maintained the basic form and shape of the Mass, adjusting it only slightly. The most aggressive reformers dispensed with all vestiges of the Mass. Others took a position between those two extremes. On the surface, many of the changes that occurred in corporate worship might appear to be stylistic changes. However, the most basic force driving these changes was a fresh look at the pages of Scripture. Without exception, the most notable reformers—from the conservative to the most extreme—spoke, wrote about, lived, and sometimes died because of a deep commitment to Scripture and doctrine. Many of the reformers did not set out in an effort to supplant Catholic liturgy. In fact, many of those who were outspoken desired to reform the Catholic Church rather than be part of establishing something outside of the Holy See. The Reformation was not an innovation of structure or form. As Luther's title of his *Ninety-five Theses* indicated, his initial dispute concerned the buying and selling of indulgences. Luther did not object merely based on his lack of trust in a corrupt Roman system. His primary objections were theological, believing that the sale of indulgences counted the grace of God as insufficient—his cry was *sola fide* (*faith* alone) rather than human work or ingenuity. In other words, the issue was first doctrine rather than form.

Luther was not alone in his desire to see fundamental doctrine renewed. The desire for theological correction and renewal of biblical doctrine drove the reformers. These changes in theology and a renaissance of Bible study brought changes to the way Christians worshiped. Where radical doctrinal changes occurred, greater stylistic changes in corporate worship followed. The most significant of these changes to corporate worship were in three areas: the Ministry of the Word, the level of congregational participation, and the meaning and function of the Eucharist. How these three areas changed was driven by the doctrinal writings and practices of men like Martin Luther, Thomas Cranmer, Balthazar Hubmaier, Ulrich Zwingli and John Calvin.

THE MINISTRY OF THE WORD
BACKGROUND AND APPLICATION

Martin Luther (1483-1546) believed that essential doctrines of the faith had become corrupt. Through centuries of practice, the truth of Scripture had become a servant of tradition. He sought to return to a time when Scripture rather than Church tradition or papal authority shaped the lives and beliefs of Christians. His efforts met with strong opposition from both Rome and those who remained loyal to the Pope and earned him a papal bull of excommunication in the autumn of 1520. Luther made his defense before the Diet of Worms in April of 1521 and, shortly thereafter, Rome declared him an enemy of the Church and State. For almost a year, he hid in the Wartburg Castle. He used this time to write many of his greatest theological works. Among his greatest contributions to the Reformation was his translation of the New Testament into German, the native tongue of his parishioners.[1] Throughout the rest of his life, he never abandoned his passion for Scripture nor his desire to see it take a position above that of tradition and papal authority. His passion for individual believers to read, understand, and absorb the truth of the Scripture had a direct impact on how he viewed corporate worship.

Luther's ministry prior to releasing his *Ninety-five Theses* (1517) had already been marked by a passion for preaching. The length and complexity of the Mass itself made preaching problematic. Apart from any sermon, the *Tridentine Mass*[2] could have easily taken more than one and a half hours and, if it were the more intricate version, it could easily exceed two hours. From a practical standpoint, the length required to attend to all the intricate ceremony had effectively squeezed preaching out of corporate worship. This reduced the sermon to little more than a brief devotional. He saw many aspects of the Mass, including prayers to the saints and an abundance of ceremony, as doing more to

---

[1] Luther's translation into German was not the first but is widely hailed as a masterpiece for his time.
[2] See CHAPTER 6, *ROMAN CATHOLIC WORSHIP.*

157

heighten mysticism than help the worshiper. Luther focused on restoring the Ministry of the Word to its rightful place in corporate worship by reducing the amount of ceremonialism and mysticism.

By 1521, he had published an alternate Latin Mass (*Formula Missae*) that trimmed the service length, and in 1526, he published a German Mass (*Deutsche Messe*) that set aside even more components of the original Catholic service. He designed these for use at the church in Wittenberg. In both of these services, Luther wrote an entry for the sermon. He expected that a significant portion of corporate worship would be devoted to preaching. This was apparent both in what he prescribed as well as in his own personal practice of preaching during Mass in the language of the people. Even though the Catholic Church had allowed preaching in the vernacular, a lack of commitment to its theological importance had left preaching in a deplorable state. Luther believed that preaching was just as important as Communion. While he maintained a commitment to the importance of the Eucharist, he felt that it had overshadowed the Ministry of the Word.

While many in the priesthood studied and read the scriptures, even preached them to each other, it was uncommon for most outside the priesthood to hear a sermon of any kind, especially in their own language. It is difficult to imagine how significant the restoration of preaching must have been for the congregation. To them, the revitalization of preaching was an extraordinary innovation. As the Reformation spread, congregants attended a worship service where they heard the Bible read and preached in their native tongue. Nearly every reformer followed Luther's lead and gave great significance to preaching in corporate worship.

Ulrich Zwingli (1488-1531), who was more aggressive in his desire to reform corporate worship than Luther, was a strong proponent of giving the Word of God its due place in corporate worship. He leaned heavily on the New Testament as the appropriate text for sermons, believing that it was the true guide for Christian faith and practice. This led him to formulate services based almost exclusively on New Testament practices. This is an interesting contrast to the Roman Church. We know from history that the Roman Church of the fourth and fifth centuries had leaned heavily on the Jewish Sacrificial System in order to build a ceremony of worship. Therefore, while Rome used the Old Testament to build a complex structure, Zwingli used the New Testament to dismantle it. As a worship reformer, Zwingli was among the most radical. Under Zwingli's direction, corporate worship in Switzerland was austere. The services primarily consisted of preaching/exhortation and prayer—much of that silent.

In general, the reformation in England moved slower and progressed less under Thomas Cranmer (1489-1556), who served as Archbishop of Canterbury from 1533 until his death. This may have been a result of instability in England.[1]

---

[1] The Reformation on the mainland of Europe unfolded during a tumultuous time for England's monarchy. After Henry VIII died, his son, Edward VI, ascended to the throne and advanced the cause of the English Reformation until his death in 1553. His

While other English reformers, like William Tyndale, typified the heart of the Reformation in England, it did not begin to progress until a conflict arose between Rome and Henry VIII. Thus, the Reformation took root in England, perhaps more for political than theological reasons. It was further advanced by Edward VI and firmly established after the death of Mary I under Elizabeth I. Cranmer's own commitment to the ideals of the Reformation seemed to shift several times over the course of his twenty-three years as Archbishop. Ultimately, he confirmed his commitment to the Reformation and was burned at the stake. One of Cranmer's earliest reforms occurred shortly after Edward VI ascended to the throne. Cranmer instructed churches to restore instructional preaching. To ensure it would take place, even if there were no one capable of delivering a sermon, Cranmer provided written messages to be read. Had it not been for the death of Edward VI and the ascendancy of Mary, he might have proved a more innovative reformer. His belief in the meaning and significance of Communion (see below) would still have proven a theological impediment to radical change. Even so, the restoration of preaching was one of Cranmer's first major adjustments to the Mass in its English expression.

Both John Calvin (1509-1564) and Balthazar Hubmaier (1480-1528) also worked to restore preaching in their respective ministries. Although Calvin did not possess a reputation as a great preacher, among the leading reformers, his command of the Scripture was unequaled. His deep commitment to see the Bible taught and understood and his deeply held theological convictions concerning Catholicism pushed him to make radical changes to corporate worship beyond those of Luther and Cranmer. For Calvin, the Word was central and occupied a place even above the commemoration of the Lord's Supper in corporate worship. Hubmaier was comparable to Calvin in the importance he placed on preaching. His services were almost completely exhortation from Scripture mixed with participation from the congregation.

In every area touched by the Reformation, there was a renaissance of the sermon in corporate worship. As the sermon resurfaced, it impacted the other ingredients in the worship service. There was a direct correlation between the amount of importance given to the sermon and the complexity of the liturgy. In most instances, the degree to which the service was simplified was the degree to which the reformers gave more focus to preaching. Therefore, the most radical reformers kept little to none of the Catholic service and gave much of the time to preaching. The pastor/priest was not the only one to participate in ministry through the Word. In some of the Anabaptist forms, the entire liturgy was removed and the Ministry of the Word passed directly to the congregation. Among some Swiss Brethren and later Mennonite gatherings, any male member of the congregation could open the Scripture and bring a word of encouragement

---

death left a controversy of succession. Ultimately, Mary became Queen and attempted to return the Church of England to Catholicism. She reversed the Protestant Reforms of her predecessor and executed many who resisted her. It was during the reign of Mary I that Cranmer was executed. She only reigned for five years and after producing no heir was succeeded by her half-sister Elizabeth I in 1557.

or exhortation. This illustrated how radically views changed, particularly with respect to the sufficiency of scriptures and the importance of the laity. Perhaps no single legacy is greater among all of the reformers than the restoration of preaching. Scripture had led the reformers to push open the doors of reform and preaching its truth opened them wider for all other aspects of worship reform.

We would be wise to learn from these reformers. In many evangelical churches there is a temptation to crowd out the preaching of the Bible with everything from music to announcements. Certainly, there is a place for many things in worship besides preaching. Moreover, many of those things, like singing, prayers, and communion are clearly called for in Scripture and represent the significant role the congregation plays in participatory worship. In all of this, the important concept is balance. *Kerygma*, *koinonia*, and *leitourgia* each have their place in corporate worship. In their desire to develop the worship form, the Greek and Roman Church had diminished preaching and teaching, giving most of the time to *leitourgia* and very little to *kerygma*. Even then, the *leitourgia* was eventually taken away from the congregation.

If a form does not provide for *kerygma*, preaching and teaching the Scripture, it is not appropriate for weekly gatherings of worshipers. Additionally, the sermon can be marginalized, not by crowding it out of the service, but by using the time allotted to do other than preach and teach the Scripture. If it is true that worship renewal accompanies a renewed focus on doctrine then we must consider the inverse corollary. The possibilities of worship renewal greatly diminish when there is a lack of biblical preaching and teaching. Churches must reconsider preaching as an essential component of corporate worship and be diligent to use the time allotted for the sermon to display the truth and beauty of God's Word. Unless we take this lesson seriously, we will squander the greatest bequeathal of the reformers and repeat a sad chapter in Church history, choosing tradition and earthly means over the Divine.

THE ROLE OF THE CONGREGATION
BACKGROUND AND APPLICATION

The Mass had developed as a sacerdotal form of worship. The priests of the Church performed the work of the Mass on behalf of the people. As such, the Supper could be undertaken and accomplish much of its theological purpose without the congregation present. Even though the *Tridentine Mass* provided some participation for the congregation, they had little real spiritual function as a congregation. This changed for all churches that followed the path of reform. Many of the leading reformers espoused some aspect of a priesthood of all believers, meaning that no human mediator was essential for believers to interact with the Almighty. This was a significant doctrinal change and a clear reversal of the sacerdotal view. Thus, in corporate worship, congregants addressed God directly and accomplished spiritual functions previously reserved for those of an ecclesiastical order.

Even the most conservative branch of the Reformation, the Anglican Church, increased the participation of the congregation. *The Book of Common Prayer*, first published under the guidance of Cranmer in 1549 and revised in 1552, improved the participation of the congregation by making participation in Communion essential to accomplish its purpose. He also expanded other aspects of participation, particularly the congregation's interaction in the liturgy. For example, he replaced the opening *Kyrie*, which had become a complex song offered by trained singers, with a congregational reading built around the Ten Commandments.

In many places, increased congregational participation often took the form of the congregational hymn and gave birth to the great body of Protestant hymnody. The most significant developments in Protestant hymnody began in Germany. The *kirchenlied* (church song), or as it is known in English, the *chorale*, utilized a single melodic line to which harmonies could be added. For those unfamiliar with the chorale, it is a strophic song having multiple verses with approximately one syllable per note just as many familiar hymns. The melody was generally simple enough for the congregation to sing but could be made more ornate by the harmonies and the accompaniment used. Luther was a strong proponent of congregational singing and depended on the chorale to achieve his goal of a truly German service. As a moderate reformer, he did not want to discard all the practices of the Roman Rite. For the services at Wittenberg, he specified chorales as an acceptable alternative to several portions in the *Proper of the Mass* and some parts of the *Ordinary*. This prompted Luther and many who followed his lead to write chorale texts in the vernacular. The chorale texts he prescribed for his congregation were comprised of both Scripture and original poems.

Luther's most famous chorale text, *Ein' Feste Burg ist unser Gott* (*A Mighty Fortress is Our God*) is an outstanding example of an original poem and archetypical of German hymnody. First, it is doctrinally weighty. The German reformers of the day did not mind singing songs that were not actually Scripture, but they were most often didactic. Considering the long dark night of doctrinal famine, this is not surprising. Luther believed that congregational songs could help educate the congregation. Perhaps for this reason it was uncommon for the German chorale to draw greatly on personal experience. The use of singular pronouns, *I* and *my,* was quite limited. Rather, as *A Mighty Fortress* demonstrates, the more typical use is plural, *we* and *our.* The effect is to have the entire congregation join in one confession rather than having individuals singing of their personal experiences.

Calvin's reforms to congregational participation exceeded Luther's in several areas. One of those was in the way the congregation participated through singing. Calvin believed that no text was appropriate for corporate worship unless the words came directly from Scripture. This was Calvin's strong reaction to the excesses of the Mass, which he described as *a vain theatrical show*[1]. While the text of the *Ordinary* was almost completely Scripture, much of the *Proper of the Mass* was not. Calvin objected to non-biblical texts, not because he necessarily disagreed with what they said; he believed that exclusively singing Scripture was the only safe way to maintain doctrinal integrity.

Ultimately, Calvin's influence became so widespread that many adopted the idea that nothing in corporate worship was appropriate unless the Scripture modeled or commanded it. This view, called the *regulative principle,* spread far beyond Calvin, even becoming part of the *Westminster Confession* (1646)*: But the acceptable way of worshiping the true God is instituted by himself, and so limited to his own revealed will, that he may not be worshiped according to the imaginations and devices of men, or the suggestions of Satan, under any visible representations or any other way not prescribed in the Holy Scripture.*[2]

This desire for a pure liturgy prompted the publication of many songbooks where the texts were all Scripture. The scriptures used were often from the book of Psalms. For this reason these songbooks were called *psalters*, although they sometimes included other Scripture passages as well. Through a process called versification, writers rephrased the scriptures in poetic meters. Early notable psalters included the *Geneva Psalter* (Huguenot) released in its full edition in 1560 and the *English Psalter*, commonly referred to as the *Sternhold and Hopkins Psalter*, first published in 1562 and bound with the *Common Book of Prayer*. It is notable that the restoration of Roman Catholicism in England, which began with the reign of Mary I in 1553, sent many reform-minded worshipers fleeing England. Many of these landed in Geneva and in Holland with other Reformed worshipers. It was in Geneva that English Psalm singing was strongly influenced by the French tradition. The *Sternhold and Hopkins* underwent multiple revisions and was widely used until the eighteenth century. The *Scottish Psalter* was published in 1564 and was closely patterned after the *Geneva Psalter*. Many others followed and, in a brief span of time, congregational singing of Psalms and Scripture exploded across Europe.

One might assume that these Psalters were like our hymn books, containing both words and music. This was not usually the case. Psalters of this period contained only the texts in a poetic or versified form. The poetic meter was indicated for each text and any melody that would fit that poetic meter could be used to sing that particular Psalm. For instance, 8.8.8.8. indicated that each verse of the poem had four lines of eight syllables. This hymn meter is known as LONG METER (L.M.). Perhaps the most famous example is the *Doxology* and first appeared in the English translation of the *Geneva Psalter* (1561).

---

[1]Jean Calvin and Henry Beveridge, *The Necessity of Reforming the Church* (Dallas, TX: Protestant Heritage Press, 1995), 31.

[2] Philip Schaff, *The Creeds of Christendom, With a History and Critical Notes, Volume III: The Evangelical Protestant Creeds, With Translations* (New York: Harper & Brothers, 1882), 646.

[8] *Praise God from whom all bless – ings flow,*

[8] *Praise Him all crea - tures here be – low,*

[8] *Praise Him a – bove, Ye heav'n – ly hosts,*

[8] *Praise Fa – ther, Son, and Ho – ly, Ghost.*

The most frequently used meter became 8.6.8.6, known as COMMON METER (C.M.). SHORT METER 6.6.8.6 (S.M.) also was used as well as doubled forms: LONG METER DOUBLE 8.8.8.8.| 8.8.8.8 (L.M.D.) and COMMON METER DOUBLE 8.6.8.6.| 8.6.8.6 (C.M.D.). This greatly enhanced the spread of congregational singing in the years following the Reformation. Rather than learn words associated with specific tunes, congregations could sing texts from the Psalter to any tune that matched its versified meter. It must have been quite an unusual sound to hear a well-known melody, whose origin was not within the Church, robustly sung with biblical text in the language of the people. Often the Psalters were released in subsequent editions, including paraphrase/prose versions of Psalms and original poetry. This illustrates the broad expansion that occurred in congregational singing in the years following the Reformation.

As for singing, Zwingli and Hubmaier took different paths and were among the most radical reformers. Like many Anabaptists, Hubmaier suffered great persecution. He was ultimately burned at the stake in Vienna (1528). Perhaps because of widespread persecution, the songs of the Anabaptists were often deeply personal and full of devotion. The first collection of these hymns was published in 1563, *Liedboeken van den Offer des Heeren*, and in each of its ten subsequent printings was always released with a volume describing the martyrdom of several Anabaptists.[1] While such songs of personal journey had predecessors in the fifteenth century Bohemian movement led by Jan Hus, they fully blossomed with the Anabaptists.

The congregational songs of the Anabaptists represented a much broader level of expression than those of their English or German counterparts. In addition to songs that were very personal in nature, the Anabaptists also utilized doctrinal songs like those of Luther and metrical Psalms like those of Calvin. With three separate genres from which to choose, a broad range of hymn singing flourished among these freeform worshipers. No less radical, but in contrast, Zwingli eschewed both instrumental and vocal music in corporate worship. This does not mean that he allowed none. He did use it sparingly. Zwingli, himself, was a trained and capable musician. Perhaps for that reason he understood the potential for music's abuse. Considering the history of the Church, his concerns were warranted.

---

[1] While the publication date of *Liedboeken van den Offer des Heeren* was signed as 1563, the publication date of the written accounts of the Anabaptists' sufferings that accompanied it, *Het Offer des Heeren*, was published in 1552. It contained letters from prison, poems, prayers, and eyewitness accounts surrounding the imprisonment and death of several Dutch Anabaptists.

While the reformers solved the issue of congregational singing differently, it is notable that they reached those conclusions from deeply held doctrinal beliefs. Just as Calvin's concern over non-biblical texts had pushed him further in reform than Luther, Zwingli's concerns about abuses of music led him to more radical measures than Calvin. Despite their differences, all of these reformers made provision for congregational participation. The common and important fact is that the congregation was again an integral partner in corporate worship. The degree to which the congregation participated was generally proportionate to the amount of structured liturgy. In some churches, this was singing; in some, reciting prayers or confessions together; in some, offering extemporaneous prayers; in some, participating in bringing a testimony or a word from Scripture; and in all, the intention for them to be active listeners to the sermon.

It is all too easy to take the role of the congregation for granted. For those who minister before people in corporate worship gatherings, we must never forget that we are not there to perform a sacerdotal worship for the people. This happens whenever our songs or our sermons become something for others to observe and not something in which to engage. God has mandated participation in corporate worship and we should do all in our power to see that it happens in the healthiest way possible. As important as it is for leaders to facilitate participation, the responsibility of those who gather is no less. They must make much of those opportunities. The lack of participation that developed in the post-Nicene era could never have happened without both leaders and followers choosing otherwise. Whether our method is structured or unstructured does not matter. Whether we are leading or following does not matter. We each share a common responsibility to participate in making His praise glorious.

THE MEANING AND FORM OF COMMUNION

Various Approaches to the Meaning of Communion
For many, the most notable change of the Reformation was the way various churches viewed and practiced Communion. The Catholic view of transubstantiation was essential in a belief system where the priest offered a sacrifice through the Bread and Cup. While only a portion of the reformers sought to eliminate all the ceremony of the Eucharist, most rejected the Roman idea that the priest offered a real propitiatory sacrifice during Mass. For the reformers, this created a dilemma. If the Elements of the Supper were not a sacrifice for sin, what were they? The reformers had a wide variety of answers to this question. The more conservative reformers were not willing to dispense with all mystery surrounding the Elements. While they were willing to reject the belief that the bread and wine transformed into the Body and Blood of Jesus, some still believed that Jesus made Himself materially present in the Bread and

the Cup. For our purposes we will refer to this view as that of *real presence.*[1] The most radical view was that the Elements were symbols, meant to remind the believer of the broken Body and shed Blood. In this view, the value was predominantly in remembering the sacrifice and is called the *memorial view.* Between *real presence* and the *memorial view* was *spiritual presence,* which espoused that the blessing in the Elements was not that Jesus was physically present, but spiritually present. Since each of these three took a unique doctrinal approach, they produced different forms of worship.

Real Presence

Among the reformers, Martin Luther was the most notable proponent of *real presence.* While he rejected the transubstantiation of Catholicism, he was unwilling to significantly reduce the importance of the Elements themselves. He defended his position on multiple occasions, perhaps most notably at the Marburg Colloquy.[2] Luther's position was broadly held by most German reformers. His colleague Phillip Melanchthon (1497-1560) clearly stated that the Bread and Cup contain the presence of Jesus.[3] While Luther held to the view of *real presence,* he rejected the view of sacrifice. Since Luther saw the death of Christ as a completed work, the significance of the Mass could not be in the Bread and Cup becoming a sacrifice. He believed that the benefit of Communion was in receiving the Body and the Blood through the Elements as a means of grace. For this reason, he could not lay aside the belief that Jesus was materially present in the Bread and the Cup. As a result, the services Luther designed for the Church at Wittenberg anticipated that believers would continue to take Communion weekly, since it was necessary for their spiritual well-being.

Thomas Cranmer's view is a bit more difficult to pinpoint. His theological writings and his entry into the ongoing debate about the nature of the Elements were much more limited than that of Luther. What he did write on the subject reveals his own struggle in defining his position. Cranmer rejected the transubstantiation of Catholicism and could not embrace the *memorial view* of radical reformers. Yet, when writing the liturgy in the *Common Book of Prayer,* he seemingly espoused both. In the prayers immediately preceding Communion, the priest prays two contradictory statements.

> WE doe not presume to come to this thy table (O mercifull Lorde) trustinge in our owne righteousnesse, but in thy manifolde and great mercies: we bee not worthye, so much as to gather up the crommes under thy table: but thou art the same Lorde whose propertie is

---

[1] We will use the term *real presence* rather than *consubstantiation* to describe the material presence of Jesus in the bread and the cup.

[2] At the Marburg Colloquy in 1529, an attempt to reconcile the dispute between Luther's view of *real presence* and Zwingli's *memorial* view failed.

[3] Leif Grane, John H. Rasmussen, *The Augsburg Confession: A Commentary* (Fortress Press, 1987), 113-114.

alwayes to have mercye: graunt us therfore (gracious lord) so to eate the fleshe of thy dere sonne Jesus Christe, and to drinke his bloud, that our synfulle bodyes maye be made cleane by his body, and our soules wasched through his most precious bloud, and that we may evermore dwel in him, and he in us. Amen.[1]

In the next paragraph the priest continues:

ALMIGHTY God oure heavenly father, whiche of thy tender mercye dyddest geve thine onely sonne Jesus Christ, to suffre death upon the crosse for our redempcion, who made there (by hys one oblacion of hymselfe once offered) a full, perfecte and sufficiente sacrifice, oblacion, and satisfaccion, for the synnes of the whole worlde, and dyd institute, and in hys holye Gospell commaund us to continue, a perpetuall memorye of that his precious death, untyll hys comynge agayne.[2]

These statements act as a counterbalance to each other: one declaring that taking the Elements is consuming the Body and Blood of Christ, the other, stating that the sacrifice has already been made complete and Communion is a 'perpetual memory' of His death. This dichotomy represents Cranmer's desire to move away from the concept of sacrifice and yet retain the concept of consuming Christ in the Eucharist. This places Cranmer more in line with Luther's theology than any of the other reformers. Therefore, for both Anglicans and Lutherans, the Lord's Supper remained an important component of weekly worship—necessary as a means of continually receiving grace.

Memorial View

The more radical reformers, like Zwingli and Hubmaier, rejected most of the mystery surrounding Communion. Instead, they saw the observance of the Supper as a memorial instituted by the Lord in which the Elements were symbols of Jesus' Body and Blood. Therefore, consuming them was not a means of receiving grace, but an act of obedience to Jesus' command to *remember Me*. Zwingli was the most prominent of the reformers to espouse this view. Zwingli began his journey much closer to Luther and Cranmer. As the Reformation unfolded, Zwingli continued to clarify his view. Perhaps concerned that retaining the mysticism of *real presence* would help maintain the power of the priesthood, Zwingli eventually dispensed with language that would indicate the real Body and Blood of Christ in the Elements.

---

[1] *The Book of Common Prayer*, 1552, The Society of Archbishop Justus, http://justus.anglican.org/resources/bcp/1552/Communion_1552.htm (accessed March 22, 2011).
   [2] Ibid.

This placed him in conflict with Luther to the point that some feared the division might undermine the progress of reform. In 1529 at Marburg, Zwingli and Luther met in an attempt to resolve the issue. Though Luther and Zwingli agreed on similar language, they both later clarified what they had meant and the conflict remained. In Zwingli's view, Luther placed too great an import on the consumption of Christ, whether completely transformed as the Catholics taught or only truly present as Luther believed. Zwingli described their difference as *two ways of salvation: the one by eating the flesh of Christ and the other by believing in him. He opposed the first as it made the atoning death of Christ unnecessary and would also restore the papacy and a religion of externals.*[1]

Spiritual Presence

Calvin provided a middle ground between Luther and Zwingli. Calvin's view focused much more on the spiritual union between God and the individual believer. Calvin believed that, as Communion occurred at the Table, there was a mystical fellowship that occurred in the spiritual realm between God and the individual. The Bread and Cup did not become or contain the physical presence of Jesus but, in a spiritual way, His presence accompanied the Elements and nourished the soul. For our purposes, we will refer to this view as *spiritual presence*. For Calvin, this made Communion an important element of corporate worship. The significance was not in any 'new grace' that was consumed by the worshiper. Instead, through the inward work of the Holy Spirit, a believer could experience close fellowship with God at the Table. Ultimately, since the significance of Communion was spiritual, it was not contingent on the Elements but on the work of the Holy Spirit. Calvin's view, distinct from that of Luther, was clear in his liturgy. [2] In the *Strassburg Liturgy* (1545), just before taking the Elements, the Minister's exhortation includes these words:

> Let us not be fascinated by these earthly and corruptible elements which we see with our eyes and touch with our hands, seeking Him as though He were enclosed in the bread and wine. Then only shall our souls be disposed to be nourished and vivified by His substance when they are lifted up above all earthly things, attaining to heaven, and entering the Kingdom of God where He dwells. Therefore let us be content to have the bread and wine as signs and witnesses, seeking the truth spiritually where the Word of God promises that we shall find it.

---

[1] W. Peter Stephens, *Zwingli: An Introduction to His Thought* (Clarendon Press, Oxford, 1992), 100.

[2] Calvin borrowed heavily from Martin Bucer's Strassburg Liturgy of 1539. Calvin's pastorates in Geneva and Strassburg produced multiple variations of his liturgy. For our purposes, when referring to Calvin's liturgy we will use the Strassburg version of 1545. See Bard Thompson, ed., *Liturgies of the Western Church.* (Philadelphia: Fortress, 1980), 207.

The Form of Communion

As the theology of the Eucharist changed, the form and frequency of Communion changed. Cranmer's plan for Communion retained a great deal of complexity. He borrowed heavily from the Roman ceremony creating the first edition of the *Common Book of Prayer* (1549). The revision of 1552 became the basis for the Anglican liturgy for centuries. While Cranmer rejected the concept that the priest was offering a sacrifice on behalf of the people, he still believed that weekly communion was essential for the spiritual life of the believer because it was an opportunity for them to ingest the Body and Blood of Jesus. Cranmer rejected sacerdotalism but could not let go of sacramentalism, believing that the Bread and the Cup contained the *real presence* of Jesus. Reformers who took this view typically understood the Supper as a means of grace: to take the physical Elements themselves was of spiritual value. This helps us to understand why there was very little structural difference between the Anglican and Catholic forms.

Luther was truly a reformer who rejected portions of Roman Catholic doctrine, rather than a rebel who sought separation from Rome. When he published his first Reformation liturgy, it was in Latin. The *Formula Missae* (1523) is a very conservative approach to reform. It was his initial attempt to reestablish the sermon and remove the mysticism surrounding Communion. When compared to the *Tridentine Mass*, Luther's appears almost identical. Luther did allow for portions of the Mass to be set aside for congregational singing but, the basic structure remained close to that of the Catholic Mass. This demonstrates Luther's belief that the form of the Mass was not past redeeming, a view he also held concerning the Roman Church. Because Luther's Latin Mass still fell short in accomplishing the goal of congregational participation, the *Deutsche Messe* was produced only three years later.

Luther was slow to abandon his hope for a purified Holy Catholic Church—Calvin had a different perspective. He had deep disdain for all Roman ceremony and symbols. Having stripped the Eucharist of these, he demonstrated his high regard for the power of the Scripture by giving the sermon the greatest significance in corporate worship. His *Strassburg Liturgy* revealed his priorities and as a result provided a balance between *kerygma*, *koinonia*, and *leitourgia*. Calvin celebrated Communion monthly in Strassburg. As a result, he prescribed corporate worship services both with and without Communion. He was one of the first leading reformers to do so. Calvin was by no means against celebrating the Supper. He celebrated it weekly during his pastorate in Zurich, believing the spiritual union between God and the worshiper at the Table was important. However, he also believed that the most essential element in advancing the work of the Holy Spirit in the believer's life was the Scripture.

Ulrich Zwingli held to the *memorial view*. He demonstrated his belief by simplifying the actual taking of the Elements. Even though his Communion liturgy maintained the use of texts from the *Gloria* and *Credo*, the latter part of the service was a radical departure from the Roman Canon. It is free and conversational. There is little fanfare. Zwingli instructed the servers to distribute

168

the bread to the congregation and for it to be passed from person to person on wooden plates. In a simple fashion, the observance followed the Pauline narrative in 1 Corinthians 11. As radical as that was, the frequency that Zwingli prescribed was the most radical among the major reformers. Zwingli specified that Communion be celebrated only four times each year. The rest of the Sunday services were devoted primarily to preaching.

Balthazar Hubmaier also influenced the more radical approach to Communion. Like Zwingli, he also subscribed to the *memorial view* of the Elements and prioritized preaching above Communion. While in Nikolsburg, Hubmaier published *A Form for Christ's Supper* (*Eine Form das Nachtmal Christi*). It likely came from his time in Waldshut where he became personally committed to Christ and introduced the Reformation in 1522.[1] An outline of that form is included later in this chapter. Rather than a strict liturgy, Hubmaier's service is a mixture of pastoral monologue and dialogue with the congregation. Significantly, he calls for the congregation to offer questions and/or comments prior to Communion and the opportunity for anyone to bring a prophetic word from Scripture. This illustrates how widely the door to congregational participation had opened for some in the Reformation.

The free approach of Zwingli and Hubmaier was visible in many worship forms of the following century, including Baptists, Moravians, Brethren, and Puritans. Many of these adopted the *memorial view* of the Supper. Even though the offshoots of the most radical branch of the Reformation may have dispensed with the idea of *real presence,* some continued to maintain regular weekly observances of the Supper. Since we can conclude that they were not doing this as a necessary means of grace or forgiveness, we may assume that the function was to experience something of the spiritual union between the believer and God.

Where post-Reformation ecclesiastical structures existed or developed and confessional statements followed, it is much easier to determine what the Reformed views of worship and the Eucharist were. In other words, between various branches of the Reformation there was not always a clear demarcation between the varied beliefs about the role of the Lord's Supper and corporate worship. This was a fluid time in which reformers vigorously debated with and borrowed from one another. It is important to state clearly that the primary difference between the various Reformed views was theological rather than liturgical. Where the Elements were seen as containing the actual presence of Jesus, the Eucharist maintained a near equal importance with preaching. Where a symbolic or *memorial view* of the Elements took root, preaching eclipsed Communion as the chief component of corporate worship.

These theological differences were the primary force in determining the worship form. Among the reformers, more complexity accompanied the view of *real presence* held by Luther and Cranmer. On the other hand, Calvin's view of

---

[1] William Roscoe Estep, *The Anabaptist Story: an Introduction to Sixteenth-century Anabaptism* (Grand Rapids, MI: William B. Eerdmans Pub., 1996), 80.

spiritual presence produced a much simpler form. Freeform worshipers, who almost universally took the *memorial view*, sometimes had no formal structure whatsoever. For the Roman Church, which retained the most mystical view of the Bread and the Cup, the Reformation prompted the Council of Trent (1545-1563), which galvanized the Catholic liturgy for another four hundred years.

The table, *Comparison of Reformation Forms*, found later in this chapter, allows us to compare the differences in structure that various theologies of Communion produced. When examining published forms from this period it is important to remember that they were in a state of flux. Except for the *Tridentine Mass*, which was published following the Council of Trent, all the other forms were frequently changed and adapted. Variants of these forms were published in the years preceding or following the date listed in the table.

Several observations from this comparison are important. First, the actual number of entries in the service was determined by the doctrine applied to Communion. As we have already mentioned, this had a practical bearing on how much time was available for preaching. The *Tridentine Mass* (far left) was a full one even without a sermon. Although Luther was committed to preaching, his first published service, *Formula Missae,* did little to solve the problem of creating room for the sermon. His commitment to congregational participation and to preaching is much more apparent in the *Deutsche Messe*. Like Luther's first offering, Cranmer desired to retain as much of the Mass as possible, creating a lengthy order of worship.

For Calvin, who was much less enthusiastic about retaining any of the Roman form, the *Strassburg Liturgy* provided time for both congregational participation and preaching. It is also important to note that fewer ingredients did not necessarily mean a shorter service. Both the *Strassburg Liturgy* and the *Deutsche Messe* included significant portions of robust singing and preaching. Calvin's sermons were typically about one hour and many times sermons were much longer than that.[1] Therefore, the services that appear simpler could have lasted as long, or even longer, than those that appeared more complex.

It is telling to examine what portions of the Mass were retained or discarded by the reformers. Calvin's order dispenses with all but one section of the *Ordinary* and there he uses the Apostles' Creed rather than the Nicene Creed. In so doing, he retains the function of a statement of faith prior to Communion. While he does not use the *Kyrie,* it is notable that he does provide a similar function by prescribing a confession of sins. From the *Proper*, there is also little remaining, primarily the Apostle Paul's narrative of the Supper from 1 Corinthians 11. This was consistent with his theological views that, beyond prayers and preaching, the service should consist primarily of Scripture.

Cranmer's theology and Luther's theology led them to a different approach. Of the five parts of the *Ordinary*, Cranmer retains and translates four: the *Kyrie, Credo, Sanctus* and *Gloria*. While he was conservative among

---

[1] *The Complete Library of Christian Worship, Volume II,* Robert E Webber, editor (Star Song, 1994), 198.

reformers, the way he used these demonstrates his innovation. He retained the concept of the *Kyrie* by combining a cry for mercy with a reading of the Ten Commandments. After each commandment was read, the congregation responded, *Lord, have mercye upon us, and encline our heartes to kepe thys lawe.* The *Credo* and *Sanctus* remained consistent in text, approximate location, and function in the service. Perhaps the most interesting innovation was Cranmer's placement of the *Gloria* at the end of the service. Apparently, he felt the celebratory nature of the *Gloria* was more appropriate following Communion, indicating the restoration and fellowship that had taken place between God and worshiper. This would have been consistent with his views of the importance and benefits of taking the Supper.

Luther's *Deutsche Messe* is less connected to the Catholic Mass than Cranmer's liturgy or his own *Formula Missae*. While Luther uses four parts of the *Ordinary* (*Kyrie, Credo, Sanctus*, and *Agnus Dei*), he lists two of them as optional, the *Sanctus* and the *Agnus Dei*. Luther permitted German hymns to be substituted for either or both of these. The fact that Luther omitted the *Gloria* in his 1526 edition does not mean that he would disallow it. The use of the *Gloria* in the Catholic Mass fluctuated depending on the season.[1] In subsequent years, the *Gloria* was used at Wittenberg and in other German churches as well. The two parts he prescribed, the *Kyrie* and *Credo,* maintained a cry for mercy and a pre-Communion statement of faith. At once this showed both his theological differences between and similarities to other reformers. All of the major Reformation forms provided a cry for mercy early in the service and all acknowledged the importance of a unified statement of faith prior to taking the Supper. To the reformers, these were important functions of corporate worship. The difference among reformers was evident in how much of the Mass they were willing to keep.

---

[1] See *The Fixed and Variable Parts of the Mass* in CHAPTER 7: ROMAN CATHOLIC WORSHIP.

A Comparison of Reformations Forms:

Tridentine Mass	Formula Missae, 1523	Holy Communion 1552 (Anglican)
Preparation and Confession		
Introit	Introit	Introit
KYRIE (9-fold)	KYRIE (9-fold)	Collect
GLORIA	GLORIA (optional)	Ten Commandments with LORD HAVE MERCY
Salutation and Collect	Collect	Collect
Gradual/Alleluia	Epistle	Epistle
Epistle	Gradual/Alleluia	Gospel
Munda cor meum and Gospel reading	Gospel	CREED
Homily (optional)	CREDO (Nicene)	Sermon or Homily
CREDO (Nicene)	Sermon	Tithes and offerings
Offertory and the Secret	Preparation of Elements	Collect
Preface	Preface	Exhortations
Sursum Corda (lift up your hearts)	Sursum Corda (lift up your hearts)	Lift up your hearts (Sursum Corda)
SANCTUS	Words of Institution	HOLY (SANCTUS)
Benedictus	SANCTUS	Words of Institution
Canon with words of institution	Benedictus	Communion (bread and wine)
The Lord's Prayer	The Lord's Prayer	The Lord's Prayer and prayer of the priest
Agnus Dei	Agnus Dei	GLORIA
Communion (priest)	Communion distribution	Words of Institution
Communion (congregation)	Post-Communion	Communion (bread and wine)
Post-Communion prayers	Collect	Benediction
Benedicamus	Benedicamus	
Last Gospel		

Deutsche Messe, 1526	Strassburg Liturgy, 1545
Hymn or German Psalm	Invocation
KYRIE (3-fold)	Confession of Sin
Collect	Scripture & Absolution
Epistle	Ten Commandments (sung)
German Hymn	Prayer for Illumination
Gospel	Scripture with Sermon
Wir glauben all an einen Gott (CREDO)	Pastoral Prayer (ending with the Lord's Prayer)
Sermon	Admonitions
The Lord's Prayer (adapted)	CREED (Apostles' Creed)
Admonition	Prayer of Dedication
Words of Institution	Scriptural Admonitions and Communion
Distribution (during the next two entries)	Psalm
Hymn or HEILIG (SANCTUS)	Prayer of Thanksgiving
Hymn or CHRISTE, DU LAMM GOTTES (AGNUS DEI)	Psalm
Collect	Aaronic Blessing (Numbers 6:24-26)
Aaronic Blessing (Numbers 6:24-26)	

Freeform Worship

Item-by-item comparisons are possible for traditions that published and maintained various orders of worship but, comparing freeform models is more difficult. The freeform style was the choice for the most radical reformers who rejected the control of both hierarchy and liturgy. *Freeform* did not mean *no form*. The truth is that all worshiping groups have some type of liturgy—a means to get from beginning to end. Those that chose the freeform approach resisted anyone outside of the local congregation prescribing a liturgy for them to follow. For this reason, it is probable that forms were very fluid among these congregations. Obviously, this complicates identifying templates used in freeform churches. Furthermore, many such worshipers often met in secret and at great peril, fearing persecution. The threat came not from Rome but mostly from fellow reformers. Prior to the Reformation, almost all Western European governments were obligated to some measure of subservience to Rome. As the Reformation took hold, government allegiances shifted away from Catholicism. Many governments became pro-Reformation, gaining a sense of independence from the threat of papal meddling. This greatly aided the spread of Reformed thought. However, this created local governments that were loyal to the particular brand of reform that had taken root in their community. At times these local governments frowned on other approaches to reform. As a result, many radical reformers found themselves on the run, not from the Roman Church but from civil magistrates. Some of Europe's leading reformers believed these radicals, many of them Anabaptists, could cause an irreparable schism in the Reformation that would destroy it. As a result, Anabaptists often suffered intense persecution at the hands of fellow Protestants. This pushed much of their worship practice underground, further complicating its study.

One of the written orders we do have for comparison is Hubmaier's *A Form for Christ's Supper* (1522) and it is included below. The record we have of this service is much more detailed than the one included. For purposes of analyzing the structure, longer segments have been condensed or paraphrased.

A Form for Christ's Supper[1]

(Condensed and Paraphrased)

    Confession and Repentance (kneeling)

    Proclamation of the Gospel (pastor)

    Questions and Words of Prophecy (congregation)

    Scripture Reading and Exhortation (blends into the next section)

    Self-Examination:

        that one is truly a believer

        that one is hungry to receive from the Lord

        that one is ready to give thanks and obedience

---

[1] See Webber, 216-224.

that one is ready to give his life for the faith
Pastoral Exhortation
Silent Meditation
The Lord's Prayer (Model Prayer)
Clarification of Bread and Wine as a memorial
Pre-Communion Confessional Dialogue (paraphrased and condensed below)

> Pastor: Will you... love others in Christ's power?
>
> Congregation: I will
>
> Pastor: Will you... be reconciled to all brothers and sisters?
>
> Congregation: I will.
>
> Pastor: Do you desire... to proclaim that this is a memorial of Jesus' death?
>
> Congregation: I desire it in God's power.
>
> Pastor: Then let us eat... Amen.

Communion
Bread
Cup
Closing Exhortation and Blessing

Whether or not this service was representative of others in the freeform movement is unknown, though several characteristics of this service are apparent in later forms of the seventeenth century. Above all, it appears that Hubmaier was most concerned that individuals had sufficiently heard, understood, and reflected on the meaning of the Lord's Supper prior to participating. Clearly, this service had little in common with the Mass and was very different from other Reformation liturgies.

Despite the obvious differences between the Reformation forms we listed in the comparison table and this one by Hubmaier, there are a few remarkable structural similarities. Hubmaier, like other reformers, retained a time for repentance and placed it early in the service. Additionally, Hubmaier, like all the reformers, retained a pre-Communion confession. Hubmaier did this without the Nicene or Apostles' Creed, instead using a series of pledges made by the worshiper. These pledges dealt with Christian actions and devotion rather than doctrine. It seems probable that Hubmaier intended for the fundamentals, those with which all approaching the Table should agree, to be clearly covered through proclaiming the gospel and preaching the Scripture. The question and answer time that followed was intended to clear up any remaining misconceptions. Therefore, instead of repeating a doctrinal statement before taking Communion, worshipers pledged to live out the faith in real actions. The pledge ended with a clear declaration that the Elements were only a memorial.

Many Evangelicals have a great aversion to fixed forms. Actually, fixed liturgies in themselves are neither good nor bad. The reformers did not change the fixed forms of Catholicism because they disliked liturgies. The majority of the reformers wrote new liturgies to replace the old ones, some of them expecting their new liturgies to be followed with the same exactness with which they had followed the Catholic Mass. Some of these Reformed liturgies have continued virtually unchanged for 500 years. Instead, they reformed the liturgy in order to reflect a Reformed theology. Their renewed attention to Scripture and subsequently to doctrine brought genuine worship renewal.

Those who have followed in the Protestant and evangelical tradition owe a great debt to these reformers. If we will listen to them, we can learn an important lesson. In an age of innovation and quick fixes, it is easy to think that changing a form or trying a new method can bring genuine worship renewal. This has led many churches searching for something that will bring genuine life to worship. For those who are looking for the way to revitalize worship, the reformers have already discovered it. Worship renewal comes from a renewed attention to Scripture and doctrine. When renewal comes, it does not look and sound the same everywhere. The Reformation produced a wide variety of forms and liturgies. That is what makes merely copying a form pointless.

This is good news for those tired of chasing some new method or hoping that some new wind will blow. The answer to renewal is already in the pages of Scripture. Our role as leaders is to go back to the Book and renew our own hearts. When this happens we can begin to address how our own methods and forms need to change. These types of transitions in a local church feed the hungry souls of our people because they address their most basic needs as defined by God in His Word. When Scripture takes root in the heart of the worshiper, renewal comes. Earlier we quoted the *Strassburg Liturgy*. Calvin's words ring just as true concerning form: *Let us not be fascinated by these earthly and corruptible elements which we see with our eyes and touch with our hands...* [Instead, let these things be] *signs and witnesses, seeking the truth spiritually where the Word of God promises that we shall find it.* This has been and remains the key to genuine worship renewal in the Church today.

CHAPTER 8

WORSHIP IN THE COLONIAL
AND POST-COLONIAL ERA
(AD 1600-1800)

By the middle of the seventeenth century, much of Europe had settled on which, if any, of the Reformation forms to follow. In some places this issue was settled fairly quickly but, in many parts of Europe the decision on which form of worship to use was resolved only through political and military conflict. England, which under changing monarchs had been both Reformed and Roman Catholic, finally settled on a very conservative variety of the Reformation. For England, this was not the end of post-Reformation conflict. Many felt that the Reformation had not gone far enough. English dissenters, like Puritans, Baptists, and Congregationalists, believed that The Common Book of Prayer had maintained far too much Catholic ceremonialism. These sought a path more along the lines of those who had followed Calvin in Scotland. During the first half of the seventeenth century, political oppression and even persecution of dissenters in England continued to increase. This created a strong undercurrent of spiritual and political unrest. Eventually, under the leadership of Oliver Cromwell, dissenters gained the majority in Parliament (1649) and created the English Commonwealth. Predictably, the years of the Commonwealth granted worshipers much greater liberty to practice and develop forms outside of the Anglican Liturgy. When the monarchy was restored to Charles II in 1661, those who had resisted the Anglican Church, and therefore the Crown, were expelled or prosecuted in large numbers. All of this made the British Isles a Reformation patchwork: Ireland was primarily Catholic; Scotland had taken the Reformed course of Calvin. All other areas were officially Anglican, although filled with Puritans and other dissenters.

On the mainland of Europe, another serious conflict was underway that would determine how the Reformation would be accepted or rejected. What began as a conflict between Catholicism and the reformers, particularly Lutherans, served as a pretext for the Thirty Years War (1618-1648). The driving force behind much of this conflict was not religion but the disputes between Europe's many monarchies and princes, including the religious monarchy that was the papacy. The story of this war, its strange alliances and its devastating effects on the population, is beyond the scope of our discussion. It is important to us because, as the political map of Europe took its shape, so did the shape of its religious practice. The war ended in 1648 with the Peace of Westphalia. Almost every major European power (except England) became a partner to this treaty. It established that the first allegiance of a region, including its religious practices, would be determined by the regional authority. This authority was usually a prince or monarch, thus limiting the political power of the papacy. This preceded and contributed to the rise of nationalism and resulted in a political map bearing the divisions that followed the Reformation.

The mainland of Europe was divided between Catholics, primarily to the south and west, and Lutherans or Calvinists to the north and east. Further to the east, Russia remained essentially unaltered by the Reformation since it had followed the liturgy of the Orthodox Church rather than the Roman Catholic Church.[1] Such an atmosphere of religious and political unrest, combined with the development and colonization of the New World, served to shape how generations would worship.

A near global move toward Western colonization burgeoned during the seventeenth and eighteenth centuries. For some, participation in the push to colonize came inadvertently as they fled their homeland, seeking to practice a form of worship other than the one sanctioned by their government. Others participated intentionally as colonists, and the governments which sponsored them, sought economic advancement by staking claims in new territories. In either case, worshipers took their worship styles with them. Therefore, the religious/political reshuffling in Europe and the race to colonize the New World played a significant role in determining how various worship styles took root in places where colonization occurred.

---

[1] For more detailed information on how the Reformation changed the map of Europe, see Hans Joachim Hillerbrand, ed. *The Oxford Encyclopedia of the Reformation*, Vol. 4 (New York: Oxford University Press, 1996), 332.

This era of colonization is significant for our study on worship because it represented the second major geographic expansion of Christianity. The first began at Pentecost and continued for almost three centuries: the expansion of Christianity from Jerusalem to the far reaches of the Roman Empire. Through colonization, Christianity spread from Europe to North and South America, encircled the continent of Africa, and eventually affected much of the Orient. This geographic expansion differed from that of the Early Church in two important ways. First, this expansion was not purely missional, in that it was not initially undertaken to spread the gospel. Second, during colonization a wide range of already developed worship forms, both liturgical and non-liturgical, accompanied the spread of Christianity. This difference was significant. During the first great expansion of Christianity, liturgies were still very fluid and generally developed in a region after the core message of the gospel had taken root. In other words, the principle truth arrived *first* and forms developed within the culture *after* the gospel had been accepted.

Since both the gospel and established forms were delivered simultaneously, colonization presents an opportunity to look at worship from a different perspective. Our study of early Christian worship reveals an initial period of health and growth, lasting until the fourth century, followed by decline and a long period of stagnation. The Reformation ushered in a new period of vibrancy. The spiritual malaise that permeated Europe for centuries doubtless occurred in concert with a decline in biblical theology—one which the Reformation sought to correct. Based only on the portions of worship history we have already studied, we could attribute that decline entirely to a Roman liturgy that became theologically aberrant. However, would that be the complete story? If the Catholic liturgy had been one that we considered doctrinally pure, would that difference have insulated worship from the decline that occurred in the centuries prior to the Reformation? By studying post-Reformation worship history, we can see whether or not having a doctrinally correct liturgy ensures that worship will remain vibrant. Furthermore, this will help us determine whether or not doctrinally pure forms remain vibrant by nature, after those who established them have passed them on to others.

Whatever our preferred form is today, we can likely find one among those of the reformers that would meet our own theological standards, one that we would consider doctrinally pure. The Colonial movement represented the export and establishment of many post-Reformation worship forms. Did any of these forms remain vibrant based solely on the fact that they were doctrinally pure? The answer could be found by studying how post-Reformation liturgies fared after they were exported on a global scale. However, examples in North America will be sufficient to demonstrate that even doctrinally pure forms eventually become spiritually stagnant unless they are constantly refilled with meaning.

LESSON 11: THE BENEFIT OF SOUND WORSHIP DOCTRINE LASTS ONLY IF IT IS CONSTANTLY RENEWED

BACKGROUND

Just as the Reformation had repainted the religious map of Europe, the broad strokes of colonization repainted the map of the world. From a perspective of worship, colonization reflected the outcome of the Reformation: allegiance to the old or alliance with the new. Those who struggled to find a place to practice their faith saw the New World as a place to worship in accordance with their conscience. Some of the first settlements in what would become the United States were established by freeform worshipers along the New England coast. These included Dutch, German, and English dissenters. From the mid-Atlantic northward, they established communities in which they could practice their own Reformation styles of worship. Settlements along the middle and southern Atlantic coastal region, distinctly sponsored and supported by the British, were established as Anglican communities.

Reformed worshipers were not the only ones who exported their worship styles. Where countries that had remained committed to Catholicism established settlements, they brought with them the Roman liturgy. In North America, Spanish settlers brought Catholicism to the Florida Peninsula and present-day Mexico, eventually pushing northward to the desert southwest and Pacific coast. Catholicism also accompanied the French settlements in the northern part of the continent as well as in the Mississippi Delta region.

In most cases, the post-Reformation styles that came to the New World were less than 100 years old. The desire to practice them freely was strong enough to drive men and women from their homeland to the New World. Generally, the colonists were more committed to the theological principles that propelled the Reformation than were those whom they left behind on the shores of Europe.[1] However, the spiritual vibrancy with which the settlers landed did not last long. In the span of 100 years, much of the passion was gone. The deep commitment to corporate worship, a commitment that prompted worshipers to leave homelands for the freedom to practice it, had ebbed away. This left the colonies in need of spiritual breath, which came through the revival of the First Great Awakening. This period of worship history is best understood in three phases: a period of impassioned **establishment, decline,** and **renewal**. Through these phases we will see that a doctrinally pure form will decline unless it is renewed. We will also see that a good form can be useful again if the heart of the worshiper is re-engaged.

---

[1] Mark A. Knoll, *America's God: From Jonathan Edwards to Abraham Lincoln* (New York: Oxford University Press, 2002), 20.

Reflecting the austerity of the settlers, Colonial worship, whether freeform or liturgical, was initially very basic. The first permanent settlement on the east coast was on the Florida peninsula, located near present day St. Augustine (1565). Like all of the settlements established by the Spanish, it was Catholic. Early Catholic missions brought only the most basic components of the liturgy and lacked much of the ornate accoutrements familiar in Europe. The first Reformation worshipers to settle in North America came to Jamestown (1607) and brought with them the Anglican form. While they practiced Anglican worship in form, these settlers initially resisted attempts to fall under the control of the Anglican Church in England. Subsequently, England placed the whole Virginia colony under the authority of the Anglican Church (1624) and enacted laws requiring conformity to the Anglican liturgy. These laws were specifically designed to diminish the influences of the Puritans, Quakers, Baptists, and Congregationalists.[1]

The Anglican Church also sought control over worship forms in the other English colonies established to the south. This scenario was repeated from present day Maryland to south Georgia, making the Anglican form the most prominent in the new colonies. There were exceptions to the Anglican form. The English allowed several communities of Lutherans and Huguenots into rural areas of the southern Atlantic region. The first Baptist congregation was not established in the south until late in the seventeenth century.[2]

One might have assumed that Anglican worship could and would become the dominant style for the New World, especially considering the English business interests that stretched from the mid-Atlantic southward. However, this was not to be the case. The fertile and open land from Virginia to the Florida peninsula was suitable for cultivation. In order to manage agricultural production, the British divided the land into large tracts, leaving the south sparsely populated and primarily rural. In these rural areas, the Anglican form was conducted with some variance because colonists in the southern Atlantic region were generally isolated from each other. This made it rare for them to share songs or any innovations that developed within their communities. Because populations were dispersed, larger cities were slower to form. Charleston was one of the only thriving cities in this region through the end of the seventeenth century. As cities eventually developed along the mid-Atlantic coast, the largest churches were most often Anglican. These congregations

---

[1] Nancy Koester, *Fortress Introduction to the History of Christianity in the United States* (Minneapolis: Augsburg Fortress, 2007) ,11.
[2] The First Baptist Church of Charleston, South Carolina, was founded in Kittery, Maine, in 1682 and relocated to Charleston in the mid-1690s.

tended to follow the English liturgy much more closely than those who lived in rural areas.[1]

If one were to map the worship forms of the thirteen colonies, the Anglican form would have appeared as the most prominent. This remained unchanged until the American Revolution. By the time population numbers were on the rise in the eighteenth century, so was the distaste for English oversight. The American Revolution ultimately was the determining factor in minimizing Anglican worship in the New World, particularly in the south, and opening it fully to freeform worship.

New England presented a different scenario. The majority of settlers in this region, unlike those who came to develop business interests in the south, came to the New World either to protest the Anglican form or to flee persecution by the government that sanctioned it. Some of the earliest objections to the Anglican liturgy had been its length and ceremony, leaving little time for emphasis on preaching or congregational participation. New England congregations all took a similar approach in addressing this concern. While there were variations in form, they all chose to use their freedom to create worship services in which preaching was a central component and congregational participation was valued. The Puritan service, which became the basis for later Congregational services, typically began with Psalm singing and prayers—both congregational and extended pastoral prayers. The remainder of the service was given to preaching. These sermons were often long, as much as an hour or more, and were usually a systematic study of a scriptural text.[2]

The first New England settlement was established at Plymouth Harbor in 1620 by English who had separated themselves from the Anglican Church. Prior to coming to the New World, they had fled to Holland, escaping the religious persecution that occurred when the Commonwealth ended and the monarchy was restored. There, they found kindred spirits among the Dutch Reformed worshipers who had embraced much of Calvin's practice. They generally shared Calvin's doctrines as well, although they would eventually reject the Presbyterian ecclesiology. Instead, they chose to have autonomous congregations. For this reason, they share a common heritage with Congregationalists as well as Baptists. They had freedom to worship freely but, they desired more. These colonists desired to establish their own communities and their own distinct homeland. This made them Pilgrims in the fullest sense. Their worship forms, like the forms of Zwingli and Hubmaier, followed a simple liturgy.

---

[1] Ruth Mack Wilson, *Anglican Chant and Chanting in England, Scotland, and America, 1660 to 1820* (Oxford: Clarendon Press, 1996), 221.

[2] Sermons in the Puritan tradition were usually exegetical, that is, taking a primary text and teaching from it, distilling the doctrine taught and its application to the life of the hearer. The listener often took detailed notes, which reveal that the structure of the sermons were quite methodical. Alden T. Vaughan, ed., *The Puritan Tradition in America: 1620-1730* (New York: Harper & Row, 1972), 82 & ff.

Opening Prayer

Psalm singing

Prayer—specifically for enlightenment during the message

Sermon

Psalm singing

Closing prayer

Singing was a key component of congregational participation and, like the tradition that had developed among Calvin and his followers, leaned heavily on the use of metrical Psalms. When these worshipers left for the New World, they brought their Psalm books with them. For those who landed at Plymouth, they carried the *Ainsworth Psalter* (1612), published by Henry Ainsworth in Holland. The *Ainsworth Psalter* contained both prose and metrical versions of the Psalms.[1] Like most of the early Psalters and hymnbooks, there were no pages containing both words and music together. Rather, as we discussed in the previous chapter, the Psalms were reworded to have a poetic meter and sung to well-known tunes. Evidently, congregational participation among these worshipers was robust. The tunes used by the Pilgrims were typically neither stiff nor overly sober. *In these, as in other early tunes generally, there almost certainly ran originally a sustained vivacity, variety and vigor akin to* [an early twentieth century] *glee or party song.*[2]

Further to the north, the Massachusetts Bay Colony was established in 1628 by Puritans. The Puritan worship style also developed among English dissenters.[3] It should be noted that, unlike the Pilgrims, the Puritans did not oppose the Anglican Church. They opposed what they perceived as the presence of Catholicism within the Anglican Church. Puritans claimed to be part of the Anglican Church, practicing the faith in a purified form (thus the name they carried). Similar to the Plymouth Harbor Pilgrims, these Puritan worshipers utilized a simple order of worship that included the same basic components. Even though they considered themselves part of the Anglican Church, they had much more in common with the worship practices of the Pilgrims. This demonstrates how closely they were influenced by Calvinists in Europe, those on the mainland as well as those in Scotland, adopting much of their practice and

---

[1] Ainsworth's approach was unique and, at times, did not follow the common metrical forms. See Richard Alfred Muller, *After Calvin: Studies in the Development of a Theological Tradition* (Oxford: Oxford University Press, 2003), 162-163.

[2] Waldo Selden Pratt, *The Music of the Pilgrims: A Description of the Psalm-book brought to Plymouth in 1620* (Boston: Oliver Ditson Company, 1921), 16.

[3] For a good summary of Puritan worship, see Hughes Oliphant Old, *The Reading and Preaching of the Scriptures in the Worship of the Christian Church*, vol. V (Grand Rapids: W.B. Eerdmans, 1998), 170 & ff.

doctrine.[1] Puritan services were often lengthy, three to four hours, with a significant amount of time devoted to prayer and singing.

Typical order of Puritan Worship in Colonial America:[2]
Opening Prayer (10-15 min)
Scripture Reading (5-10 min)
Psalm Singing (20-30 min)
Sermon (60-90 min)
Psalm Singing (20-30 min)
Closing Prayer (60 min)
Blessing (5 min)

The popular Psalter for this colony became the *Bay Psalm Book* (1640), which replaced the *Ainsworth* as the one most widely used in the early colonies. Most likely printed under the guidance of Richard Mather, the *Bay Psalm Book* was historically significant as the first book of any type printed in the original Thirteen Colonies. The poetry of the *Bay Book* was awkward and simple, lacking the poetic flow found in other psalters. For example, the most popular English Psalter of the day was *The Whole Book of the Psalms*, published in its first full version in 1562 and referred to as the *Sternhold and Hopkins*. When comparing texts from the *Bay Book* and the *Sternhold and Hopkins*, the unique approach of the *Bay Book* is apparent. For the *Bay Book*, the primary purpose was not to create beautiful verse, but a metrical version of the text that followed the English Bible as closely as possible. By comparing passages from both the *Sternhold* and the *Bay Book*, the more straightforward and less poetic rendering of the latter is apparent. The text of the *Twenty-Third Psalm* from both is included below. The similarities between the *Bay Book* and the *Authorized Version* of the Bible (1611) are apparent. Conversely, the *Sternhold* takes much greater liberty with the biblical text in order to create more fluid poetry. Both are based on Common Meter, 8.6.8.6.

Bay Book Psalms	*Sternhold and Hopkins*
The Lord to me a shepherd is,	*My Shepherd is the living Lord,*
Want therefore shall not I.	*nothing therefore I need;*
He in the folds of tender-grass	*In pastures fair near pleasant streams,*
Doth cause me down to lie:	*he setteth me for to feed:*

---

[1] They also adopted the ecclesiology of the Calvinists, choosing to employ elder authority rather than congregationalism.

[2] Times are estimated based on contemporaneous writings. Closing prayers could go as long as two hours. See Jon Butler, Grant Wacker, Randall Balmer, Randall Herbert Balmer, *Religion in American Life: A Short History* (Oxford: Oxford University Press, 2008), 54.

To waters calm me gently leads	He shall convert and glad my soul,
Restores my soul doth he:	and bring my mind in frame:
He doth in paths of righteousness:	To walk in paths of righteousness,
For his names sake lead me.	for his most holy Name.

Yea though in the valley of death's shade	Yea tho' I walk in vale of death,
I walk, none ill I'll fear:	yet will I fear none ill:
Because thou art with me, thy rod,	thy rod and staff do comfort me,
And staff my comfort are.	and thou art with me still.

For me a table thou hast spread,	And in the presence of my foes:
In presence of my foes:	my table thou shalt spread:
Thou dost anoint my head with oil,	Thou wilt fill full my cup, and thou
My cup it over-flows.	anointed hast my head.

Goodness & mercy surely shall	Thro' all my life thy favour is,
All my days follow me:	so frankly shew'd to me:
And in the Lords house I shall dwell	That in thy house for evermore,
so long as days shall be.[1]	my dwelling-place shall be.[2]

During this period of establishment, theological differences between Puritans and Pilgrims that would affect worship were insignificant. There were differences among New England churches, e.g., the Pilgrims took the congregational approach to ecclesiology. Nevertheless, New England achieved a stylistic uniformity in worship because most all congregations held a common commitment to the Ministry of the Word and based congregational singing primarily on the Psalms. The greatest variation among these worshipers was how they handled the frequency of Communion. The Congregationalists tended to celebrate Communion weekly, while Puritan congregations typically did not. Even with this difference, the influence of Calvin was apparent in both. Puritans and Congregationalists tended to adopt the *Spiritual Presence* view of the Bread and Cup.

Between the New England and Southern Colonies, the Middle Colonies were settled by many Dutch Reformed and pietistic German worshipers. Like their English neighbors to the north, these worshipers came to the New World to practice their faith freely. The Dutch began seeking a place for a permanent settlement along the Hudson River in 1617, finally establishing New Amsterdam on present day Manhattan Island in 1624. Similarly, many German worshipers settled in what is now Delaware and Pennsylvania. The first settlement of Germans in the New World was established just north of present day Philadelphia in 1683 in the Pennsylvania District.

Unlike other European countries, Germany never officially settled a colony in North America. Settlers who came from Germany did so primarily for two

---

[1] *The Bay Psalm Book: a Facsimile Reprint of the First Edition of 1640* (Chicago: University of Chicago Press, 1956), n.p.

[2] Sternhold, Thomas, and John Hopkins. "Facsimile: Metrical Psalms - Sternhold and Hopkins (1720 Edition)." Digital image. Gallery Music. http://psalmody.co.uk/library/OV1720.html (accessed December 19, 2010).

reasons. The first was to escape religious persecution and the second was to escape the devastation of the *Thirty Years War* (1618-1648). As the Lutheran form became the one sanctioned among many German Christians, persecution increased toward freeform worshipers. Additional pressure was applied to them from the Holy Roman Empire which sought to return rebellious portions of Europe to a counter-reformed and resolute Catholicism. For German-speaking Christians who were committed to the Reformation but did not want to practice the Lutheran form of worship, the New World presented the hope of free religious expression.[1] When they arrived along the Atlantic coast, they found themselves in colonies either under the control of the Anglican Church or worshiping in Dutch services in the Middle Colonies. Rather than live in turmoil with the English over worship styles or worship in a language not their own, many of these colonists pushed to the west of the frontier. This created a natural flow of German settlers into the Pennsylvania District. There they separated themselves from the influence and control of English colonists and established communities that preserved their language, customs, and worship styles.[2]

Dissenters were not the only Germans who made their way to the New World. The ravages of the *Thirty Years War* were by any standards, ancient or modern, severe. The conflict went far beyond that which existed between the German Lutherans and the Roman Catholic Church. In fact, other religious sects may have fared even worse since both Lutherans and Catholics bitterly persecuted freeform worshipers such as Quakers, Moravians, and Anabaptists. The devastation of war made normal civil life nearly impossible in many parts of Germany. Often villages were forced to keep constant vigil and be ready to flee invasion at a moment's notice. Everyday necessities were scarce, devastated by mercenaries who waged war for various sides. This bolstered the attraction of the New World, not only for those who sought a place to worship freely, but also for those who wanted to escape widespread poverty and destruction.

Since the first wave of German immigrants in the seventeenth century were dissenters, their worship style had a great deal in common with colonists in New England. Their services were primarily Word-centered and congregational participation was important. They utilized both Psalm singing and, at times, drew upon the German tradition of chorale singing. The success of those establishing a place to worship in the style, language, and customs of their choosing eventually brought the second wave of German settlers to the New World in the eighteenth century. Many of these were practicing Lutherans, who chose not to follow their freeform predecessors into Pennsylvania. Instead, many turned southward, following the eastern rim of the Appalachian Mountains into Virginia and the Carolinas, forming some of the earliest Lutheran Synods on the

---

[1] Nelson, Clifford E., *Lutherans in North America* (Minneapolis, Minnesota, 1980), 21.

[2] The worshipers were known as the Pennsylvania *Deutsch*. This term was eventually Anglicized to *Dutch*. Vestiges of the culture, language, and worship practice among these settlers remain today among the Pennsylvania Dutch.

east coast. These types of migrations continued to bring unique language, cultural practices, and worship forms to America.[1]

It is noteworthy that the non-liturgical forms, developed after the Reformation, took deepest and most permanent root in the New World. There they flourished and, in their vibrancy, far outlasted much of the Reformed tradition on the mainland of Europe. During the Colonial period, from Georgia to Maine, nearly every congregation worshiped in forms born out of the Reformation.[2] Because many settlers came to the New World to practice their faith freely, worship and spiritual health were given great attention. Among the first structures raised in any community was a house of worship. This structure was the spiritual and social center of the community, creating a tight bond between these settlers in both civil and religious matters. This bond was strengthened by the common foe of hardship. The New World was a harsh place where annual mortality rates of around 20% were not uncommon. Furthermore, difficulties, such as disease and famine, were often viewed in terms of God's remedial judgments.[3] The Colonists

> themselves were deeply troubled by the existence of personal sin in their own lives and by the presence of unconfessed corporate sins in the churches and in the nation. They regarded natural calamities as manifestations of the displeasure of God Almighty against sin and allowed such events as earthquakes, fires, volcanoes, epidemics, floods, and droughts to prompt them to special seeking of God's face in fasting, prayer, and corporate repentance.[4]

The concept of corporate repentance shaped both sermons and services. Even hardship became something for the people to work through together, enhancing a collective sense of identity. Such a perspective strengthened the connection among like-minded believers and, in many cases, furthered the spiritual resolve which had led them to leave Europe.

The shared commitment to Word-centered and participatory worship played a key role in making the first century of colonization one of great spiritual vibrancy. The backbone of this spiritual vibrancy stretched from the

---

[1] Like the Germans who came with the intent to preserve their culture and worship style, Moravians also came to the New World. The first Moravian attempt to settle was in Georgia in 1735. That attempt failed, but was followed by successful attempts in the Pennsylvania District beginning in 1741.

[2] The only notable exception to this was the first English-speaking Catholic settlement founded around 1634 near the mouth of the Potomac along the Chesapeake Bay.

[3] This was often spoken of in sermons and writings of the New England pastors. For an example, see Increase Mather, *Doctrine of Divine Providence Opened and Applied: Also Sundry Sermons on Several Other Subjects* (Whitefish, MT: Kessinger Publishing, 2003), 84.

[4] Richard Owen Roberts, *Sanctify the Congregation: A Call to the Solemn Assembly and to Corporate Repentance* (International Awakening Press, 1994), 7.

Middle Colonies to New England, serving as an incubator for American democracy. Here the concepts of Puritanism, Congregationalism, and Calvin's Doctrines of Grace melted into one substance that greatly defined who these settlers were and what the United States would become. By the time of the American Revolution, over 75% of inhabitants in the New World had grown up with significant Puritan influence and half of the remaining ones had other roots in European Calvinism.[1] They shared both theology and practice, creating a sense of homogeneity and, therefore, identity that would fan the flames of a cooperative revolution. This collective spirituality, combined with the desire to establish the New World as a sustainable homeland, made the seventeenth century a Christian highpoint in American history.

DECLINE

By the beginning of the eighteenth century, many of the worst hardships of colonization had passed. To be sure, there were difficulties that remained. However, working from established colonies, growing cities, a developing commerce, and trade with Europe, life on the east coast was much more welcoming than the first or second generation of settlers had found it. Almost as quickly as the colonies were well established, a general spiritual decline ensued. We will briefly discuss some of the factors that contributed to the spiritual decline in the New World. The deep need for spiritual awakening in the settlers was noted by those who led the Great Awakening. They often pointed out how settlers of the eighteenth century no longer carried the passion of those who originally left all to come and worship freely in the New World. For our purposes, it is important to understand that what was born in spiritual vibrancy did not remain that way and was found in need of genuine renewal. Of the many factors that contributed to the decline of healthy worship, we will look briefly at three: Quaker libertarianism, New England legalism, and a general prosperity that touched almost all of the colonies.

Libertarianism

One of the contributing factors to the loss of spiritual vibrancy in worship came quite inadvertently. In the Middle Colonies, particularly in the Pennsylvania District where Quakers had the strongest influence, religious freedom meant a benevolent tolerance of all Christian faiths. Known as the *Holy Experiment* by William Penn, its primary proponent, Pennsylvania was a place that sought to accept all who embraced Christianity regardless of customs or practices. Acceptance among Quakers of various faith expressions was not undertaken without conflict which, at times, *resulted in political rancor and turmoil.*[2] Even so, the pervasive spirit was toleration. As new settlers arrived,

---

[1] James Reichley, *Faith in Politics* (Washington, D.C.: Brookings Institution Press, 2002), 54.

[2] Frank Lambert, *The Founding Fathers and the Place of Religion in America* (Princeton, NJ: Princeton University Press, 2003), 112.

they were welcomed and encouraged to practice their own faith according to the dictates of their consciences. Toleration was not new with the Quakers. It was a hallmark of Moravians and Anabaptists in Europe following the Reformation. However, the Quaker influence was unique because of their belief that worship was an internal, spiritual matter and did not necessarily or systematically express itself in corporate worship.

The form of Quaker worship itself was one of systematic introspection rather than any definable order. This made corporate worship among Quakers the most austere among freeform worshipers. Quaker worship developed in England in the seventeenth century and, having rejected formalism in Anglican worship, went even further, eschewing all forms, even those of freeform worshipers. To Quakers, worship occurred between man and God in the spirit only. For this reason, planning a worship service in advance was problematic. Quakers did assemble weekly for worship, however, those gatherings were characterized by long periods of silence, as individual worshipers sought to commune with God. A spoken word of exhortation, a Scripture, or a public prayer could be shared with the congregation. By allowing for this type of freedom, neither the silence that characterized much of Quaker worship nor those things which broke the silence were prescribed.

Whereas, in New England congregational worship sparked discussion and sharing among various congregations, the Quakers in the Pennsylvania District took a different approach. Quaker worship itself was an inner-personal experience and its practice was not intended to be shared with others outside of the faith community. This curtailed the zeal to spread the Quaker faith and inhibited its cross-pollination with other worship styles. As the population grew in the Pennsylvania District so did the belief that one's faith practice was not a matter for public display. Understandably, Quakerism was strongest during the years of its early growth. By the eighteenth century its decline became apparent:

> The passionate outreach that swiftly swelled [the Quaker] ranks in the seventeenth century had now cooled, and while there was a widespread movement of visiting in the ministry that welcomed and often drew in seeking strangers, the Quakers were largely dependent on heredity, on the allegiance of their own children, for their continuance.[1]

As a result, corporate worship was significantly weakened in areas where Quaker influence was strong. When the spread of Quakerism cooled, what remained was an understanding that the means by which individuals worshiped was a private matter and therefore it was not necessarily shared nor meant to be formally practiced with others. This type of libertarianism espoused an attitude of *Do whatever works best for you—just don't tell me about it.* This had the effect of privatizing worship in the Pennsylvania District, valuing the individual

---

[1] Douglas V. Steere, *Quaker Spirituality: Selected Writings* (New York: Paulist Press, 1984), 50.

experience to the exclusion of the shared experience. Although the concepts of individual freedom and religious toleration were important in the development of American democracy, they ultimately had an adverse effect when applied to corporate worship, undermining its significance.

Legalism

To the north, religious freedom was also a driving force, though how the concept of that freedom was understood and applied was quite different. To the Puritans and Congregationalists that settled in New England, religious freedom meant freedom *from* faith practices that they considered erroneous, namely those from the Catholic and Anglican Church. A deep desire for purity in the approach to worship led these settlers to enact civil laws that demanded adherence to Sunday worship practices. In many cases, failure to follow the liturgy approved by the civil government could result in significant consequences. For instance, all settlers were required to practice Sunday worship and to do so in the Puritan form. This not only included the worship service itself but also a very strict sabbatarianism. Penalties for not following these laws ranged from fines to death.[1] Local laws also prohibited Anglicans from building churches or practicing their faith in the New England colony.[2] As a reaction to this, England revoked the charter of the New England colony and enacted a new one that provided for freedom of expression within the bounds of the Christian faith. What had been a worship style born in the freedom of the Reformation came to be practiced in a very strict legalism.

We should not overlook the irony that those who came to the New World for the purpose of freely worshiping subsequently enact laws requiring a specific faith practice. Nor should we overlook what this tells us about spiritual vibrancy at the time. Except for the Quakers, the actual variance of practices among freeform worshipers during the Colonial era was miniscule. However, suspicion and a Puritan zeal for a pure form leveraged those differences to the point of division. *By the mid-eighteenth century, Catholic and Anglican liturgies would still stoke the older Puritan polemic, but most on-the-ground battles were fought now over evangelical styles of worship.*[3] Therefore, even among like-minded groups that existed in New England, such as Presbyterians and Baptists, cooperation was difficult. It was difficult, not because they disagreed over key doctrinal issues, but because there was a pervasive resistance to anything not practiced by the sects located in New England. For this reason, many New

---

[1] Between 1659 and 1661, four Quakers were hanged in the square in Boston for failing to conform.

[2] Steere, 98.

[3] Edwin S. Gaustad and Leigh Eric. Schmidt, *The Religious History of America: the Heart of the American Story from Colonial Times to Today* (New York, NY: Harper One, 2004), 62.

England dissenters collected in Rhode Island, where there was both tolerance and active outward expression of Christian worship.[1]

Previous history taught us that worship styles cannot successfully be standardized unless there is a standardized culture. The twist in this story is that culture among most colonists *was* shared and therefore the fact that they shared worship styles was not a problem. However, this did not ensure that the faith and worship practices of the colonists would remain healthy. The laws that required adherence to worship practices and their civil enforcement indicate that passion was no longer a sufficient force to hold the religious culture together. The transfer of the faith's deepest meaning to subsequent generations and newcomers had failed. While it is admirable that those who led in New England sought to preserve the distinctive nature of their freeform worship, making it a legal requirement could only void its essential component of being free.

Prosperity

Other factors contributed to the decline of corporate worship; perhaps none more significant than the success of the colonies themselves. As subsequent generations were born in the New World, commerce and trade were growing rapidly. In a society that was becoming more affluent, corporate worship took on a greater sense of professionalism and preparedness. This occurred along with the development of a refined society. The colonies had become established and had grown in prosperity. This created a self-reliance that clearly weakened the desperate cries of dependence on God that had marked the original colonists. The eventual economic success of the colonies had disastrous consequences on the spiritual health of the churches and led *to a great decline of vital Christianity, and although partial revivals took place, the all-pervading piety that characterized the first generation suffered a great diminution. The light of holiness grew faint and dim, and morality, in general, degenerated in a like degree. The Fathers had gone to the tomb, and were succeeded, upon the whole, by inferior men.*[2]

Like the Church, which had suffered greatly until she became favored in the Roman Empire, believers in the New World had a similar change of circumstances. Fleeing persecution in Europe, they came to the New World at great cost. By the beginning of the eighteenth century, the second and third generations of colonists were beginning to enjoy the fruit of a bountiful land, one of seemingly unlimited opportunity and abundance. The success of the colonies produced a self-sufficiency that, more than any other single factor,

---

[1] This contributed to making Rhode Island a cradle for Baptist development in Colonial America.

[2] Robert Baird, *Religion in America, or, An account of the origin, progress, relation to the state, and present condition of the evangelical churches in the United States: with notices of the unevangelical denominations.* (Harper, New York, 1844), 100-101.

struck at the very heart of what biblical worship should be. This placed the colonists in need of a genuine work of God.

WORSHIP RENEWAL

The Great Awakening that began in both Massachusetts and in Georgia in the 1730's and spread across the colonies was a benchmark event in the spiritual life of America. Lasting for roughly twenty years and centering on revitalizing the individual's acceptance of the gospel, the First Great Awakening transformed many aspects of religious life in Colonial America. The Awakening is generally associated with the ministries of men such as George Whitefield (1715-1770), Jonathan Edwards (1703-1758), and Gilbert Tennent (1703-1764), but also included less Reformed men such as John Wesley (1703-1791) and Charles Wesley (1707-1788). During this period of revival, all aspects of corporate worship were revitalized, including preaching and congregational singing. Ministers preached the new birth with passion and renewal traveled between churches, up and down the eastern seaboard.

Active church membership among evangelicals grew as much as six times faster than the burgeoning population of the colonies. By the end of the eighteenth century, all Christian denominations in America had experienced significant growth. Some of this was related to the growth of the colonies themselves. However, the denominations that participated in the Great Awakening and, therefore, aggressively preached personal conversion during this period were, by far, the ones that saw the largest percentage increases. This is significant since the great majority of this growth came through individuals expressing a commitment to follow Christ.

While the first Puritans and Pilgrims may have assumed the necessity of personal conversion, the Christians of the Great Awakening were explicit by calling for it. Of the denominations that existed in the Colonies, Presbyterians and Baptists saw the greatest percentages of growth (see the table below). The Methodist Episcopal societies, which formed out of the preaching of John Wesley, also saw extraordinary growth.[1] Whether a denomination viewed redemption as general or particular, both preached conversion and both had measurable success.

---

[1] The effects of the Great Awakening continued in some areas for much more than 20 years. In Virginia alone, the number of Methodist Episcopal societies grew more than 1,400 percent in the 10 years between 1774 and 1784. See Ian Murray, *Revival and Revivalism: The Making and Marring of American Evangelicalism* 1750-1858 (Edinburgh: Banner of Truth Trust, 1994), 73-74.

The religious affiliations of the British colonies, 1660-1780 (thousands)[1]			
	1660	1740	1780
Congregationalists	75	423	749
Episcopalians	41	246	406
Dutch Reformed	13	76	127
German Reformed	-	51	201
Catholics	12	20-40?	56
Presbyterians	5	160	495
Lutherans	4	95	-
Baptists	4	96	457
Quakers	-	-	200
Total (approximate)	150	1200	2500

The focus on personal conversion went hand-in-hand with the desire for personal freedom and the development of a national identity. This would ultimately affect how corporate worship would be viewed. The transition that was beginning to take place would move worship more toward personal expression in corporate worship. This type of individualism was evident in the American Revolution and would be given full expression through the Enlightenment. It is not surprising that the Great Awakening and the Enlightenment occurred during the same period. The awareness of self, both intellectually and emotionally, played an important role in both movements, and the clear call for personal spiritual conversion was key to the Great Awakening. The impact on corporate worship would prove enormous.

Much of this followed naturally out of the Reformation, since in medieval Catholicism there had not been a great deal of attention on the individual. Initially, the Reformation had decentralized authority and doctrine, moving it from Rome to the local church or presbytery. The same could be said of corporate worship and its form. However, what had not yet been fully realized was how a renewed commitment to the truth of personal faith in Christ would affect an individual's expression in freer forms of corporate worship. From the Reformation to the period we are now discussing, the majority of congregational singing had been versified Psalms, especially by those who had followed the teachings of Calvin. Where other groups ventured beyond the Psalter, the songs of the Reformation were characteristically doctrinal and often voiced in the

---

[1] Data from Phillip Jenkins, *A History of the United States* (Macmillan, 1997), 32.

plural (we, us). This enhanced corporate identity rather than individual identity. Generally speaking, the Reformation answered the question of how worship would be taken from Rome and brought to the local church, but had not dealt with the issue of how a fresh focus on personal conversion might be expressed and celebrated by the individual within a corporate setting. For this reason, songs voiced in the first person (I, we) were uncommon prior to the Great Awakening. In fact, when such songs were used in the early years following the Reformation, they were not widely accepted and thought scandalous at the time.[1]

Songs that were more personal in nature were used among some non-Calvinistic worshipers, but were very rare among those influenced by Geneva, including Puritans, Congregationalists, Baptists, and Presbyterians. This changed during the Great Awakening as hymns gained wide acceptance among most freeform worshipers. This meant that those who had previously been committed only to Psalm singing had to change their beliefs. The *Philadelphia Confession* (1742) illustrates how the new practice of singing original hymns required a change to long held convictions. The *Philadelphia Confession* (Baptist) was strongly Calvinistic and nearly identical to its predecessor, the *Second London Confession* (1688). However, note the article that was added to the *Philadelphia Confession* (Chapter 23), opening the door beyond the Calvinistic practice of singing only from the Psalter.

> We believe that (Acts 16:25, Eph. 5:19, Col. 3:16) singing the praises of God, is a holy ordinance of Christ, and not a part of natural religion, or a moral duty only; but that it is brought under divine institution, it being enjoined on the churches of Christ to sing psalms, hymns, and spiritual songs; and that the whole church in their public assemblies, as well as private Christians, ought to (Heb. 2:12, Jam. 5:13) sing God's praises according to the best light they have received. Moreover, it was practiced in the great representative church, by (Matt.26:30, Matt. 14:26) our Lord Jesus Christ with His disciples, after He had instituted and celebrated the sacred ordinance of His Holy Supper, as commemorative token of redeeming love.

This demonstrates how the Awakening was changing the worship practices of those within the Reformed tradition. The use of the words *psalms, hymns,* and *spiritual songs* in this application gave a nod to the use of songs outside their modern day Psalters. The preaching of personal conversion resulted in a desire for personal expression that was fulfilled in original hymns. This was one of the lasting impacts of the Awakening on the practice of corporate worship and would open the flood gates for hymns and spiritual songs over the next two centuries.

---

[1] For instance, the poem *Jesu meine Fruede*, which is intensely personal, was written by Johann Frank around 1650 and was set to a tune by Johannes Crüger around 1653. It is best known in the later adaptation by J.S. Bach, *Motet No. 3 in E Minor,* Bach-Werke-Verzeichnis 227.

The songs of this era are typified in the work of two primary hymnists, Isaac Watts (1674-1748) and Charles Wesley (1707-1788). The work of these men represent the best hymn writing from two streams of evangelicalism that were both gaining strength in the eighteenth century. For our understanding of this period, it is helpful to briefly mention these two streams. The more Calvinistic branch is typified in the sermons and writing of George Whitefield and Jonathan Edwards. Both of these men preached personal conversion and, at the same time, held firmly to election, believing that God in His sovereignty had limited salvation to those whom He had chosen. The other branch is typified in the writings and sermons of John and Charles Wesley. While John and Charles Wesley preached and taught the sovereignty of God in salvation, they also believed that God's love was universal and personal redemption was contingent on man's choice. This difference would become more apparent in hymns that developed in the nineteenth century, but was already present in the theologies of both groups.

Even among many of those who disagreed on these matters, civility remained the goal though not always the result. This conflict led to a break in the partnership of George Whitefield and the Wesley brothers. However, the civility between George Whitefield and Charles Wesley remained. In an exchange of letters between the two, Wesley wrote and Whitefield responded:

> "Many, I know, desire nothing so much as to see George Whitefield and John Wesley at the head of different parties, as is plain from their truly devilish plans to effect [sic] it, but be assured, my dearest brother, our heart is as your heart. O may we always continue to think and speak the same things!" For Whitefield's part, he later wrote to John Wesley saying, "For Christ's sake, if possible dear Sir, never speak against election in your sermons; no one can say I ever mention it in my public discourses, whatever my private sentiments may be. For Christ's sake, let us not be divided amongst ourselves."[1]

In congregations across Colonial America, the differences between the two camps may have been less than apparent to many congregations, since both coexisted during the Great Awakening and at times shared pulpits and songs. Furthermore, because many of the revival meetings occurred outdoors, they served as common gatherings beyond the walls of individual churches. This gave congregations the opportunity to share hymns with one another. Such was the case with many of those by Watts and Wesley.

The works of these two hymnists signaled the beginning of one of the greatest periods of Christian hymnody. For this reason, it is difficult to overstate the impact of Watts and Wesley. Wesley was, by far, one of the most prolific

---

[1] See John R. Tyson, *Assist Me to Proclaim: the Life and Hymns of Charles Wesley* (Grand Rapids, MI: William B. Eerdmans Pub., 2007), 106.

hymnists in Christendom, composing over 9,000 hymn texts and poems, including his own versification of the Psalms. Wesley's impact was grand, partly because of the sheer volume of his work and how frequently his texts were sung. It would not be until the next century that the enormous impact of Wesley would be fully realized. Both John and Charles Wesley eventually broke from the Reformed tradition and, as a result, produced many texts that found their greatest acceptance in the nineteenth century among those who held to general redemption. The text below is an excerpt from the thirty-six stanzas of the hymn, *Universal Redemption.* Scholars generally attribute the hymn text to Charles Wesley. It was originally published in 1739 and accompanied John Wesley's sermon *Free Grace.* *Universal Redemption* demonstrates that, even in hymn texts, the conflict between the two camps was, indeed, theological.

When God invites, shall man repel? Shall man th' exception make?
"Come, freely come, WHOEVER WILL, And living water take!"

Thou bidd'st; and would'st thou bid us choose, When purposed not to save?
Command us all a power to use, Thy mercy never gave?

Thou canst not mock the sons of men, Invite us to draw nigh,
Offer thy grace to all, and then, Thy grace to most deny!

Horror to think that God is hate! Fury in God can dwell,
God could an helpless world create, To thrust them into hell!

Doom them an endless death to die, From which they could not flee,
No Lord! Thine inmost bowels cry, Against the dire decree!

Believe who will that human pain, Pleasing to God can prove:
Let Molock feast him with the slain, Our God, we know, is love.

Lord, if indeed, without a bound, Infinite love thou art,
The HORRIBLE DECREE confound, Enlarge thy people's heart!

Ah! Who is as thy servants blind, So to misjudge their God!
Scatter the darkness of their mind, And shed thy love abroad.[1]

Even with the significant conflict between the two camps, the result of the Great Awakening brought many of Wesley's hymns into Reformed congregations. This meant that while there was ongoing conflict among theologians of the period, congregations sang and absorbed aspects of Wesley's view of both God and salvation and blended it with their own.

---

[1] [Charles Wesley(?).] "Universal Redemption." In John Wesley's *Free Grace*, 31–35. Bristol: Farley, 1739. Accessed December 01, 2010 through the website of The Center for Studies in the Wesleyan Tradition, Duke Divinity School, http://divinity.duke.edu/initiatives-centers/cswt/wesley-texts/poetry-hymn (accessed May 12, 2010).

Isaac Watts was not nearly as prolific as Wesley. However, a greater percentage of his texts became standards among worshipers in both camps. Those who believed in particular redemption eventually sang songs by Wesley. Those who reject particular redemption sang the hymn texts of Isaac Watts. In fact, when John Wesley published his first hymnal, *A Collection of Psalms and Hymns* (Charleston, South Carolina, 1737), almost half of the texts were written by Isaac Watts.

As for transforming the literature of worship, there is no greater figure in post-Reformation worship than Isaac Watts. We mentioned earlier that through the Great Awakening personal emotive songs gained much wider acceptance. Much of this came through the pen and thinking of Watts, a London Congregational pastor. Many of his hymn texts, like *When I Survey the Wondrous Cross,* are still widely cherished. Yet his contribution was far more significant than the texts he wrote. As a thinker and writer in the Reformed theological tradition of Calvin, his use of hymn text beyond the Psalter gave personal and, at times, deeply emotive expression to the doctrines of grace. Furthermore, and perhaps more *avant-garde* for his time, was his treatment of the Psalms themselves. Watts' approach to the Psalms was unique in that he wanted them sung in view of the New Covenant. He believed that Christians should sing the Psalms, but that they should do so from this side of the cross. On the subject he wrote:

> Why must Christians be forbid all other melody, but what arises from the victories and deliverances of the Jews? — David would have thought it very hard to have been confined to the words of Moses... And yet the special concerns of David and Moses were much more a-kin to each other, than ours are to either of them ? [sic] and they were both of the same religion, but ours is very different.[1]

Watts applied the view to his treatment of the Psalms. The result of his work was not simply a versification of the Psalms, but a distinctly Christian interpretation of them. Archetypical of Watts' New Covenant adaptation is his treatment of David's words in Psalm 40:5-10. Compare the Authorized Version with the verse (Long Meter) of Watts:

---

[1] See Isaac Watts, *The Psalms of David: Imitated in the Language of the New Testament and Applied to the Christian State and Worship* (Boston: Manning & Loring, 1803), 99-100.
http://babel.hathitrust.org/cgi/pt?seq=106&view=image&size=100&id=nyp.3343308164 1320&q1=psalm+40&u=1&num=99 (accessed June 6, 2010).

Authorized Version	Watts
⁵Many, O LORD my God, *are* thy wonderful works *which* thou hast done, and thy thoughts *which are* to us-ward: they cannot be reckoned up in order unto thee: *if* I would declare and speak *of them*, they are more than can be numbered.	The wonders, Lord, thy love has wrought, Exceed our praise, surmount our thought, Should I attempt the long detail, My speech would faint, my numbers fail.
⁶Sacrifice and offering thou didst not desire; mine ears hast thou opened: burnt offering and sin offering hast thou not required.	No blood of beasts on altars spilt, Can cleanse the souls of men from guilt; But thou hast set before our eyes An all-sufficient sacrifice.
⁷Then said I, Lo, I come: in the volume of the book *it is* written of me,	Lo-! Thine eternal Son appears, To thy design he bows his ears, Assumes a body well prepar'd An[d] well performs a work so hard.
⁸I delight to do thy will, O my God: yea, thy law *is* within my heart.	Behold, I come (the Saviour cries, With love and duty in his eyes) I come to bear the heavy load Of sins, and do thy will, my God.
⁹I have preached righteousness in the great congregation: lo, I have not refrained my lips, O LORD, thou knowest.	'Tis written in thy great decree, 'Tis in the book foretold of me, I must fulfil the Saviour's part, An[d] lo! thy law is in my heart.
^{10a}I have not hid thy righteousness within my heart; I have declared thy faithfulness and thy salvation:	I'll magnify thy holy law And rebels to obedience draw, When on my cross I'm lifted high, Or to my crown above the sky.
^{10b}I have not concealed thy lovingkindness and thy truth from the great congregation.	Thy Spirit shall descend and show What thou hast done, and what I do: The wond'ring world shall learn thy grace, Thy wisdom and thy righteousness.

Such a distinctly Christian rendering was revolutionary for someone who lived and worked in the tradition of Geneva Psalm singing. Prior to the Great Awakening, the only texts common among all freeform worshipers were those of the Psalms. Freeform worshipers who ventured beyond them were, by far, a minority. Watts' adaptation of the Psalter was accepted among Psalm singing churches, making them more open to original hymn text. Once original hymn texts were accepted among Congregationalists, Puritans, and Presbyterians, the whole dynamic of Protestant worship changed. Within a hundred years, most congregations, regardless of their views on particular or general redemption, were open to using distinctly Christian rewrites of the Psalms as well as original hymn texts. For the first time in Christian history, a large cross-section of believers was learning to share a varied tapestry of congregational music.

This launched multiple innovations in congregational worship. Among the most significant was the proliferation of hymn writing and, in the subsequent century, a similar rise in the publication of hymnals. Additionally, the desire to see the congregation improve in its ability to sing spawned the establishment of a singing school movement. This movement began in Massachusetts, moved through New England, and eventually spread to the southern colonies. During these *singing schools,* Christians would gather solely for the purpose of hymn singing, trying out new tunes and texts. This became so popular that whole communities would set aside their work and gather, as an itinerate teacher taught them to sing hymns. Among the chief teachers and contributors to this movement was William Billings (1746-1800). Considered the father of American music, Billings published the first book of completely American music in 1770, the *New England Psalm-Singer.* This early American hymnal contained both text and tunes. It included settings of 126 texts, most of them from Isaac Watts, and the rest from other Great Awakening leaders. The last text in the hymnal was one by George Whitefield. The tradition among previously Psalm singing congregations was changing and popular original hymn texts from their pastors were a confirmation. Billings subsequently wrote five additional volumes, each more progressive in nature than its predecessor.[1]

The importance of Billings' innovation was not in writing verse, but in providing new melodies to which metrical verse could be sung. The custom had been for a local congregation to make use of only a few tunes. Billings sought to significantly broaden that number. Billings' musical style was awkward, *but after a century and a half of dull monotonous drawling of a few threadbare psalm tunes the spirited style that Billings introduced must have delighted the young people of his day. He gave local music a new meaning, a fresh impulse, a greater freedom.*[2] In great measure, Billings' hymn tunes gained wide acceptance through the singing schools he instituted. This was a harbinger of a

[1] See Stephen A. Marini, *Sacred Song in America: Religion, Music, and Public Culture* (University of Illinois Press, 2003), 79.

[2] William Arms Fisher, *Notes on Music in Old Boston* (Oliver Ditson Company, 1918), 13.

broader interest in musical education that accompanied a refinement of Colonial society and growth in literacy. For a season, the mythical breach between secular and sacred music was closed and song leaders like Billings were as welcomed in the local cultured concert as in the Sunday service. The widespread expansion of singing represents the depth and breadth of the corporate worship renewal that occurred during the Great Awakening.

SUMMARY THOUGHTS ON THIS PERIOD

The period between 1600 and 1800 is one of two great spiritual peaks: the years of Colonial establishment and the Great Awakening. As we stated earlier, this period of history allows us to see if a theologically pure form can ensure long-term vibrancy in worship. No matter your preferred worship liturgy, if you are a Protestant, one of the forms used by Puritans, Congregationalists, Baptists, Anglicans, Presbyterians, etc., would likely meet your theological criteria. That being the case, the need for revival was real among worshipers of all types, no matter what form they inherited—and the need for and the effects of the revival were shared among the wide variety of congregations that existed. None of the post-Reformation forms that were used in the New World could, in themselves, sustain spiritual vibrancy. It is true that bad theology can kill corporate worship; we saw that in the millennium that preceded the Reformation. But it is equally true that good theology, expressed in form alone, does not guarantee spiritual vibrancy. What every generation needs, besides theological orthodoxy, is for hearts of individuals to be constantly rekindled with passion for God.

For us today, the need for scriptural truth to come alive in the hearts of individuals remains. My own denomination has undergone a resurgence of biblical orthodoxy and a renewal of conservative doctrine. For that, I am grateful. History decisively teaches that to have a high view of Scripture and a solid biblical theology is far better than the alternative. However, all movements to purify theology or maintain orthodoxy fall short of accomplishing their goals unless the hearts of the people are renewed. Anglicans and Congregationalists, like so many children of the Reformation, found themselves in desperate need of spiritual renewal. Certainly, the Puritans came to realize that no amount of purified form, even if conscripted by law, could ensure that hearts would be individually inclined toward God. It took a genuine move of God in the hearts of the people to revitalize corporate worship. We must take note: it is simply too easy to assume that cleaning up a form means that hearts will be clean as well. Simply maintaining a theologically pure form does not mean those practicing it will remain spiritually engaged.

We previously learned that there are three essential components for a worship encounter to occur with the Almighty: God must reveal Himself, we must respond in willingness, and there must be sufficient truth to guide the encounter according to God's will. The early colonists had both the desire to respond and sufficient truth to guide the encounter. As a result, it was a period of spiritual life. What happened in the years of decline was neither the loss of biblical truth nor the addition of unscriptural forms. It was simply a loss of passion among many to live out what it means to be the people of God. When passion returned to individual hearts, real renewal came and vibrancy in corporate worship returned with greater force than had previously existed.

This places a great responsibility on those who lead, since maintaining a proper form cannot ensure spiritual vibrancy. For those who have done the hard work of examining the Scripture to find what God wants, there remains another greater work—to shepherd our people toward a passion for God. Worship is first and foremost about who we are (*being*)—our passion, our humility, our submission—rather than the form we use (*doing*). Without hearts that seek after God, the exactness of our theology and form yield nothing of the genuine work of His Spirit in us. Admittedly, even shepherding our people toward a passion for God only yields benefits if the sheep follow. This points to our limitation as leaders. We can only teach the truth of the Bible, do our best to be as scriptural as possible in the forms we use, and maintain our own passion for God. We must remember that awakening and renewal can come only through a sweet, God-sent work of revival. And just because God has moved does not mean that we will automatically maintain our passion for Him simply because we know the truth and have experienced a deep work of God in our own lives. Even churches touched by the Great Awakening needed renewal not long after the generation that had experienced it passed away. Only when our hearts are passionate about God will we see theologically pure forms remain vibrant. And even then, they must be renewed each day, each week, and by each subsequent generation or, even in their theological purity, they will become devoid of spiritual life.

CHAPTER 9
A PARTING OF WAYS
(AD 1800-1900)

The way churches came to understand the purpose of worship changed significantly in the nineteenth century. This change was primarily a shift in the reason for having a weekly gathering. In previous centuries, the Sunday gathering generally assumed the conversion of those present. Because of this, songs and sermons were intended to be used in an environment of believers. During the Great Awakening, outdoor meetings had often focused on those who needed salvation. Sermons and, to some extent, songs in those meetings addressed those who were lost. As a result, many gatherings during the Great Awakening were not actually worship services, at least not in the strictest sense—a group of believers gathered for the purpose of worshiping God. Instead, these meetings could better be described as evangelistic meetings in which the focus was calling the lost to repentance.

In varying degrees, churches absorbed this focus into their regular Sunday services. During the nineteenth century, the shifting of focus, either toward evangelism or away from it, set a course for two very different approaches to corporate gatherings. In some aspects, this was a new twist on the division that already existed between the views of general and particular redemption. Churches of both varieties were comfortable sharing songs and preachers with one another during the Great Awakening. However, the two camps ended the nineteenth century separated by a great distance. In many cases, the fellowship enjoyed in the Great Awakening was broken during the nineteenth century and remains so to this day. While various churches may consider themselves united around the gospel of Jesus Christ, most of our own present worship styles have developed out of one of these two approaches and, therefore, reflect something of this division.

The challenge in studying this century is that we now begin to discuss the rudiments of our own present styles and preferences. History can be an objective voice, but hearing that voice is difficult when it begins to tell us that our own preferred approach has weaknesses. Often, our commitment to a particular method is based more on our level of familiarity with it than on a theological or philosophical viewpoint that shaped its development in a previous generation. This period provides us an opportunity to see how changes in nineteenth century theology and methodology continue to shape today's worship practice. This type of examination is an important part of ensuring our own approach to worship is appropriate. While we may claim Scripture as the defender of our style, we have seen in our study of worship that the Bible sanctions no style. Therefore, it is never beneficial to make our deepest commitment to a human method or system—both allegiance to Scripture and a willingness to see our own weaknesses are crucial for a continued healthy development of our own faith and practice.

There were benefits for churches that embraced the innovations of the nineteenth century and benefits for those who shunned them. There were downsides as well. Both produced offspring that went so far from biblical truth that they separated themselves from the evangelical tradition and, in some cases, from orthodox Christianity. For example, some churches attempted to employ methods that they believed would ensure conversions during services. As some saw it, human ingenuity could move the heart of a man to cry out to God. This pushed worship toward an unhealthy emotionalism and an attempt to establish a cause and effect relationship between the fervor of the worshiper and God's activity.

Other churches attempted to avoid emotionalism, but fared no better. Not only did many forgo the expectation for God to manifest Himself during corporate worship, but an increasing number of churches viewed emotional passionate worship as unsophisticated or vulgar. Wherever this occurred it became increasingly rare to hear messages that sought to persuade men to repent before a righteous and holy God. Instead, messages exhibited an increasing fascination with human ability and ingenuity. For those who went in that direction, it was a short step to believe that a sovereign God had given humanity enough tools to better himself. This led straight toward humanism. By the beginning of the twentieth century, it was unusual for many of the New England churches, which had been at the epicenter of the Great Awakening, to preach repentance and conversion. The same could be said for the colleges that they founded. Suppressing emotional passion for the lost, but sophisticated in intellectual pursuits, many of these churches were ripe to fall to the onslaught of liberalism.

The lessons taught by this century are profound. The division between those who passionately entreat men to repent and those who trust the sovereignty of God to quicken hearts did not mean a complete breakdown of fellowship in the eighteenth century, nor did it mean the development of incompatible worship styles. Corporate worship can benefit from aspects of both approaches. However, in the nineteenth century we can see that leaning too heavily in either direction is injurious to corporate worship. Worship is healthier when leaders recognize God's sovereignty—He is solely responsible for moving the hearts of those present—*and* explore the full force of human emotions—hoping for hearts to be moved. Scripture calls us to worship God with the heart (emotion) and the head (intellect). If congregations worship without both intellect and emotion, unhealthy practices are bound to develop—to negate one necessarily harms the other. Admittedly, there is a tension, but that tension exists in Scripture and is there for a reason. Herein is the most profound lesson of this century.

LESSON 12: HEALTHY WORSHIP DOES NOT CHOOSE BETWEEN INTELLECT AND EMOTION; IT FULLY ENGAGES BOTH AND TRUSTS GOD'S SOVEREIGNTY FOR THE RESULTS.

To demonstrate the truth of this lesson, we will examine how various developments widened the gap between an emotional and intellectual approach to worship. We will see how styles of worship took on a much greater variety. Some of this variety came from an increasing diversity of culture. In the nineteenth century there were many cultural developments that pushed styles further from one another. The Civil War separated the North from the South. The success of industrialists in the northeast fueled a growing high society that lived in a totally different world than the labor class. The push to settle the west created a division between the frontiersmen and the city dweller. And a wide variety of cultures arrived with increasing force as waves of immigrants flooded into the United States. In each case and many others, subgroups who sought their own style of worship services developed. However, underlying these cultural differences were more significant theological ones. As theological differences became more distinct, so did the variety of approaches to congregational singing. This was evident in an explosion of printed resources, including hymnals and songbooks for congregational use.

In the first half of the nineteenth century there were only a handful of hymnals published in the United States. In the second half of the century nearly every denomination was producing its own resources for congregational singing. A list of hymnals published during the nineteenth century is included on the following pages. It is not exhaustive but, it demonstrates the dramatic increase in hymnal publications in the second half of the century.

1831	1866 (continued)
Lyre, Leavitt...Pres. Cong.	*Collection of Hymns*... ... ... Meth. So.
Spiritual Songs, Hastings, Mason ... .Pres. Cong.	*Common Praise*, Waterbury............................Epis.
1839	*New Hymn A Tune Book*, Phillips....................Meth.
Hymns of Zion, Thomas..................................Univ.	*Presbyterian Hymnal* ....Old School Pres.
1850	**1867**
Christian Psalmist	*Christian Hymnal*, Sewall ....Swedbg.
1851	*Church Hymn Book*, Salter (tunes apart) ....Cong.
Christian Melodies, Cheever, Sweatzer................Cong.	*Jubilee Harp*... ... ... Advt.
Temple Melodies, Jones... ... ...Cong.	**1868**
1854	*Book of Praise* ... ...Cong.
Congregational Church Music, Bacon.................Cong.	*Hymn & Tune Book*, Livermore ....Unit.
1855	*Book of Common Prayer*, Hodges ....Epis.
Plymouth Collection, Beecher... ... ... Cong.	*Spiritual Harp* ... ...Spirit.
1857	*Vestry Harmonies*, Adams ....Univ.
Hymns for the Use of the M. E. Church... ... ...Meth.	**1869**
1858	*Hymns of the Church*, Thompson.
Church Melodies, Hastings... ... ...Pres.	Vermilye, Thompson ....Ref. Dutch
Songs of the Church, Davies ....Epis.	*Hymns of the New Life* ... ...Pres. Cong.
1859	**1870**
Baptist Chorale, Manly, Everett... ... ...Bapt.	*Christian Hymn & Tune Book*, Hayden
Choralist, Day, Tappan, Curtis, Cheney.....Free-W. Bapt.	*Christian Praise* ... ...Ref. Dutch
Collection of Sacred Song, Hopkins......... ....Epis.	*Hymnal*, Hutchins... ... ...Epis.
Evangelical Psalmist, Seise, McCron, Passavant... ... Luth.	*Parish Hymnal*, Tucker ....Epis.
New Congregational Hymn: A Tune Book., Nason...Cong.	**1871**
Pastor's Selection, Hurt... ... ...Pres.	*Baptist Praise Book*, Holbrook ....Bapt.
Puritan Hymn: A Tune Book... ... ... Cong.	*Christian Hymnal*... ... ...Disciples
Sabbath Hymn: A Tune Book. Park, Phelps, Mason..Cong.	*Collection of Hymns*, Shuey, etc.,... ... ...Unit. Breth.
1860	*Tribute of Praise*, Tourjee,... ... ...Cong.
American Hymn: A Tune Book, Stevens,	**1872**
McDonald... ... ... N/A	*Brethren's Hymn; A Tune Book*....................Dunkers
A Book of Hymns Tunes, Longfellow..... ... ...Unit.	*Church Hymn Book*, Hatfield... ... ...Pres.
Church Choral-Book, Baker, Tufts... ... ...Cong.	*Hymnal*, Goodrich, Gilbert... ... ...Epis.
Psalmist, Edmands ....Bapt.	*Hymnal*, Tucker... ... ...Epis.
Psalms of David, Jones (tunes apart)	*Hymns of the Morning*, Barker ....Advent.
Wesleyan Hymn: A Tune Book, Everett ... ...Meth. So	*Sacrifice of Praise*, Murray, Oilman ....Pres.
1861	*Church Book*, Schmucker, Bird ....Luth.
Gospel Psalmist, Adams... ... ...Univ.	**1873**
1862	*Baptist Hymn A Tune Book*, Evans ....Bapt.
Songs for Social & Public Worship, Msonn...........Cong.	*Church Harmonies*, Bolles, Washbum ....Univ.
Songs of the Church, Robinson... ... ...Pres.	**1874**
1863	*Hymns A Songs of Praise*, Hitchcock,
Psalms of David, Keys...............................Pres.	Eddy, Schaff ....Pres.
1864	*Hymns for the Sanctuary* ... ... Unit. Breth.
Church Pastorals, Adams... ... ...Cong.	**1874**
Devotional Hymn A Tune Book,	*Presbyterian Hymnal*, Duryea ....Pres.
Rowland. Bradbury... ... ...Bapt.	**1875.**
1865	*Hymns for Christian Devotion*... ... ...Univ.
Songs for the Sanctuary, Robinson... ... ...Pres. Cong.	**1875**
1866	*Psalms A Hymns A Spiritual Songs*, Robinson ....Pres.
Book of Worship, Bacon ....Pres.	*Service of Praise* ... ...Cong.

[1] Waldo Selden Pratt, Charles N. Boyd, *Groves Dictionary of Music and Musicians, Volume 6, America Supplement* (New York: The MacMillan Company, 1920), 250-251.

1876
Bible Songs ... ...Cumb. Pres.
Book of Worship (chants, not tunes)... ... ...Swedbg.
Christian Hymn Book... ... ...Christ.
Hymns & Tunes... ... ...7th-D. Advt.
1877
Christian Hymnal, Burton, Parker, Twichell ... .Cong.
Hymn; A Tune Book... ... ...Unit.
1878
Methodist Hymnal... ... ...Meth.
Reformed Church Hymnal. ... ...Ger. Ref.
Selection of Spiritual Songs, Robinson ... ... Pres. Cong.
1880
Book of Worship... ... ...Luth.
Christian Praise, Thompson... ... ...Ref. Dutch.
Evangelical Hymnal, Hall, Lasar... ... ... Pres.
Manual of Praise, Mead, Rice... ... ...Cong.
Songs for the Lord's House, Bridgman... ... ...Bapt.
Songs of Christian Praise, Richards... ... ...
Cong.
Worship in Song, Holbrook
1881 Choice Collection of Spiritual Hymns.... Mennonite
Church Praise Book, Stryker, Main... ... ...Pres.
Hymns of the Advent.... ... ...Adv.
1882
Evangelical Hymn; A Tune Book,.... ... ...Ev. Assoc.
New Christian Hymn A Tune Book,
      Fillmore... ... ...Disciples
New Hymn Book... ... ...Meth. So.
1883
Baptist Hymnal, Johnson, Doane... ... ...Bapt.
Church Book, Bacon... ... ...Cong.
Sacred Songs for Public Worship, Savage, Dow.....Unit.
Duplex Hymn; A Tune Book, Shotwell... ... ...Pres.
Wesleyan Hymnal... ... ...Wesl. Meth.
1884
Baptist Hymn Book, Thompson... ... ...Prim. Bapt.
Brethren Hymnody... ... ...Dunkers
English & Latin Hymns (later, Catholic Hymnal)....R. C.
Laudes Domini, Robinson... ... ...Pres. Cong.
1885
Carmina Sanctorum, Hitchcock, Eddy, Mudge.... ... Pres.
1886
Book of Common Praise, Moore, Gilchrist... ... Ref. Epis.
Hymn; A Tune Book, Durand, Lester... ... ... Prim. Bapt.
Hymnal Companion... ... ...Ref. Epis.
Songs of Pilgrimage, Hastings... ... ...N/A

1887
Christian Hymnal, Wilson... ... ...7th-D. Advt.
Church of God Selection ... ...N/A
Hymns of the Faith, Harris, Tucker, Glesen... ... ...Cong.
New Hymn A Tune Book... ... ...Afr. Meth. Zion
Psalter, with Music... ... ...Unit. Pres.
Seventh-Day Adventist Hymn & Tune Book... 7th-D. Advt.
1888
Hymns for the Sanctuary... ... ...Unit. Breth.
1889
Church Song, Stryker... ... ...Pres.
Evangelical Lutheran Hymn Book... ... ...Luth.
Hymn & Tune Book... ... ...Meth. So.
1890
Church Hymnary, Bedell... ... ...Ref. Dutch.
Hymnal — Amore Dei, Williams ... ...Unit.
Hymnal ... ...Ger. Ref.
Hymns A Tunes ... ...Mennonite
Hymns of the Church Universal, Foote... ... ...Unit.
Otterbein Hymnal, Lorens ... ...Unit. Breth.
Primitive Hymns, Spiritual Songs & Sacred Poems,
      Lloyd ... ...Prim. Bapt.
1891
Hymns of the Ages, Kerr ... ...So. Pres.
1892
Christian Science Hymnal ... ...Chr. Sci.
New Laudes Domini, Robinson... ... ...Pres. Cong.
1893
Church Book, Krauth... ... ...Luth.
Hymnal, Messiter... ... ...Epis.
Hymnal ... ...Afr. Meth.
Magnificat ... ...Swedbg.
Plymouth Hymnal, Abbott ... ...Cong.
1894
Hymnal, Hutchins... ... ...Epis.
Hymnal, Tucker, Rousseau ... ...Epis.
1895
Church Harmonies, Tenney, Lewis ... ...Univ.
Hymnal, Benson... ... ...Pres.
Sacred Hymns A Tunes, West,... ... ...Meth.
1897
Hymnal, Darlington... ... ...Epis.
In Excelsis ... ...Pres. Cong.
1898
African M. E. Hymnal ... ...Afr. Meth.
Sursum Corda, Johnson, Ayres ... ...Bapt.
1899
Hymnal ... ...Luth.

Such a multiplicity of styles and approaches was a new development for post-Reformation Christianity. What had been a fairly unified style of American Protestant hymnody became a patchwork of approaches for congregational participation. It is amazing that the lineage of many groups that published specialized hymnals and songbooks in the nineteenth century had shared a common hymnody in the Great Awakening.

In all of these variations, there were two basic approaches among nineteenth century churches: 1) those that embraced the revivals of the nineteenth century and subsequently adopted a more emotional approach to worship, and 2) those who shunned the revivals and opted for a more intellectual approach to worship. In both cases, preaching and music exhibited strengths and weaknesses. The hope is that we can identify and retreat from the weaknesses within our own approach and move toward the strengths of the other. In so doing, perhaps some of the blessings that were shared by churches in the Great Awakening can be ours again today.

DEVELOPMENTS IN WORSHIP ORIENTED TOWARD EMOTION

What had been a long season of unhindered economic expansion for the Colonies stalled during the Revolutionary War. Meanwhile, the spirit of revival so strong during the Great Awakening had cooled and left many churches struggling. Early in the nineteenth century the young nation experienced a new spiritual revival. This was known as the Second Great Awakening (1800-1840). It was during the Second Great Awakening that many churches moved toward weekly gatherings that were constructed more for the purpose of evangelism than worship. Understanding the theology and thought behind this transformation is essential for our study of worship and is clearly demonstrated in the ministries of Francis Asbury and Charles Grandison Finney. These two men played an integral role in the Second Great Awakening, influencing how churches looked at the corporate gathering and the way they viewed and understood how God works in the lives of people.

The benchmark event that propelled the Second Awakening occurred at Cane Ridge, Kentucky in 1801, where many gathered to see what was described as an outpouring of God's presence.

> Between August 6 and August 12, thousands of people—perhaps as many as 25,000—gathered at Cane Ridge to fast and pray and take communion. This was the largest attendance at a religious revival in America up to this time. ...Cane Ridge became an instant legend. Never before had religious piety and fervor been so openly expressed or conversions so numerous. By early 1801, only about 10 percent of all Kentuckians were formal members of a church; ministers complained about the pervasiveness of deism, rationalism, and religious indifference. Then, in the course of six months, in a series of religious revivals, at least 100,000 Kentuckians, hungry for intense religious

experience and eager for a sense of community, joined together in a search of religious salvation.[1]

This set off a wave of such meetings that often lasted for days. During these protracted meetings, multiple speakers preached evangelistic sermons and long periods of robust singing encouraged people to repent and come to Christ. Evangelical denominations flourished, exploding in numbers and transforming American Protestantism's demographics and theology.

> Before the Awakening there were about three hundred Methodists in the country. When the indefatigable Francis Asbury died in 1816, there were two hundred thousand. By 1812 there were also two hundred thousand Baptists, and both groups continued to grow exponentially: by 1850 there were more than a million Baptists in the United States.[2]

This spirited style of revival preaching and singing not only became part of an *instant legend,* but also buoyed a very different approach to Sunday worship services for a significant portion of American Christians.

The Beginning of Evangelism as Worship: Francis Asbury
The ministry of Francis Asbury (1745-1816) was a major catalyst of the Second Great Awakening. Born in England and raised in the Wesleyan movement, he made his way to the New World where, as a circuit rider, he was relentless in advancing the teachings of John Wesley and particularly his method of preaching for conversions. Methodism had expanded rapidly under Wesley in England. However, its growth in America was initially slow, hindered by a lack of communication between the few hundred adherents in the Colonies and their counterparts in England. Such communication was made nearly impossible during the Revolutionary War.[3] Following the American Revolution, it was clear that American Methodism could no longer be attached to the Church of England as it had been under John Wesley. In 1784, Wesley appointed Asbury as the first Bishop of the Methodist Episcopal Church in America. Until this separation between American Methodism and the Church of England, corporate worship among American Methodists was patterned after the Common Book of Prayer. Following Wesley's death, this began to change. Asbury led Methodists to a

---

[1] Steven Mintz, *Moralists and Modernizers: America's Pre-Civil War Reformers* (John Hopkins University Press, 1995), 24.

[2] Milton Gaither, *American Educational History Revisited: A Critique of Progress* (Teachers College Press, 2003), p. 39. Some estimates run much higher. See Phillip Jenkins, *A History of the United States* (Macmillan, 1997), 32.

[3] The suspicion of Asbury as a British subject was significant in the years leading up to and following the American Revolution. Because of Asbury's British roots and his connection to the Anglican Church (via Wesley), he was forced to seek refuge in the home of a judge in Delaware for two years during the height of the war.

much simpler format for corporate worship, prescribing basic elements that included prayer, hymn singing, Scripture reading, and a sermon. While this was later revised and became much more complex as the nineteenth century concluded, the significant change reflected Asbury's impact among Methodists.

The reasons for Asbury's changes to the Methodist worship order were both practical and theological. Far from the established church houses of New England, much of Asbury's work occurred on the western frontier and in rural areas of the south, often in outdoor brush arbor meetings. Like the gathering at Cane Ridge, Asbury's meetings would often last several days or weeks and utilize numerous sermons interspersed with robust congregational singing. Many such meetings are described by Asbury in his journal:

> Preaching and exhortations, and singing, and prayer—we had all these without intermission on the campground, and we have reasons to believe that many souls will be converted. The number of traveling and local preachers present, are about three hundred. There are people here with their tents who have come one hundred and fifty miles. The prospects of doing good are glorious. We have already added two new circuits, and gained six preachers. There may have been from two to three thousand persons assembled.[1]

Asbury's driving concern for these meetings was the conversion of *many souls.* This passion drove and shaped much of the development of Methodist worship practices. As the Second Great Awakening spread and Methodism was experiencing unparalleled growth, revival fervor swept across the brush arbor meetings and came to rest in the Sunday services of many churches. Congregations that had experienced a move of God in the camp meetings brought the songs and evangelistic preaching back to the worship services in their own churches. Whereas worship had been geared toward believers expressing praise to God, many worship services became Sunday morning camp meetings, preaching the message of salvation to the lost. By the time Asbury died in 1816, Methodist congregations dotted the landscape of Georgia, North and South Carolina, Virginia, and the western frontier. It is interesting that many of these areas were previously Anglican during the Colonial era. The spread of Asbury's style of worship effectively transformed worship in this region from forms built around the Common Book of Prayer to a simple liturgy.

> For some Methodists, what became identified as the revival style of hymn singing, ardent prayer, and fiery preaching that flourished on the frontier exemplified the basic and most fruitful means of winning souls. This often meant adopting a practical approach so that worship reached its commonly understood goal: the conversion of heart and mind, which often was

---

[1] Written from Milledgeville, GA on December 25, 1809. See Francis Asbury and Ezra Squier Tipple, *The Heart of Asbury's Journal* (New York: Methodist Book Concern, 1904), 606.

dramatically confirmed by kinetic and vocal responses in the pew or at the altar rail.[1]

The decision was immediate and so were the visible results.

For the first time in the history of Christian worship, Church Music sought to fully explore the emotional aspect of singing as a tool to affect the congregation—specifically, as an attempt to produce a *response dramatically confirmed by kinetic and vocal responses.* A focus on such responses represented a strong shift toward heightened emotion in worship and was even beyond Wesley's view of hymns as useful for teaching doctrine to the church. Songs moved away from being didactic and toward stimulating the emotions of those singing and listening.[2] As the function of music in the Church changed, congregations were flooded with a glut of songs fashioned with the primary intent of elevating the emotions. As much as the purpose of these songs was to charge the emotions, the thrust of the message was to secure a decision. Wherever such an approach was used, the function of the Sunday gatherings was no longer worship. While much of this transition did not occur in Asbury's lifetime, the groundwork was laid during his ministry. As the mantle of Revivalism was assumed by Charles Finney, many of the developments that began during Asbury's ministry found full expression.

The Solidification of the Evangelistic Method: Charles Grandison Finney

Charles Grandison Finney (1792-1875) was born in Connecticut and grew up in the New England Presbyterian tradition. Originally he undertook the study of law, but experienced a dramatic and highly emotional conversion in 1821. Soon after, he undertook his own preparation for ministry outside the Reformed tradition in which he had grown up. Setting aside his denomination's confession (Westminster), he studied the scriptures seeking to establish his own views about redemption and atonement. His resulting theology led him to believe that man was responsible for the will to repent for salvation (justification) and to perform the work necessary to maintain his purity (sanctification).[3] In 1832 he took a pastorate in New York and later would serve as professor and president of Oberlin College (1851-1866).

---

[1] Karen B. Westerfield Tucker, *American Methodist Worship* (Oxford: Oxford University Press, 2001), 11.

[2] See Mark A. Noll and Edith Waldvogel Blumhofer, *Sing Them over Again to Me: Hymns and Hymnbooks in America* (Tuscaloosa: University of Alabama Press, 2006), 26.

[3] For a complete study of Finney's theology in his own words, see Charles Grandison Finney, et al., *Finney's Systematic Theology: Lectures on Classes of Truths, Moral Government, the Atonement, Moral and Physical Depravity, Natural, Moral, and Gracious Ability, Repentance, Faith, Justification, Sanctification, Election, Divine Sovereignty & Perseverance of the Saints* (Minneapolis, MN: Bethany House Publishers, 1994).

Finney's impact did not come from riding the revival circuits. Whereas much of Asbury's work had been in rural frontier areas, Finney's work was primarily in the populated cities of the northeast. Beginning in New York City and moving in the upstate regions around Troy and Rome, Finney sought to demonstrate that the power of God in conversion and revival could be experienced whenever people sought it, as long as the message was presented in the right way. Finney's new approach was tested when he preached a message entitled, *Make Yourself a New Heart*. In recalling the message, Presbyterian minister, Rev. Moses Gillett recounted how the attendees were urged to get right with God. *The people responded by saying, "We cannot change our own hearts." The command was urged, "Make you a new heart and spirit, for why will ye die?"*[1] For those who had been schooled in the belief that salvation and repentance were solely dependent on the work of God, such a thought—that it was in the individual's power to make a new heart for himself—was unprecedented.[2]

Beyond Finney's work in the cities of the northeast, his writing as a teacher and tactician of revival deeply impacted nineteenth and twentieth century worship. Most of Finney's writing and teaching was not geared toward corporate worship services. Instead, he focused on developing services that would move the unsaved to make a public decision at an altar call. Finney's services sought to bring unbelievers to a place of deep anguish for their sinful condition. To accomplish this, he taught believers to set aside joyous singing and, instead, enter into the travail of prayer for the lost. Finney's instructions for conducting meetings were spelled out in his *Lectures on Revivals of Religion,* first published in 1835. In the section entitled *Measures to Promote Revivals,* Finney described what he called the *new measures.* In contrast to the Old Divinity, which leaned heavily on an understanding of God's sovereignty, Finney sought to design his meetings to produce a specific result. *Before the 1820's the altar call, or its equivalent, was little known in most churches.*[3] That changed with Finney. He planned the service to culminate with sinners coming to the anxious seat or mourners bench, where they could express their desire to be saved and, if possible, immediately be confirmed before the congregation.

Finney's instructions included all aspects of the service, from how to preach the sermon and how to handle late arrivals to dealing with detractors and how the congregation should or should not sing. Finney's teaching on music was quite restrictive considering the robust singing that had developed by the early nineteenth century. Finney gives the following instructions concerning music in revival meetings:

---

[1] Robert Evans, *Fire From Heaven: A Description of the Revivals from the "Burned-Over District" of New York, 1800-1840, and Spiritual Deceptions* (Hazelbrook, N.S.W.: Research in Evangelical Revivals, 2005), 195.
[2] Deborah Vansau McCauley, *Appalachian Mountain Religion: A History* (University of Illinois Press, 1995), 137-139.
[3] Ian Murray, *Revival and Revivalism: The Making and Marring of American Evangelicalism 1750-1858* (London: Banner of Truth Trust, 1994), 277.

A great deal of singing often injures a prayer meeting. The agonizing spirit of prayer does not lead people to sing. There is a time for everything; a time to sing, and a time to pray. But if I know what it is to travail in birth for souls, Christians never feel less like it, than when they have the spirit of prayer for sinners. Singing is the natural expression of feelings that are joyful and cheerful. The spirit of prayer is not a spirit of joy. It is a spirit of travail, and agony of soul, supplicating and pleading with God with strong cryings, and groanings that cannot be uttered. This is more like anything else than it is like singing...

... If the hymn be of a joyful character it is not directly calculated to benefit sinners, and is highly fitted to relieve the mental anguish of the Christian, so as to destroy that travail of soul which is indispensable to his prevailing in prayer.

Finney goes on to describe how he has seen music used appropriately in the service:

When singing is introduced in a prayer meeting, the hymns should be short, and so selected as to bring out something solemn; some striking words, such as the Judgment Hymn, and others calculated to produce an effect on sinners; or something that will produce a deep impression on the minds of Christians; but not that joyful kind of singing, that makes everybody feel comfortable, and turns off the mind from the object of the prayer meeting.

I once heard a celebrated organist produce a remarkable effect in a protracted meeting. The organ was a powerful one, and the double bass pipes were like thunder. The hymn was given out that has these lines:

See the storm of vengeance gathering
O'er the path you dare to tread,
"Hear the awful thunder rolling.
Loud and louder o'er your head."

When he came to these words, we first heard the distant roar of thunder, then it grew nearer and louder, till at the word "louder," there was a crash that seemed almost to overpower the whole congregation.

Such things in their proper place do good. But common singing dissipates feeling. It should always be such as not to take away feeling, but to deepen it.

Often a prayer meeting is injured by calling on the young converts to sing joyful hymns. This is highly improper in a prayer meeting. It is no time for them to let feeling flow away in joyful singing, while so many sinners around them, and their own former companions, are going down to hell. A revival is often put down by the church and minister all giving themselves up to singing with young converts. Thus by stopping to rejoice, when they ought to feel more and more deeply for sinners, they grieve away the Spirit of God, and they soon find that their agony and travail of soul are all gone.[1]

We can draw several important conclusions about how Finney viewed congregational singing. First, and foremost, Finney was suggesting a different focus of the singing itself. Rather than providing an opportunity for the believer to sing to or about God, Finney indicated that songs should focus on the misery of those who were lost. This was obviously a departure from previously existing notions of the role of hymns and songs. Hymns proliferated that were directed to the unbeliever rather than God. As these became commonly used in Sunday services, the voicing of the service was fundamentally altered—it was no longer primarily addressed to God. The second important insight into Finney's understanding was the character of the music itself. For him, the joyful songs of faith, assurance, and victory, once prized by children of the Reformation, were *highly improper* in a meeting where there were lost who need salvation. Of course Finney's point is that the emotional thrust of a song is not for the believer to express his confidence in God but, rather, to bring a solemnity of heart *calculated to produce an effect on sinners*.

The above excerpt is somewhat typical of much that Finney wrote. His statements have a natural logic but they also demonstrate a short-sightedness. If joyful singing is inappropriate for believers *while so many sinners around them, and their own former companions, are going down to hell*, it begs the question: should believers sing joyously only when unbelievers are not present? Either Finney did not consider the broader implications of his instructions or they were unimportant to him in the larger scope of utilizing the *new measures*. To be fair, we should note that Finney's language here and elsewhere in his *Lectures* describes the service as a *prayer meeting*, a *revival meeting*, or a *protracted meeting*. Clearly, Finney was not giving very much thought that the function of such gatherings might be for the purpose of believers to worship God. For this reason, the widespread use of Finney's methods in worship services was a misapplication of his intent to create evangelistic services rather than worship services. Nevertheless, his teachings were applied far beyond revival meetings or evangelistic prayer meetings and had a significant influence on regular Sunday worship services in churches that embraced the revivals of the Second Great Awakening.

The Effects of Revivalism on Worship

Much of what was taught and practiced in the nineteenth century revival meetings stood in stark contrast to what was taught in the seventeenth and eighteenth centuries. Of all the differences, none is greater than the way in which the activity of God was sought and understood. The concept of *revival* in the

---

[1] Excerpt from Charles Grandison Finney, *Lectures on Revivals of Religion.*, ed. William G. McLaughlin (Cambridge: Belknap of Harvard University Press, 1960; reprint, New York: Leavitt, Lord & Co., 1835), 123-124.

first Great Awakening was understood as a sovereign move of God—something to which *humankind* responded. The Second Great Awakening offered something more akin to *Revivalism*—the development of human means to which *God* would respond. For Asbury, if God's love were universal then fervent prayer and preaching could affect the salvation of souls. Finney's ministry went still further. His belief that the use of specific means (*new measures*) could produce salvation in men led him to conclude that revival among God's people was not the choice of a sovereign God to pour out His blessings on His people. Instead, it was the result of a concerted work of human beings who had the ability to pray or 'work revival down.' As such, extraordinary moves of God could be perpetual if the proper human actions were undertaken.

In a broad sense, Revivalism affected the way many viewed the Christian life. In the eighteenth century, Wesley had taught that believers, through discipline, could attain a level of spiritual perfection. In his later years, he greatly moderated on this view, but Finney took Wesley's teaching still further. He taught that just as a man could muster up the faith and will to be saved completely of his own accord, so he could also choose a life of perfection if he fell under the complete control of the Holy Spirit. This sent many of those who had professed conversion in a revival meeting looking for a special portion of God's Spirit to make such a life possible. By the last quarter of the nineteenth century, some sought a life of perfectionism in the *Holiness Movement*. For others, it led them to seek a second blessing or baptism of the Holy Spirit.[1] The momentum created in Revivalism continued well into the twentieth century as denominations divided and splintered. Even the *Charismatic Movement*, which can be traced to a late blooming camp meeting at Azusa Street Church in 1907, grew out of nineteenth century Revivalism.

Finney's model was so focused on conversion that when churches absorbed his approach into their regular services they gave very little attention to discipleship.[2] The push for numerical growth and expediency without spiritual depth left many wide open to the influence of cults that grew like thistles in the second half of the nineteenth century. Mormons, Oneness Pentecostals, Christian Scientists, Jehovah's Witnesses, and others all grew as offshoots of nineteenth century Revivalism, splintering the cause of Christianity and abandoning its essential teachings.

For churches that remained in the Christian faith, many saw the Sunday gathering repurposed and the components in their services substantially altered. Three areas where this was felt most acutely were: the Ministry of the Word, the function of the congregation, including the proliferation of Gospel songs that reshaped much of Church Music.

---

[1] See Daniel L. Akin, David P. Nelson, and Peter R. Schemm, *A Theology for the Church* (Nashville, TN: B & H Academic, 2007), 654-655.

[2] Jerald Finney, *God Betrayed: The Separation of Church and State: The Biblical Principles and American Application* (Xulon Press, 2008), 97.

Redefining the Ministry of the Word

Fiery sermons, calling the lost to repent, were not an innovation of the 1800's. Sermons like Jonathan Edwards' *Sinners in the Hands of an Angry God* (preached July 8, 1741), were clearly intended to have a deep emotional impact and move the heart of the hearer.[1] But what began in the outdoor meetings of the Great Awakening as a passionate sermon delivered with the hope of conversion became, for many, the *raison d'être* following the Second Awakening. The function of the sermon became evangelism. Finney's *new measures* became the benchmark by which many churches evaluated the effectiveness of their worship gatherings—primarily, by visible signs of conversion. For instance, *to obtain the sought end of worship, Methodists of the early nineteenth century and beyond willingly exhibited the liturgical pragmatism popularized by Finney.*[2] By the time Finney had left his imprint on evangelical preaching, those who followed him evaluated sermons almost exclusively on their ability to produce visible manifestations of God's activity.

Since the Reformation, nearly all Protestant worship services had held one thing in common: the significance of the Ministry of the Word. From the Calvinist and Lutherans in Europe, to the Puritans in the New World, to the Congregationalists in New England, and Baptists along the Atlantic coast, the preaching of Scripture was the primary focus of corporate worship. The desire of the reformers to set other things aside and make room for preaching the Scripture was one of the greatest bequeathals of the Reformation. For two hundred and fifty years that commitment was expressed in worship services, both liturgical and freeform, where the Bible was preached and taught to those within the Church.

The role of the sermon in weekly worship changed little during the first Great Awakening, continuing the practice of delivering messages that were theologically rich and built around exegesis of biblical texts. This began to change with the meteoric rise of Methodism in the nineteenth century, where producing a sermon that demonstrated an essential connection to the Scripture was not the main goal.

> The primary intention of Methodist preaching was never exegetical accuracy, but rather the need to inflame stone-cold hearts and rekindle the lukewarm by the power of the gospel, through the agency of the Holy Spirit. Indeed, preachers from the first century of American Methodism would often boast that though their sermons (which "took" a Scripture text and elaborated on it)

---

[1] Warren Wiersbe described Edwards' sermon as, *perhaps the most terrifying sermon ever preached.... marked with utter sincerity and profound conviction.* See, Warren Wiersbe, *Treasury of the World's Great Sermons* (Grand Rapids: Kregal Publications, 1993), 198.

[2] Karen B. Westerfield Tucker, *American Methodist Worship* (Oxford University Press, 2001), 11.

or exhortations (testimonies of the faith not connected to a specific text) might not be erudite or systematic, they were effectual.[1]

This represented a significant shift in the role of the sermon in worship. The success of a sermon was not judged on its faithfulness to the text, but on whether or not it produced visible results—was it *effectual*? In this style of sermon, the job of the preacher was no longer to be a Bible expositor, but a motivator—responsible to move the listener to action.

Finney's approach to the sermon built on this concept, teaching that *it was the preacher's task to secure a decision of faith, applying whatever means seemed useful.*[2] This placed the outcome of the service on the means used by the preacher instead of on the power of God's Word to transform. If the sermon could not produce a movement of God, then something was wrong with the way the sermon or service was conducted. By the end of the century, techniques for giving an invitation that produced results were widely shared and taught. In 1898 the Rev. C. H. Yatman, then secretary of the Y.M.C.A. of Newark and leader at Ocean Grove Camp Meeting (a Methodist Campground on the coast of New Jersey), wrote the following in his training material for Christian workers. The excerpt is long, However, it is provided to show how much was being expected of the minister who sought to handle the invitation properly:

> In the majority of cases *in the general invitation,* it is best to so give it as to have the sinner take a bold stand on the side of Christ. The exceptions are where the sinner will in a quiet way take a first step, and thereby get confidence both in himself and Christ for a bolder stand. Make sure of all this in all invitations, that the sinner understands there is salvation in nothing, or nowhere but in Christ. Every invitation must mean at the bottom, "The full surrender of all to God. The complete giving of all we have and are to the service of Christ, and trusting him."

> SPECIAL KINDS OF INVITATION. Who will come to the altar or anxious seat to seek Christ? Who will come to the inquiry room? Will you come and be one of the class to be instructed "how to be saved?" Will you rise up in your seat? While all Christians are standing or bowed in prayer, get them to rise or lift a hand for prayer; this is a first step. Ask all who have decided to become Christians to rise and say, "I have," or "I will." Have them repeat "Christ for me." Make the seat an altar of prayer. Get them first to rise for prayer, then to come forward as seekers for salvation. Get them to lift the hand or rise for prayer or as seekers, then invite them to an after service. Have them remain in their seat, and some Christian worker will talk with them. "Who will meet with the others and hear the plan of salvation?" Who will sign an "I will" card? Then get a book like "Good news for you." Have all who want Christ, or will seek him, to walk out of their seat to the inquiry room. Give the plans of salvation, and then get them to say, "I will trust," "I will take," or "I will choose." While heads are bowed in prayer, get them to rise and say, "I take

---

[1] Tucker, 36.

[2] John MacArthur, *Ashamed of the Gospel, When the Church Becomes Like the World* (Crossway Books: Wheaton Illinois, 1993), 159.

217

Christ." Ask, "Who will receive Jesus?" Give full plan of salvation, then get Christians and all who will give themselves to God to stand and sing "My God is reconciled." Ask those who have or will give themselves to God to come forward and shake hands with the leader or minister. Get the Christians and the sinners to the altar. Ask all who will seriously listen to the truth to stand. Get them to ask for prayer by written request. Invite them to meet you in your own room. Sing "Who will go," and ask who will. Who will promise to meet me in heaven? Who will meet loved ones in heaven? Ask the older Christians to stand, then "who will take their keeping Saviour?" Who will accept the King's invitation to be present at the marriage supper of the Lamb? Who will pray, "God be merciful to me a sinner?" Who will call on the name of the Lord? Who will meet the pastor of the church? Go from seat to seat seeking sinners. While preaching, stop and urge an immediate giving of themselves to God. Between the verses of song or solo get them to decide. While singing an invitation hymn, get them to decide and come. Ask, "Will you be a Christian now?" and get them to decide then and there. Let unsaved seekers come forward and seek till they find that light. Ask, "Who will give up all sin and serve God?" Who will write their names after "fear not" in Isa.XLiii. Who will receive and who will reject Christ? Get those who have the most influence with the individual to invite them. Get them to come to the unconverted people's meeting.[1]

It is not difficult to see that a great deal of responsibility for procuring a response is placed on the one conducting the invitation. The most important part of the sermon was not the preaching of Scripture; instead it was the way in which the invitation time was handled. In other words, the content of the sermon was not as important as the call for response. As a result, emotional responses and visible decisions became the primary focus of the gathering. As this model was absorbed into Sunday worship services, sermons shared one common focus: a time of invitation where the repentant would somehow visibly manifest that he had made a decision of some type.

The Changing Role of the Congregation and Proliferation of Gospel Songs

Beginning with the Reformation, congregational singing had revolved around two scriptural functions: to address God directly and to testify to one another concerning His redemptive work. Songs directed to God were by far the majority of the two. In the revival-style service, songs directed to God became less important because the voicing of the service (to whom it was addressed) was moving away from addressing God and, instead, seeking to direct a stirring message to the congregation. How songs addressed those present was different from the testimony songs that were common in the first Great Awakening. For instance, the popular eighteenth century song by Isaac Watts, *When I Survey the Wondrous Cross,* was written to be sung as a declaration shared by all who had experienced redemption—a testimony shared in the congregation. In a revival-

---

[1] Charles H. Yatman, *Temple Themes and Sacred Songs with the Christian Workers' Training Class* (John H Hood: Philadelphia, 1898), microfilm, 92.

style service, testimony song texts no longer addressed other believers but directly addressed the unbelievers, encouraging them to repent and make a decision. This was part of the reordering of the function of music in worship. No longer simply concerned with voicing songs to God and between believers about God, Church Music in the nineteenth century exploded with songs that addressed the lost and the backslider, bidding them come to Christ or back to Christ before it was too late to do so.

Such hymns were chosen for their ability to move the hearts of the sinner to a decision. The example below is archetypical of such texts. Written in the first quarter of the nineteenth century and published in 1821, songs like this were common in the camp meetings of the nineteenth century, both in the U.S. and in England. The entire song is an emotional plea to the lost person.

HYMN 28. P. M.[1]
v.1 Stop, poor sinner, stop and think, // Before you farther go,
Can you sport upon the brink // Of everlasting woe?
Hell beneath is gaping wide, // Vengeance waits the dread command,
Soon to stop your sport and pride, // And sink you with the dam'd.

Chorus:
Once again I charge you stop, // For unless you warning take,
Ere you are aware, you'll drop // Into the burning lake.

v. 2 Say, have you an arm like God, // That you his will oppose?
Fear you not that iron rod // With which he breaks his foes?
Can you stand in that great day, // When he judgment shall proclaim,
And earth shall melt away, // Like wax before the flame?

v. 3 Pale-fac'd death will quickly come, // And drag you to the bar;
Then to hear your awful doom, // Will fill you with despair.
All your sins will round you crowd, // Sins of blood and crimson die;
Each for vengeance crying loud, // And what will you reply?

v. 4 Tho' your heart be made of steel, // Your forehead lin'd with brass,
God at length will make you feel // He will not let you pass;
Sinners then in vain will call, // (Tho' they now despise his grace,)
Rock and mountains on us fall, // And hide us from his face.

v. 5 But as yet there is a hope, // You may his mercy know,

---

[1] Hymn 28, from Hugh Bourne, *A Collection of Hymns for Camp Meetings, Revivals, &c.: for the Use of Primitive Methodists* (Bemersley near Tunstall [England]: Printed at the Office of the Primitive Methodist Connexion, 1821), 28-29.

Tho' his arm be lifted up, // He still forebears the blow.
'Twas for sinners Jesus died, // Sinners he invites to come,
None who come shall be denied, // He says there still is room.

A chorus would have followed each verse and this format became a
trademark feature of the camp meeting song. The song leader would line out
(recite or sing the opening line of) the verse or chorus and the congregation
would follow along. As a result, such songs could be repeated freely and last for
an extended period during an invitation or a particularly emotional climax in the
service. The invitation hymn became a distinct genre and, as the century
progressed, many hymnals delineated a section of hymns for such a purpose.
This type of song became typical in regular Sunday services well into the
twentieth century. While the poetry became more refined, the basic function of
the song remained the same. Phillip Bliss' (1838-1876) *Almost Persuaded*,
written in 1871, represents this genre at its best. Note that the role of the
congregation is both exhorter and intercessor.

"Almost persuaded" now to believe;
"Almost persuaded" Christ to receive;
Seems now some soul to say,
"Go, Spirit, go Thy way,
Some more convenient day
on Thee I'll call."

"Almost persuaded," come, come today;
"Almost persuaded," turn not away;
Jesus invites you here,
Angels are ling'ring near,
Prayers rise from hearts so dear;
O wand'rer, come!

Oh, be persuaded! Christ never fails—
Oh, be persuaded! His blood avails—
Can save from every sin,
Cleanse you without, within—
Will you not let Him in?
Open the door!

"Almost persuaded," harvest is past!
"Almost persuaded," doom comes at last;
"Almost" cannot avail;
"Almost" is but to fail!
Sad, sad that bitter wail—
"Almost—but lost!"

Be now persuaded, oh, sinner, hear!
Be now persuaded, Jesus is near;
His voice is pleading still,

220

Turn now with heart and will,
Peace will your spirit fill—
Oh, turn today![1]

Invitation hymns caused concern for those outside of the revival movement. Their objections were based partly on distaste for emotionalism and sentimentality and partly on the concern that they were becoming so popular that they were displacing songs directed to God. The defense to these objections was that such texts used during invitations worked. In a book compiling popular hymns near the end of the century, editor, W.T. Stead, wrote the following defense and commentary on *Almost Persuaded*:

> The sad, wistful wail of the music to which this hymn was set has made it an instrument of power to many souls. The task of clinching a decision almost crystallized into action is one of the most necessary and difficult of all the tasks of the religious teacher. In its performance, such hymns as this have proved too useful to permit their exclusion on the pedantic ground that they are not addressed to the Deity. The purists are in danger of provoking a reaction which will result in objections being taken to any hymns which are not directly addressed to those whose course may be altered by touching melody or sacred song.[2]

The immediate results were validation enough. By the end of the century many evangelical churches were conducting Sunday worship services built almost totally on the Revivalism model. In services where this occurred there were few, if any, hymns that addressed God directly. Instead, the typical service in this genre was comprised of songs that addressed the unbeliever rather than the believer, a sermon crafted for a final gospel presentation and an invitation hymn like the one above. All of these changes were intended to move the listener directly to a decision that could be announced publicly in the service.

Revivalism produced other genres of congregational music as well. The *camp meeting song* is similar to the invitation hymn in encouraging the sinner to repent. However, the music to these was much less sober and quite lively. The roots of the camp meeting song are musically tied to folk music, including songs used among African Americans, slaves and free, as well as folk music of Appalachia and the rural South. As such, they share a common heritage with twentieth century Southern Gospel, Blues, and Bluegrass. Many of these songs were published and shared regionally in small pamphlet-style collections.

The popularity of regional music, which had begun in the singing schools of William Billings in the eighteenth century, spurred the development of *shape note singing*. Shape note singing became widely popular among revival minded

---

[1] "Hymn: Almost Persuaded," Hymnal.net.
http://www.hymnal.net/hymn.php/h/1046 (accessed December 19, 2010).
[2] W. T. Stead, *Hymns That Have Helped: Being a Collection of Hymns Which Have Been Found Most Useful to the Children of Men* (New York: Doubleday and s

Christians in the same rural areas that utilized the camp meeting songs. Rather than reading traditional notation, in which the pitch is specified by where a note is written on the musical staff, the shape note system utilized different shapes for each note. Singers read the shape to determine what pitch to sing. This movement spawned a succession of shape note publications including *Kentucky Harmony* (1817), *Southern Harmony* (1835), and *The Sacred Harp* (1844).

By the end of the century, the use of all Church Music forms had seen significant growth. The number of hymnals published in the second half of the nineteenth century was more than double the number published in the first half of the century.[1] Hymns, Gospel songs, camp meeting songs, and short refrains were all being used widely in worship services and Sunday Schools. Many of these were made famous in the meetings of evangelist, Dwight L. Moody (1837-1899), and his song leader, Ira D. Sankey (1840-1908). Together these men preached and sang the gospel in evangelistic services to tens of thousands and brought the revival movement full force into the twentieth century. The mid-twentieth century evangelistic crusades of Billy Graham became the heirs of their revival legacy.

Beyond the kind of songs that the congregation sang, there were other changes in the way they participated in the service. In a gathering where the full thrust of all elements was intended to produce a visible effect on the congregation, Revivalism spawned many physical manifestations that were previously uncommon in Protestant worship. This was apparent from the beginning of the Second Great Awakening at Cane Ridge, Kentucky. *Tales of "physical exercises" that people experienced at Cane Ridge spread far and wide: weeping, shrieking, groaning, shouting, dancing, trembling, jerking, swooning. The outpouring of religious feeling at Cane Ridge soon erupted across the entire country.*[2] In many services, such manifestations became common and were seen as a sure sign that the Spirit had fallen on the people with great power. Such visible signs had been observed in the previous century and, while John Wesley affirmed them, they were not generally accepted. Writing in 1874, Henry Clay Fish summarized how the leaders of the first Great Awakening viewed such physical manifestations:

> John Wesley looked upon these physical agitations as proofs of the divine presence. Charles Wesley suspected and discouraged them. Whitefield was incredulous. Edwards puts in an apology for them. But very few ministers favored them. Finding by careful examination that they were often accompanied with rational conviction and sound conversion, they treated them gently, but did not ascribe them to divine influence, nor hold them to be parts of a revival. It were better, no doubt, had there been a more decided discouragement of them. Even with the aids of science in its present advanced state, it is not possible to account for these physical effects; nor is

---

[1] See above, *Hymns Published between 1800 and 1900.*
[2] Robert R. Mathisen, *Critical Issues in American Religious History* (Waco, TX: Baylor University Press, 2006) 202.

it important. Agitations quite as marked have occurred when in no way connected with religion, and also with fanatical heresies.[1]

Despite the fact that such *physical exercises* had been observed among heretical groups, they became commonplace in revival meetings and would continue to sporadically appear through the twentieth century. For those who were convinced that visible manifestations were the confirmation that God had moved, this gave both believer and unbeliever a clear indicator of the Spirit's activity. While this sort of freeform participation may have seemed liberating, it created an unfortunate circumstance where the benefits and results of the corporate gathering were judged on extra-biblical criteria—how many demonstrated through some *physical exercise* that they had experienced an outpouring of the Spirit? Clearly, the Scripture has its own indicators that confirm whether or not one has come to faith in Christ or has experienced a deep work of God: namely, the fruit of righteousness that comes from a heart submitted to God.

Final Thoughts on the Effects of Revivalism on Worship

Our earlier discussions demonstrated that there are three types of communication in Christian worship: mono-directional (*kerugma*), bi-directional (*leitourgia*), and omni-directional (*koinonia*). In each of these, Scripture presumes the belief of those involved. These three types of communication are what distinguish a worship gathering from an evangelistic meeting. In a worship gathering, the one who teaches the Scripture does so to those who know the Lord and are growing in the knowledge and application of the Word. Similarly, the liturgy (*leitourgia*) of the people and Christian fellowship (*koinonia*) are limited expressions for those who are saved.

Nineteenth century Revivalism presumed a very different scenario. It presumed the probable lostness of those present and constructed the sermon accordingly. While a sermon may still be mono-directional and have the same look as *kerugma*, it is no longer primarily teaching the Scripture to believers when its principal concern is moving the emotions of the lost. Instead, it is evangelism, declaring the gospel to unbelievers. When the sermon becomes primarily evangelistic, those who have already made a decision are no longer listening for how the Word applies to them, but for how it will move the lost person toward salvation. This relieves the believer from making primary application to himself—the primary application is not intended for him. This creates an unhealthy circumstance where sermons can be crafted in a way that only incidentally addresses the believers in the congregation. The New Testament demonstrates that, in a gathering of believers, evangelism is not the primary goal of teaching the Scripture. Instead, evangelism should be a healthy by-product—the Word is preached primarily for the edification of the believer

---

[1] Henry Clay Fish, *Handbook of Revivals: for the Use of Winners of Souls* (Harrisonburg, VA: Gano, 1988; reprint, Boston: James H. Earle, 1874), 19-20.

and the greater work of evangelism happens when the transforming work of God's Spirit and His Word compel believers to go and share the gospel.

This does not mean that evangelism does not and should not occur in corporate worship settings. When unbelievers are present in a worship gathering, they hear the truth of God's Word. They see the genuine love and affection that believers have for Christ and for each other. Each of these can be effectively used by the Spirit to draw the unbeliever to salvation. For this reason it is always important to be aware that there are likely unbelievers present in a worship gathering. We must stand ready to assist them in any way we can as they respond to God's work in their lives, whether by coming forward during an invitation or by some other means. However, the real power of evangelism is not demonstrated in the worship gathering. It is demonstrated by believers who have been ignited by the work of God and go into the world as salt and light. Preaching in the Revivalism model for worship addresses the unbeliever, saying, "Come, and we will tell you about Christ." The New Testament model of preaching in worship gatherings addresses the believer, saying, "Be transformed and go tell others about Christ."

Evangelism will occur in worship services when God chooses to move in the hearts of unbelievers who are present. Sermons should be preached with the hope that God *will* grow the hearts of believers and quicken the hearts of unbelievers. With that hope and expectation, churches should be ready to provide people an opportunity to profess their newfound faith. Additionally, churches may find it helpful to have gatherings for the purpose of evangelism, but such gatherings should never supplant the place of biblical worship. Turning our regular worship services into evangelism meetings cannot be the best approach for reaching a lost world—most of the lost people in our world will never attend any Christian gathering until after they have heard the message. Getting the gospel to them means, for the most part, going to them. In the end, our passion for the lost will be best expressed by demonstrating our sensitivity to their presence in our worship gatherings and by providing them a way to respond to God. Above all, we must do all in our power to strengthen believers so that they live fully for the glory of God outside of our worship gatherings. That remains the best hope for the millions who are lost and without Christ.

The reason for which we gather is the crux of the issue—is it first and foremost for worship as demonstrated in the Scripture? If success in our services is judged primarily by whether or not we see immediate and visible signs of God's activity, we are not evaluating our services on biblical grounds and aberrations are predictable. These may include the *physical exercises* described above or great emotional outpourings, none of which in themselves advance the cause of Christ. But more tragically, those who have been pressed by the combined efforts of a sermon and congregation to have an experience may lift a hand, be overcome with a great outpouring of emotion, or respond to an invitation, without ever knowing the transforming power of salvation. As well-meaning as it may be, declaring that someone is saved based solely on an emotional experience, without demonstrating any other fruit, dilutes the witness of what it means to be a follower of Christ. The state of much of Christianity today exhibits that this tragedy is real and ongoing. The surest protection is to allow the focus of the worship gathering to be just that—people gathered to submit themselves to God's power and majesty, to hear the Word preached and be transformed by its power, and to join in genuine fellowship with other believers. All of this must be done, trusting God for the outcome. These must comprise the fundamental elements of the corporate gathering—however it looks, wherever it occurs, or whatever style it assumes—because that is what Scripture demonstrates it to be.

WORSHIP IN CHURCHES THAT RESISTED REVIVALS AND REVIVALISM

Background

While many churches in New England were touched by revival in the first Great Awakening, there was significant resistance to the methods used. Many who preached in large outdoor meetings were considered radical by the 'old lights' of the Congregational and Presbyterian churches. They opposed the use of such a passionate, emotional style of preaching, as well as much of the hymnody that went with it. This was evidence of two developing schools of thought. *One emphasized emotionalism and found its expression in the Great Awakening. The other emphasized reason and found its expression in "rational Christianity" and deism, both products of the Enlightenment.*[1] The tension between these two views was exacerbated by the Second Great Awakening. If the 'old lights' could not approve of Jonathan Edwards and George Whitefield, they could certainly not approve of Asbury and Finney. They feared that Revivalism would be the undoing of the worship style used in many Reformed churches; and, in some cases, it was.

However, worship practices in the Reformed churches of New England and the upper Atlantic coast were facing a greater enemy than the aberrations found among the meetings of Asbury and Finney. Having opposed emotionalism, those who chose "rational Christianity" soon found themselves inundated with a very humanistic concept that embraced a God-given goodness in humankind and affirmed the individual's ability to better himself through learning and understanding. This was nurtured in New England, particularly at Harvard, which became *a breeding ground for "Unitarian moralist theology."*[2] This rational approach went far beyond rejecting emotionalism in worship. Churches born of Puritanism or orthodox Congregationalism, who in one century held to a strong Reformed theology, embraced ideas which attempted to alter the nature of the atonement, the sinfulness of man, and dismiss the deity of Christ.

---

[1] Timothy Miller, *America's Alternative Religions* (Albany: State University of New York Press, 1995), 88.
[2] Ibid.

By the end of the century, there were three distinct approaches that shaped worship practices in New England:

1) those who embraced the First Awakening and subsequently received aspects of Finney and/or Asbury in the Second Awakening,

2) those who maintained orthodox Reformed theology, but resisted revival preaching altogether, and

3) those who in the optimism of the Enlightenment and prosperity of the new democracy opted for an immanent God who helps men help themselves.[1]

It is this third group to which we now turn our attention because although they rejected the revivals, their influence equaled or exceeded that of the Revivalism movement. Most churches which comprised this group were initially in New England. There, some of the same churches that had been bellwethers in the first Great Awakening were embracing humanism.[2] Many of these churches had rejected the revivals and had witnessed a large decline in their growth rates. This was in contrast to those who embraced revivals: Baptists, Methodists, and revival minded Presbyterians.

> During the late eighteenth and early nineteenth centuries, the Congregationalist and Episcopal churches grew relatively slowly. The number of Congregationalist churches rose from 750 in 1780 to 2,200 in 1860; the number of Episcopal congregations from 400 to 2,100. At the same time, other denominations—particularly the more pietistic and evangelical sects—expanded at a staggering pace. Baptists from 225 to 2,100; Presbyterians from 500 to 6,400; Methodists from 50 in 1783 to 20,000 in 1860.[3]

By 1895 this trend was even more pronounced. The number of Presbyterian churches had risen to 14,530; Baptists to 46,871; Methodists to

---

[1] A division into three groups also appeared in the first Great Awakening. Thomas Kidd writes: "On one end were the *anti-revivalists* who dismissed the revivals as religious frenzy or 'enthusiasm.' In the middle were the *moderate evangelicals,* who supported the revivals at their outset but became concerned about the chaotic, leveling extremes that the meetings produced. Finally, on the other end were the *radical evangelicals,* who eagerly embraced the Spirit's movements, even if social conventions had to be sacrificed." See Thomas S. Kidd, *The Great Awakening: the Roots of Evangelical Christianity in Colonial America* (New Haven: Yale University Press, 2007), xiv.

[2] The movement toward liberalism in Congregational churches flourished under the leadership of Congregationalist William E. Channing (1780-1842), who was instrumental in the formation of a liberal association of Congregational churches. This would later become the American Unitarian Association in 1825.

[3] Mathisen, 202.

52,550. Meanwhile, all branches of the Episcopal churches numbered only 5,979 and Congregationalist churches numbered only 5,500.[1]

Even though many New England churches slowed in their rate of growth, their influence expanded greatly. The significant economic development that occurred in the second half of the nineteenth century created some of the wealthiest and most influential families in American history. Many of the nation's top political and religious thinkers were part of the cultural elite and most of them spent their lives in New England churches that had rejected the revivals. It was not that these churches necessarily opposed all aspects of the revivals. However, most pastors of established and affluent New England churches preferred to remain in their comfort rather than brave the frontier. Sociologists Finke and Stark identified this as a choice by the established mainline denominations in the northeast to lose momentum and hand it over to the Baptists and Methodists:

> It was abundantly clear to all parties that enthusiastic preaching, revival campaigns, and camp meetings were potent methods for mobilizing religious participation. Thus, it was well known, even among professors at Harvard and Yale, that Baptists had benefited greatly from Whitefield's crusade, and even popular press recognized the rapid growth of Methodism following the Revolution. Moreover, because 94 percent of Americans lived on farms in 1800, the camp meeting was even more important for church growth than were urban revivals. None of these, however, prompted the colonial mainline denominations to adopt similar "marketing" tactics. To the contrary, the leading lights condemned all such methods while ridiculing Methodist and Baptist preachers as ignorant, even dangerous fools.[2]

The cultural distinction between affluent churches which rejected revivals and less cultured churches that embraced them is an important one in understanding how worship styles developed. It was not unusual to find New England pastors who supported aspects of the revival movement in the nineteenth century. Men such as Lyman Beecher (1775-1863), a leading Presbyterian minister, actually supported many of Finney's new measures. However, there was a growing distinction between pastors who embraced an established cultured form of worship and those who embraced the forms common among the revivals.

---

[1] Henry King Carroll, *American Church History Series*, Phillip Schaff, et al, General Editors, *The Religious Forces of the United States: Enumerated, Classified and Described on the Basis of the Government Census of 1890, with an Introduction on the Condition and Character of American Christianity,* revised (New York: The Christian Literature Co., 1893), 454.

[2] Roger Finke, Rodney Stark, *The Churching of America, 1776-2005: Winners and Losers in Our Religious Economy, 2nd Edition* (Rutgers University Press, 2005), 106-107.

Comfortable, well-paid mainline clergy rarely desired to go West and had no taste for ministering to the ignoble vulgus. They earned more esteem from publishing their sermons in books than from bellowing them to multitudes in open fields. In any case, clergy flirting with Unitarianism or who thought Methodists and Baptists were literally "out of their wits" would have been of little worth out where the great harvest of souls was under way, even had they been willing to venture forth. It is impossible to imagine Lyman Beecher exhorting the "muscular" sinners at Cane Ridge.[1]

This confirms that some of the division that occurred over worship styles during the nineteenth century was based on cultural difference. If the revivals were happening among the *ignoble vulgus*, those in established affluent churches wanted no part in them or the type music they employed. Rather, they chose alternate approaches to worship that further distinguished them from those who embraced the revivals. What followed was a natural shift away from that which they considered coarse emotion. Concomitantly, congregations embraced refinements in preaching styles, liturgical forms and architecture. This pushed their music toward professionalism and moved preaching toward intellectualism, making the end of the nineteenth century a cultural zenith for Protestant churches in music and architecture while, at the same time, eschewing Revivalism and dismissing historic Reformed theology. We will briefly examine how these areas of worship changed in the churches that rejected the emotionalism of the revivals and chose, instead, to embrace a more refined, intellectual approach.

Effects on Preaching

The shift toward intellectualism and later, liberalism, was not sudden and in many cases proceeded under various banners of noble causes, such as the abolition of slavery, women's suffrage, and prohibition.[2] The transition in thought was well underway in the first quarter of the nineteenth century. Churches fueled by a growing fascination with human ability saw themselves as the engine that could drive away suffering and lead humankind into a golden age. The greatest impact this had on worship was how the sermon was approached and prepared. Revivalism diminished the Ministry of the Word by moving toward emotionalism. Those who rejected the revivals suppressed the Ministry of the Word in an effort to appeal to the intellect and to reason. Their approach was based on an increasingly popular belief that the sovereign God had provided humankind with sufficient resource to work out its own problems through human achievement—that man could suppress his own demons and cure the world's ills. For pastors attempting to preach in this new style, this meant

---

[1] Finke, 112.

[2] Causes provided the impetus for sermons in churches for those who embraced emotionalism and those who chose intellectualism. By the end of the nineteenth century, many Methodist pastors were preaching sermons built around social causes. See the discussion below *Concluding Thoughts on This Period.*

presenting God as the loving Creator who had endowed man with enough goodness to blossom, if properly nurtured. This was a departure from sermons that presented God as transcendent and human beings as totally lost, with no capacity for true good apart from redemption.

Perhaps no one exemplified this type of preaching more than Henry Ward Beecher (1813-1887). While he was not the primary theologian of nineteenth century liberalism in America, he did become its most famous spokesman.[1] The son of Lyman Beecher and schooled in the Reformed tradition, H.W. Beecher began his ministry as a Presbyterian. After serving for a brief stint in Indianapolis, Beecher moved to Brooklyn Heights, New York in 1847, and assumed the pastorate of Plymouth Congregational Church. He remained there until his death. During those forty years, he built a reputation as a leading voice for the abolition of slavery and as a powerful spokesman on other social ills. But beyond that, Beecher was highly regarded as a practitioner of a new preaching style which embraced theological liberalism. *In Brooklyn Heights Beecher put liberal Protestantism on the map.*[2]

A great deal of Beecher's approach to preaching was summarized in a series of lectures he presented at Yale in 1872 in which he described two historic approaches to preaching. One was found in the liturgical church, where the sermon took a secondary or complimentary role to symbol and form, and the other in the Reformed tradition, where preaching was propositional, teaching doctrine from Scripture. Beecher proposed a new approach to supersede both, which he called the *Life School* approach.

> [I]t may be said that there have been but two schools of Preachers. One may be called the Ecclesiastical school; in which term I include the whole body of men who regard the Church on earth as something to be administered, and themselves as channels, in some sense, of Divine grace, to direct the flow of that Divine institution. Ecclesiastical preachers are those who administer largely and preach incidentally, if one might say so. There is also the Dogmatic School of Preachers, or those who have relied upon a pre-existing system of truth, which has been founded before their day and handed down from generation to generation, and who apparently proceed upon the supposition that their whole duty is discharged when they have made a regular and repetitious statement of all the great points of doctrine from time to time.

---

[1] The key American liberal theologian of the nineteenth century was Horace Bushnell (1802-1876). His key role in American liberalism, his influence on Beecher, and Beecher's transition, from reformed Presbyterian to Liberal spokesman, is examined by Gary J. Dorrien, *The Making of American Liberal Theology: Imagining Progressive Religion, 1805-1900* (Louisville, KY: Westminster John Knox Press, 2001).

[2] Gary J. Dorrien, *The Making of American Liberal Theology: Imagining Progressive Religion, 1805-1900* (Louisville: Westminster, John Knox Press, 2001), 191.

Now, the school of the future (if I am a prophet, and I am, of course, satisfied in my own mind that I am!) is what may be called a *Life School.*[1]

Beecher goes on to explain that this new style of preaching is not based in liturgy or established doctrine. Instead, the sermon, above all, is grounded in an understanding of human nature.

> This style of preaching is to proceed, not so much upon the theory of the sanctity of the Church and its ordinances, or upon a pre-existing system of truth which is in the Church somewhere or somehow, as upon the necessity for all teachers, first, to study the strengths and the weaknesses of human nature minutely; and then to make use of such portions of the truth as are required by the special needs of man, and for the development of the spiritual side of human nature over the animal or lower side — the preparation of man in his higher nature for a nobler existence hereafter. It is a life-school in this respect, that it deals not with the facts of the past, except in so far as they can be made food for the present and factors of the life that now is; but rather studies to understand *men,* and to deal with them, face to face and heart to heart, — yea, even to mold them as an artist molds his clay or carves his statue.[2]

The influence of humanism and intellectualism changed both the process and focus of nineteenth century sermons. In the Reformed tradition, the concept was systematic and propositional. It was the pastor's role to go to the Scripture, plumb the truths it contained, and deliver them as the great doctrines of the faith. The teaching of Scripture was a focal point of corporate worship. For Beecher, preaching was not a matter of delivering the meaning of a particular Scripture or teaching a particular doctrine. Beecher's concept was that the Scripture would be ancillary, making *use of such portions of the truth as are required by the special needs of man.* Thus, the careful study of *the strengths and the weaknesses of human nature* inform the Scripture rather than *vice versa.* Once human nature was studied and the needs were determined, Scripture could then be applied as necessary to move the hearer and *mold them as an artist molds his clay or carves his statue.*

As different as Beecher's intellectual approach was from Finney's Revivalism, there is an inescapable similarity. In both, the sermon began its development by first looking at the particular needs and interests of the hearer and then determining how to structure the sermon to produce a specific result. For Finney, the outcome was a salvation experience and for Beecher, it was to touch the *higher nature for a nobler existence hereafter.* In both cases, the

---

[1] Henry Ward Beecher, *Yale Lectures on Preaching: Delivered before the Theological Department of Yale College, New Haven, Conn., in the Regular Course of the Lyman Beecher Lectureship on Preaching. First, Second, and Third Series* (New York: Fords, Howard, & Hulbert, 1889), 76-77.

[2] Ibid, 77-78.

exegesis of Scripture suffered since the sermon no longer grew from the text itself. Instead it began with the hearer, his needs, his concerns, and his nature.

Beecher's departure from the historic view of preaching is most vividly revealed in his view of the Scripture, particularly how it takes a secondary role in the sermon. Rather than seeing the text of the Bible as eternal truth that had the power to transform the hearer, it contained only seminal truths that are applied after understanding human nature. As Beecher put it, the Scripture was the acorn and human experience was the tree:

> The kingdom of God and of truth, as it is laid down in the New Testament, is a kingdom of seeds. They have been sown abroad, and have been growing and developing in the world; and, whereas, when they were initiated they were but seminal forms, now they have spread like the banyan-tree. And shall I go back and talk about acorns after I have learned about oaks? Shall I undertake to say that the Infinite Truth that is in Jesus Christ is, all of it, comprised in the brief and fragmentary histories that are contained in the four Evangelists...?

> All that has been evolved in human existence you may find as germ-forms in the Bible; but you must not shut yourselves up to those germ-forms, with stupid reverence merely for the literal text of the gospel. It is the gospel *alive,* the gospel as it has been made victorious in its actual conflict with man's lower nature, that you are to preach.[1]

This approach was well suited to the northeast where intellectualism, humanism, liberalism, and refined society flowed and mixed freely. The Puritan concepts of God's transcendence, man's depravity, and sermons rooted in Scripture gave way to a God who was near, human beings who were not so bad after all, and sermons rooted in the study of human nature.

The Concept of the Church House as God's Sanctuary[2]

The prevailing concept of God in nineteenth century New England was not the same as the transcendent One preached in the first Great Awakening. Humanism was much more comfortable with God's immanence than His transcendence, seeing, in some way, His love and goodness in all people. His presence was not to be feared but celebrated. This meant that the place where Christians gathered for worship need not be austere. The stigma of ornate cathedrals that had existed since the Reformation was fading. The church house was a place where God's presence dwelt, where people could meet with Him and engage the whole person—socially, economically, intellectually, and spiritually;

---

[1] Ibid, pp. 78-79.

[2] The changing face of church architecture in the nineteenth century and its relationship to changing views of God is covered in the excellent work of Jeanne Halgren Kilde, *When Church Became Theater: The Transformation of Evangelical Architecture* (New York: Oxford University Press, 2002).

a sanctuary where the gap between God and man had been closed and His nearness could be seen in the goodness of those gathered. In some aspects, this was a renewal of the Old Testament concept of the Temple: the Sanctuary where God's presence dwelt. The idea that God's presence would particularly be associated with a building was *far from that of Colonial Calvinists, who would have no more sought God's presence in the meetinghouse than in the jailhouse.*[1]

At the same time, many believed that man's potential goodness could be realized in the nurturing environment of the home. An expanding middle class absorbed the Victorian view of the home as a place of solace and refuge from the press of urban and industrial development. By the second half of the nineteenth century, church architecture synthesized the concepts of the home as a place of refuge and the church as a place to celebrate God's immanence.

> In the late 19th century this "meeting with God" meant not simply coming together as Christians to hear the Word; it also meant active worship, which was directed toward God. Hymns and anthems addressed the divine, stressing the presence of God, his witness to worship. The great distance between God and humanity conceived by the Calvinists had been overcome. An immanent God required a holy locale, and the meetinghouse became the "house of God," merging flawlessly with the domestic, familial ideology prominent within the middle class.[2]

This changing view of God greatly altered the spaces in which American Christians worshiped. If the church house was God's house, then neither the folksy songs of the revivals nor the simple church architecture of previous generations were suitable. To find a suitable architecture and appropriate music, New England church leaders looked to the opera houses and symphony halls. During the last quarter of the nineteenth century, numerous mainline churches in major cities erected large edifices that demonstrated their concept that the gathering house was the sanctuary—the "house of God." For the first time since the Reformation, Protestant churches were using what had been a Roman Catholic concept—the cathedral as the sanctuary where a special measure of God's presence dwelt. Clearly, Protestant churches were employing the pre-Reformation connection between the Jewish Temple and the house of worship. In the 1883 inaugural issue of *Church Building Quarterly*, the editors placed Exodus 25:8 on its front cover: *"And let them make me a sanctuary that I may dwell among them." Such ideas about the presence of God within religious space are not surprising for evangelicals who since the 1850's had been growing comfortable with both Gothic Revival churches and expanding liturgies.*[3] The choice of architectural style (Gothic Revival) harkened to a pre-Reformation idea about the house of God. While the humanistic concept of God's immanence

---

[1] Jeanne Halgren Kilde, *When Church Became Theater: The Transformation of Evangelical Architecture* (New York: Oxford University Press, 2002), 147.
[2] Ibid.
[3] Ibid.

was different than that of pre-Reformation Catholicism, both placed a great importance on the role of the building itself to affect corporate worship.

While the exterior of these structures demonstrated their view that the worship house was a temple for God, the inside communicated a growing fascination with the congregation as consumers. By the end of the century, interior spaces were patterned after the best opera houses and symphony halls in the world. The preacher, who often enjoyed near star status, was located on an elevated stage at the focal point of a well of curved seats. The stage itself was large enough to accommodate a choir and space was designed to the rear of the choir loft to house a large, Romantic Era pipe organ. The side walls of the stage and the ceiling above were often surrounded by a proscenium arch (just as those that framed the stages in theaters). The congregation was positioned as an audience, outside the proscenium, and seated in individual theater seats to watch the best musicians and pulpiteers perform an increasingly refined liturgy. While this was not intended to disconnect the congregation from those who were on the stage, there is little doubt that such an arrangement placed the preacher, et al, in virtually the same relationship to the congregation as the stage performer had with his audience.

Changes in Congregational Music

Refinements in church design and architecture went hand in hand with a growing complexity in liturgy and in the music that was used. By the end of the century, affluent churches were using hymns for congregational singing interspersed with classical music performed by trained singers. The need for a trained musician to oversee the use of such music and musicians led churches to hire a staff coordinator for the job. Colleges and seminaries took note and by the end of the century had developed *programs to train and credential musicians for church work; a number of church musicians were able to derive their income mainly or totally from their parish work and to be considered on a level with clergy, even to bearing the title "minister of music."*[1] Beyond the effort to elevate the quality of the performance to honor God, music programs in church became a huge draw, rivaling the popularity of the preacher.

The drive for churches in larger metropolitan areas to mount larger music programs led by the best singers became competitive, understanding *that a reputation for a fine church choir was a powerful recruiting tool for new members.*[2] The focus was to procure the best singers possible, often hiring a professional quartet, one voice for each section of the choir. This made it possible for the choir to attempt more complex choral works. Orders of worship from New England churches in the latter half of the century regularly included

---

[1] John Ogasapian, *Church Music in America, 1620-2000* (Macon Georgia: Mercer University Press, 2007), 163.

[2] Charles D. Cashdollar, *A Spiritual Home: Life in British and American Reformed Congregations, 1830-1915* (University Park. Pa.: Pennsylvania State University Press, 2000), 93.

separate performance anthems. These were often masterworks from classical composers. Additionally, new pieces were often commissioned or written by the choirmaster or organist in a classical style.

The increasing appetite for high quality classical music was evident in church houses as well as in symphony houses and concert halls. Publishers that specialized in sacred music became profitable by the end of the century. By the term *sacred music*, we are describing Church Music that was classical in nature, a genre distinct from the Gospel-style music of the revival movement. In New England, sacred music was becoming much less a type of music that could be performed by the members and was becoming a subset of classical music, as it had been in Europe for several centuries. Just as European churches had once retained the services of master composers and musicians for the weekly service, the church went in search of the best musicians it could afford. *By the end of the century, when the evolution of choirs had been completed, there were two types of church choristers—volunteers and salaried professionals. Nearly all town and city churches paid at least some of their singers in order to achieve the quality that was expected by increasingly critical churchgoers.*[1]

With the addition of featured musical selections set in a classical concert style, worship services began to utilize more complex forms. In a service where quality musicians were paid, effort was made to use them for more than to bolster congregational singing. Affluent churches of all denominations added additional components to the worship service. Organ and orchestral settings for preludes and postludes as well as choral settings to provide a call to worship, responses to prayers, benedictions, etc., became common. In major New England cities, such as Boston and New York, newspapers and magazines reported on and critiqued musical performances in churches with the same attention to detail as they reviewed and critiqued performances of the opera or symphony.

The interest in classical music in the church blossomed and by the early twentieth century, societies and guilds developed for the purpose of raising the level of Church musicianship. Organizations such as the American Guild of Organists (founded in 1896) became a place where issues of classical music in the Church were discussed and championed. At the heart of this approach to Church Music was a conviction that anything other than the highest artistic form of music was less than befitting the majesty and glory of God. Therefore, music should represent the finest in poetry, the finest in composition, and the finest in performance. This was an attempt to make a distinction between revival-style Gospel music and classically-oriented *sacred music*. In an address presented at the Thirteenth Church Congress of the Protestant Episcopal Church (1890) and published in the 1912 edition of *The New Music Review and Church Music Review*, Peter Christian Lutkin stated:

---

[1] Ibid.

Broadly speaking[,] music in our church services serves two distinct objects. On the one hand it may assist in our formal worship of Almighty God in praise, in thanks giving, in supplication. On the other hand the primary object may be to touch the souls of men and by softening their hearts draw them nearer to God. At times both these objects may be subserved at once by the judicious selection of music, but more frequently there is a line of more or less marked differentiation between them, and for the following reasons:

As a formal act of worship the music that we offer to Almighty God should naturally be the best that we are able to provide. Not only should the music in itself have artistic value, but its performance should be upon as high a plane of excellence as circumstances will permit. We should strive to eliminate the concert room attitude and not look for pleasant musical sensations or enjoyment from a purely esthetic standpoint. The idea of worship should ever be foremost in our minds, of worship expressed in worthy musical terms, the worthiness of which should not be determined by the idiosyncrasies of untrained minds but by the judgment of mature artistic experience.[1]

Lutkin was championing Church Music as a worthy artistic pursuit. The 'fine art' concept of Church Music was a new development for American Protestants, who had typically chosen much simpler forms of music. Church Music as an art form was much more in line with the liturgical approaches of churches that the colonists had left behind in Europe. Such an approach to Church Music sought to attain the highest artistic level possible because it was directed to God, irrespective of the artistic sensibilities of the hearer. In this approach the art value of the music justified its usage, because God is worthy of the best that human creative energy can offer. He goes on to distinguish his approach from that of the revivalists:

As a matter of fact the musical appreciation of people in general is decidedly under-rated for the reason that it is not always in evidence upon the single hearing of an art work. An essential element in the effect of good music is adequate performance, and adequate performances are unfortunately rare. But given an adequate performance, it takes but few repetitions indeed to carry to the average listener the real purport of so-called classical music in its simpler forms. To give a concrete example I firmly believe that in the course of a revival of the Moody and Sankey type, a really great artist could make more effect with Mendelssohn's "For the Lord is mindful of His Own" than could possibly be made by the revival songs manufactured for the occasion, *provided* that it be sung at least three times during the meeting. It might fail upon the first singing, but if repeated at the psychological moments I am convinced that it would profoundly move the most miscellaneous audience one could gather together. Of course revivalists aim to make immediate appeal and trust to the catchy jingle and cheap sentiment of their songs to accomplish this result. They succeed temporarily, but it is an open question

---

[1] Peter Christian Lutkin, *The New Music Review and Church Music Review: Music as an Aid to Religion*, December ed., vol. 12 (New York: H. W. Gray, 1906), 549.

whether the superficial and ephemeral character of the means employed does not promote religious feelings of a similar sort, and whether a stronger and more wholesome musical diet would not produce a more substantial religious product.[1]

Both Revivalists and the Fine Art church musicians saw music as a means to affect the worshiper—a molding process that fit neatly with the concept of humanity's self-betterment prevalent in the nineteenth century. Obviously, Lutkin's view of Church Music is different from Finney's. The assertion that the results of revival style music *succeed temporarily*, while more classical music might produce a *more substantial religious product,* demonstrates that the difference between the two approaches was beyond a stylistic one. To one, music was a practical tool—a spade used to dig at the heart; to the other it was a masterpiece meant to elevate the mind and heart to a higher place.

Beyond that, there was still a greater and more fundamental difference in the emotional and intellectual approach. In some measure this difference is related to the conflict that was addressed in the opening pages of this chapter, namely, general or particular redemption—the nature of how God's Spirit moves and works in a person's life in salvation and beyond. The revivalist sought music to move the raw emotions and affect an immediate decision, believing that if a person could refuse the grace of God, the moment could be lost and so could the person. In a view where God's grace is ultimately irresistible, there is not the same sense of urgency in the moment. Such had been the background of many New England churches. They could embrace the Fine Art approach to Church Music, in part, because they did not feel the press of the revivalists and could give time to grow the person, to raise his awareness intellectually, culturally, and spiritually—letting God deal with his soul. If a man has no part in his own salvation, he will be saved if God's grace woos him.

In part, this explains why so many who came out of the Reformed tradition had a greater propensity to choose the complexities of Sacred/Classical over Gospel music. In their estimation, Gospel-style music stimulates only the emotions, which is temporary, while the other stimulates the emotions as well as the deeper and higher parts of the intellect and soul. The ability of higher art forms to stimulate the mind was a fitting companion for the type of preaching made popular by Henry Ward Beecher.

Final Thoughts on Churches that Resisted the Revivals and Revivalism

While the greatest weakness of Revivalism proved to be a redefinition of the purpose of the weekly gathering (from believer's worship to evangelism), the great weakness of those who resisted the revivals was a loss of passion to see conversion as it had been understood in the first Great Awakening. For many who stood outside of the revivals of the nineteenth century, salvation was increasingly viewed as a gradual lifting of man away from his lower demons to a higher plane. The sermon, the architecture, and the music were all built to

---

[1] Ibid, 551.

advance man's nature through cultural refinements, believing that was the best way to move him toward God. In doing so, the sermon revolved around the intellectual prowess of the preacher and his ability to demonstrate that he understood the needs of the listener. Concurrently, music in these churches moved increasingly toward a classical style and left more and more congregations sitting like an audience at the symphony hall.

This raises an important question for us. Can a sermon possess intellectual depth and still honor the spirit of biblical worship? Or, can music move toward a classical style, performed at very high level of competency, and still be worship? Simply put, the answer to both is *yes*. The problem arises when these are substituted for what is rightfully essential to worship. Even if these churches had not drifted toward liberalism, the reorientation of the sermon toward human nature rather than the Scripture, and the increasing lack of participation by the congregation, would have been enough to rob them of elements essential for worship. These changes did not go unnoticed, even within the denominations where it was occurring. In the late nineteenth century, Robert MacArthur and Francis Bellamy discussed this in the introduction to *The People's Worship and Psalter.* MacArthur and Bellamy identified that, among the problems that were developing, there was a lack of participation by the congregation. The suggestions they offered are telling:

> Each Congregation already has its order, written or unwritten, and many orders are more elaborate than this. Most of them, however, are confessedly unsatisfactory. Their faults are:

> 1. Their lack of naturalness. This is not surprising when one reflects how hastily they are often thrown together, with an eye for expediency rather than for spiritual meaning, copying stray features from here and there without reference to their origin and proper place.

> 2. The fact that they are often constructed for effectiveness of display, under the suggestions of the choir-master, who sometimes may prove a misleading master of worship.

> 3. The fact they have not adequately recognized that public worship ought always to be the People's Worship. The exercises previous to the sermon should not be considered as "preliminaries," a kind of introduction to the Sermon, — but Worship; the people's word to God, as the sermon expresses God's word to the people. Here the ordinary Sunday service is at fault. It seems to have been conceived in a forgetfulness that an order of service ought to be primarily a natural and familiar vehicle in which the people can express their feelings to God, and with the notion that the exercises are primarily an agency through which the people are to be acted upon by minister and choir. This is also a fatal error in the Roman Catholic service.

These are the leading blemishes in most of our modern orders of service. Few are contented with them. They are ornate and varied and long enough; but they are bewildering both because of their frequent changes, and of their remoteness from any familiar form of devotion either of the closet or of the prayer meeting. Devout Christians who have gone to the house of God to worship, and have felt themselves disappointed, have grown weary of services which depend for their effectiveness upon the minister's mood or personal power, and upon the choir's performances. Ministers, in multitudes, have realized what spiritual opportunity is being lost every Lord's Day in the inadequacy of the ordinary service, and have wished for some order which might avoid the above faults, and afford the people a simple and natural expression of their worship.

Numerous attempts, on a limited scale, have been made for the accomplishment of this purpose. But most of them, though excellent within their scope, have failed to win general acceptance, largely because they have not recognized the instinctive fondness which a regular Congregation has for regularity of exercises. Of course there should be margin for some variation; we want no inflexibility like that of the Episcopal Prayer-book. Yet it is natural for us to want certain general grooves for our devotion; we are disturbed by not knowing what to expect when we attend public worship.

This little service-book is a reverent attempt to offer to Christian Congregations an Order which embodies the following characteristics: —

1. It has, first of all, sought naturalness. It has endeavored to seize upon the class of Scriptural passages which are most familiar in the prayer-meeting and in the personal experience of the Evangelical believer. It has sought to compass the chief phases of the believer's relation to God, and to express, with a natural sequence, in public the familiar thoughts of the closet.

2. It has sought to dethrone the spectacular and display element which finds too large a place in much of our modern public service. The choir has a place of no less importance than before, but its voice is to fall unobtrusively into the trend of the people's worship, and to assist in expressing the people's thought rather than to divert it by an unexpected effect. The function of the choir is exalted, and its opportunity enlarged, while its personnel is more retired.

3. This Order has aimed to express the people's worship. In this service less depends on the minister's personality; more, on his desire to assist the people to worship. The preaching and his manner of conducting the service will give to his personality sufficient opportunity; it is the personality of the people which is here accented.

4. Very little that is entirely new is suggested; and what is new may remain unused without serious detriment to the significance of the service. The aim has been rather to re-arrange existing usages so as to secure the above

238

desiderata of naturalness, spirituality, and emphasis of the people's part. A few venerable forms, to be found in most of our hymnals, although hitherto seldom used, are suggested because of their simple grandeur and their exalted spirituality above most of our modern productions. They originated in the Primitive Church, and are the property of no one denomination, but belong to the whole Body of Christ. They have stood the test of time, and the people have never wearied of them.

The authors put forth this offering in the belief that it is timely. There is a growing demand for a people's worship which shall be both natural and spiritual. The Church of the Apostles had nothing else. Responsive psalms, general hymns, general prayers, general responses by all, made up the early worship. The Papacy gradually silenced the people's voice, and substituted pageantry by priest and choir. The English Reformers made their first struggle to win back worship for the people. The American Puritans, rejecting the English liturgy as still too ritualistic, nevertheless stoutly maintained, in general psalm, in requests for prayer, in reverent standing during prayer, and in final response, the people's privilege in public worship. It was the successors of the early American fathers who allowed choirs and artistic singers and great organs to take away again, like the Papacy of old, the people's voice, and finally to leave us with the present elaborate, but changeful and often unmeaning, patchwork style of service.

So, not with haste, but after prolonged and careful study of the history and meaning of the various forms of Christian worship; not as hostile innovators, but rejoicing in all the steps already taken towards a true utterance of the people's devotion; not as heralds of any untried and undesired fashion of service, but as endeavoring to express the scriptural idea of spiritual worship by "all the people" in familiar forms of modern usage; and finally, with no disrespect for the past, but in affectionate harmony with the Evangelical faith delivered to us from the fathers, the authors devoutly put forth this book of worship.[1]

In their own words, MacArthur and Bellamy were addressing deficiencies in two of the three types of communication essential to worship. Concerning preaching, they would go on to remind their readers, *The sermon is but the elucidation of God's word to us.*[2] As such, its success does not rest on the preacher's gifts, his personality, his intellect, or his understanding of human nature. Just as extremes of Revivalism had dispensed with systematically preaching the Scripture to believers, many churches that resisted the revivals did the same—not for the sake of evangelism, but opting for inspiring messages based on the study of humanity. While the sermon can be delivered with great intellectual depth and verbal skill, it is not preaching if it does not deliver God's Word to His people. It does not have to be erudite but, it must focus on the text

---

[1] Robert MacArthur and Francis Bellamy, *The People's Worship and Psalter, A Complete Order of Service for the Morning and Evening Worship of Christian Congregations* (Boston: Silver, Burdett & Co., 1891), 5-8.
[2] Ibid, 9.

rather than the speaker or the hearer. In a similar fashion, music can be more classical in nature and still be used by God. Like a finely crafted sermon, a skillful composition can be a powerful tool to move the heart toward God. However, it no longer serves the function of worship when it takes the place of *leitourgia*—again, the words of MacArthur and Bellamy are instructive: *public worship ought always to be the People's Worship*. Certainly, musical selection in a worship service can utilize mono-directional communication. However, even if such music reaches the highest artistic achievement, it will fall short of its stated purpose (worship) if it ultimately supplants participation by the congregation.

FINAL THOUGHTS ON THIS LESSON

The nineteenth century was a true melting pot of developments. We have focused on one of the key factors that shaped worship in the nineteenth century: the division that widened between a more emotional approach to worship and one that was more intellectual and refined. This was exacerbated by the economic landscape in the United States after the Civil War. A poorer South in Reconstruction proved to be much more furtive for the development of a passionate revival-style of worship, where Folk and Gospel music seemed much more at home. The economy in the North fared much better after the Civil War and was naturally more apt to reflect a refined society both inside and outside the church building.

Our focus might lead one to believe that liberalism developed only in the Reformed congregations that rejected the revivals and moved toward intellectualism. That would not be true. There was a general consensus among both religious liberals and evangelical revivalists that American Christianity *would take the lead in spreading Christian influence around the globe and combating all forms of tyranny and injustice.*[1] This desire to combat social wrongs led many revival minded denominations toward liberalism almost as quickly as it did those who rejected the revivals. Both believed they had found means to accomplish God's work beyond those known to their fathers and in doing so believed they could shape humanity into a better version of itself. By the end of the century *the social gospel was especially prominent in the life and work of Presbyterians, Baptists, and Methodists of the North, and among Congregationalists and Episcopalians.*[2] Obviously, even among the evangelical denominations that had embraced the revivals (Methodists and Baptists, particularly in the North) there were those that eventually moved toward liberalism.

Whether a church initially rejected the revivals or accepted them, they often turned to liberalism if they failed to lead their congregations to stay both

---

[1] Steven Mintz, *Moralists and Modernizers: America's Pre-Civil War Reformers* (Baltimore: Johns Hopkins University Press, 1995), 32.

[2] Williston Walker, Richard A. Norris, David W. Lotz, Robert T. Handy, *A History of the Christian Church,* Fourth Edition (New York: Scribner, 1985), 665.

intellectually and emotionally connected. There must be a fundamental connection to both in our preaching and our singing. The shift toward liberalism in Episcopal churches during the nineteenth century illustrates this clearly:

> When the old Evangelical party failed to think—or failed to train a new generation to think—of a new way to talk about Christ's satisfactory atonement and human sin, young Episcopal leaders abandoned the party of their forebears, rejecting the distinctive doctrines of the movement, and embraced liberalism. When the Evangelical party most desperately needed to reassert its theology in a new way, it failed to meet the challenge. Its genius, through the century, had been its ability to maintain its theological and experiential core in the face of successive changes.

> The younger Evangelicals-turned-liberals did attempt to modify evangelical theology for a new generation. They modified it so much, however, that it bore little resemblance to traditional orthodoxy. Some of them recognized that, in essence, they had rejected the faith of their forebears.[1]

For this reason, this lesson demonstrates that corporate worship must constantly reassert orthodoxy in terms that are both theological and experiential, both emotional and intellectual. This brings us full circle to the lesson with which we began this chapter: *Healthy worship does not choose between intellect and emotion; it fully engages both and trusts God's sovereignty for the results.*

The nineteenth century parting of ways did begin with differing views of how a person comes to faith in Christ—whether by free will or by God's sovereignty. While these two views generated vastly different approaches to the corporate gathering, they had acted as counter balances to each other. When they became separated from one another, they lost that ability. The results were destructive, producing aberrations from hyper-Pentecostalism to humanistic liberalism. These two approaches do not have to be enemies, nor do churches have to choose between a dry intellectual approach to worship and one that is filled with shock and awe to get people to make a decision for Christ. The great nineteenth century pastor, C.H. Spurgeon, saw the conflict in his day and when pressed to choose between the free will of man and the sovereignty of God responded:

> I never try to reconcile to friends, never. These two doctrines are friends with one another; for they are both in God's Word and I shall not attempt to reconcile them. If you show me that they are enemies, then I will reconcile them. "But," says one, "there is a great deal of difficulty about them." Will you tell me what truth there is that has not difficulty about it? "But," he says, "I do not see it." Well, I do not ask you to see it; I ask you to believe it.

---

[1] Diane Hochstedt Butler, *Standing Against the Whirlwind: Evangelical Episcopalians in Nineteenth-Century America* (Oxford: Oxford University Press, 1995), 229.

There are many things in God's Word that are difficult, and that I cannot see, but they are there, and I believe them. I cannot see how God can be omnipotent and man be free; but it is so, and I believe it.[1]

Such a full embrace of both free will and God's sovereignty was rare in the nineteenth century. Many drew a hard line between the two and, in doing so, lost something very useful. Namely, they lost the protection that comes from embracing the full orb of what Scripture teaches, even if it is beyond one's limited rational ability to grasp it. This does not mean that all churches should be alike. Again, the first Great Awakening proved otherwise. However, over the course of the nineteenth century the methods and approaches by each side became codified, each pushing further from a safe middle. *Theologically, the Awakening popularized a shift in American Christianity from a focus on God's sovereignty and human degradation to God's benevolence and the possible human agency in personal and spiritual regeneration and social transformation.*[2]

Where the approach was intellectual, a clear call for conversion was not an integral component in the weekly gathering. Instead, the sermon sought to advance the congregation through intellectual and cultural refinement. Ultimately, this made many churches easy targets for academic liberalism, which exploded in the second half of the nineteenth century. Where the approach tilted toward the emotional, visible signs of God's activity were essential in the weekly gathering. Therefore, methods were developed in an attempt to ensure such a result. This left churches wide open to seeking greater and more spectacular manifestations of God's power. In less affluent areas, the revivals became less and less about preaching repentance for salvation and more and more about the preacher's ability to move someone to a spiritual experience. *Charismatic preachers, scorning pessimistic Calvinist views of human nature and recognizing people's ability to speed their own salvation, expressed exuberant confidence in their ability to save souls and promote revivals.*[3]

As the diagram below illustrates, there is some latitude between being more intellectual or more emotional. However, the nineteenth century demonstrates that moving too far in either direction results in unhealthy consequences.

---

[1] Charles Hadden Spurgeon, "Jacob and Esau," The Spurgeon Archive. http://www.spurgeon.org/sermons/0239.htm (accessed December 01, 2010).

[2] Milton Gaither, 39.

[3] Steven Mintz, *Moralists and Modernizers: America's Pre-Civil War Reformers* (Johns Hopkins University Press, 1995), 172.

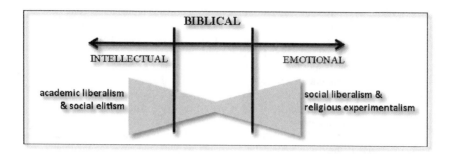

What began as two approaches, different but still within biblical boundaries, ended the century having moved beyond those boundaries and separated by a great distance. In both cases, the more extreme results produced those who rejected Orthodox Christianity. And, for those who may not have gone quite that far, there was still the high price of chasing after special manifestations of the Spirit, or catering to the 'higher nature' of man.

Today, the same division underlies much of evangelicalism. The danger to choose one side or the other is a trap into which many fall. Our call should be to enter into and celebrate the tension that exists between an intellectual approach and one that is more emotional in nature, even to go as far as Spurgeon and embrace free will and God's sovereignty as two friends that need no reconciliation. A full affirmation of both emotion and intellect was at the root of the first Great Awakening. Preachers like Jonathan Edwards delivered sermons with enormous passion but trusted God for the results. *In a time when some believers thought one had to be either intellectually or emotionally inclined in their religious practice, Edwards proved that one could do both. Indeed, his preaching strongly affirmed the need to be both intellectually rigorous and emotionally vulnerable to God's grace.*[1]

Spurgeon, himself fully convinced of God's absolute sovereignty in all things, laid before his congregation the deepest of doctrinal truth and the strongest of passionate appeal. Speaking to his people about their responsibility to pray for and work for the salvation of those whom they knew, he preached these words:

> Oh, let not the fierce regret sting you like an adder,—"Oh that I had prayed for my children! Oh that I had taught them before they departed." I pray you so live, that when you stand over your child's dead body you may never hear a voice coming up from that clay, "Father, thy negligence was my destruction. Mother, thy want of prayer was the instrument of my damnation." But so live, that when you hear the funeral knell, for a

---

[1] Mary Jo Weaver and David Brakke, *Introduction to Christianity* (Belmont, CA: Wadsworth, 2009), 112.

neighbour even, you may be able to say, "Poor soul, whether he is gone to heaven or to hell, I know I am clear of his blood." And with double earnestness be it so with your children. "Yes," says one "but I have thought of teaching my children more of Christ, and being more earnest in prayer for them bye-and-bye," but what if they should die to-morrow? "Yes," says the wife, "I have thought of speaking to my ungodly husband, and trying to induce him to attend the house of God with me, but I was afraid he would only laugh at me, so I put it off for a month or two." Ah! what if he dies before you have cleared your conscience of him? Oh, my brothers and sisters in Christ, if sinners will be damned, at least let them leap to hell over our bodies; and if they will perish, let them perish with our arms about their knees, imploring them to stay, and not madly to destroy themselves. If hell must be filled, at least let it be filled in the teeth of our exertions, and let not one go there unwarned and unprayed for.[1]

It is my prayer that churches could once again see intellectual acuity and fervent passion as integral, *essential* to corporate worship. If we can commit ourselves to corporate worship that is emotionally engaging and doctrinally pure, and to preaching that is biblical in both its passion and its truth, perhaps our own churches can see a great move of God, a genuine awakening in our day.

---

[1] C.H. Spurgeon, *Sermons of Rev. C. H. Spurgeon of London,* seventh series (New York: Robert Carter & Brothers, 1883), 333-334.

CHAPTER 10

FROM WORSHIP STYLES
TO WORSHIP BUBBLES
(AD 1900-2000)

In 1970, sociologist Alvin Toffler released his bestselling book, *Future Shock*. Toffler hypothesized that changes can be so numerous and so rapid that living through them causes people enormous stress. While Toffler wrote his book before the dawning of the Information Age (PC's, cell phones, the Internet, etc.), he had identified a telling mark of the twentieth century: rapid cultural change. In many ways the twentieth century could also be described as a period of *worship shock*. Changes in worship styles occurred with increasing rapidity through the twentieth century. By the end of the century, worship styles were changing significantly within a decade or less. What once lasted for generations, or even centuries, changed so quickly that single generations lived through multiple changes to worship music and Church culture. For this reason, worship music in the twentieth century became increasingly difficult to speak of in terms of a musical form.

The factors that led to such rapid changes and the effect they had on corporate worship will be the focus of this discussion. A great deal of this change was the harbinger of a new epoch. Modernism, which had characterized Western Civilization since the Renaissance, was giving way to Postmodernism. By the end of the century this transition became clearly visible in the Church as long lasting worship styles gave way to short lived bursts of cultural expression. This trend continued into the twenty-first century. A clear understanding of the lesson taught by the twentieth century explains a great deal of the worship shock experienced by numerous churches.

LESSON 13: WORSHIP EXPRESSIONS HAVE BECOME LESS LIKE FORMS OR STYLES AND MORE LIKE BUBBLES

BACKGROUND
Worship Forms and Styles

For readers who have not studied musicology or music history, it is necessary to provide a brief explanation of how musical styles form. Since music is a component of a culture's language, changes to culture precipitate changes to the music it produces. Small changes in culture can produce small changes in music. However, whenever significant components of the culture change—thought, philosophy, technological advancement, etc.—significant changes in music are likely to occur. When changes to music become so pervasive that the fundamental structure of the music changes, it normally produces new forms and may result in a completely new *stylistic period*. In the study of Classical Music in Western Civilization, there were five stylistic periods prior to the twentieth century: Medieval, Renaissance, Baroque, Classical, and Romantic. While scholars vary on exact beginning and ending dates for each of these periods (this leads to overlapping and a variety of proposed dates), these five are commonly accepted as periods in which most of the music was written under shared conventions and thus shares common traits. Twentieth Century Music was so varied in its development that it is not possible to clearly define one style that describes the period. Instead, it was a period of significant experimentalism.

To understand when these transitions occurred, the following table below shows each stylistic period name, the approximate dates of its beginning and end, and cultural changes that precipitated the change or unique characteristics that the musical period produced. It should be noted that the dates of similar periods in literature, sculpture, and painting have tended to precede those of music. Generally speaking, when the Fine Arts exhibit changes they come first in literature, followed by painting and sculpture, music, then finally, architecture. For the non-musician, the musical aspects of each style are less important than understanding how the timing of major shifts in musical style coincided with major changes in Western Civilization.

Period Name	Period Dates	Cultural Characteristics	Musical Developments
Medieval	500-1300	lack of widespread literacy, art and learning occurred almost exclusively in the Church	multiple melodic lines, the development of music notation
Renaissance	1300-1600	the rebirth of learning, writing, printing and the Reformation.	refinement of modal composition, advanced forms of polyphony
Baroque	1600-1750	rise of European powers, the push toward colonization.	modern tonal structure, birth of opera, the development of classical vocal technique
Classical	1730-1825	nationalism, revolution, democracy	development of the sonata structure, the modern symphony
Romantic	1815-1900	industrialization, individualism and introspection	highly emotive music, whether grand symphonies, or art songs. expressing longing
Twentieth Century	1900-2000	modernization, computers, information, globalization	Neo-Classicism, atonality, dissonance, experimentalism

Whether one is a student of music or not, a basic understanding of the history of Western Civilization reveals that significant changes in Western culture happened in each of these periods. The stylistic periods of music are simply one of the ways those changes were expressed. For instance, in the transition from the Medieval period to the Renaissance, there were multiple developments. A rapid expansion of literacy and learning, the birth of the European university system, the invention of the printing press, the Reformation, significant advancements in painting techniques, etc., were all part of a wide scale cultural shift. This also reflects the transition that occurred from pre-Modernism to Modernism. Subsequently, each of the transitions from one stylistic period to the next indicated major cultural changes.

This basic concept is essential to understand how developments in the twentieth century affected corporate worship. In the twentieth century there was not a single group of cultural changes that resulted in one major style, but multiple ones that layered and overlapped one another, creating a complex web of diverse cultural expressions. This was one of many indicators that the change from Modernity to Postmodernity was underway. This proved to be a massive transition, altering the way people in Western Civilization, and eventually, Global Civilization viewed the world in which they lived. Since musical styles tend to change whenever there are massive cultural changes, the twentieth century is a valuable laboratory for observing how massive cultural changes can affect the formation of worship styles.

Changes in the Twentieth Century
1900-1950

In the first fifty years of the century, Americans experienced multiple changes. Transportation moved from horse-drawn carriages and rail to widespread use of the automobile, and from no human flight to the establishment of commercial airlines that connected many major cities. In communications, the century began with a dependence on print media for news, the telegraph, and no widespread use of radio. By 1950, people were heavily dependent on radio for their news and entertainment and on telephones for personal communication. In media, black-and-white silent, short films became full length color motion pictures. And in recorded music, wax cylinders were subsequently replaced by massed produced vinyl records. A raft of other amazing advancements in medicine and manufacturing were added. Many of these advancements were hastened by two World Wars and the first fifty years ended with two super powers having entered the nuclear age headed toward a stalemate. Despite all of these changes, a glance at corporate worship could lead one to believe that it had changed very little in the first fifty years of the twentieth century. The two basic divisions between a more intellectual approach and one geared more toward emotion were still evident. However, a closer look reveals that even within these two approaches change was coming.

The more intellectual and cultured approach to worship became common in almost every large city in the United States. The mainline denominations flourished in these growing cities and during the first half of the twentieth century became enormously wealthy.[1] Operating with a continued optimism that the Church could cure many of society's ills, many used their resources to extend a variety of benevolent ministries. Despite these outward successes, there was an underlying problem developing in Europe that would place American mainline denominations in a precarious position later in the century. The optimism in humanity, which many had adopted in the nineteenth century, was unraveling.

> Therefore, when two world wars and the events surrounding them gave lie to the dreams of the nineteenth century, Protestant liberalism was shaken to its foundations.... In the twentieth century, partially as a result of the failure of Liberalism and its optimistic hopes, those areas where Protestantism had been traditionally strong—Germany, Scandinavia, and Great Britain—also witnessed a decided increase in skepticism and secularism.[2]

---

[1] Mike Liles, Jr., *Christian Faith in Contemporary Society: The Framework for Belief* (Lincoln, NE: iUniverse, 2005), 338.

[2] Justo L. González, *The Story of Christianity* (San Francisco: Harper & Row, 1984), 360.

This precipitated a decline in church attendance in Western Europe during the first half of the twentieth century. While mainline denominations in the United States were able to maintain a status quo, they, too, were becoming skeptical. They witnessed the Great Depression, two World Wars, and the Holocaust. It would not be until the second half of the century that both growing skepticism and secularism would similarly manifest themselves in the United States; and when they did, it was clear in large numbers of mainline Protestant worshipers, who abandoned their faith altogether or left their reasoned approach to worship for something more experiential and organic.

Meanwhile, the more emotional, Gospel-style service continued to expand. This expansion was significant in rural areas throughout the United States, particularly among Methodists and Baptists. The great revival tradition had flourished continued under the leadership of men such as Billy Sunday (1862-1935) and his frequent musical leader, Homer Rodeheaver (1880-1955). Their work continued to fuel an interest in Gospel-style songs. Rodeheaver published hundreds of them and many were widely used.

The demand for Gospel songs led to the formation of publishing companies specializing in these types of songs. In 1924 the Stamps-Baxter Publishing Company was established, circulating thousands of Gospel songs in small pamphlet-like songbooks. These were often performed in revival meetings, youth camps, and in fifth-Sunday-singings. The growing popularity of this music birthed recording businesses as well, using radio to broadcast Gospel music to remote areas. Since these rural areas became highly dependent on radio for their understanding of the world in which they lived, people in the rural South and Mid-West were hearing many of the same types of songs. This explains how rural areas developed a strong stylistic unity around Gospel music.

Revival/Gospel-style worship further expanded with the rise of Pentecostalism. In fact, this movement grew so rapidly that by the second half of the century it would become a significant influence on the worship practices of most evangelical Christians. Developing out of the Wesleyan and Holiness movements of the late nineteenth century, the Pentecostal movement had its beginnings in the same region where Gospel music was most popular.

[T]he American South became the first region in the world where Pentecostalism put down deep roots and significantly changed the spiritual landscape. As a religion of the poor and disinherited, Pentecostalism found fertile soil in the impoverished South, where blacks and whites struggled to eke out an existence on the economic and social margins of society. The first Pentecostal denominations in the world, including the Church of God in Christ, the Pentecostal Holiness Church, the Church of God (Tennessee), and the Assemblies of God, took root in the states of the old confederacy. Indeed, in the decades to come, the southern Pentecostal groups would play major roles in developing the ethos and character of the movement.[1]

Expressions of Pentecostalism in worship were destined to become much more than a regional movement following the revival meetings that occurred at Azusa Street in Los Angeles (1906-1909). Over the course of three years, thousands came to California to experience a mighty movement of God's Spirit—in particular to have a Pentecost-like experience. Like the Pentecost-style meetings that had become common in the South, the services at Azusa Street were patterned after the brush arbor meetings of the nineteenth century. Gospel-style songs were interspersed with sermons delivered by numerous preachers and teachers. The services themselves had a distinct Pentecostal flavor, yielding many of the same physical manifestations seen in the meetings of John and Charles Wesley. Through the revival, *the dynamic forces of Azusa Street soon transcended all boundaries of culture, nationality, and theological tradition.*[2]

By the middle of the twentieth century, the Pentecostal movement had spread as a loose affiliation of churches that practiced Pentecost-type gifts in regular worship services. Whether one accepts these manifestations as genuine or not, it is important to understand the common worship heritage shared by Pentecostals and those who had chosen a more altar call oriented approach. Both developed out of nineteenth century Revivalism and became widely popular in the twentieth century. Despite theological differences within these streams, they shared a common approach to worship—a sermon and service designed to produce immediate visible results. Even with the rise of Pentecostalism, there were still only two major approaches to worship: 1) the emotional (Revival/Gospel-style), which shaped the service toward a moment where God's work would become immediately apparent; and 2) the intellectual approach, which valued classical music/art and shaped the sermon to stimulate the mind and move the hearer toward godliness. Thus, worship styles in many non-Pentecostal churches that valued the altar call approach had much more in common with Pentecostal worship than with the styles common in mainline denominations. This would prove to be significant in the second half of the century as worship styles mixed and mingled with each other.

1950-2000

The second half of the century was one of even greater cultural change. Following a decade of respite after the Second Word War, which resulted in the Baby Boom, the undercurrents of a changing society began to become more apparent. Teenagers and young adults rejected their parents' optimism that the

---

[1] Vinson Synan, *The Holiness-Pentecostal Tradition: Charismatic Movements in the Twentieth Century* (Grand Rapids, MI: Wm. B. Eerdmans Publishing Co., 1997), 129-130.

[2] Ibid, 130.

system, whether religious or governmental, could fix man's problems. A raft of continuing social ills reminded them that neither the Enlightenment nor an optimistic, theological liberalism really helped. Injustices and suffering remained; and if the Second World War taught anything, it taught that humanity's demons had not been eradicated. Skepticism and secularism which had emptied the churches in Europe in the first half of the century now went to work in American churches. Rather than remaining in their parents' churches, many turned to almost anything except the *establishment*, including other faiths.

> During this time, ideas of multi-cultural spiritualties came into public focus. The religions of the East began to make an impression on the youth seeking a greater spiritual awakening. Buddhism, Hinduism and Taoism were among the major Eastern philosophies that created the biggest impact. Artists, painters and musicians all began to reflect this aura of social change, and popular culture in American youth itself began to shift its focus to a more enlightened mind frame. All over the country protests, violence and cultural movements emerged in the name of positive social change.[1]

Concurrently, technological development was picking up speed. The age of space travel, instant worldwide satellite news, cell phones, the personal computer, and the Internet all changed the way people communicated with each other and the way they viewed and understood their world. And, while historians may differ on when globalization began, by the end of the century, there was a pervasive understanding that it had arrived.[2] By the end of the century, the world was substantively different, intertwined in a technological web and bound together in increasing global economic interdependence. All of this was reflected in multiple, rapid changes in culture and, therefore, in music.

We have discussed how changes in culture generally appear in the Fine Arts, first in literature and later in music. By the end of the twentieth century changes in music occurred in such close proximity to other cultural changes, at times it appeared that music itself was causing change rather than reflecting it.[3] For churches that based their worship on Classical Music, many of these changes came and went without ever entering the church house. However, for churches that had taken the more Gospel music approach—in itself a popular, non-Classical style—this created a problem. As culture changed and produced (or was shaped by) musical changes, the late nineteenth century and early twentieth century Gospel songs seemed very outmoded. Churches that used them could not, like those who used Classical Music, appeal to a higher artistic rule to avoid

---

[1] Christopher Ericson Etter, *A Study of Qualitative Non-Pluralism* (Lincoln, NE: iUniverse, 2006), 222.

[2] Robert K. Schaeffer, *Understanding Globalization: the Social Consequences of Political, Economic, and Environmental Change* (Lanham: Rowman & Littlefield Publishers, 2003), 9-10.

[3] See Roy Shuker, *Popular Music: the Key Concepts*, 2nd Edition (New York: Routledge, 2002).

change. As a result, musical change came early and often to parts of Protestantism that had rejected the nineteenth century trend to use Classical Music in worship. Certainly, there were churches in the Gospel camp that refused change as there were churches in the Classical camp that embraced change. However, the most frequent worship transitions occurred earliest among churches that had already rejected Classical Music as the primary style of music for corporate worship. In these churches, musical form often came and went so fast that it is difficult to use the term *form* to describe them at all, since that same term is used to describe practices that lasted decades or centuries.

Twentieth Century Revivalism in Worship

During all of these cultural shifts, the Revival/Gospel-style of worship remained popular, even as it began to absorb newer cultural styles. In fact, the denominations that tended to use the revival format in worship were the ones that were growing. An examination of five major denominations between 1950 and 1988 reveals growth in only two: Southern Baptists (SBC) and Assemblies of God (AOG). Attendance declined between 1950 and 1988 among United Methodists (UMC), Presbyterians (PCUSA), and Lutherans (LCMS).[1] Growth among churches that used the Revival/Gospel-style occurred concurrently with a growing popularity of large inter-denominational evangelistic crusades. Between 1950 and 1980, millions from almost every Christian denomination attended city-wide evangelistic crusades.

The leading figure in the twentieth century crusade evangelism movement was Billy Graham (1918). Taking the mantle from men such as Dwight L. Moody and Billy Sunday, Graham's ministry rose to prominence following a hugely successful crusade in Los Angeles in the fall of 1949. Aided by his music director, Cliff Barrows (1923), the *crusade evangelism* format set the Revival/Gospel-style of worship on the national stage. Graham's meetings were often held in large stadiums, featuring huge choirs, robust congregational singing, and special music by both secular and sacred recording artists. The service featured an evangelistic message and culminated with an altar call. These crusades were not only attended by millions, but viewed by millions more through the expanding medium of television. Having seen or experienced a freeform, Gospel-style service, many went looking for a similar format in weekly worship. This bolstered the attendance among churches whose worship style was more Revival/Gospel oriented and helped keep overall church attendance numbers from declining, even when they were doing so in mainline denominations.[2]

The earlier movement toward liberalism in the northeast and a growing unchurched population in the west meant that the Revival/Gospel-style of

---

[1] David A. Roozen and C. Kirk. Hadaway, *Church and Denominational Growth* (Nashville: Abingdon Press, 1993), 51-52.

[2] James T. Patterson, *Grand Expectations: the United States, 1945-1974* (New York: Oxford University Press, 1996), 456.

worship had been concentrated in the South in the first half of the century. The influence of Graham's crusades spread a stylistic unity among evangelical churches across the nation. The rise in popularity of network television helped introduce the style to a national audience. The crusades, both in the stadiums and on television, became an archetype from coast to coast. The style of music used in the crusades became an example of what church could be. For churches that had steered away from Classical Music, whether for socio-economic reasons or theological ones, Graham's crusades offered a prominent style they could embrace.

Charismatic Trends—Praise and Worship

At this point, it is helpful to give a brief explanation of the terms *Pentecostal* and *Charismatic*. We have previously used the term Pentecostal to describe churches that sought Pentecost-like experiences in their worship services—specifically, the sign gifts of tongues, healings, words of knowledge, various physical manifestations, etc. By the end of the twentieth century, the term 'Charismatic' became more popular to describe a wide variety of churches or individuals who practiced the sign gifts or taught that the Baptism of the Holy Spirit was a subsequent event to salvation. In the first half of the century, Pentecostal worship practices were discounted by mainline denominations, both for their use of Gospel-style music and their Pentecostal practices. However, it was clear that by the late 1960s, these practices were spreading to individuals within mainline denominations.[1] *Individuals* who belonged to mainline denominations and practiced Pentecostalism were called Charismatics, while the term Pentecostal indicated *churches* and *denominations* that embraced the practice. The use of 'Charismatic' took on a more comprehensive meaning as Pentecostal practices and teaching spread.

> With the development of 'nondenominational' Charismatic churches and organizations…, the term was broadened to refer to all those movements outside denominational or 'classical' Pentecostalism where spiritual [sign] gifts are exercised. It is often impossible now to distinguish between 'Pentecostals' and 'Charismatics', and there are often as many theological and liturgical differences between classical Pentecostals themselves as there are between them and Charismatic churches.[2]

The main idea of Charismatic worship was still attached to the Revival/Gospel-style. Like the services of the Second Awakening, Charismatic

---

[1] *Most observers consider that the Charismatic Movement, the practice of Pentecostal phenomena or of spiritual gifts in the 'mainline' Protestant churches began in the Episcopal Church in the USA in 1960, and in the Roman Catholic Church in the same country in 1967,* Allan Anderson, *An Introduction to Pentecostalism: Global Charismatic Christianity* (Cambridge: Cambridge University Press, 2004), 144.

[2] Ibid.

worship was designed for a specific public response. However, the sought-after result in Charismatic churches was different. Their approach was often explained in biblical terms using the Jewish Temple as an archetype, where the worshiper began outside the walls of the city and figuratively journeyed into the Holy of Holies.[1] While only the High Priest could go into the Holy of Holies in the Old Testament, the work of Christ had torn the veil and made the place of nearness to God available to all believers. In this analogy, the Holy Place was where a special portion of God's presence resided and therefore the place where intimacy and special manifestations, including ecstatic utterances, could occur.[2]

During the 1960s and 1970s, Charismatic churches and evangelical denominations, such as Southern Baptists, were the ones growing, while most mainline denominations had plateaued or were declining. Both mainline Protestants and evangelicals began to incorporate aspects of Charismatic worship into their regular services. For mainline denominations, this may have been an attempt to grow again. For evangelical denominations, such as Southern Baptists, it was a predictable fit since the Charismatic renewal shared the same Gospel heritage and was seen as *a revivalist movement within Christianity.*[3] Blending between Charismatic and non-Charismatic worship styles occurred as Gospel songs and choruses in non-Charismatic churches were replaced with those used among Charismatic churches. *The Gospel chorus had been a staple of non-charismatic Christian youth groups in the 1940s and 1950s, but these songs had been used primarily as fellowship or campfire material, not as songs to be sung in church. However, the emotionalism of Pentecostal-style worship and its music appealed to many people and both elements were widely adopted in non-charismatic churches.*[4]

The poetic style of those songs was similar to those of the 1950s and 1960s, but the music was different, creating what became known as Praise and Worship music and spawning the *Praise and Worship Movement.* Praise and Worship music had a different sound than the old Gospel-style music that had been used among revival minded churches. The traditional revival choruses were based on the Southern Gospel style, while Praise and Worship choruses shared more in common musically with Pop/Rock folk songs. Acoustic guitars that had been much more at home in a Country or Bluegrass style became a primary instrument of early Praise and Worship choruses. During the 1960s, Praise and Worship choruses were very similar to Folk/Rock-style protest songs. As popular music developed and Rock and Roll music utilized more electric instruments in the 1970s, the style of Praise and Worship music followed suit.

---

[1] For a detailed explanation from the Charismatic viewpoint, see Judson Cornwall, *Let Us Worship* (So. Plainfield, NJ: Bridge Pub., 1983).

[2] Donald P. Hustad, "Foreword," Foreword to *The New Worship: Straight Talk on Music and the Church* (Grand Rapids, MI: Baker Books, 1996), 10.

[3] Stephen Hunt, *Alternative Religions: a Sociological Introduction* (Aldershot: Ashgate, 2003), 90.

[4] David W. Music, *Christian Hymnody in Twentieth Century Britain and America: an Annotated Bibliography* (Westport, CT: Greenwood Publishing, 2001), 7.

By the 1980s and 1990s, Praise Music was no longer a definable musical genre, but broadly reflected various Pop styles. The popularity of this music spread across denominational and theological lines and helped propel the rise of Contemporary Christian Music (CCM).

Praise and Worship choruses often had simple texts, typically consisting of only one or two couplets. Like the choruses of the nineteenth century revivals, they were repeated freely. A survey of popular Praise and Worship choruses of the 1970s and 1980s reveals that a majority of those that became popular were either quotes of well-known Scripture passages or adaptations set as a single verse (Example 1). Alternately, these choruses were written with a two part structure (A-B). Like Revival/Gospel-style hymns, they had both verse and chorus; however, multiple verses were not common (Example 2).

Example 1.
Praise The Name Of Jesus
Roy Hicks, Jr. ©1976

Praise the Name of Jesus! // Praise the Name of Jesus!
He's my Rock // He's my Fortress
He's my Deliverer // In Him will I trust!
Praise the Name of Jesus!

Example 2.
Ah, Lord God
Kay Chance ©1976
(Jeremiah 31:17)

Verse:
Ah, Lord God, Thou has made the heavens
And the earth by Thy great power
Ah, Lord God, Thou has made the heavens
And the earth by Thine outstretched arm

Chorus:
Nothing is too difficult for Thee // Nothing is too difficult for Thee
Great and mighty God // Great in counsel and mighty in deed
Nothing, nothing, absolutely nothing // Nothing is too difficult for Thee

While some evangelical churches resisted all musical influences of the Praise and Worship movement, others sought a middle ground. They utilized traditional hymns with organ and piano (or orchestral accompaniment) in morning services and allowed more pop/rock musical styles, along with the instruments used to play them, in evening or youth services. Not all Praise and Worship songs were written in a Pop/Rock style. Some retained a traditional Gospel sound. Songs such as these became a bridge, a safe alternative for churches not ready to embrace pop/rock elements, but looking to branch out beyond older Gospel sounding musical forms, or to move beyond traditional denominational forms. One of the key contributors to this style was William (Bill) Gaither (1936). Gaither was born in Indiana and began his career singing Southern Gospel music. His compositions built on the Southern Gospel model and brought a tempered, quasi-pop version of it into the mainstream of many churches. Both choruses and hymns such as Gaither's *Alleluia* and *Because He Lives* became standards in both Charismatic and non-Charismatic churches and were included in various denominational hymnals by the 1980s.

The Charismatic influence on Christian worship has been significant. As a worship leader for more than thirty years and teacher on the subject, I have learned a great deal from the Praise and Worship movement. Approaching the corporate gathering with a sense of anticipation and freedom was a boost to many who gathered weekly to sing to, for, and about God. Additionally, a renewed focus on biblical expressions and postures of worship was helpful. At the same time, many churches experienced bitter divisions over the introduction of Praise and Worship music into their local churches. Some of these divisions were predictable as newer musical styles met old traditions. But more significantly, divisions were theological in nature. Non-Pentecostal churches had to address an influx of people who practiced sign gifts and in many cases sought to encourage fellow church members to do the same.

Beyond the discussion of whether or not sign gifts are acceptable today, it is important to address aspects of worship theology that developed in the Charismatic movement. Some of the teaching in the movement has been well-meaning but misguided. One such teaching sees a parallel between worship and a journey into the Holy of Holies—a view widely absorbed into many evangelical churches. In this concept, praise is the vehicle that precedes the encounter with God, i.e., worship. Texts such as Psalm 100:4 seem to suggest this: *Enter His gates with thanksgiving And His courts with praise.* The Psalmist is using the architecture of the Temple to describe coming before the LORD in worship. The *gates* are referring to the Temple gates and the *court* to the outer section of the Temple. In the Psalmist's mind he is approaching the Holy Place to worship.

However, the biblical definition of worship would strongly argue against any application of this passage that suggests that acceptable praise can occur without a heart already submitted to God. Praise, extolling the person and character of God, is always unacceptable to Him unless there is already a heart of worship—*the proper state of submission.* God declares that our praise is odious to Him unless our hearts are in the right place. In Isaiah 29:13 the Lord delivered an indictment to His people, saying, they *draw near with their mouth and honor me with their lips, while their hearts are far from me, and their fear of me is a commandment taught by men.* Jesus renewed the same charge in Matthew 15:8: *This people honors me with their lips, but their heart is far from me.*

A heart not properly submitted to God cannot give Him praise. As we discovered in Chapter 1, worship describes the lowering of self in submission to God. All the other biblical vocabulary for worship—praise, honor, glorify, thanksgiving, bless, etc.—describes ways to outwardly express such a heart. Worship is not a higher plane of spiritual existence or a journey into a special place to meet with God. Rather, worship, *the state of proper submission before God*, should be normative for the believer. Living a life of submission before God is our reasonable act of service as living sacrifices. Therefore, it is impossible to separate praise, or any other outward expression toward God, from true worship. Furthermore, we do not go to find God in the Holy of Holies and worship Him there. While the analogy is certainly biblical, it is not New Covenant. Both the veil of humanity and the Temple were torn apart when Jesus, the Son, came to seek and save us—God incarnate giving His life for us on the cross. Because of His salvific work we are saved and, even now, are raised to life and seated *with him in the heavenly places in Christ Jesus*.[1] By grace we have been brought into the true place of God's dwelling, of which the earthly Holy of Holies was only a copy.[2]

This is a significant difference between the First and Second Covenant and this must have a direct bearing on how we view worship. In spiritual terms, this error is similar to that of the Roman Catholic Mass. There, the congregant starts the service at some distance from God and approaches Him through the liturgy, until he has a personal encounter with Christ through His Blood and Body in the Elements.[3] This is very similar in shape to the Holy of Holies concept of worship popularized in the Charismatic movement. Again, the believer starts at some distance from God and approaches Him through praise until meeting Him in the Holy Place of worship.

The primary issue is not whether churches of divergent beliefs can share the same songs. In the history of worship, that has happened often. The problem arises when significant doctrinal differences are ignored. As wonderful as it may sound, setting aside significant doctrinal differences in order to worship together cannot be healthy in the long term. Whatever approach to worship one takes, history has taught us it *must* be doctrinal. Churches that resisted musical changes simply because they preferred a traditional style were not making decisions about worship based on doctrine. They were making choices based purely on preferences. In a similar way, churches that embraced Praise and Worship music based solely on a preference for a particular musical style were also making decisions based on something other than doctrine. Certainly, everyone has preferences. However, churches are in a precarious position when they become so consumed with their preferences that decisions are made to avoid or embrace styles apart from doctrinal considerations. For evangelical churches that adopted Praise and Worship music without having a firm biblical foundation, many unwittingly absorbed and retained Old Covenant worship theology. This has continued to pose a problem. Services may be structured to provide the 'Holy of

---

[1] Ephesians 2:6.
[2] Hebrews 9:24.
[3] See Chapter 6, *ROMAN CATHOLIC WORSHIP*.

257

Holies moment' in churches where there is no theological provision for freeform ecstatic expression.

The Church Growth Movement

In the twentieth century, developments in four areas comprised what became known as twentieth century modernity: *capitalism, technology, urbanization, telecommunications.*[1] These became evident at the beginning of the twentieth century and had run their full course by its end. The effects of modernity's last gasp were visible in everything from product development, production and marketing, to the way people moved *en masse* to the city. By the last quarter of the century, a national identity of rural life was swallowed up in the vastness of cities. Culture that had been closely attached to a sense of community and local mores was relinquished to larger and larger population centers. As these population centers grew, so did a shared urban and suburban culture. Technological developments made the study of this growing culture possible. Studies in psychology and sociology sought to identify and explain the wants and needs of large blocks of people. This data became a tool in the developing science of research-based marketing. Realizing that such data was useful for designing mega marketing campaigns, corporations reoriented themselves. By utilizing market studies and finding the specific needs of consumers, companies could capitalize on niche markets, designing and advertising products with pinpoint accuracy. By the last quarter of the century, all of this converged to create a consumer driven society.

It was in this environment that the Church Growth Movement began. The idea that consumer research and targeted marketing could make a product successful was leveraged into a strategy for evangelism and church growth. The beginnings of the Church Growth Movement can be traced to Donald McGavran (1897-1990), a former missionary to India, who spent much of his career teaching missions at Fuller Theological Seminary. His basic premise was that healthy churches should grow naturally. McGavran believed that the biggest impediments to church growth were cultural rather than theological. Therefore, if churches were not growing, finding the cultural barriers and removing them would allow growth again. If a church could identify and address those barriers, they could successfully grow. The science of market research and targeted advertising became tools in the hands of churches and *were applied to the North American cultural context beginning in the 1970's.*[2]

By the 1980s, two key leaders had emerged in the Church Growth Movement: William (Bill) Hybels (1951), the founding pastor at Willow Creek Community Church, and Richard (Rick) Warren (1954), the founding pastor of Saddleback Community Church. Separately and nearly simultaneously, they

---

[1] David F. Wells, *God in the Wasteland: the Reality of Truth in a World of Fading Dreams* (Grand Rapids, MI: W.B. Eerdmans, 1994), 7-8.

[2] Frank C. Senn, *The People's Work: a Social History of the Liturgy* (Minneapolis: Fortress Press, 2006), 278.

began to experiment with a targeted approach to evangelism. Based on market data and neighborhood surveys, they designed Sunday services intended to bring Baby Boomers back to church by removing the barriers that were keeping them away. The focus on those not attending church would earn this movement the name *Seeker Sensitive* or *Seeker Driven*. Hybel's and Warren's popularity and influence were widespread and imitators covered the gamut, from Charismatic to liturgical churches. Marketing and target evangelism became a driving force for planning the Sunday gathering. *While McGavran himself did not think these principles would affect worship, worship was massively affected by being turned into an evangelistic tool that made use of the expressions of contemporary popular culture to target particular audiences.* [1]

While the transition from worship to evangelism seemed to be an innovation, it was not. The writings of Second Awakening revivalists like Finney had already laid the foundation, repurposing the Sunday gathering from worship to evangelism in thousands of churches. The innovation with the Church Growth Movement was marketing and targeting toward a specific audience. After surveying communities about what they wanted church to be, services were designed with those specifications in mind. Long periods of congregational singing and expository sermons were generally suppressed. Instead, sermon topics were derived from the expressed needs of the people. Music was almost exclusively in a Pop/Rock style and eschewed nearly everything that used words or sounds that might be familiar to the church memory of the Baby Boomer. Other entries such as videos and short dramas rounded out the rest of the service, which normally did not exceed an hour.

It was certainly no surprise that lost people who were surveyed wanted little congregational worship, nor was it shocking that they did not request exegetical sermons. Instead, those surveyed spoke about their needs and struggles, such as marital and parenting issues, financial problems, and the like. While a desire to exalt God for His work in salvation or hear exegetical sermons might be expected from someone who is a believer, it would be unnatural for someone without Christ. The criticisms and praises for this approach have been frequent. The fact is that the Church Growth Movement and the subsequent Seeker orientation brought both rain and drought. The Seeker Movement did set many thinking freshly about reaching lost people. We may ask, if Finney and others had already laid the groundwork for making Sunday gatherings evangelistic, then weren't churches already thinking about lost people? While many churches preached evangelistic sermons and faithfully gave invitations every Sunday, as if they were at an evangelistic crusade, in reality, the lost were not coming in great numbers to hear those Sunday sermons nor the appeals to be saved.

The Seeker Movement used the concept of targeted marketing to get lost people back in the building, so to speak. Whether those who came back to the church during the Seeker Movement actually heard the gospel, or really

---

[1] Ibid.

responded to it if they did, remains a topic of intense debate. We do know this: of all the God-honoring things we can do in heaven, we cannot tell a lost person about Jesus. The local church was never established by God to be a closed membership club. Every church and every person needs a deep and unwavering passion for lost people, and even in our worship gatherings, to be sensitive to those who may be seeking Christ. Inasmuch as churches were awakened by the Church Growth Movement to preach the *true* gospel to the lost, it was a benefit. The Seeker Sensitive Movement produced as many detractors as supporters but, at least many eyes were opened to see the people beyond the walls of the church.

Resistance to the Seeker Movement was understandable. To ask the lost person what he needs or wants in a worship service and then to design the weekly gathering around that is to assume that the lost person knows what he needs. In addition, to plan a worship service to meet the needs of the unbeliever is to attempt the impossible. While unbelievers will one day worship (*every knee will bow*), they cannot enter into the fellowship of believers who join to worship God for salvation in Jesus Christ. If unbelievers gather, whatever you may call it, it is not corporate worship—they can observe it and be moved by it but, they cannot participate in it. Churches that totally embraced the Seeker Movement, like those who fully embraced Revivalism, forfeited worship for evangelism. The same caution that we gave to those who designed services for visible decisions at the altar is the same one that would have applied to the Seeker Movement. While Seeker oriented services generally dispensed with the altar calls, the design of the service was, like those of the revivalists, to produce a visible result. Again, evangelism is a natural component and byproduct of worship, but should never be provided as an alternative to corporate worship.

As the Sunday gathering was again redesigned to become something other than worship, some churches looked for other ways to accomplish corporate worship. In the case of Willow Creek, Wednesday night services were designed with more participatory worship and sermons were geared more toward believers. The lack of wide-spread effectiveness of this aspect of their approach was acknowledged by Willow Creek. Over twenty years after the movement began, Willow Creek conducted and released its own, highly publicized self-study, describing how the huge numbers that came to weekend services never translated into huge numbers that came Wednesday evenings for believers' worship services.[1] For those of us who plan, this means that it is possible to design weekend services that draw large crowds without meeting the biblical criteria for, nor reaping the benefits of, corporate worship. This is a sobering thought, no matter what methodological approach is used.

Synthesis and Short Life Spans
The rapid changes of urbanization and 'suburbanization' had produced a broad, thin veneer of homogeneity. However, the explosion of the music

---

[1] Willow Creek's findings are contained in the book by Greg Hawkins and Cally Parkinson, *Reveal: Where Are You?* (Barrington, IL: Willow Creek Association, 2007).

industry in the latter half of the twentieth century told another story. Radio station programming became more varied, each station identifying with a particular style of music. Musical tastes were becoming more segmented. By the beginning of the twenty-first century, satellite radio and mp3 players made it possible to deliver custom mixes of music to a wider and wider spectrum of diets. The proliferation of various musical styles was a clear indicator that culture was dividing and subdividing. As a greater variety of popular musical styles developed, each was marketed with great accuracy to an increasingly diverse culture.

The Christian music industry was also expanding. Radio, once the home of Revival/ Gospel style music, became an expanding avenue for the distribution of Contemporary Christian Music. In the last quarter of the century, the number of CCM radio stations skyrocketed, as did the number of those listening. *In 1974, there were no full-time CCM stations, and even as late as 1990, CCM radio networks and formats were rudimentary. As of 2000, the Gospel Music Association claims that over 20 million people listen to Christian/Gospel radio every week.*[1] Pop-style Christian music reflected the same type of subdivision that was occurring in secular music. More specificity in musical tastes translated to increased demand for all types of Christian music, including CCM, Praise and Worship, Black Gospel, Rap, Hip Hop, Southern Gospel, etc. Between *1984 and 1995, gospel music* [all forms combined] *experienced a 290 percent increase in sales.*[2]

Much of the industry's growth began in the 1980s with marquee artists like Sandi Patti, Steve Green and Larnelle Harris. Their music was in a Pop style and added orchestral instruments and vocal techniques that found acceptance in a wide variety of churches from traditional to contemporary. Sales of recordings and radio airtime helped make their music widely popular and created a demand for published versions of their music. Sheet music, album collections, and seasonal musicals featured written arrangements of these popular recordings and were sung by a growing number of churches who combined choirs, orchestras, guitars, and drums to recreate the same songs for Sunday morning worship.

By the 1980's, the Praise and Worship style was reaching maturity, leaving behind the Folk-style choruses, yielding fully produced recordings that shared much in common with adult contemporary music (sometimes called Easy Rock). Publishers like Maranatha! Music and Vineyard Publishing released multiple recordings where the marquee was not the singer, but the song, already produced and packaged for sale to the local church. For churches using a more

---

[1] "The Production of Contemporary Christian Music: A Geographical Perspective," in *Sound, Society, and the Geography of Popular Music*, ed. Ola Johansson and Thomas L. Bell, by John Lindenbaum (Burlington, VT: Ashgate, 2009), 289.

[2] Jay R. Howard, John M. Streck, *Apostles of Rock: The Splintered World of Contemporary Christian Music* (Lexington, KY: The University of Kentucky Press, 1999), 44.

contemporary style, this gave them a steady supply of new music for choir or congregation from which to choose.

The last two decades of the century featured a succession of styles that arrived, were wildly popular, and receded within a decade or less. The spread of some of these styles was a result of an increased effort to record, publish, and market Praise and Worship and Contemporary Christian Music to targeted markets. Other factors also contributed to the spread of new worship music. The first, and perhaps most significant was the popularity of the Seeker Movement, itself. Between 1980 and 2000, tens of thousands of pastors and church leaders attended conferences like those at Willow Creek and Saddleback. Conferences such as these superseded denominational affiliations and shaped contemporary worship styles for many churches. This served not only to spread the concepts of the Church Growth Movement, but also became sharing points for worship songs and contemporary worship techniques.

Promise Keepers (PK) had a similar effect. From a small beginning in 1990, PK held meetings in major cities throughout the US. According to the Promise Keeper's website, during the last decade of the twentieth century, combined attendance at all PK conferences exceeded 4.7 million.[1] The format of the services at Promise Keepers was similar to the brush arbor revival meetings: a variety of speakers and preachers interspersed with robust singing. However, the style was far from traditional Gospel music. These meetings utilized the latest in well produced Praise and Worship and Contemporary Christian music. The significance of both church growth conferences and Promise Keepers should not be overlooked. As leaders and pastors experienced contemporary worship music, they went back to their churches asking for more of the same on Sundays. Like the Billy Graham crusades in the 60's and 70's, the nineteenth century brush arbor meetings, and the gatherings of the First Great Awakening, these gatherings provided a visible expression of congregational worship that, once experienced, was imitated in numerous local congregations.

In addition to these, several artists also played a major role in shaping the direction of contemporary worship or, in some cases, at least providing an indicator where worship culture was headed. Darlene Zschech (1965), a singer/songwriter, and Hillsong Church in Australia became a major influence by the mid-1990s. Combining elements of Praise and Worship, CCM, and Gospel, the worship ministry of Hillsong Church and the recordings of Zschech became popular among both Charismatic and non-Charismatic churches. The significance of Hillsong's influence goes beyond the music itself and demonstrates that Christian worship was undergoing globalization. Over the span of twenty years, Hillsong's music provides a vivid picture of how worship music transitioned. The Gospel and adult contemporary feel (and thus, the Baby Boomer appeal) with which it began transitioned to the postmodern sounds of groups like U2 and Coldplay. This gave Hillsong music (and its daughter style, Hillsong United) a staying power that lasted well into the twenty-first century.

---

[1] See http://www.promisekeepers.org/about/pkhistory (accessed October 5, 2010).

This type of ongoing development was also apparent in various college campus movements, such as the Passion Movement in the US. Beginning in the 1990's and lasting well into the twentieth century, the Passion Movement provided an important connecting point for tens of thousands of college age adults to experience the latest developments in worship music.

WHAT DID THESE CHANGES MEAN?
A Cultural Shift

By the mid-1990s, the multiple and rapid changes in music indicated that a large cultural shift was well under way. The age of Modernism was setting and Postmodernism was rising. *While some scholars are convinced that postmodernism is a fad that will fade quickly, most scholars are convinced that postmodernism is anything but a fad; postmodernism is a cultural shift, the likes of which have not been experienced since around 1500, the beginning of the modern period.*[1] During the nearly five hundred years of the Modern era, worship forms developed by a predictable process. People identified a set of beliefs and planned worship services as a reflection of those beliefs. As a result, Modernism produced worship styles that could be studied and understood by examining the belief systems on which they were based. This was true for the gatherings of the Reformation all the way through the Church Growth Movement. Postmodern gatherings are another story.

Defining and understanding postmodern worship styles is not possible by simply defining the belief system behind the practice. This is where we begin to see a significant difference between Modernism and Postmodernism. To reject or embrace a worship style in Modernism was to embrace or reject the belief system on which the style was based. In contrast, worship styles in Postmodernism are accepted or rejected according to the experience of the individual. The validity of the personal experience rather than the belief system is the determining factor in shaping the worship style.

The table below lists five characteristic differences between Modernism and Postmodernism. Each of these impacts how postmodern thinkers view and practice worship. While Postmodernism is marked by some aspects of globalization, note that many of the changes move a person from one who is an individual within a group, to one who is more isolated both in his experience and his expression.

---

[1] Franklin M. Segler and C. Randall Bradley, *Christian Worship: Its Theology and Practice* (Nashville, TN: B & H Pub. Group, 2006), 91.

MODERNISM ⟹	POSTMODERNISM
from regional	**to global**
Since the Renaissance, governments, economies, language, and Fine Art had been definable based on regional, racial, or national associations.	Colonization in the nineteenth century laid the foundation for globalization. By the end of the twentieth century, economies, Fine Art, culture, and, in some sense, government itself became more globalized.
from homogeneous communities	**to interconnected cells**
Social grouping was based on shared values, religious practice, social standing, etc. These created tightly connected local communities where extended families birthed and buried their own.	Urbanization and sub-urbanization emptied rural communities. Whereas Moderns tended to eschew relationships outside homogeneous cells, the postmodern values them, frequently crossing most traditional barriers.
from industrialism	**to technological**
Farming gave way to industry. A trained labor force became the primary economic engine. By the twentieth century, the use of tools and machines pushed industrial development to its limits.	Technology overtook industry as a primary mark of economic strength, becoming the glue of the global economy and the means of interpersonal communication and relationship.
from rationalism	**to intuition**
The rise of learning that began in the Renaissance continued. The age of reasoning and humanism celebrated man's intellectual achievement. Status was accorded to those with knowledge, and truth itself was an objective commodity that could be acquired through study.	No longer acquired from an objective standard, truth is known through personal experience. Contradictions unacceptable to a modern thinker may be acceptable to a postmodern, since truth is subject to the individual experience. To the postmodern, truth is intuitive rather than objective.
individualism	**self-expression**
The trajectory of Modernism took the individual on a progressive journey toward education, career apprenticeship and training, and, finally to humanism where individuals believed they had gained the power to tackle the world's greatest problems. In Christianity, the rise of individualism meant casting off the authority of the Church and renewing the concept of salvation of individuals through belief in the objective truth of Scripture.	In the wake of failed humanism, individualism moved toward introspection and a unique personal expression. *This focus on a consciously constructed self goes beyond modernism's emphasis on individualism.*[1] Modernism built up the individual so humanity could accomplish great things. Postmodernism explores self in order to discover one's own personal truth. That process itself is the means by which humanity is improved.

Globalization in worship meant both music and worship practices were shared across cultural lines. This became possible as new music and methods could travel almost instantly from one side of the world to the other. Whereas worship practices were once developed in the local community where mores and

---

[1] James L. Golden, *The Rhetoric of Western Thought* (Dubuque, IA: Kendall/Hunt, 2007), 25.

culture were shared, there is now a global community where worship practices are shared across cultural lines. In this sense, technology has made the world seem small. At the same time, the concept of globalization has meant a loss of local community. For many, this void is filled through virtual community and social networking, often with people who are separated by miles or even by oceans. While Moderns experience community through physical proximity, Postmoderns may experience community via technology. This community is made up of interconnected cells that do not necessarily depend on physical proximity or shared culture and values. Exploring how much community can be experienced without proximity or shared values may further stretch the definitions of concepts such as 'congregation,' 'corporate worship,' and 'fellowship.'

Effects on Preaching

Modernism explored and expanded knowledge and learning. However, it worked under the assumption that there was objective truth that was both discoverable and reasonable. This truth could be used to evaluate everyone's experience. As Western Civilization progressed through Modernity, individualism pushed truth into a smaller and smaller box, making it less applicable to everyone. *The age of reason, in spite of its intentions, was the unhappy progenitor of subjectivism: an intellectual calamity which led ineluctably to skepticism and nihilism, so descriptive of the postmodern malaise.*[1] Thus, subjectivity has the ability to trump objectivity by declaring 'that may be true for you but, it is not true for me.' In Postmodernism, intuitive knowledge and personal experience become the means by which reality is measured. *Postmodernism rejects the possibility of absolutes except for what is observed personally.*[2]

As sermons developed through the nineteenth and twentieth centuries, they increasingly appealed to reason. This was visible both in more Bible based apologetic sermons—*why God and the Bible are real and you should believe*—as well as sermons based more out of perceived human needs—*Ten ways Jesus can make your life better*. Even in Finney's revivalist approach there is an appeal to logic. In each of these cases, messages attempted a reasoned approach to get someone from unbelief to faith. An approach seated primarily in reason may appeal to the Modern mind, but will often be dismissed by the Postmodern. This has led some Postmodern thinkers to suggest that the sermon as proclamation is passé, proposing instead that sermons of the future should be conversations rather than proclamation. Brian McLaren sees this approach in Jesus' teaching method, describing it as, *short on sermons, long on conversations; short on answers, long on questions; short on abstractions and proposition, long on stories and parables; short on telling you what to think, long on challenging you*

---

[1] Roman T. Ciapalo, *Postmodernism and Christian Philosophy* (Mishawaka, IN: American Maritain Association, 1997), 282.
[2] Ibid, 93.

to think for yourself; short on condemning the irreligious, long on confronting the religious.[1]

So what approach to preaching will work for corporate worship in a Postmodern world? By this time, you should guess that the answer should be 'a biblical one.' Perhaps the greatest mistake any generation can make is to think that God takes sides in the cultural shifts of humanity. If Postmoderns are satisfied with seeing Jesus through the myopia of their own culture, they will fare no better than the Modernists, who ultimately put God in their own box. The Moderns eventually fell short, thinking too much of their own ability. They increasingly set the gospel aside and gravitated toward preaching conversion either as finding a better version of self, or as a logical response to a reasoned presentation of God's truth. We should acknowledge the error, no matter how subtle. Man cannot make himself better, nor can reason bring anyone to saving faith. Both reveal a cultural myopia. Likewise, Postmoderns will fall short if they develop a picture of Jesus taken through the lens of their culture. After 2000 years it appears the Church has still not learned that the transforming power of the sermon is not in its cultural approach—Modern or Postmodern. The power is, of course, in the message itself—in the Word of God, all human accoutrements aside. The gospel is neither Postmodern nor Modern. The gospel will always be culturally transcendent and culturally relevant at the same time. It will touch the mind, the emotions, and the will, and in every epoch it will crucify all that is distinctly human and therefore incapable of knowing God apart from repentance and new birth.

A presentation of the gospel that ultimately calls for a repudiation of self (including one's own cultural biases) is essential. We know this from our foundational definition of worship. Whether we are proclaiming the gospel to the Modernist or the Postmodernist is not the issue. All need to hear and repent to be saved. The Modernists may err by assuming that since the Bible is true it can be used to reason someone into a relationship with Jesus Christ. The Postmodern may err by assuming that no one accepts the Bible is true and therefore fails to proclaim its objective unchanging truth. Considering the transcendence of the gospel, it would be foolish to allow cultural variations to modify any aspect of it. In every epoch, men and women will stand before a mire of cultures and be called upon to faithfully declare the message. Like Paul at the Areopagus in Acts 17, we must declare that God *commands all people everywhere to repent, because he has fixed a day on which he will judge the world in righteousness by a man whom he has appointed; and of this he has given assurance to all by raising him from the dead* (vs. 30-31).

To do less than call people to genuine repentance is to deprive them of the message they must hear to be saved. The reactions will be just as varied as they were for Paul: *Now when they heard of the resurrection of the dead, some mocked. But others said, "We will hear you again about this." So Paul went out*

---

[1] Brian D. McLaren, *More Ready than You Realize: Evangelism as Dance in the Postmodern Matrix* (Grand Rapids, MI: Zondervan, 2002), 15.

from their midst. But some men joined him and believed, among whom also were Dionysius the Areopagite and a woman named Damaris and others with them (vs. 32-34).

Postmodernism and Worship Music

The rate at which worship styles have changed in the last fifty years should come as no surprise. We have already discovered that cultural changes often precede changes in worship styles. The two diagrams below illustrate this. The first shows the rate of cultural change and demonstrates that events such as the fall of the Roman Empire, the rise of Islam, the discovery of the New World, and technological developments can all lead to significant cultural change. There have also been times when culture changed rapidly and worship styles did not, creating some notable exceptions. For example, during the fall of the Roman Empire and the rise of Islam, culture was undergoing significant change and worship was relatively static. When there are significant changes in culture and worship expression remains static, worship is generally unhealthy. This does not necessarily mean that all changes in style that accompany cultural change make worship healthier. However, we may safely assert that if culture is changing rapidly and it is not reflected in any adjustments to worship practice, it will be less healthy.

Rate of Cultural Change

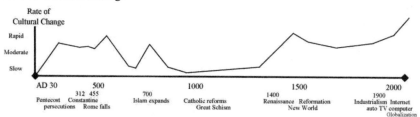

Rate of Worship Change

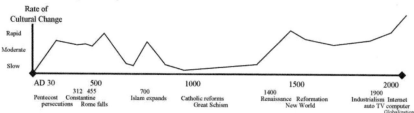

So where did all of this leave music, going into the twenty-first century? The last two decades of the twentieth century clearly indicated massive cultural division and subdivision. In this environment it is clear that whereas musical styles once lasted decades or generations, the rapid rate of cultural change in the twentieth century altered the fundamental way in which music styles rise and fall, making worship forms more like bubbles than styles. This is the key lesson of this century and one that is essential to grasp for those seeking to understand twenty-first century worship.

When we refer to a *worship bubble* we are speaking of a definable style of worship. Unlike styles of previous centuries, however, a *worship bubble* can rise very quickly and fall quickly as well. The reason *worship bubbles* can rise and fall so quickly is that they represent a sub-culture's attempt to make a unique expression of worship. While all people desire to have a way to express their own faith, their own song, the Postmodern desire for self-expression goes much further. In Postmodernism it is *no longer enough for people to simply focus on themselves—as in individualism; rather, they feel the urge to define themselves and to express this definition publicly.*[1] Therefore, worship styles can be as customized for a congregation as a musical diet can be customized on an MP3 player. Each new subtle cultural shift can produce a new *worship bubble*. *Worship bubbles* can be very flexible and can vary in size, becoming large and influential or remaining as small as worship in a home group.

The size of a *worship bubble* (how large its influence is) may be determined by its ability to combine with other bubbles produced before it or after it. However, once a *worship bubble* is defined, it begins to age, moving forward on the conveyor belt of time. At some point it will combine with other bubbles, become inflexible, or evaporate completely. How quickly new bubbles form depends on how quickly sub-cultures attempt to create their own unique style of worship. How quickly they become passé depends on the rate at which time moves the bubbles forward. The speed with which culture is producing new bubbles is generally seen when looking at young adults who are graduating from high school and entering college. The culture is now changing so quickly that almost each new graduating class is producing new bubbles. The following illustration, *How Worship Bubbles Form and Develop,* provides a way to see how *worship bubbles* form and how they move forward on the conveyor belt of time. To the left of the diagram, a Student Minister sits atop the hourglass watching seniors graduate. When they do, they begin to move forward on a conveyor belt representing time. The speed with which culture is changing is easily viewable as the Student Minster sees how students that graduated just a few years ago are different from those that will graduate a few years from now.

---

[1] Golden, 25.

How Worship Bubbles Form and Develop:

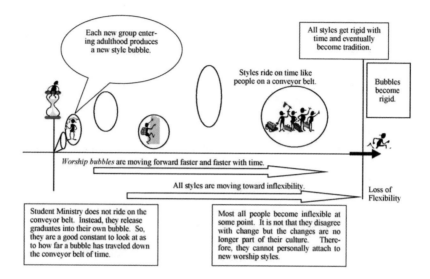

If we were to track how styles and bubbles have emerged in the history of Christian worship, an interesting picture would begin to emerge. Long lasting styles occurred from about the time of Constantine until about 1900. In the twentieth century, styles became very fluid. The worship bubbles of the twenty-first century share a striking similarity to the way worship styles developed in the first century.

How bubbles have formed with worship style changes:

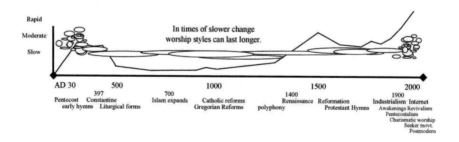

FINAL THOUGHTS ON THIS LESSON

The multiple layers of culture and the rapidity with which those layers can now change present some very real challenges for the twenty-first century worship leader. This is further exacerbated because, while the transition to Postmodernism is well under way, *not everyone today lives equally in the postmodern milieu—some live in quite premodern or modern settings. This situation, coupled with the fact that an ideology of diversity departs radically from modernism's emphasis on similarity—means that differences can become a controversial and contested value.*[1]

For those who already consider themselves deeply immersed in Postmodernism, there is still the need to be understanding with those who grew up in and only see through eyes of Modernity. Conflicts that occur within churches over musical styles exist, in part, because each worshiper adopts a style or a *worship bubble* based on music that they personally associate with significant spiritual experiences in their own lives. Whenever a person has significant spiritual memories attached to a type of music, that music becomes their preferred style. As new believers associate significant spiritual events with a wider and wider variety of *worship bubbles*, finding stylistic unity becomes more and more difficult. While worshipers in previous centuries could have easily used much of the same music as their grandparents and even great grandparents, that changed in the twentieth century. For most of the twentieth century, preferred styles were shared less and less between generations. By the beginning of the twenty-first century, taste variations among individuals within the same congregation rivaled what would have been differences between multiple successive generations.

Where all of this will head is not immediately evident. With such a growing variety of personal musical experiences, getting everyone to enter into corporate worship across quickly rising and changing *worship bubbles* could become increasingly difficult. The fact is that, with so many bubbles forming, fewer people are likely to share common preferences. While some Postmoderns may enjoy the juxtaposition of traditional and new, ancient and contemporary, liturgical and freeform, the musical language of such diversity is itself a mark of Postmodernism and rarely appeals to Moderns. Even today's practice of incorporating older hymns does not always close the gap. The hymns may have such a different musical sound that many Moderns may be unable to embrace them as the songs that they associate with their own spiritual experiences years ago. Because the association between spiritual experiences and certain hymns creates such a strong bond, many may actually feel that changing the musical style of cherished hymns is offensive.

This could mean that the mega church, as it developed in the latter half of the twentieth century, is headed for significant changes. Remember, Modernity valued similarity. If mega churches were able to form because thousands of

---

[1] Ibid.

Christians liked the same style and wanted to worship in the same way at the same time, Postmodernism is likely to have a significant impact on that. The Postmodernist concept of self-expression is much more likely to opt for smaller bubbles that are closer to their own preferred expression. Or, at least, they are likely to prefer unique expressions within smaller communities. The probability exists that twenty-first century churches may be naturally smaller in their local expression. This does not necessarily mean that mega churches will go away. In any large metropolitan area, it is conceivable that enough Postmodern worshipers may prefer the same style for many Postmodern mega churches to form. However, it could also mean that within a given church more and more styles of worship may develop.

This leaves some church leaders scratching their heads about what constitutes unity in a church and raising the question: *Does everyone in the church have to worship together?* This question is not about whether families should worship together. I believe they should. This question is specifically aimed at exploring whether or not a church in a given locale can maintain an organic unity based on something besides stylistic conformity. Whereas unity among Modern churches was achieved through common culture and shared liturgy, perhaps the future will present another option, which could be positive. Mega churches of the future could find their unity primarily in doctrine and theology. This could mean that a local church could have many different liturgies, spread across multiple locations. If this were to happen, mega churches of the future could eventually reflect the type of unity experienced among first century churches. For example, believers in Jerusalem constituted the 'Church in Jerusalem.' James was the chief pastor of that flock. Yet, they did not worship together. They could not have—the church numbered in the thousands and therefore met in various houses. The point is this: unity came from a shared theology not a shared worship style. While some bemoan the passing of Modernity, it is also possible to look with a sense of anticipation at what God may do in the twenty-first century. The determining factor will be whether or not the spread of the gospel and the development of new worship styles is grounded and tethered to solid theology and fixed to the Word of God. That is what made the Early Church effective and will determine whether or not Postmodernism will be a blessing or a liability.

SECTION III:

APPLICATIONS AND POSTLUDES

CHAPTER 11

APPLYING THE LESSONS
AND MOVING FORWARD

The study of worship history helps us see how our decisions today can impact worship tomorrow. Many of today's ills are a result of yesterday's mistakes and, similarly, today's strengths often represent yesterday's wise choices. It is a sobering thought that the decisions we make will directly affect how those who come after us may worship and how effective their corporate worship experiences might be. Therefore, it is crucial for those who make decisions about worship to do so with godly wisdom. In this chapter we will discuss additional ways to determine what should and should not change, how we can change without compromise, and ways to lead healthy change.

WHEN CHANGE COMES

The subject of change can be difficult for everyone because spiritual experiences are so often connected to our preferred style of worship. This is further complicated because leaders may approach transition in the wrong way. Too often, attempts to revitalize or transition worship stall because leaders begin by making external, cosmetic changes. This is rarely effective. Healthy change is a process that begins by clearly defining the spiritual reasons that make change necessary. Answering the 'why' of change must go beyond the preferences of the leaders or the members. Since there are things that must change to keep people engaged in corporate worship, God has surely provided us with a healthy way to make those changes. After working through worship transitions with various churches over the last thirty years, I believe leaders can help cultivate a healthier attitude toward change by answering three questions before they begin:

1) *Why do we need to change?*

2) *What will or can change?*

3) *What will not and cannot change?*

Why do we need to change?

We change because our ways are secondary to God's ways.

Despite our own opinions, the prime consideration in worship must always be what God wants rather than what we want. Accepting this is an important first step because it places everyone in the church, member and leader alike, on the same level playing field. God has already spoken, telling us much about what He wants worship to be. We must start there. Only after that can we begin to discuss our own opinions. I have seen leaders and congregations equally stubborn about issues in the outer ring of methods. Such human stubbornness only reveals our pride and is an affront to God. His indictment delivered through the Psalmist in Psalm 81:10-13 is stinging:

I, the LORD, am your God, Who brought you up from the land of Egypt; Open your mouth wide and I will fill it. But My people did not listen to My voice, And Israel did not obey Me. So I gave them over to the stubbornness of their heart, To walk in their own devices. Oh that My people would listen to Me, That Israel would walk in My ways!

Like the Children of Israel, churches are often gripped with stubbornness because each individual or each faction desires their own way. The one who demands his own way is foolish and presumptuous. God is rightfully jealous that we walk in His ways rather than our own. Many churches would see a totally different attitude toward change if they started with the following truth: the personal preferences of individuals concerning worship styles and methods mean little to God. While our own spiritual experiences may have made a particular style of worship dear to us, God stands outside and above our traditions, innovations, and preferences, saying to everyone equally: *Walk in My ways.* While His ways are everlasting, our methods and forms are only temporary. To walk in *His* ways means our agenda becomes secondary. This calls us to relinquish our personal preferences and make changes without grumbling and strife.

We change to make worship beneficial for those who practice it.

It is God's desire that worshipers benefit from properly following His ways. The Pharisees did not understand this. They made an idol of the Law of God, distorting its requirements. It became a god to be served rather than a guide to show people their need for a relationship with the Living God. The Pharisees demonstrated this by how they understood the Sabbath. Mark 2:23-28 describes an encounter between the Pharisees and Jesus. As He and His disciples walked through the fields on the Sabbath, the disciples picked some of the heads of grain to eat. The Pharisees chided Jesus for not requiring His disciples to observe the strict traditions of the Sabbath. Jesus went straight to the root of their misunderstanding saying, *The Sabbath was made for man, not man for the Sabbath. So the Son of Man is Lord even of the Sabbath.*[1]

Not only was Jesus making a claim of divinity, he was calling the Pharisees out for serving the form with more fervor than they served God. Jesus was telling those, who spent their whole lives refining a form of worship, that the *form* was to serve man rather than for man to serve the form. While this does not mean that our faith practice is all about us, in God's design, form is the servant of function. Worship is for God (Jesus declared himself *Lord even of the Sabbath*), but He intends for our form, whatever it is, to benefit us. This may seem a strange thought to us, just as it must have been to the Pharisees. If the form of worship does not benefit the worshiper, God is no more glorified in it than He was in the practices of the Pharisees. Like many of us, the Pharisees failed to see that the Sabbath was intended to benefit them. Application of this truth should be broad and lead us to examine what we are doing. We can perform our acts of worship with such rote precision that we can faithfully gather for worship, hear the Word, be in the presence of God's people, sing the songs, without any of the benefits of a relationship encounter with God. This consideration alone should prompt us to make significant changes to our worship practices.

We change to make adjustments for those who know or experience less of God than we do.

This truth is apparent in Paul's instructions to the churches at Corinth and Rome. In a discussion on the use of spiritual gifts, he calls on those who have the gift of tongues to limit their worship expressions to accommodate the ungifted or unsaved.[2] His point is very clear. If the whole church comes together and everyone is speaking in a tongue, the unbeliever or those who do not understand will not benefit from that part of the gathering. Instead, Paul instructs them to major on the proclamation of the Word (prophecy) since that will benefit everyone, even declaring that the unbeliever will hear the truth and be converted.

---

[1] Mark 2:27.
[2] 1 Corinthians 14:16, 23.

277

To clarify, Paul is not suggesting that unbelievers determine the content and conduct of corporate worship. Instead, he is helping us see our obligation to evaluate our worship services and make appropriate adjustments. The type of adjustments he is suggesting make it possible for the weakest (the unbeliever and the uninformed) to receive maximum benefit from the gathering. This is the principle of deference, where those who believe and understand are called upon to make changes for the sake of those who do not.

This principle of changing or deferring for the sake of the weaker one is repeated in Romans 14. Paul is addressing the conduct of believers concerning what is eaten (daily life) and the observance of Holy days (functions of worship). He makes it clear that the mature should be willing to make changes for the sake of the weaker rather than vice versa. Paul writes in Romans 14:1-5:

> Now accept the one who is weak in faith, but not for the purpose of passing judgment on his opinions. One person has faith that he may eat all things, but he who is weak eats vegetables only. The one who eats is not to regard with contempt the one who does not eat, and the one who does not eat is not to judge the one who eats, for God has accepted him. Who are you to judge the servant of another? To his own master he stands or falls; and he will stand, for the Lord is able to make him stand. One person regards one day above another, another regards every day alike. Each person must be fully convinced in his own mind.

While it may be acceptable before God to eat various types of foods or to observe various days as holy, Paul concludes in verses 13-16,

> Therefore let us not judge one another anymore, but rather determine this—not to put an obstacle or a stumbling block in a brother's way. I know and am convinced in the Lord Jesus that nothing is unclean in itself; but to him who thinks anything to be unclean, to him it is unclean. For if because of food your brother is hurt, you are no longer walking according to love. Do not destroy with your food him for whom Christ died. Therefore do not let what is for you a good thing be spoken of as evil.

The application of the principle should not be ignored in regards to worship. In 1 Corinthians, the practice of tongues was to be curtailed for the common good of all present, particularly in consideration of the weaker ones. Similarly in Romans 14, the freedom to eat meat or observe special days of worship should be limited if they are harmful to the weaker brother. If worship is to be of maximum benefit to everyone, practices should be changed if the way in which mature believers express their worship creates a barrier for the less mature to participate. This may seem like a call to 'dumb down' the truth of the message or lessen the devotion with which mature believers worship. This is not what Paul was teaching. Instead, he taught that in order for everyone to benefit, the truth is proclaimed boldly while the mature defer to the weaker ones in other areas of practice.

For churches involved in the spiritual process of self-examination, it is the mature that should be quick to lay aside their preferences in non-essentials for the sake of others. Paul clearly speaks to the more mature when he says, *Now accept the one who is weak in faith, but not for the purpose of passing judgment on his opinions.* In fact he goes on to say in the same passage; *Now we who are strong ought to bear the weaknesses of those without strength and not just please ourselves.*[1] Unfortunately, a major factor in determining style and method is often the personal opinion and the personal comfort of the most seasoned worshipers. According to this scriptural principle, it cannot be right for mature believers to decide what style of worship they will choose based solely on what pleases them or makes them most comfortable. Since God and His truth are the only things that do not change, we must constantly be willing to surrender methods, culture, and style.

It is my own experience that many seasoned believers struggle with this. They either become selfish, demanding that they should not have to change for the sake of others, or they equate a call for change with a call to dumb down the corporate worship experience. This often leads to deadlock. Paul's prophetic word speaks to the *whole church.* To the selfish who think their way is best, he calls them to keep it between themselves and God.[2] To the super fervent who want to have the special experience while others reap no benefit, he says to 'cool it.'[3] To those who would say to let the essentials slide, he renounces any attempt to elevate human methods over the Word of God.[4] With so many churches arguing over style, it would be wise to embrace Paul's teaching as the way to move forward.

If we applied Paul's teaching in Romans 14 to our struggles over worship styles, it would loosen the tight hold many keep on their preferred form. Imagine approaching the subject of worship transition in a church where everyone applied Paul's teaching to their own convictions about corporate worship:

> Now accept the one who is weak in faith, but not for the purpose of passing judgment on his opinions. One person has faith to worship one way, but he who is weak does not worship in that way. As one who is in the Lord Jesus, I am fully convinced that no form of worship of the true God is bad in itself.

---

[1] Romans 15:1.

[2] *The faith which you have, have as your own conviction before God.* Romans 14:22.

[3] *But if there is no interpreter, he must keep silent in the church; and let him speak to himself and to God.* 1 Corinthians 14:28.

[4] *But we have renounced the things hidden because of shame, not walking in craftiness or adulterating the word of God, but by the manifestation of truth commending ourselves to every man's conscience in the sight of God.* 2 Corinthians 4:2.

But if anyone finds a form offensive or unapproachable, then for him it is bad. If you do not care that someone weaker is put off by your style of worship, you are no longer acting in love. Do not let your worship form destroy him for whom Christ died. Do not allow what you consider good to become something spoken of as evil. For the kingdom of God is not a matter of hymns or choruses, contemporary or traditional, but of righteousness, peace, and joy in the Holy Spirit. If you will serve Jesus in this way you will please God and gain the approval of those who really matter. So let's make every possible effort to pursue what leads to peace and helps build up those who need building up. Do not inhibit the work of God just because you like your worship style. All kinds of true worship may be okay, but it is wrong if you practice it at the expense of offending one who is weaker. It is good not to practice a form of worship if it is a stumbling block. If you have a conviction about your style of worship, keep that conviction between yourself and God. Do not condemn yourself by what you choose.

adapted from Romans 14: 1-2, 14-22

So what can change and what should not change?

Several years ago I was asked to help a church work through a conflict between those who wanted to change the style of worship and those who did not. Before I arrived, I was told that the leaders were in a virtual standoff. Each group had already decided what they were willing to change and what they were not willing to change. This left them with no way to move forward.

After praying with the group and briefly teaching on the biblical meaning of worship, I asked them to share what was important them. It was easy to see the division, and the root of that division was tragic. In nearly every area where the various factions were unwilling to change, change could have occurred without violating anything in Scripture. In the same way, those who were demanding change were generally seeking cosmetic or external changes. Sadly, most in the group were more willing to sacrifice something Scripture required or modeled than to set aside something they preferred. I was struck with how foolish our arguments are, at times.

I asked them to list all the ingredients used in their current worship services as they existed and as some wanted them to be. This list included the comfortable traditions and the desired innovations. On a dry erase board, I listed those things in a column to the left. Then, I asked them to use their knowledge of the New Testament to list things they knew were a part of the first century Church. I wrote those things in a column to the right. They did not finish the list but had named enough things to help them learn an important lesson.

Slowly, they began to realize that several areas where they were intransient had little to do with what Scripture mandates or models. Many things which they were doing or wanted to do were not part of the first generation of Christian worshipers. The two lists looked something like this:

My Church	The First Century Church
Sound system	Preaching
Offerings	Offerings
Band	Bible
Bible	Pastor(s)
Choir	Lord's Supper
Pastor(s)	Deacons
Buildings	Prayer
Preaching	Fellowship
Lord Supper	Singing
Hymnals	Greeting
Buildings	Public Bible Reading
Piano	Baptism
Drums	
Greeting	
Announcements	
Projectors	
Singing	

Then, we worked our way through the list on the left, circling those things in their services that were part of worship in the New Testament and striking through those things which were not. The result looked something like this:

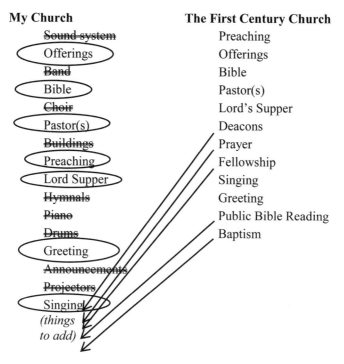

Those things we struck through were not bad in themselves, but they were the things that had the greatest potential to divide. The things that we share with the churches of the first century are those things that make our worship gatherings distinctly Christian and therefore must never change. Everything else is part of our own worship culture, our methods, and traditions. If we become unwilling to change those things, or we demand those things, we are elevating our own culture to the level of Scripture. The sobering aspect of this exercise was that the people with whom I was meeting were ready to make war over things that, according to the Bible, were not even essential. To have such a deep commitment to these temporal things is dangerous. All aspects of our worship culture must ultimately be expendable. Because they are not something the Bible models for us or instructs us to do, they should last only as long as they are effective to accomplish the things which must never change.

If we never stop to look at our own practices, it is possible to continue to add layers of extra-biblical practices to our worship. *Extra-biblical* is not necessarily *anti-biblical*, but neither is it *biblical*. If something is not a part of worship in the Scripture it CANNOT be theologically essential to the present-day practice of worship. Otherwise we are affirming an open revelation—the addition of *essentials* for Christian worship beyond what we can find in the written Word. Each generation has the responsibility to examine its own practices in the light of Scripture, reaffirming those things that God desires, and constantly surrendering cultural practices to God so they can be changed as needed. We do this to keep ourselves firmly attached to the Scripture, while maintaining the ability to make necessary changes to our methods.

Worship Constants: Truths that keep us from changing and require us to change

For worship to be pleasing to God, we all must conform to a set of truths that apply to everyone at all times. We will call these *Worship Constants*—a set of unchanging truths that govern the practice of worship. The things we discussed in the opening chapters are all *worship constants*: the heart of submission, the supremacy of God's glory, worshipers who live holy lives in service to a holy God, etc. Such truths rightfully limit our freedom to make changes to that which defines worship. At the same time, there are some truths in the Bible about worship that make change essential. Therefore, *worship constants* can keep us from changing or require us to change. We will call those truths that keep us from changing *formational constants*. Understanding and maintaining the *formational constants* help us see which aspects of corporate worship should never change, ensuring that we share common traits with all true Christian worshipers who preceded us or will come after us. On the other hand, *transitional constants* are truths that require us to change. For instance, some changes to language and culture must be reflected in worship if the gathering of worshipers is to remain participatory. When *worship constants* superintend our practices, we will utilize established methods that are appropriate and be willing to set them aside when they are no longer effective. Examples listed below are not exhaustive, but demonstrate how some *constants* keep us from changing and others instruct us to change. As you study worship in the Scripture and find applicable truth, it is good to ask the diagnostic question, *Does this truth keep us from changing or require us to change?*

Formational Constants	**Transitional Constants**
Worship requires submission of the individual worshiper.	Corporate worship is to be participatory.
Corporate worship is conducted in a gathering.	Corporate worship includes cultural expressions that are unique.
Only believers are God's children and can worship Him as Father.	Worship requires some deference for the weaker ones present.
Worship is the activity of a kingdom of priests, with Jesus as the sole mediator.	Worship utilizes the spoken word to communicate the message.
Worship of Holy God cannot be worldly.	Corporate worship involves music, which constantly changes.

Constants, whether *formational* or *transitional,* are those things about worship that we can see in God's Word. They may be explicit or implicit, modeled or mandated but, because they are found in the Bible, we are bound to them. Methods originate with human beings and may be useful for only a season. That makes understanding and applying *transitional constants* crucial for those who plan and lead corporate worship. If we ignore them, we will avoid essential changes to our methods and forms. Clearly, we can see how the Church of Rome ignored *formational constants* as they added to or ignored clear teaching in the Bible. But they also faltered by ignoring *transitional constants,* holding on to a language and form that made active participation improbable for the common worshiper. The changes required by *transitional constants* keep our methods fresh and effective as time passes. As the popular saying goes, *Methods are many; principles are few. Methods may change, principles never do.*

CHANGE WITHOUT COMPROMISE

A church may be concerned that changes made to reflect culture only serve to make the church worldly. This concern is not without merit and no full understanding of planning and leading corporate worship can ignore it.

According to Jesus' prayer in John 17, we are not of the world but we are not yet to be taken out of it. Instead, Jesus asks that we be left in the world and protected from the evil one.[1] Maintaining a clear perspective that we are in the world but not of the world is essential. The struggle to be in the world but not overtaken by its evil presents a constant and palpable tension in the life of the believer. In a local congregation, there are few places this tension is more evident than in the ongoing debate over changing worship practices.

Setting a Scriptural Standard

John tells us in 1 John 2:15: *Do not love the world or the things in the world. If anyone loves the world, the love of the Father is not in him.* This draws a very clear line of separation—the love of the world[2] and the love of the Father cannot exist in the same space at the same time. They are mutually exclusive.[3] Therefore, we cannot lead our people to love God more deeply and obey Him with greater devotion by teaching them to love the world's system and the things in it. This does not mean that we are to become isolationists. In 1 John 3:17, the Apostle also tells us that we are to use the world's goods to bless others. The word for *world* is the same word he used in 1 John 2:15 (*kósmos*). Interestingly, the word translated *goods* is the word *bios* [βίος]. *Bios* indicates far more than wealth. The *world's goods* include our span of time in this world, as well as the world's resources, the world's means, and the world's way of life.[4] So there is an aspect in which we cannot isolate ourselves from what is in the world because we are actually to use it for the good of others.

However, before we feel free to make *any* change, we must also come face to face with a stark reality. The inducements of the world are bait, concealing a painful and deadly hook. In corporate worship, just as is every other area of life, the love of the world is enmity with God. While each congregation must work out the issues of what is acceptable, all fall equally under the same obligation to follow Scripture, whether it limits our ability to make worship more attractive to our culture or whether it pushes us to change our methods to accommodate cultural changes. To be in the world, aware of its culture, and able to navigate it

---

[1] John 17:14-16.

[2] *kósmos* [Κόσμος].

[3] This differs from the way in which God loved the world (*kósmos*) and gave His one and only Son for it (John 3:16). *In these epistles [1,2,3, John] and the Gospel, John employs this term [kósmos] in three distinct and basic ways: (1) the created universe ([1 John] 3:17; 4:17; John 1:10); (2) the world of human persons (John 3:16; 1 John 2:2); and (3) an evil organized earthly system controlled by the power of the evil one that has aligned itself against God and his kingdom ([1 John] 4:3–5; 5:19; John 16:11). In these verses John uses the third meaning.* See Daniel L. Akin, vol. 38, *1, 2, 3 John*, electronic ed., Logos Library System; The New American Commentary (Nashville: Broadman & Holman Publishers, 2001), 108.

[4] *Bios, from which the word "biography" is derived, refers to duration, means, and manner of life.* See Spiros Zodhiates, *The Complete Word Study Dictionary: New Testament, electronic ed.* (Chattanooga, TN: AMG Publishers, 2000).

without violating Scripture, requires us to constantly examine why we are making changes in the first place. This brings us to a key question we must ask ourselves: *Are we using methods or considering methods because they appeal to the flesh?* If so, the battle is already lost. To use the flesh and a worldly system as inducements to a holy God defies all that the Bible teaches about worship. The roots of fallen humanity that are visible in every culture are incompatible with the holiness of God.

So where does that leave us? The Apostle John summarizes the problem by identifying three faces of worldliness. Each can help us delineate the line between holy and unholy in corporate worship. In 1 John 2:16-17 he states: *For all that is in the world, the lust of the flesh and the lust of the eyes and the boastful pride of life, is not from the Father, but is from the world. The world is passing away, and also its lusts; but the one who does the will of God lives forever.* This gives us three areas to examine, each having a direct impact on planning and leading worship services.

The first is the *lust of the flesh.* The word translated *lust* is *epithumía* [ἐπιθυμία], meaning to desire greatly. The English word *lust* has a negative connotation, as it should in this context. Surprisingly however, the intense desire is not the problem. Jesus uses a verb form of the same word[1] to describe His longing to eat the Last Supper with His disciples,[2] as does Paul describing his longing to be with Christ.[3] The problem is not the *desire* but the *object of the desire.* John is speaking of a desire which is from the flesh, focused on the flesh, and seeks to gratify the flesh. This makes the desire worldly and therefore sinful.

All of us should be able to agree that certain things in our world, in our own culture, are indisputably worldly. We would be quick to understand that the lust of the flesh would include misguided sexual desire, greed, covetousness, jealousy, and the like; that would be correct. The deeds of the flesh are evident.[4] These things pose a significant threat to the spiritual health of our people. This calls for modesty, restraint, and discernment. What each of us approves or prohibits will not be the same. Nevertheless, worship has a much higher probability of being God-focused if worship leaders are careful to avoid anything that would encourage fleshly desires.

It is also important to remember that everything worldly does not look evil and everything that is flesh does not have the easily identifiable stench of carnality. Worldly things, fleshly things, are not necessarily vile or repulsive things. They can actually be attractive, generally appreciated, and socially acceptable things—beautiful flesh so to speak. There are many things in this world that are not apparently or intrinsically evil, but they become evil to us when they draw our hearts away from God. We can see this illustrated in the story of man's fall in Genesis 3. When the serpent lured Eve she *saw that the*

---

[1] *epithuméō* [ἐπιθυμέω].
[2] Luke 22:15.
[3] Philippians 1:23.
[4] Galatians 5:19.

tree was good for food, and that it was a delight to the eyes.[1] It appealed to her flesh. The fact that it was beautiful did not make it evil. God had created the heavens and the earth and *everything* in them was good. He did not place the tree there to tempt Eve: *Let no one say when he is tempted, "I am being tempted by God"; for God cannot be tempted by evil, and He Himself does not tempt anyone.*[2] The evil was not in the tree itself. It was in Eve's disobedience to the command of God to not eat of or touch the tree.[3]

Some things may be beautiful to the eye or the ear, pleasing to the senses, able to excite the mind and appetite of the multitudes. They can be enjoyed for what they are. Had Eve simply enjoyed the beauty of the tree and trusted in God's command to not eat its fruit, the story would have had a different ending. In fact, the tree could have been something beautiful to look at, reminding her of who created it and set its boundaries. Eve discovered that her appreciation for beauty could have tragic consequences if she allowed the voice of the serpent to guide her desire.

Our situation is more precarious than Eve's. Her desire did not come from a corrupted flesh (she had not yet sinned); ours does. The corruption of the flesh that occurred in the Fall of Man leaves us with an even greater Achilles heel. Beauty can declare the wonder of God but it can also become a worldly pursuit. So subtle is the line between the two that many churches are filled with things that are beautiful flesh: a delight to eye and ear, appealing to the senses but a distraction to following God with a devoted heart. We must realize that, like the tree in the garden, God does not always put a fence around beautiful things to keep us from misusing them. This makes that which is 'beautiful flesh' all the more dangerous. Whether flesh is beautiful or not, all believers have an ongoing battle with it: *Beloved, I urge you as aliens and strangers to abstain from fleshly lusts which wage war against the soul.*[4]

Therefore, worship must never incorporate that which is designed to leverage the natural and corrupt fleshly desires of those who participate. While we may have differing views on what those things would be, it is reckless to plan and lead worship without giving serious consideration to this boundary. Anything that moves the worshiper toward a pursuit of the flesh must by definition lead him away from God. All flesh, whether it is repulsive or beautiful, is still flesh and adroit at disrupting our obedience to God. *For the flesh sets its desire against the Spirit, and the Spirit against the flesh; for these are in opposition to one another, so that you may not do the things that you please.*[5]

---

[1] Genesis 3:6.
[2] James 1:13.
[3] The command was given to Adam (Genesis 2:17). Clearly, Eve knew it as well; she quoted God's prohibition verbatim (Genesis 3:2-3).
[4] 1 Peter 2:11.
[5] Galatians 5:17.

The second face of worldliness is the *lust of the eyes*. Again, the *desire* is not the problem but the *object of that desire*. Recognizing the power of the eye to distract the worshiper, David writes: *I will set no worthless thing before my eyes.*[1] We have already discussed that our propensity to be drawn away by what we see is as old as temptation itself.[2] Every marketing company understands this, leveraging our own weaknesses against us. For believers, the eye must never drive us or we will be perpetually disoriented. Paul reminds us in 2 Corinthians 4:18 that what we see is merely temporary and has no eternal value. Because human beings have a natural weakness to be absorbed with what is seen, care must be taken to avoid that which encourages the lust of the eyes.

There is nothing wrong with making use of beautiful things. Worship and creative arts ministers, church architects, and others who have input into the visual aspects of corporate worship, understand the power of image. Beautiful things can direct the mind toward God—*the heavens are telling the glory of God.*[3] As a worship pastor it has been my privilege to work with some incredible artists. I have seen them use their skills to create extraordinary moments of beauty and I can say, without exception, the masterworks of art they helped create have never pointed to the art or the artist. In every instance, they used the beauty of paint and canvas, sculpture, lighting and set design, all out of their God-given creativity, to draw the eye of the worshiper to focus on the glory of God and His gospel. So that which is beautiful can be useful when it declares the glory of God and brings the heart of the worshiper toward Him. As leaders, we must be vigilant, understanding that the *lust of the eyes* can naturally and quickly draw us into a worldly system that separates us from a close relationship with God.

The third face of worldliness is *the boastful pride of life*. This is as deadly as the lust of the flesh and the lust of the eyes. It should be clear by now that while there is great liberty to practice worship in a variety of ways, there are some things that are so antithetical to the nature of worship and the character of God that, if present, make acceptable worship impossible. Among these is pride. The phrase John uses here speaks of doing anything for the purpose of being seen. This includes *showing off to fellow mortals; the pride, pomp, or manner of life; the ambitious or vainglorious pursuit of the honors, glories, and splendors of this life; the luxury of life for the purpose of showing off.*[4] American Christianity, in much of its worship expression, fails on nearly every one of these points. Jesus' exhortation is applicable and piercing:

> Beware of practicing your righteousness before men to be noticed by them; otherwise you have no reward with your Father who is in

---

[1] Psalm 101:3.
[2] Genesis 3:6.
[3] Psalm 19:1.
[4] Spiros Zodhiates, *The Complete Word Study Dictionary: New Testament*, electronic ed. (Chattanooga, TN: AMG Publishers, 2000), 212.

heaven. So when you give to the poor, do not sound a trumpet before you, as the hypocrites do in the synagogues and in the streets, so that they may be honored by men. Truly I say to you, they have their reward in full.[1]

Nothing we do for God can also be done so that others will see it and think more of us. Those who attempt such will have no reward from the Father. That does not mean there is not a reward. Three times in this discourse Jesus uses the refrain, *they have their reward in full*.[2] When we assemble the best worship band, the finest orchestra, a stellar choir, or craft an excellent sermon in order to be seen, we do get a reward (*Truly I say to you, they have their reward in full*). That reward is the honor of men. Could it be that we have become addicted to that reward instead of longing for the reward that comes when we have the Father's approval? Despite knowing that God rejects anything we do in order to be seen by others, we may preach, sing, plan, and lead with more concern about what others think than what God thinks. While we are busy outwardly impressing others, God sees inside where the ugliness of self-promotion has displaced Him from the throne of our hearts.

Properly handling these things—the lust of the flesh, the lust of the eyes, and the pride of life—is a weighty responsibility. Each of these plays to the inherent weaknesses of humanity and can be used to motivate people for all the wrong reasons. This makes it possible for us to create an aura of success, receive the affirmation of our people, and enjoy our own accomplishments, all in the name of worship without any of its true blessings or benefits. For this reason, we must maintain boundaries that minimize our human predilection to accommodate worldliness. Churches of all shapes and styles incorporate aspects of worldliness into their Christian practice without even considering these scriptural truths.

Finding Usable Boundaries

While individuals are responsible for their own actions, leaders must remember that they will give an account to God for how they lead His people. For things that are not specifically addressed in Scripture, it can be difficult to determine what is right and wrong, holy and unholy, worldly or honoring to God. This does not release us from the responsibility of establishing boundaries that guide us in planning worship. It is the leaders' job to know and understand how to take the truths of Scripture and apply them to issues not addressed in Scripture.

This does not mean that our boundaries will all be identical. In fact, they are likely to vary greatly. I began to see this in my young adulthood. I was born in western North Carolina. When I was still a young boy, my family moved to

---

[1] Matthew 6:1-2.
[2] Matthew 6:2, 5, and 16.

South Carolina. My father died when I was eight years old. From that time on, I was welcomed into a loving Southern Baptist church. There, I was taught the Bible, came to faith in Jesus Christ, and was afforded many opportunities to grow in His knowledge and grace. As I became a young man and periodically traveled back to western North Carolina, I was surprised to find that some believers there thought that my church was worldly. Others even thought that my denomination was apostate—a tool of Satan. I soon discovered that what they understood as worldly differed greatly from what I was taught. Naming those things that they thought were worldly would be superfluous. The point is this: on issues not addressed in Scripture, acculturation itself has a direct bearing on what one believes to be holy or unholy. In this case, two different cultures produced two different standards.

Forty years later (more than thirty of which were spent leading worship in churches), I am still trying to understand how one can be in the world and use its resource to do good, without leading people to become worldly. It is difficult to define a universal line that separates ministry *to the culture* from accommodation of the wickedness *in the culture.* Ignoring the issue does not make it go away. Whatever we choose to do in corporate worship is communicating that which has our approval.

For this reason, I hope to remain a lifelong student of this subject, trying to clarify where the line really is between holy and worldly. Our motivation for defining this is not to get as close to the line as possible—living on the edge can be deadly. Our motivation should be, as the Apostle Paul states, that our conscience can be clear, being one *who does not condemn himself in what he approves.*[1] Over the years I have continually tried to reevaluate and adjust. Below are three standards that lead me to deep and sober reflection as I attempt to understand what may be acceptable and what is not.

1)   We should approve of nothing in corporate worship that would cause us to be ashamed if the Master returned in that very moment.

Luke 12:45-46 describes a scene in which the Master returns to find the unsuspecting servant doing that which was evil. The consequences were swift and brutal. I must ask myself, if the Lord comes back and finds His people following my lead in worship, would we rejoice in His nearness; or, would our actions, our songs, our music, our sermons, our attitudes be embarrassing? We must seek to lead so that *we may have confidence and not shrink away from Him in shame at His coming.*[2] If He returned in that moment would He bring with Him His approval or His anger? This is not a call to live under self-condemnation. Instead, it helps me remember that the only one who really needs to be 100% pleased with what we are doing is the Lord for whom we are doing it.

---

[1] Romans 14:22.
[2] 1 John 2:28.

2)   We must always craft our plans to move the spirit of the worshiper.

This helps us get straight to the heart of the matter. The worship plan should move the worshiper on a direct path toward God for the sake of God. The worship experience is all at once spiritual, physical, and emotional. However, if we are not intentional, we will excite the emotions, involve the body, and neglect the spirit. The spirit of the worshiper must be the first consideration; emotional and physical responses can follow and God has sanctioned many. Even so, they are only acceptable to God in as much as they represent one who is *in a proper state of submission to God.* If the heart is not inclined toward God, then in reality, we have only excited the flesh. Before I can decide whether something is holy or unholy, I must think about its initial appeal. Is it first spiritual, physical, or emotional?

3)   We must understand the Scripture and the culture of those we lead.

I previously shared my own experience growing up in a Southern Baptist church. While it was a Bible-teaching, Bible-believing church, there are those who could never affirm a church like the one in which I came to know Christ. Suppose God had called me to serve in one of those mountain churches. To the people in such a church, the way I worshiped God in my home church violated the line between holy and unholy. Having an agenda to get them to see worship my way would not have been fruitful. To help the people in that church have a meaningful worship encounter with God, I would have needed to defer and accept them where they were, leading them, not to embrace my style of worship, but to find fullness and freedom in biblical worship within their cultural context.

Our role as leaders is not to get people to worship like we do, whether that is more traditional or more innovative. Our job is to understand the faith language of the people we lead and understand the culture of the community in which they live. Then, taking the panoply of scriptural truth on the subject, we are called to lead people into a meaningful encounter with God. While there are churches that I think could loosen up and churches that I think have gone too far, I cannot answer for them. They will have to answer to God for what they do, just as we all will. When looking at potential changes to worship styles, we must first see if they are within the bounds of biblical truth. Second, we should assess whether or not those changes are likely to benefit the congregation or the culture into which God has planted those people. Our desire should be to faithfully lead people to worship God in a way that is beneficial to them and acceptable to Him. To do that requires both a commitment to obey Scripture and an understanding of the culture.

Standards for Song Selection

One additional area that we should address with respect to *Change without Compromise* is the issue of song selection. We will not analyze individual styles of music. Doing so requires a meaningful evaluation of musical acculturation (how a person came to understand what is right and wrong) and association (what particular events in a person's life become attached to a particular style). This makes evaluation somewhat subjective. Even describing a particular style of music as acceptable is unhelpful. Virtually every style of music has been used for evil purposes at some point. A survey of Western Music since 1600 would illustrate this all too well. Having served in worship ministry for many years, I can say that a *very* wide variety of music can be used to glorify God. It will suffice at this point to say that the guidelines laid out by the Apostle John concerning worldliness should be applied to musical styles. All music has the power to move the heart away from God and much of it has the power to move the heart toward God. Whatever style of music is ultimately used in a church, no worship leader should become one who *condemn*[s] *himself in what he approves.*[1]

As for the text of a particular song, it is much easier to be objective. Churches of all types choose poorly simply because they fail to maintain criteria for analyzing and evaluating lyrics. These are important for regulating the quality of songs, including theological and doctrinal content. They also help us identify and understand the function that a particular song can have in corporate worship. These are essential considerations for all worship leaders.

Voicing: Some songs are addressed to God, some to believers or unbelievers, and sometimes combinations of these. Being aware of a song's voicing means the worship leader knows what he is asking the congregation to say and to whom he is asking them to say it. In a service, there should be some variety in voicing; and, over the course of several weeks there should also be a healthy balance of voicing. For instance, I have been in services where every song was testimonial, i.e., the congregation speaking to one another. In such a service, God may never be addressed by the congregation. Imagine that believers gather to worship God and He never hears them address Him at all. Hopefully, when this happens it is an oversight. Check to make sure the congregation actually has one or more opportunities to address God together as His people. And, if needed, help them understand how that should direct their thoughts as they sing.

Doctrine: Considering the ease with which people absorb song lyrics, it is critical to examine the doctrine of every song. This review should be done by someone who is facile with biblical theology. No matter how 'nice' a song is, good music can never overcome bad theology. This argues for worship leaders who will take it upon themselves to study and understand the great doctrines of the faith. If you serve in a church where you are the only pastor and others are choosing songs, it is your responsibility to review them—someone must. This extends beyond statements that are blatantly wrong and also involves evaluating what may be inferred from the text. There is no excuse for singing songs that teach wrong theology.

Along these same lines, lyrics must be examined in the light of the New Covenant. It is certainly acceptable to sing texts from the Old Testament.

---

[1] Romans 14:22.

However, doing so can omit New Covenant truth. For example, let's suppose we constructed a song on David's confession in Psalm 51. Verse 11 says, *Do not cast me away from Your presence And do not take Your Holy Spirit from me.* This would need some explanation. The removal of God's Spirit was a real possibility for David—it had happened to his predecessor. However, that must be understood and explained in light of the way in which the Holy Spirit indwells believers after Pentecost. There are numerous examples we could cite that would illustrate how singing texts directly from the Old Testament can ingrain Old Covenant doctrine into New Covenant hearts. Again, the point is that we must evaluate what each lyric is actually teaching. Is it true orthodox theology? Is it New Covenant teaching? Each of these issues must be considered when evaluating the text of song.

Imagery: Poetic language can express abstract or complex truths with cognates we can understand. For example, Scripture uses imagery to help us grasp concepts about God and about ourselves. Even though He is very different from us, anthropomorphisms help us understand aspects of God by using human images that are common to us, i.e., the *eyes of the LORD*, the *face of the LORD*, the *right hand of the LORD*.[1] These are images that relate to our own experience and, as a result, help us have some way to understand more about who God is. The Bible also uses images to help us understand who we are. The Bible says that His people are the *sheep of His pasture*, the Church is the *body of Christ*, we are the *light of the world*.[2] The use of scriptural images in songs can help us become familiar with the language of the Bible and, at the same time, help us understand broader truth represented by the image.

Song lyrics may also use contemporary images. Recalling a shared event can become an effective image to illustrate a spiritual truth. Because these types of images are attached to a specific culture or locale, they tend to lose their ability to communicate effectively as culture changes. For example, Edwin S. Ufford used the image of a lifeline quite effectively in his 1888 hymn, *Throw out the Lifeline*. In a day when the fear of being lost at sea was much more common and many immigrants had faced that fear to come to a new country, the image of a lifeline would have been very poignant. Today that same image may not have the same impact—some not even aware of what a lifeline actually is. When evaluating imagery in lyrics, ask the following series of questions:

1) What imagery is used?

2) Is it biblical or extra-biblical?

3) If it is biblical, how can we take the opportunity to teach the meaning of that image as it is used in the Bible?

4) If it is extra-biblical, does it still communicate biblical truth accurately and effectively?

---

[1] *The eyes of the Lord*, 2 Chronicles 16:9; *the face of the Lord,* Psalm 34:16; *the right hand of the Lord,* Psalm 118:16.
[2] *Sheep of His pasture,* Psalm 100:3; *the body of Christ,* 1 Corinthians 12:27; *light of the world,* Matthew 5:14.

Understanding and applying biblical imagery can be helpful. Knowing the culture of your people will help you choose imagery that clearly communicates biblical truth and encourages meaningful worship.

Objective or Subjective: Song texts will either be objective or subjective. Objective texts state truth that is applicable to everyone. For instance, lyrics that describe the character of God often fall into this category. The popular hymn, *Holy, Holy, Holy,* is almost completely objective in its statements. Whether recited by a believer or unbeliever, a seasoned saint or a novice Christian, the words are true. That is part of the power of a text that is objective. On the other hand, song texts can be subjective—true only for those who have had a particular experience. Songs that use the first person to describe aspects of the Christian life are subjective. I do not mean by that they are not true, but that the truth they contain is subject to a particular experience. When someone sings the words to Isaac Watts', *When I Survey the Wondrous Cross,* the words are true only for a believer. Such a division between objective and subjective is easy to grasp.

The difficulty with subjective texts is that they can be so subjective that only a small percentage of the people can relate to them. The effectiveness of a subjective text is dependent on the number of people who have had a shared experience. Themes such as forgiveness and grace are common to all believers. On the other hand, very intimate terms may express how a particular writer understands his/her relationship with Christ. However, if the whole congregation is asked to sing such an intimate poetic verse, they may feel disengaged. Singing very personal poetry in a congregational setting has been an ongoing problem. A hymn such as *In the Garden,*[1] which describes a poet's encounter with Jesus in mildly romantic terms, may be very popular with some may seem awkward to others. Lyrics that describe the relationship with Jesus in romantic terms increased in popularity in the late 20th and early 21st centuries, leaving many uncomfortable with singing them at all. According to recent studies, many men disassociate from the church and corporate worship because they do not relate to Jesus in any way that is romantic, nor are they comfortable with singing about Him as if He were a feminine counterpart in a relationship.[2]

This is only one example of the way subjective texts can be so personal that they disinvite rather than invite participation. Therefore, it is vitally important to choose songs that can provide as much expression as possible for the widest number of those participating. While believers' worship is subject to conversion (unbelievers cannot honestly sing songs about being redeemed),

---

[1] Written by Charles Austin Miles (1912).

[2] For a brief summary of this topic see *The Feminization of the Church: Why Its Music, Messages and Ministries Are Driving Men Away,* Holly Pivec, "Spring 2006 - Biola Magazine - Biola University," Biola University - A Private Christian University in Southern California, Spring 2006, accessed May 17, 2011, *http://www.biola.edu/news/biolamag/articles/06spring/feminization.cfm.*

there is a whole gamut of poetic imagery and expression that may be useful in private but, by its own subjectivity, is not be useful for corporate worship.

Proclamation: One of the chief functions of corporate worship is to rehearse the redemption story. To do this, lyrics should display the character and activity of God, the lostness of humankind apart from redemption, the substitutionary death and resurrection of a victorious Jesus Christ, and the consummation of human history in the world to come. As we have previously discussed, rehearsing the activity of God is a common theme in the Old Testament and still just as appropriate for those on this side of Calvary. No matter how varied musical styles become, the story does not change. If corporate worship does not recount the redemption story, what real worship can take place? Being in the *proper state of submission to God* requires that we constantly see our condition as we were before He saved us and rejoice in our present position as objects of His adoption through grace. While there are many activities in which churches may be involved, who else will recount the story of the perfect God-man dying on the cross in order to pay our sin debt; rising from the dead on the third day, and now sitting at the right hand of the Father interceding for us? Songs must declare the gospel! If we offer any offense, let it be that which should offend—the message of the cross. No matter what style of music you choose, make sure that you make it a habit to sing the gospel! Sing the character of God, the hopeless condition of humankind without Christ, the cross where God in Christ closed the gap between His holiness and our sinfulness, the living, resurrected Savior, and the hope of His return.

LEADING HEALTHY CHANGE

While we have discussed constraints that limit our adaptation to culture, inevitably change must come if we obey *transitional constants*. Often, this is a source of bitter division within a church. Even in the best of situations, change will be difficult for some people. Therefore, when it is time to proceed, do so deliberately and carefully. All of the helps included in the discussion that follows are given presuming that the leader(s) have sought the Lord and believe that areas where change is planned will not violate Scripture. Instead, the changes being considered are the type called for by one or more *transitional constants*. Leading transition out of a spiritual conviction rather than a personal preference is important. When conflict does come, and it likely will, leaders need to have the confidence before God that the types of changes being considered are those that would be pleasing to Him.

For leaders charged with navigating the choppy waters of changing worship styles, there are some spiritual examples to follow. There is none better than the way God leads us. As students of the Bible know, the Greek word for pastor is *poimḗn* [ποιμήν]. It is the word used to describe a shepherd and the same word Jesus used when He described Himself as the Good *Shepherd* in John 10:11. Since Jesus is the perfect Shepherd, His example should be our benchmark. As the Shepherd leads His sheep, so leaders should also care for the needs of the sheep they lead. At the same time, leaders must make sure that they are also allowing God to shepherd and lead them. The observations below are from the Twenty-third Psalm. As David shares how God shepherds his own heart, we can learn how to shepherd those whom God has placed under our care. Each observation provides a pattern for us to imitate—a way in which God leads David that should be our standard for how we lead. We will also see some things that we need to avoid.

A Psalm of David.
The LORD is my shepherd, I shall not want.
He makes me lie down in green pastures;
He leads me beside quiet waters.
He restores my soul;
He guides me in the paths of righteousness
For His name's sake.
Even though I walk through the valley of the shadow of death,
I fear no evil, for You are with me;
Your rod and Your staff, they comfort me.
You prepare a table before me in the presence of my enemies;
You have anointed my head with oil;
My cup overflows.
Surely goodness and lovingkindness will follow me all the days of my life,
And I will dwell in the house of the LORD forever.

v.1   *The Lord is my shepherd, I shall not want.*

Pattern to follow: *The Lord always feeds His sheep. Never stop feeding your sheep.*

The Lord understands the needs of the flock and is always careful to make sure they have what they truly need. The Lord can superintend the universe and at the same time be fully aware of and able to make provision for each individual person. We do not have the same ability to focus our full attention on everything simultaneously. Instead, we must carefully allocate our time and attention. During times of transition, the extra planning, the extra thinking, the extra meetings, etc. can become overwhelming. This makes it easy to become focused on the logistics of change and neglect the primary pastoral function of providing spiritual food. People that are not receiving spiritual nourishment will usually lack the ability to grasp the spiritual reasons for the change you are leading. In other words, malnourished sheep may be irritable and not very spiritually minded toward change. Do not undermine the whole process by giving so much attention to methods that you neglect what matters most.

Warning Sign: an over-emphasis on methodology rather than spiritual health.

Resolution: Jesus is the Bread of Life. Keep the sheep well fed by focusing their attention on Him.

v.2-3a *He makes me lie down in green pastures, he leads me beside still waters, he restores my soul.*

Pattern to follow: *The Lord makes sure that we have places to rest. Keep some green pastures where the sheep can feed and rest.*

In our lives, circumstances constantly buffet us. Our Shepherd always provides some place to rest, to be refreshed. In the middle of everything else, God is our refuge. Even when He tills the soil of our hearts, He does so as a vinedresser with a spade rather than as a farmer with a backhoe. As transitions begin to unfold in a church, areas that are not changing act as a counterbalance to those areas which are changing. If you plow under everything at once, where will the sheep find rest? Leaders make this mistake and find themselves feeling like they are fighting a war on all fronts. This can usually be avoided by making sure there are 'safe' areas where members of the congregation do not feel disturbed. Since the Good Shepherd makes sure we always have some green pastures, good earthly shepherds would be wise to do the same. You will rarely have success in transition if you change everything at once. Every group of people has a stretch factor. If you exceed the amount of stretch your people can take, your transition will become unnecessarily divisive. Ask God to help you stay in touch with how stretched your people feel. You can help your people avoid feeling overstretched by providing them some places where they are not being asked to change.

Warning Sign: too many areas are in simultaneous conflict.

Resolution: Seek God's wisdom so you will not transition too many different things at one time—don't be unwilling to slow down!

v.3b *He leads me in the path of righteousness for his name's sake.*

Pattern to follow: *The Lord leads us for the glory of His own name. We must walk people through change ONLY for the glory of God.*

Such a tender Shepherd does not lead His sheep so they will have better pastures, better lives, be healthier or for any other reason except one—He does it for His own name's sake. God's work in our lives is not ultimately about us. He leads us for His name's sake. He does not lead us to enhance our lives, grow our churches, or expand our importance. Jesus prayed that we would be fruitful for one purpose—that the Father would be glorified.[1] As a leader it is very easy to measure our success by earthly standards rather than by God's standards. Externals like growth in numbers, facilities, or programs cannot confirm whether or not our actions are glorifying to God.

---

[1] John15:8.

If we accomplish anything that really matters, it will only be because it draws attention to the glory of God. All of our 'successes' in ministry should fulfill Jesus' instruction that our good works should be seen by men and cause them to glorify our Father in heaven.[1]

Warning Sign: We gauge our 'success' by any standard other than whether or not the endeavor brings glory to God.

Resolution: Jesus was pleased to please the Father. Let that be your only and ultimate pursuit.

v.4a   *Even though I walk through the valley of the shadow of death, I fear no evil, for You are with me;*

Pattern to follow: *The Lord knows we will face trouble but promises His presence through it. Prepare your people for difficulty but reassure them of the outcome.*

The Psalmist reveals two important personal convictions. The first is that he *will* walk through difficulties and the second is that he will be *personally* guided by the Shepherd. Surprisingly, his comfort does not come because he believes he will avoid the valleys. It is the presence of the Shepherd in the depths of those valleys that quiets his soul. Oftentimes, leaders make the mistake of talking about how wonderful everything will be when the music changes, when the building changes, when the style is right. In doing so, pastors place themselves more in the business of salesmen than shepherds. Leaders can gain more traction by being open and honest. Saying to someone, *This will not be easy but in God's strength we can get through this difficult thing,* goes much farther than ignoring the challenges and doing a hard sell. Everything is not going to be in our comfort zone. Beyond the benefits of change (many of our people will not be able to look ahead and see them), there is a greater comfort we can offer. Obedience is its own best reward. If God calls us to do something difficult, He will provide everything we need to lead us through it.

Warning Sign: To get people to follow, you realize that you are candy-coating or hard selling needed changes.

Resolution: Clearly communicate that while change is not easy, God can always be trusted to walk with us through every place He takes us.

v.4b   *Your rod and Your staff, they comfort me.*

Pattern to follow: *The Lord always protects, directs, and corrects. Our role as shepherds should be no less.*

The rod and the staff may represent two separate instruments used by the shepherd. The shepherd could use the rod to count his sheep as well as to correct

---

[1] Matthew 5:16.

and protect them.[1] The staff, on the other hand, actually carries the meaning of support and is often used to specify something trustworthy on which to lean.[2] The rod and staff can also be the instrument which the shepherd holds up to offer guidance.[3] For those of us who walk with God, we know Him as faithful, caring, supportive, guiding—all of this and more. As we attempt to lead others toward change, compassionate godly guidance can accomplish more than almost any single thing. Our confidence in God is based totally in His character and consistency. It should be no surprise that people are drawn to leaders when they know their leaders truly care for them. Sometimes it is a difficult path. Even so, knowing that a leader truly has the best interest of his followers at heart can go a long way in soothing the difficulties of change. Leaders who want faithful and compassionate followers must be faithful and compassionate leaders. During transitions we ask difficult things of people without considering the struggles and difficulties that those changes bring. When this happens, the trust in leadership is precarious at best and irreparably harmed at worst. Change is a daunting prospect for many people and requires a caring and trustworthy leader who will lead out of love for his people more than his desire to make changes.

Warning Sign: You do not feel compassion for what your people are going through in transition.

Resolution: As God comforts, guides, and corrects you, ask Him to grow the same compassion for those whom you lead.

v.5 *You prepare a table before me in the presence of my enemies. You anoint my head with oil; my cup overflows.*

Pattern to Follow: *The Lord provides the intimacy of fellowship even in the face of our enemies. Set the table of fellowship for your people and lavish them with love.*

In the Sacrificial System, a communal meal was the symbol that fellowship between God and His people had been restored.[4] For Christians, the Table was given to us by the Lord as a place where we go to remember what He did for us on the cross. The Scripture is full of examples of meals that have spiritual significance, often providing fellowship and affirming covenant. The symbolism used here is exactly that. When surrounded by adversaries, the Good Shepherd offers us close fellowship with Himself rooted in the surety of His covenant. At His table, He lavishes us with His grace and love. In David's day it was customary *to receive a guest by anointing him with fragrant perfume and with a*

---

[1] Robert Laird Harris, Gleason Leonard Archer and Bruce K. Waltke, *Theological Wordbook of the Old Testament*, electronic ed. (Chicago: Moody Press, 1999), 897.

[2] Ibid, 945.

[3] Carl Friedrich Keil and Franz Delitzsch, *Commentary on the Old Testament*. (Peabody, MA: Hendrickson, 2002), Ps 23:4–5.

[4] See above, CHAPTER 2, OLD TESTAMENT ARCHETYPES AND CHRISTIAN WORSHIP.

cup filled with a choice wine. In this way, the host indicated that nothing was to be considered too good for his guest.[1] Here, the Psalmist sees such an extravagant expression of love from the Shepherd that his cup is filled to overflowing.

During times of transition or change, we often forget to express love to our people by affirming, encouraging, and fellowshipping with them. Instead, we are more likely to think about the ways they can help us accomplish our goals. In doing so, we fail to recognize how God leads us and we miss an important opportunity to lead our people in the same way. By the indwelling of the Holy Spirit, we have the seal of His love upon us—a deposit of His presence in us and with us. God has made an incredible provision to lead us by means of a close and personal relationship. In leading our people to make needed changes, the journey is as important as the destination and, in fact, makes the destination all it can be. The authority granted by God to lead is not given for the purpose of *commanding* change, but lovingly *leading* change. To use the metaphor of this Psalm, we can accomplish much more with our people in the dining room than we can in a boardroom. If you must remind everyone that they should follow you because you are the leader, it is likely that you are not successfully leading through relationship.

Warning Sign: You are dictating change rather than leading it.

Resolution: Pour your life, love, and vision into others. They are much more likely to follow.

v.6 *Surely goodness and mercy will follow me all the days of my life and I will dwell in the house of the Lord forever.*

Pattern to Follow: *The Lord points us to the ultimate goal throughout the entire journey of our lives. Point your people to the ultimate goal.*

God does not lead us by dangling temporal things in front of us. Instead, He offers us an *inheritance which is imperishable and undefiled and will not fade away, reserved in heaven for* [us].[2] David found his strength in looking past the ups and downs of his own life to something that was better, something perfect. His hope rested in the promise of being with God forever. If we draw people toward change by using temporal things, such as a larger church, a bigger building, better music, etc., they *may* follow. However, we have cheated them— we have motivated them to do something for *themselves* instead of for God. This robs them of the great joy of knowing that what they did was for God's glory. Without the ultimate goal in front of us, we are left to bring significance to that which moth and rust destroy. Give your people a cause that is greater than themselves or this life. Regularly remind them that forever with God is an

---

[1] Roger Ellsworth, *Opening Up Psalms* (Leominster: Day One Publications, 2006), 51.

[2] 1 Peter 1:4.

eternal weight of glory far beyond all comparison.[1] Goodness and mercy will follow you but God must remain in front of you.

Warning Sign: Your rallying cry is anything that is temporary.

Resolution: Keep the ultimate goal in front of your people throughout the process.

Additional guidelines for leading change

Having led both successful and unsuccessful transitions at churches during the last thirty years, the following principles are given from my own personal experiences. They are not necessarily from the Scripture, although each of them has a connection to truths taught in the Bible.

1)   Start with the willing ones and be patient with late bloomers.

When change begins, leaders will encounter those who embrace change and those who resist it. In the process you will pray through an area where change is needed, study the options extensively, and arrive at a deep spiritual conviction. That will all seem great until some people begin to react as if you had suggested they forsake the Faith. Often when change begins, the initial reactions will include distrust. The leader's motives, wisdom, even his relationship with God may all be questioned. As a leader it is easy to attribute this to the spiritual immaturity of people, to write them off as 'being in the flesh.' To be sure, a congregation may have people who come against the leader(s) and do so in the flesh; some may not even be regenerate. However, deep emotional aversion to changing worship styles does not always come from people who are evil. For this reason, patience with them is a better approach.

How can these people who undergo, endure, and even embrace change in their workplace and in their communities be so intransient when it comes to making changes at church? We easily overlook how songs function in the life of the Christian. While Scripture never changes, culture does. Like other aspects of cultural expression, music provides a way for a believer to express eternal truths in a deeply personal, contemporary way. Because of this, an individual learns to associate songs with aspects of his or her spiritual pilgrimage. The songs they love become an integral part of their spiritual pilgrimage, a way to chronicle and understand their own history with God. This creates a profound connection between God's work in their lives and certain songs or styles. Because musical language is always in transition (now faster than ever), worshipers will live to see others come along who do not value that which has become dear and meaningful to them. When the new comes, people often feel that the validity of their spiritual journey is being questioned, even devalued, as the music they hold dear is no longer treasured by the group to which they belong. As a result, the initial negative reaction to change may have nothing to do with whether or not the people are good or bad, spiritual or unspiritual. It may simply be the grief

---

[1] 2 Corinthians 4:17.

300

associated with setting aside something that has had a profound meaning in their life.

If leaders will be patient with the honest struggles of their people, they may be rewarded by seeing many join with those who initially responded positively, accepting or even embracing change. And although some may never really like the changes, they come to see the greater value in terms of Christ's Kingdom. That is what makes patience so important. Leaders should never present change as if it were the last boat leaving—*if you miss it, you are not with us*. Start with the willing ones, but do so without any condemnation for those who find change difficult. Leaders gain little and lose much by creating a culture within any group of those who 'get it' and those who do not. This cuts off some well-meaning people who, given some time and understanding, not only come to accept change, but possess the ability to influence others who are even less likely to accept change.

2) Lead toward a willingness to change rather than a particular style.

In watching churches through the years, it has been my conclusion that, if a church handles change well, they have an opportunity to create an ongoing culture of change. To do this, leaders must avoid presenting any style as the final destination. Let's assume that a church sees the need to make a change. Perhaps they are located in a transitional neighborhood where language and culture have changed around them. Realizing they must change, the leaders place before the people the singular goal of adopting a new cultural language that better reflects the people God has placed in their neighborhood. If that transition is successful, what happens when the neighborhood changes again in five to ten years? Rather than starting the process all over again, the leaders would have been much wiser to make the singular goal that of building an ongoing cultural flexibility into their congregation.

Too often, enormous amounts of energy are expended at a very high price only to get the church to embrace a new style of worship. Because those churches have not been led to embrace a culture of change, they will be frustrated when asked to change again. We can help our people by constantly reminding them that their own preferred worship culture is temporal. The Word of God is eternal and God is the one to whom they must cling. Transition, if truly successful, is never complete. As long as new people are being added to the conveyor belt of time behind us (see the Worship Bubble in the previous chapter), the need for change will be ongoing. Considering the rapid pace of change in the twenty-first century, this may prove more important than it has ever been.

This principle goes beyond the mere pragmatism of making change easier. It reminds us that all we create—our culture, our buildings, our songs, our styles—lasts only for a moment. For *"All flesh is like grass, And all its glory like the flower of grass. The grass withers, And the flower falls off, But the word of the Lord endures forever.*[1] Continuing to remind our people of the temporal nature of worship culture is a constant reminder that only the Word of the Lord is forever.

3) Work first to revitalize what you are currently doing (create the appetite).

The goal of all worship transitions should be to keep its expression biblically faithful and spiritually vital. Often congregations begin to consider transition because they (or a segment within the church) are dissatisfied with the current practices. When corporate worship becomes flat, congregations may look to find a new style. While change may be warranted, there is something wrong with moving to a new style to solve 'flat worship.' If all we have come to understand about the temporal nature of style is true, then changing style alone will not revitalize worship. Change may be exciting to some people but, that is not necessarily the same thing as revitalization. As we saw in the Reformation, revitalized worship comes from refocusing on the God of Scripture—a renewed focus on the object of our worship, rather than the means. God is never looking for a new style, although He may not object to it. He wants to see 're-newed' hearts of people passionate again for Him.

Therefore, a change in the heart needs to precede any transition of style. If we place a style change in front of our people as the means by which to renew their hearts, we are communicating the wrong thing about the nature of worship. No style can renew us, only the fresh work of God in our hearts. I have seen many congregations tinker over and over with various forms trying to find one that will bring life back to corporate worship. Since virtually any style can be effective, start with what you are doing now and refill it with meaning, Once people refocus their eyes on eternal things they are much more likely to release temporal things. If a congregation fills its *existing* style of worship with meaning, there will likely be a new hunger for God. People that are hungry for God are more likely to embrace the right kind of change for the right kind of reasons.

4) If at all possible, start the music transitions with the people you have now.

One of the most tragic mistakes made in worship transition is to push capable people aside. I suspect that churches are full of thousands of talented musicians who no longer use their gifts in the church because they have not yet recovered from being pushed aside during a worship transition. While nearly everyone who has served in ministry has had to set someone aside for good reasons, a change in worship style is not always one that requires a total change in personnel. God began to teach this lesson to me some years ago.

In the mid-1990's I came to serve a church in Houston, Texas. After being in the church for several months, I found that there were several professional-grade musicians in the church, many of whom were not leading Sunday worship.

---

[1] 1 Peter 1:24-25.

Instead, the piano and organ were being played by capable musicians and several orchestra members joined them each Sunday. In thinking through how to use the gifts of those not participating, I had a dilemma. The quality musicians who were not serving played instruments such as drums, acoustic guitar, electric guitar, and bass. I talked to them about 'playing along' with the others but, they knew as did I, what an awkward mix that would be. So after much prayer, I decided the music needed to change styles. My main intent was to fully utilize what God had placed in the body. To do this meant finding music that would utilize the exceptional skills of the musicians God had brought to that church. A piano could work with this type of music but, what would I do with the organist? Her name was Rosemary. She was a precious, feisty little widow. How could I go to her, knowing she had given years of service, and ask her to step aside so the others could take over? I could not do it. One day an idea came to me (I am now sure it was God's idea, not mine). Why not ask Miss Rosemary to play some B3 (an organ sound often used in pop/rock/country) and to add some string or synthesized sounds on an electric keyboard? While it would mean a change of instrument for her, it would still give her a chance to be a part and use her gifts.

I made an appointment to meet with her. I told her how much I valued her for who she was as a sister in Christ, her years of experience, and the gifts God had given to her. I explained the need to involve the other musicians. Later I learned she thought I was about to retire her! Instead I finished what I had to say by asking her, "Miss Rosemary, would you be willing to be a keyboard player in a Rock-style band?" I could not have been more pleased with her response. "Well," she said slowly, "I have never done anything like that but, I sure will try." For almost five years she played with our worship band. She became the proud 'den mother' of the group and, while she was with us, many rehearsals included some freshly baked treat that she brought to share. I found out later that, when she heard criticism of the music from her contemporaries, she was quick to remind them how much fun she was having and how everyone in the band treated her so nicely. What could they say? One of their own was in the middle of it, helping make it all happen. I will never forget seeing her playing with us one night as we shared the gospel on Bourbon Street in New Orleans. There she sat behind her keyboard, having the time of her life, wearing her Blues Brothers glasses.

During the last two years she played with us, she contracted Amyotrophic Lateral Sclerosis, or ALS. She continued when she only had one usable hand. Despite her repeated offers to retire, I encouraged her to continue. Finally, when it went beyond that, she told me that she hated to drop out of the band but, she needed to do so. The week before she went to be with the Lord, we talked, laughed, and cried at all we had experienced together. I am convinced that, to a great extent, the transition at that church happened because of how God used her.

Having been part of a successful worship transition, I was receiving invitations to speak on the subject. It seemed to be an incomplete story if I left out Miss Rosemary. It was not something I had accomplished, it was something

God had done and He had used Miss Rosemary in an extraordinary way to do it. When we last spoke, I promised her that I would never teach on the subject of worship transitions without telling her story. So in part, I have shared this to keep that promise. Beyond that, I believe there is a lesson for the wise observer. I have often tried to imagine what we all would have missed if I had taken the well-worn path of dismissing those who were part of the 'old worship style' so the new people could do the 'new thing.' I know it was not my wisdom. God intervened and helped me do something that would change the course of many lives, including my own. If you are considering changes to your congregation's worship style, do not assume that you must only use new people. While there were a few musicians who decided not go forward with the change, that was their own choice, not mine. I could not have asked for the whole transition to have gone any better. I would not trade anything for what I learned from Miss Rosemary. She taught me and all who watched a valuable lesson.

FINAL THOUGHTS ON MOVING FORWARD

When my children were small, I loved to hear them try to learn our colloquialisms. One of my favorite was associated with the way they learned the phrase 'on purpose.' They learned to use that phrase to describe that an intended action had a desired result. What made it funny was when the opposite happened—an unintended action with an unintended result, or an intended action that had an unintended result. When this happened, I would hear them explain, *I did it 'on accident.'* To them, that must have been the logical antonym to 'on purpose.'

It strikes me that a considerable amount of what happens in churches, with respect to corporate worship, is done *on accident.* We do things without thinking them through and we wind up a far cry from where we meant to be. Or, we make choices without understanding what the results will be. In either case, our actions may have consequences that we never intended. We could go back to many of our lessons from worship history and see such a pattern. In retrospect, we can probably see such unintended consequences in our own ministries.

By God's sovereign design, many issues are not spelled out in Scripture. The New Testament does not provide an exhaustive list of do's and don'ts like the one under which the Jews lived. We do not have Pharisees (though some are self-appointed) who can tell us with pinpoint accuracy what is holy or unholy, what is acceptable in corporate worship and what is not. We do not have point-to-point instructions on how to lead our people to maintain a spirit of flexibility with regards to their worship preferences. As a result, many choose to act as if nothing restrains us from using anything that works. This is a misuse of the liberties afforded to us and a waste of the direction we have been given. Our charge remains: *we are responsible to take the clear guidelines in Scripture and deal with them.* We cannot afford to ignore them. If nothing else, we must be able to say that we have taken what the Bible says and have applied it fully to our ministries. I do not want to stand before God knowing that I made worship into what I wanted it to be, rather than what He wants it to be. We must each be faithful stewards of the ministry to which we have been called so that *we may have confidence and not shrink away from Him in shame at His coming.* [1]

POSTLUDE

There will be a time when we will no longer see through a glass darkly and every tribe and tongue will join in one song around our everlasting Redeemer. Until that day comes, style will be debated. As long as we are on this earth, there will never be one style that suits everyone for all time. While we will (and should) continue to have a healthy and rigorous debate over styles and methods of worship, the actual content of our worship services is another matter. We have no excuse for becoming lax in the content of our worship services. This has been an ongoing source of frustration for me. I have seen churches of all varieties—megachurches, store-front churches, contemporary churches, postmodern churches, traditional churches, house churches, and everything else in between and beyond—get sloppy with what they include or exclude in corporate worship services. I have seen the Bible become a prop or an ornament rather than the Book around which God's people gather for spiritual food. I have seen churches sing syrupy hymns or songs, one after the other, with virtually no theological content. I have seen stage presentations that rival anything the world can offer but with no more spirituality than the programs they are imitating. I have known churches that prided themselves in being 'spot on' in their doctrine but they stretch my definition of what it means to be *the dead in Christ*.

I do not say this to be cruel; I say it bewildered, wondering what Bible we are looking at in order to guide our people into meaningful encounters with God. I have looked at services that I have planned or led and wondered the same thing. I constantly have to go back to the Bible, reboot my own views, and clear the cache of my practices. Almost every time I have taught the material contained in this book, I return home to find some area I have neglected. The practice of worship is like a marriage—it is relational. If a husband does not continue to pursue his wife, he will miss the subtle changes that are happening in her and lose his sense of connectedness to her. Of course the same is true for the wife toward the husband. Worship is such a pursuit as well. It must be constantly reevaluated and renewed. Worship is relational and, as such, it is dynamic. The moment we stop digging in the Word, evaluating our experiences, working to understand our people, we fail to capture worship's vibrancy in our own lives and subsequently in the lives of many people we lead.

My prayer for students of worship is that they will take the information in this book and genuinely think about it with respect to what they do. Beyond what the Scripture says about worship and what actually happened in the history of worship, what I have written represents my best understanding when put into practice. Students who dig deep may draw different conclusions from history or might address certain topics differently, if not better. Had I written this book twenty years ago my opinions would have been different and if I were to revisit the subject in another twenty years, I am sure it would change again. No matter how fluid our opinions (the outer ring of methodology), we are all equally bound to orthodox theology and Scripture. As we have seen, the Bible has plenty to say about the subject of worship; and history has plenty to teach. What bothers me is how few give serious, ongoing consideration to applying what is said and taught when it comes to making application to their actual ministry. As is often the case, we know significantly more than we practice—and that is a dangerous position. It is our responsibility to lead people in such a way that we can stand before the Lord and say *I have tried to follow the Scripture and have not forsaken the true gospel handed to me.*

Because of the broad liberties that Scripture gives concerning methods and styles for worship, each of us must define how our beliefs look when put into practice. You may have never really nailed down what you think. Or, like me, you may have nailed it down, revisited it, pulled the stake up, and moved it farther out or brought it closer. That is the kind of thoughtful analysis in which all of us as leaders should be engaged. Whether we can articulate our convictions or not, the way in which we lead worship is communicating our convictions to others. I have been amazed at how few pastors have really given thought to many of the issues discussed in this book. As long as the sermon is planned and goes well, most are satisfied. Likewise, many who assist in leading congregational worship may go home pleased that the songs went well, or the testimony went well. In each case, myopia is a problem. If leaders never stop to consider what God actually wants worship to be, or take time to seriously examine worship in light of both Scripture and the culture in which their people live, who will?

Worship practices, during particularly vibrant portions of Church history, demonstrate worship as it should be: a beautiful marriage of deep vibrant theology and broadly expressive passion for God. Sadly, that marriage is seldom

308

seen in many of our churches. We may be discontent with congregational worship in our churches but, we are not discontent enough to make any substantive evaluations or adjustments. Perhaps we fail to see the gravity of the situation. The proliferation of available Bible teaching (not all of it good), the popularity of Christian music, the rise of a new generation of theological thinkers, even relative success in our own churches, may keep us from looking at the larger picture.

I would be remiss to write a book on worship without bringing the subject full circle to ask this question: *If worship among our churches is indeed vital and transforming, then how is that demonstrated in our desire to see the nations join us in worshiping Jesus?* We must come to grips with this truth: there is an unbreakable connection between genuine worship and the proclamation of the gospel. John Piper writes: *Missions exists because worship doesn't.*[1] Despite the many things we could debate, we do know this: redemption through Jesus Christ is the *only* possible way that the peoples of the world can joyfully and willingly worship Him. Tragically, our lack of vibrant worship is clearly exposed when we look at our real progress toward inviting the nations to worship Him. In 2000, the percentage of the world population that was unevangelized stood at around 29.9%. By 2025, that percentage is projected to be 29.4%, a percentage gain of 0.5%. But in real numbers, human beings, that means there are presently over 1.8 billion who have no access to the gospel and, because of population growth, that number will rise to over 2 billion by 2025. That is another 200 million people who will have no access to the gospel.[2]

This should be a wakeup call to everyone who professes the name of Jesus Christ. I cannot help but think that a lack of vital Christian worship adversely impacts the spread of the gospel. The passion to obey the Great Commission and share Christ with others should well up from a deep and loving commitment to Him. Whether we are general or particular in our view of redemption, everyone should agree that we are speaking of 2 billion people who cannot believe in Jesus if they have never heard his name. That number will continue to rise if something does not change significantly. Too many times we separate our understanding and practice of worship from other key elements of the faith. The connection between vital worship and aggressive evangelism is clear in Scripture and the history of the Church is a case study of that connection. During times of rapid expansion in the Church, indicated by high levels of evangelism, the practice of Christian worship has been biblically focused and organically connected to the lives of the people.

---

[1] John Piper, *Let the Nations Be Glad! The Supremacy of God in Missions* (Grand Rapids, Michigan: Baker Academic, 2004), 17.

[2] *Status of Global Mission, 2011, in Context of 20th and 21st Centuries*, from the Center for Study of Global Christianity, Gordon-Conwell Theological Seminary, http://www.gordonconwell.edu/sites/default/files/StatusOfGlobalMission.pdf (accessed May 13, 2011).

We must come face to face with this truth again: there is no such thing as vital corporate worship unless there are individuals who *hear* and *obey* the Master. We hold gatherings and call them *worship* services without knowing if true worship occurs or not. Despite all our planning and flawless execution, the spiritual fruit of corporate worship can be no greater than the sum of its individual parts. This draws the circle around us as individuals. Unless there is a genuine connection between our corporate worship experiences and the other aspects of our Christian life (a desire to evangelize the lost, concern for the widow and orphan, freedom from greed and pride, etc.), we are really only fooling ourselves. We have become people who play at worship. Until we are ready to set aside ourselves for something far greater, the situation will not improve. Like John the Baptist, until our hearts are ready to say, *He must increase, but I must decrease,*[1] we will never know the true joy that comes from a heart fully submitted to Him. And as a result, our participation in the expansion of Christ's Kingdom will be diminished.

We know little of Enoch, but I remain intrigued by the simple description of him in Hebrews 11:5, *By faith Enoch was taken up so that he should not see death, and he was not found, because God had taken him. Now before he was taken he was commended as having pleased God.*[2] Genesis 5:24 describes him this way, *Enoch walked with God; and he was not, for God took him.* Enoch was a man of faith, so he pleased the LORD and received His commendation. He *walked with God*—that statement alone is a challenge to my comfortable Christianity. Beyond that, Enoch is a true picture of what worship can accomplish. He *walked with God; and he was not*—he walked so closely with God that he was no more. If I were so enamored with the glory, the goodness, the holiness, and the majesty of God, that I lowered myself to the *proper state of submission* before Him, that I walked with Him so closely that the entirety of my *self* disappeared, and only the radiance of Christ's glory in me remained—that would be *worship, from the ground up*. I long to live it.

Much Jesus, Less...

Stuart Sheehan
Houston, Texas
2013

---

[1] John 3:30.
[2] Hebrews 11:5.

310

BIBLIOGRAPHY

Abbington, James. *Readings in African American Church Music and Worship*. Chicago, IL: GIA Publications, 2001.

Akin, Daniel L., David P. Nelson, and Peter R. Schemm. *A Theology for the Church*. Nashville, TN: B & H Academic, 2007.

Anderson, Allan. *An Introduction to Pentecostalism: Global Charismatic Christianity*. Cambridge, U.K.: Cambridge University Press, 2004.

Asbury, Francis, and Ezra Squier Tipple. *The Heart of Asbury's Journal*. New York: Methodist Book Concern, 1904.

Baird, Robert. *Religion in America, Or, An Account of the Origin, Progress, Relation to the State, and Present Condition of the Evangelical Churches in the United States: with Notices of the Unevangelical Denominations*. New York: Harper, 1844.

Ball, Warwick. *Rome in the East: the Transformation of an Empire*. New York: Routledge, 2000.

Barnes, Timothy David. *Constantine and Eusebius*. Cambridge [Massachusetts]: Harvard University Press, 1981.

Bass, Diana Butler. *Standing against the Whirlwind: Evangelical Episcopalians in Nineteenth-century America*. New York: Oxford University Press, 1995.

The Bay Psalm Book: a Facsimile Reprint of the First Edition of 1640. [Chicago]: University of Chicago Press, 1956.

Beecher, Henry Ward. *Yale Lectures on Preaching: Delivered before the Theological Department of Yale College, New Haven, Conn., in the Regular Course of the Lyman Beecher Lectureship on Preaching. First, Second, and Third Series*. New York: Fords, Howard, & Hulbert, 1889.

Blumhofer, Edith Waldvogel. *Pentecostal Currents in American Protestantism*. Urbana, IL: Univ. of Illinois Press, 1999.

Boak, Arthur E. R. *A History of Rome to 565 A. D.* New York: Macmillan, 1921.

Bourne, Hugh. *A Collection of Hymns for Camp Meetings, Revivals, &c.: for the Use of Primitive Methodists*. Bemersley near Tunstall [England]: Printed at the Office of the Primitive Methodist Connexion, 1821.

Boyer, Paul Samuel, Clifford Edward Clark, and Joseph F. Kett. *The Enduring Vision: a History of the American People*. Boston: Houghton Mifflin, 2008.

Brackney, William H. *A Genetic History of Baptist Thought: with Special Reference to Baptists in Britain and North America*. Macon, GA: Mercer University Press, 2004.

Brockway, Robert W. *A Wonderful Work of God: Puritanism and the Great Awakening*. Bethlehem [PA]: Lehigh University Press, 2003.

Bukofzer, Manfred, and Claudio Monteverdi. *Music in the Baroque Era*. London: Dent, 1978.

Butler, Jon. *Awash in a Sea of Faith: Christianizing the American People*. Cambridge, MA: Harvard University Press, 1990.

Butler, Jon, Grant Wacker, and Randall Balmer. *Religion in American Life: a Short History*. Oxford: Oxford University Press, 2008.

Calvin, Jean, and Henry Beveridge. *The Necessity of Reforming the Church*. Dallas, TX: Protestant Heritage Press, 1995.

Carroll, Henry K. *The Religious Forces of the United States Enumerated, Classified, and Described; Returns for 1900 and 1910 Compared with the Government Census of 1890: Condition and Characteristics of Christianity in the United States*. New York: C. Scribner's Sons, 1912.

Cashdollar, Charles D. *A Spiritual Home: Life in British and American Reformed Congregations, 1830-1915*. University Park, PA: Pennsylvania State University Press, 2000.

The Center for Study of Global Christianity, Gordon-Conwell Theological Seminary. "Status of Global Mission, 2011, in Context of 20th and 21st Centuries." http://www.gordonconwell.edu/sites/default/files/StatusOfGlobalMission.pdf (accessed May 13, 2011).

Chadwick, Henry. *The Church in Ancient Society from Galilee to Gregory the Great*. Oxford: Oxford University Press, 2003.

Chartrand, René. *The Spanish Main 1492-1800*. Oxford: Osprey, 2006.

Chilcote, Paul Wesley. *Recapturing the Wesleys' Vision: an Introduction to the Faith of John and Charles Wesley*. Downers Grove, IL: InterVarsity Press, 2004.

Christensen, Thomas Street. *The Cambridge History of Western Music Theory*. Cambridge: Cambridge University Press, 2002.

Ciapalo, Roman T. *Postmodernism and Christian Philosophy*. Mishawaka, IN: American Maritain Association, 1997.

Cox, Harvey Gallagher. *Fire from Heaven: the Rise of Pentecostal Spirituality and the Reshaping of Religion in the Twenty-first Century*. Reading, MA: Addison-Wesley Pub., 1995.

Cornwall, Judson. *Let Us Worship*. So. Plainfield, NJ: Bridge Pub., 1983.

Daniels, Morris S. *The Story of Ocean Grove Related in the Year of Its Golden Jubilee, 1869-1919*. New York: Methodist Book, 1919.

Dargan, William T., and Isaac Watts. *Lining out the Word: Dr. Watts Hymn Singing in the Music of Black Americans*. Berkeley: University of California Press, 2006.

D'Onofrio, Giulio, and Matthew J. O'Connell. *History of Theology: The Middle Ages*. Collegeville, MN: Liturgical Press, 2008.

Dorrien, Gary J. *The Making of American Liberal Theology: Imagining Progressive Religion*. Louisville, KY: Westminster John Knox Press, 2001.

Downs, Philip G. *Classical Music: the Era of Haydn, Mozart, and Beethoven*. New York: W.W. Norton, 1992.

Dreyer, Frederick A. *The Genesis of Methodism*. Bethlehem, NJ: Lehigh University Press, 1999.

Dyrness, William A. *A Primer on Christian Worship: Where We've Been, Where We Are, Where We Can Go*. Grand Rapids, MI: W.B. Eerdmans Pub., 2009.

Edersheim, Alfred. *The Life and Times of Jesus the Messiah*. Peabody, MA: Hendrickson, 1993.

———. *The Temple, Its Ministry and Services as They Were at the Time of Jesus Christ*. Grand Rapids, MI: Kregal Publications, 1997.

Estep, William Roscoe. *The Anabaptist Story: an Introduction to Sixteenth-century Anabaptism*. Grand Rapids, MI: William B. Eerdmans Pub., 1996.

Etter, Christopher. *A Study of Qualitative Non-pluralism*. New York: iUniverse, 2006.

Eusebius, and Arthur Cushman McGiffert. *The History of the Church*. Stilwell, KS: Digireads.com Pub., 2005.

Finke, Roger, and Rodney Stark. *The Churching of America, 1776-2005: Winners and Losers in Our Religious Economy*, 2nd Edition. New Brunswick, NJ: Rutgers University Press, 2005.

Finney, Charles Grandison, Dennis J. Carroll, Bill Nicely, and Louis Gifford Parkhurst. *Finney's Systematic Theology: Lectures on Classes of Truths, Moral Government, the Atonement, Moral and Physical Depravity, Natural, Moral, and Gracious Ability, Repentance, Faith, Justification, Sanctification, Election, Divine Sovereignty & Perseverance of the Saints.* Minneapolis, MN: Bethany House Publishers, 1994.

Finney, Charles Grandison. *Lectures on Revivals of Religion.* Ed. William G. McLaughlin. Cambridge: Belknap of Harvard University Press, 1835. Reprint, New York: Leavitt, Lord & Co., 1960.

Finney, Jerald. *God Betrayed: The Separation of Church and State: The Biblical Principles and American Application.* Xulon Press, 2008.

Fish, Henry Clay. *Handbook of Revivals: for the Use of Winners of Souls.* Harrisonburg, VA: Gano, 1988. Reprint, Boston: James H. Earle, 1874.

Fisher, William Arms. *Notes on Music in Old Boston.* New York: AMS Press, 1976.

Gaither, Milton. *American Educational History Revisited: a Critique of Progress.* New York: Teachers College Press, 2003.

Gaustad, Edwin S., and Leigh Eric Schmidt. *The Religious History of America: the Heart of the American Story from Colonial Times to Today.* New York, NY: HarperOne, 2004.

Golden, James L. *The Rhetoric of Western Thought.* Dubuque, IA: Kendall / Hunt, 2007.

Golz, Reinhard, and Wolfgang Mayrhofer. *Luther and Melanchthon in the Educational Thought of Central and Eastern Europe.* Münster: Lit, 1998.

González, Justo L. *The Story of Christianity. Volume 1, The Early Church to the Reformation;* and *Volume 2, The Reformation to the Present Day.* New York, NY: HarperOne/HarperCollins, 2010.

———. *The Story of Christianity:* San Francisco: Harper & Row, 1984.

Grane, Leif, and John H. Rasmussen. *The Augsburg Confession: a Commentary.* Minneapolis: Augsburg Publishing House, 1987.

Greene, Jack P., and J. R. Pole. *A Companion to the American Revolution.* Malden, MA: Blackwell Publishers, 2000.

Grout, Donald Jay, J. Peter Burkholder, and Claude V. Palisca. *A History of Western Music.* New York: W.W. Norton, 2006.

Haines, Michael R., and Richard H. Steckel. *A Population History of North America.* Cambridge, UK: Cambridge University Press, 2000.

Harper, George W. *A People so Favored of God: Boston's Congregational Churches and Their Pastors, 1710-1760.* Lanham, MD: University Press of America, 2004.

Harrell, David Edwin. *Unto a Good Land: a History of the American People.* Grand Rapids, MI: William B. Eerdmans, 2005.

Harris, Robert Laird, Gleason Leonard Archer and Bruce K. Waltke, *Theological Wordbook of the Old Testament*, electronic ed. Chicago: Moody Press, 1999.

Hartman, Lars. *'Into the Name of the Lord Jesus': Baptism in the Early Church.* Edinburgh: T & T Clark, 1997.

Hefele, Karl Joseph Von, William Robinson Clark, Henry Nutcombe Oxenham, and E. H. Plumptre. *A History of the Councils of the Church: from the Original Documents.* Eugene, OR: Wipf & Stock, 2007.

Herring, George. *An Introduction to the History of Christianity: from the Early Church to the Enlightenment.* London: Continuum, 2006.

Hillerbrand, Hans Joachim., ed. *The Oxford Encyclopedia of the Reformation.* Vol. 4. New York: Oxford University Press, 1996.

Hood, Edwin Paxton. *Isaac Watts: His Life and Writings, His Homes and Friends.* [Whitefish, MT]: Kessinger Pub., 2008.

Howard, Jay R., and John M. Streck. *Apostles of Rock: the Splintered World of Contemporary Christian Music*. Lexington: University Press of Kentucky, 1999.

Hunt, Stephen. *Alternative Religions: a Sociological Introduction*. Aldershot: Ashgate, 2003.

Hustad, Don. *Jubilate II: Church Music in Worship and Renewal*. Carol Stream, IL: Hope Publishing, 1993.

———. "Foreword." Foreword to *The New Worship: Straight Talk on Music and the Church*. Grand Rapids, MI: Baker Books, 1996.

"Increasing Diversity Predicted in U.S. Population by 2030." America - Engaging the World - America.gov. March 18, 2004. http://www.america.gov/st/washfile-english/2004/March/20040318124311CMretroP0.4814264.html (accessed March 01, 2010).

Jenkins, Philip. *A History of the United States*. New York: St. Martin's Press, 1997.

Johansson, Ola, and Thomas L. Bell. *Sound, Society, and the Geography of Popular Music*. Farnham, England: Ashgate, 2009.

"John Wesley's Poetry and Hymn Collections: Hymns and Sacred Poems, 1740." Through the website of The Center for Studies in the Wesleyan Tradition, Duke Divinity School. http://divinity.duke.edu/initiatives-centers/cswt/wesley-texts/poetry-hymn (accessed December 01, 2010).

Jones, Cheslyn, Geoffrey Wainwright, Edward Yarnold SJ, and Paul Bradshaw. *The Study of Liturgy*. Revised ed. London: SPCK, 1992.

Katz, Steven T. *The Cambridge History of Judaism*. Cambridge: Cambridge University Press, 2006.

Kaufman, Charles H. *Music in New Jersey, 1655-1860: a Study of Musical Activity and Musicians in New Jersey from Its First Settlement to the Civil War*. Rutherford [NJ]: Fairleigh Dickinson University Press, 1981.

Keil, Carl Friedrich, and Franz Delitzsch. *Commentary on the Old Testament*. Peabody, MA: Hendrickson, 2002.

Kidd, Thomas S. *The Great Awakening: a Brief History with Documents*. Boston: Bedford/St. Martin's, 2008.

———. *The Great Awakening: the Roots of Evangelical Christianity in Colonial America*. New Haven: Yale University Press, 2007.

Kilde, Jeanne Halgren. *When Church Became Theatre: the Transformation of Evangelical Architecture and Worship in Nineteenth-century America*. New York: Oxford University Press, 2002.

Kittel, Gerhard, Geoffrey William Bromiley, and Gerhard Friedrich. *Theological Dictionary of the New Testament*. Grand Rapids [MI]: Eerdmans, 1985.

Koester, Nancy. *Fortress Introduction to the History of Christianity in the United States*. Minneapolis: Fortress Press, 2007.

Kurtz, J. H. *Offerings, Sacrifices and Worship in the Old Testament*. Peabody, MA: Hendrickson, 1998.

Lambert, Frank. *The Founding Fathers and the Place of Religion in America*. Princeton, NJ: Princeton University Press, 2003.

"Lectionary Statistics." Catholic Resources - Felix Just, S.J. 2009. http://catholic-resources.org/Lectionary/Statistics.htm (accessed December 01, 2010).

Leonard, Bill. *Baptists in America*. New York: Columbia University Press, 2005.

Liesch, Barry Wayne. *The New Worship: Straight Talk on Music and the Church*. Grand Rapids, MI: Baker Books, 2001.

Liles, Mike. *Christian Faith in Contemporary Society; The Framework for Belief*. New York, NY: iUniverse, 2005.

314

Lutkin, Peter Christian. *The New Music Review and Church Music Review: Music as an Aid to Religion*. December ed. Vol. 12. New York: H. W. Gray, 1906.

MacArthur, John. *Ashamed of the Gospel: When the Church Becomes like the World*. Wheaton, IL: Crossway Books, 1993.

———. *Preaching: How to Preach Biblically*. Nashville, TN: Thomas Nelson, 2005.

MacArthur, Robert Stuart, and Francis Bellamy. *The People's Worship and Psalter: a Complete Order of Service for the Morning and Evening Worship of Christian Congregations*. Boston: Silver, Burdett & Company, 1891.

Marini, Stephen A. *Sacred Song in America: Religion, Music, and Public Culture*. Urbana: University of Illinois Press, 2003.

Marsden, George M. *Jonathan Edwards: a Life*. New Haven [CT]: Yale University Press, 2004.

Marshall, Madeleine Forell, and Janet M. Todd. *English Congregational Hymns in the Eighteenth Century*. Lexington, KY: University Press of Kentucky, 1982.

Mather, Increase. *Doctrine of Divine Providence Opened and Applied: Also Sundry Sermons on Several Other Subjects*. Whitefish, MT: Kessinger Printing, 2003.

Mathisen, Robert R. *Critical Issues in American Religious History*. Waco, TX: Baylor University Press, 2006.

Maxson, Charles Hartshorn. *The Great Awakening in the Middle Colonies*. Chicago, IL: University of Chicago Press, 1920.

McCauley, Deborah Vansau. *Appalachian Mountain Religion: a History*. Urbana: University of Illinois Press, 1995.

McKibbens, Thomas R. *The Forgotten Heritage: a Lineage of Great Baptist Preaching*. Macon, GA: Mercer, 1986.

McKim, Donald K. *The Cambridge Companion to John Calvin*. Cambridge: Cambridge University Press, 2006.

McLaren, Brian D. *More Ready than You Realize: Evangelism as Dance in the Postmodern Matrix*. Grand Rapids, MI: Zondervan, 2002.

McManners, John. *The Oxford History of Christianity*. Oxford: Oxford University Press, 2002.

Merriam, Alan P. *The Anthropology of Music*. [Evanston, Ill.]: Northwestern University Press, 1980.

Miller, Calvin. *Preaching: the Art of Narrative Exposition*. Grand Rapids, MI: Baker Books, 2006.

Miller, Perry, and Thomas Herbert. Johnson. *The Puritans: a Sourcebook of Their Writings: Two Volumes Bound as One*. Mineola, NY: Dover Publications, 2001.

Miller, Timothy. *America's Alternative Religions*. Albany: State University of New York Press, 1995.

Mintz, Steven. *Moralists and Modernizers: America's Pre-Civil War Reformers*. Baltimore: Johns Hopkins University Press, 1995.

Missale Romanum: Ex Decreto SS. Concili Tridentini Restutum Summorum Pontificum Cur Recognitum. Church Music Association of America, *Musica Sacra*: 1962.

Morgenthaler, Sally. *Worship Evangelism: Inviting Unbelievers into the Presence of God*. Grand Rapids, MI: Zondervan Pub. House, 1999.

Muller, Richard A. *After Calvin: Studies in the Development of a Theological Tradition*. Oxford: Oxford University Press, 2003.

Murray, Iain H. *Revival and Revivalism: the Making and Marring of American Evangelicalism, 1750-1858*. Edinburgh: Banner of Truth Trust, 1994.

Music, David W., and Paul Akers Richardson. *"I Will Sing the Wondrous Story": a History of Baptist Hymnody in North America*. Macon, GA: Mercer University Press, 2008.

Music, David W. *Christian Hymnody in Twentieth Century Britain and America: an Annotated Bibliography*. Westport, Conn.: Greenwood Press, 2001.

Music, David W. *Hymnology: a Collection of Source Readings*. Lanham, MD: Scarecrow Press, 1996.

Nelson, E. Clifford. *The Lutherans in North America*. Philadelphia: Fortress Press, 1980.

Netland, Harold A. *Encountering Religious Pluralism: the Challenge to Christian Faith and Mission*. Downers Grove, IL: InterVarsity Press, 2001.

Noll, Mark A. *America's God: from Jonathan Edwards to Abraham Lincoln*. New York: Oxford University Press, 2002.

Noll, Mark A., and Edith Waldvogel Blumhofer. *Sing Them over Again to Me: Hymns and Hymnbooks in America*. Tuscaloosa: University of Alabama Press, 2006.

Ogasapian, John. *Church Music in America, 1620-2000*. Macon, GA: Mercer University Press, 2007.

———. *Music of the Colonial and Revolutionary Era*. Westport, CT: Greenwood Press, 2004.

Old, Hughes Oliphant. *Worship: Reformed According to Scripture*. Louisville, KY: Westminster John Knox Press, 2002.

———. *The Reading and Preaching of the Scriptures in the Worship of the Christian Church. Volume 1: The Biblical Period*. Grand Rapids: W. B. Eerdmans, 1998.

———. *The Reading and Preaching of the Scriptures in the Worship of the Christian Church, Volume 2: The Patristic Age*. Grand Rapids: W. B. Eerdmans, 1998.

———. *The Reading and Preaching of the Scriptures in the Worship of the Christian Church, Volume 3: The Medieval Church*. Grand Rapids: W. B. Eerdmans, 1999.

———. *The Reading and Preaching of the Scriptures in the Worship of the Christian Church, Volume 4: The Age of the Reformation*. Grand Rapids: W. B. Eerdmans, 2002.

———. *The Reading and Preaching of the Scriptures in the Worship of the Christian Church, Volume 5: Moderatism, Pietism, and Awakening*. Grand Rapids: W. B. Eerdmans, 2004.

———. *The Reading and Preaching of the Scriptures in the Worship of the Christian Church, Volume 6, The Modern Age*. Grand Rapids: W. B. Eerdmans, 2007.

———. *The Reading and Preaching of the Scriptures in the Worship of the Christian Church, Volume 7: Our Own Time*. Grand Rapids: W. B. Eerdmans, 2010.

Palisca, Claude V. *Baroque Music*. Englewood Cliffs, NJ: Prentice Hall, 1991.

Patterson, James T. *Grand Expectations: the United States, 1945-1974*. New York: Oxford University Press, 1996.

Perl, Paul, Jennifer Z. Greely, and Mark M. Gray. "How Many Hispanics Are Catholic? A Review of Survey Data and Methodology." 2005. http://cara.georgetown.edu/Hispanic%20Catholics.pdf (accessed December 01, 2010).

Peterson, Mark A. *The Price of Redemption: the Spiritual Economy of Puritan New England*. Stanford, CA: Stanford University Press, 1997.

Piper, John. *Let the Nations Be Glad! The Supremacy of God in Missions*. Grand Rapids, Michigan: Baker Academic, 2004.

Plantinga, Leon. *Romantic Music: a History of Musical Style in Nineteenth-century Europe*. New York: W.W. Norton, 1984.

Placher, William Carl. *Readings in the History of Christian Theology*. Louisville, KY: Westminster John Knox Press, 1988.

Pratt, Waldo Selden, and Charles N. Boyd. *Grove's Dictionary of Music and Musicians: American Supplement*. New York: Macmillan, 1920.

Pratt, Waldo Selden, and Henry Ainsworth. *The Music of the Pilgrims: a Description of the Psalm-book Brought to Plymouth in 1620.* Boston: Oliver Ditson, 1921.

"The Production of Contemporary Christian Music: A Geographical Perspective." In *Sound, Society, and the Geography of Popular Music*, edited by Ola Johansson and Thomas L. Bell, by John Lindenbaum. Burlington, VT: Ashgate, 2009.

Reichley, James. *Faith in Politics.* Washington, D.C.: Brookings Institution Press, 2002.

Rieser, Andrew Chamberlin. *The Chautauqua Moment: Protestants, Progressives, and the Culture of Modern Liberalism.* New York: Columbia University Press, 2003.

Roberts, Alexander, James Donaldson, A. Cleveland Coxe, Allan Menzies, Ernest Cushing Richardson, and Bernhard Pick. *The Ante-Nicene Fathers: Translations of the Writings of the Fathers down to A.D. 325: Volume I: The Apostolic Fathers; Justin Martyr, Irenaeus.* New York, NY: Cosimo, 2007.

Roberts, Richard Owen. *Sanctify the Congregation: a Call to the Solemn Assembly and to Corporate Repentance.* Wheaton, IL: International Awakening Press, 1994.

Roberts, Richard Owen. "When God Comes Near - Online Magazine Archives - NavPress." NavPress Home. http://www.navpress.com/magazines/archives/article.aspx?id=14745 (accessed December 01, 2010).

Robinson, Haddon W. *Biblical Preaching: The Development and Delivery of Expository Messages,* 2nd Edition. Grand Rapids, MI: Baker Academic, 1980, 2001.

Robinson, Haddon W., and Craig Brian Larson. *The Art and Craft of Biblical Preaching: a Comprehensive Resource for Today's Communicators.* Grand Rapids, MI: Zondervan, 2005.

Roozen, David A., and C. Kirk Hadaway. *Church and Denominational Growth.* Nashville: Abingdon Press, 1993.

Ryken, Leland. *Worldly Saints: the Puritans as They Really Were.* Grand Rapids, MI: Zondervan Publishing House, 1990.

Sadie, Stanley, and John Tyrrell. *The New Grove Dictionary of Music and Musicians.* New York: Grove, 2001.

Schaeffer, Robert K. *Understanding Globalization: the Social Consequences of Political, Economic, and Environmental Change.* Lanham: Rowman & Littlefield Publishers, 2003.

Schaff, Philip. *Ante-nicene Christianity: A.D. 100-325.* Grand Rapids: W. B. Eerdmans, 1950.

———. *The Creeds of Christendom, With a History and Critical Notes, Volume III: The Evangelical Protestant Creeds, With Translations.* New York: Harper & Brothers, 1882.

———. *History of the Christian Church.* Peabody, MA: Hendrickson Publishers, 1996.

———. *Nicene and Post-Nicene Christianity from Constantine the Great to Gregory The Great, A.D. 311-600.* Grand Rapids: W. B. Eerdmans, 1974.

Scheid, John, and Janet Lloyd. *An Introduction to Roman Religion.* Bloomington: Indiana University Press, 2003.

Schofield, Tracey Ann. *Rome.* Dayton, Ohio: Teaching and Learning Company, 2002.

Segler, Franklin M., and C. Randall Bradley. *Christian Worship: Its Theology and Practice.* Nashville, TN: B & H Pub. Group, 2006.

Senn, Frank C. *The People's Work: a Social History of the Liturgy.* Minneapolis: Fortress Press, 2006.

Shuker, Roy. *Popular Music: the Key Concepts,* 2nd Edition. London: Routledge, 2002.

Snyder, C. Arnold, and Linda A. Huebert Hecht. *Profiles of Anabaptist Women: Sixteenth-century Reforming Pioneers.* Waterloo, Ont.: Published for the Canadian Corporation for Studies in Religion by Wilfrid Laurier University Press, 1996.

The Society of Archbishop Justus, *The Book of Common Prayer*, 1552, http://justus.anglican.org/resources/bcp/1552/Communion_1552.htm (accessed March 22, 2011)

Soderlund, Jean R. *William Penn and the Founding of Pennsylvania: a Documentary History*. Philadelphia: University of Pennsylvania Press, 1983.

Spinks, Bryan D. *Early and Medieval Rituals and Theologies of Baptism: from the New Testament to the Council of Trent*. Aldershot, England: Ashgate Pub., 2006.

Spurgeon, Charles Hadden. "Jacob and Esau." The Spurgeon Archive. http://www.spurgeon.org/sermons/0239.htm (accessed December 01, 2010).

——. *Sermons of Rev. C. H. Spurgeon of London,* seventh series. New York: Robert Carter & Brothers, 1883.

Stark, Rodney. *The Rise of Christianity: a Sociologist Reconsiders History*. Princeton, NJ: Princeton University Press, 1996.

Stead, W. T. *Hymns That Have Helped: Being a Collection of Hymns Which Have Been Found Most Useful to the Children of Men*. New York: Doubleday and McClure, 1897.

Steere, Douglas V. *Quaker Spirituality: Selected Writings*. New York: Paulist Press, 1984.

Stegemann, Ekkehard, and Wolfgang Stegemann. *The Jesus Movement: a Social History of Its First Century*. Minneapolis, MN: Fortress Press, 1999.

Stephens, W. P. *Zwingli: an Introduction to His Thought*. Oxford, England: Clarendon Press, 1992.

Streett, R. Alan. *Effective Invitation: a Practical Guide for the Pastor*. Grand Rapids, MI: Kregel Pub, 2004.

Strong, James. *Strong's Exhaustive Concordance of the Bible*. Peabody, MA: Hendrickson Publishers, 2007.

Synan, Vinson. *The Holiness-Pentecostal Tradition: Charismatic Movements in the Twentieth Century*. Grand Rapids, MI: W.B. Eerdmans Pub., 1997.

Tenney, Merrill C., Walter M. Dunnett, and Merrill C. Tenney. *New Testament Survey, Revised*. Grand Rapids, MI: Wm. B. Eerdmans Pub., 1985.

Terry, John Mark, Ebbie C. Smith, and Justice Anderson. *Missiology: an Introduction to the Foundations, History, and Strategies of World Missions*. Nashville, TN: Broadman & Holman Publishers, 1998.

Thompson, Bard, ed. *Liturgies of the Western Church*. Philadelphia: Fortress Press, 1980.

Thwaites, Reuben Gold. *The Colonies, 1492-1750*. New York: Longmans, Green and Co., 1910.

Tyson, John R. *Assist Me to Proclaim: the Life and Hymns of Charles Wesley*. Grand Rapids, MI: William B. Eerdmans Pub., 2007.

Umphlett, Wiley Lee. *From Television to the Internet: Postmodern Visions of American Media Culture in the Twentieth Century*. Madison, NJ: Fairleigh Dickinson University Press, 2006.

Vaughan, Alden T., ed. *The Puritan Tradition in America: 1620-1730*. New York: Harper & Row, 1972.

Vischer, Lukas. *Christian Worship in Reformed Churches Past and Present*. Grand Rapids, MI: W.B. Eerdmans, 2003.

Walker, Williston, Richard A. Norris, David W. Lotz, Robert T. Handy. *A History of the Christian Church,* Fourth Edition. New York: Scribner, 1985.

Wainwright, Geoffrey, and Karen B. Westerfield Tucker. *The Oxford History of Christian Worship*. Oxford: Oxford University Press, 2006.

Ward, W. Reginald. *The Protestant Evangelical Awakening*. Cambridge: Cambridge University Press, 1992.

Watson, J. R. *The English Hymn: a Critical and Historical Study*. Oxford: Clarendon Press, 1999.

Watts, Isaac. *The Psalms of David: Imitated in the Language of the New Testament and Applied to the Christian State and Worship*. Boston: Manning & Loring, 1803.

Weaver, Mary Jo., and David Brakke. *Introduction to Christianity*. Belmont, CA: Wadsworth, 2009.

Webber, Robert. *The Complete Library of Christian Worship*. Vol. 1. Nashville, TN: Star Song Pub. Group, 1993.

———. *The Complete Library of Christian Worship*. Vol. 2. Nashville, TN: Star Song Pub. Group, 1993.

Wells, David F. *God in the Wasteland: the Reality of Truth in a World of Fading Dreams*. Grand Rapids, MI: W.B. Eerdmans, 1994.

———. *No Place for Truth; Or Whatever Happened to Evangelical Theology?* Grand Rapids, MI: W.B. Eerdmans, 1993.

Wesley, Charles. *Short Hymns on Select Passages of the Holy scriptures*. Bristol: E. Farley, 1762. Through the website of The Center for Studies in the Wesleyan Tradition, Duke Divinity School. http://divinity.duke.edu/sites/default/files/documents/cswt/02_Universal_Redempti on_%281739%29_Mod.pdf (accessed December 12, 2010).

Westerfield, Tucker Karen B. *American Methodist Worship*. Oxford: Oxford University Press, 2001.

Westermeyer, Paul. *Te Deum: the Church and Music: a Textbook, a Reference, a History, an Essay*. Minneapolis: Fortress Press, 1998.

White, James F. *A Brief History of Christian Worship*. Nashville: Abingdon Press, 1993.

———. *Protestant Worship: Traditions in Transition*. Louisville, KY: Westminster/John Knox Press, 1989.

Whitefield, George. *George Whitefield's Journals*. London: Banner of Truth Trust, 1978.

———. *Selected Sermons of George Whitefield; with an Introduction and Notes by the Rev. A.R. Buckland, M.A.*. Philadelphia: Union Press, 1904.

Wiersbe, Warren W., Grenville Kleiser, and Robert Scott. *Treasury of the World's Great Sermons*. Grand Rapids: Kregel Publications, 1993.

Wilson, Ruth Mack. *Anglican Chant and Chanting in England, Scotland, and America, 1660 to 1820*. Oxford: Clarendon Press, 1996.

Woolsey, Theodore Dwight. *The First Century of the Republic: a Review of American Progress*. New York: Harper & Bros., 1876.

Wuthnow, Robert. *The Restructuring of American Religion: Society and Faith since World War II*. Princeton, NJ: Princeton University Press, 1988.

Yatman, Charles Henry, John R. Sweney, and William James Kirkpatrick. *Temple Themes and Sacred Songs with the Christian Workers' Training Class Lessons*. Philadelphia: J.J. Hood, 1888. Microfilm.

Zodhiates, Spiros, ed. *The Complete Word Study Dictionary: New Testament*. Chattanooga, TN: AMG Publishers, 1992.